MUSICAL EXCELLENC

MUSICAL EXCELLENCE

Strategies and techniques
to enhance performance

Edited by

AARON WILLIAMON

Royal College of Music, London

OXFORD

UNIVERSITY PRESS

OXFORD
UNIVERSITY PRESS

Great Clarendon Street, Oxford OX2 6DP

Oxford University Press is a department of the University of Oxford.
It furthers the University's objective of excellence in research, scholarship,
and education by publishing worldwide in

Oxford New York

Auckland Cape Town Dar es Salaam Hong Kong Karachi
Kuala Lumpur Madrid Melbourne Mexico City Nairobi
New Delhi Shanghai Taipei Toronto

With offices in

Argentina Austria Brazil Chile Czech Republic France Greece
Guatemala Hungary Italy Japan South Korea Poland Portugal
Singapore Switzerland Thailand Turkey Ukraine Vietnam

Published in the United States
by Oxford University Press Inc., New York

© Oxford University Press 2004

A catalogue record for this book is available from the British Library

Library of Congress Cataloging in Publication Data
(Data available)

ISBN-10: 0 19 852534 6 (Hbk)   ISBN-13: 978 0 19 852534 9 (Hbk)
ISBN-10: 0 19 852535 4 (Pbk)   ISBN-13: 978 0 19 852535 6 (Pbk)

10 9 8 7 6 5 4 3

Typeset by Newgen Imaging Systems (P) Ltd., Chennai, India
Printed in Great Britain
on acid-free paper by
Biddles Ltd., King's Lynn, Norfolk

ACKNOWLEDGMENTS

I should like to thank the contributors to this book, whose attention to detail, general erudition, and insight into musical performance have been both professionally rewarding and personally inspiring. I am also grateful to the Royal College of Music (RCM) and to Oxford University Press for their support at every stage of this venture.

My own involvement in research to enhance musical performance was sparked by the multidisciplinary project "Zoning In: Motivating the Musical Mind." The project was based on a partnership between the RCM and The Leverhulme Trust, and its aim was to enable musicians to improve their performance skills and manage the high levels of stress that often accompany performance situations. From 1999 to 2002, over 150 students at the College worked with a team of scientists and musicians to learn complementary mental and physical training routines drawn from four areas: (1) physical fitness, (2) Alexander technique, (3) neurofeedback, and (4) mental skills training (each of which is detailed in Chapters 9–12 of this volume). Since the inception of the project, there has been a burgeoning interest in applied music research among RCM faculty and students, and research outcomes have now been embedded into the curriculum of the College. For this, I am most grateful to my esteemed collaborators on the project, whose commitment to enhancing musical performance has been steadfast: Christopher Connolly, John Gruzelier, Tobias Egner, Brian Hawkins, Judith Kleinman, Janet Ritterman, Yonty Solomon, Adrian Taylor, Sam Thompson, Elizabeth Valentine, and David Wasley.

Finally, I wish to acknowledge the discerning advice of several individuals who have, in numerous of ways, made this book possible: Paul Banks, Jennifer Barnes, Martin Baum, Roger Chaffin, Eulalie Charland, Steve Cothran, Bob Crenshaw, Hubert Eiholzer, Nick Foster, Scott Gwara, Patrik Juslin, Andreas Lehmann, Tânia Lisboa, Karin Marson, Gary McPherson, Janet Mills, Javier Negrin, Karen Rayner, John Rink, Karin Rosenkranz, Charles Wiffen, and David Wright.

Aaron Williamon
London, 2004

FOREWORD

Performers strive for excellence. Whatever the genre or specialism, at the highest level, expressive impact supported by flawless execution is the goal to which professional musicians aspire, knowing that only by this means will they be able to communicate effectively with their audiences and derive personal fulfilment from performing.

But the road is far from easy, as many professional performers can testify. In his monograph on performance (with its evocative subtitle, *Revealing the Orpheus Within*) Anthony Rooley, lutenist and director of The Consort of Musicke, writes of the journey that he has traveled as a performer. He contrasts the experience of performance when it feels as though nothing can prevent the "Orpheus within" from being revealed, with earlier occasions when he found himself hampered by aspects of his mental or physical preparation. Rooley's account of a situation in which he had "never felt less like a performer" will have familiar resonances for many: there can be few musicians who have not felt at some point in their career that their performances have fallen below the standards that they believe they can achieve.

It is to assist musicians in developing personal strategies that will enable them to "feel like performers" and to perform to the best of their ability that this book, *Musical Excellence*, has been produced. Bringing together the findings of applied research on performance enhancement, based in many cases on insights and intuitions contributed by experienced performers themselves, this volume offers guidance to musicians on types of performance preparation that have been shown to help in developing and maintaining musical excellence. Many of these are techniques that can also assist in reducing the performance-related anxiety that can make the experience less rewarding than it should be.

Admittedly, there are performers for whom such uncertainties seem not to hamper artistic development. Their performances are distinctive, often from an early age, and they appear to achieve and maintain high standards in a range of performance situations, with the minimum of self-questioning. Perhaps it is because we all know performers like this that there has been some reluctance among musicians to consider scientifically grounded ways—commonly explored in other performance fields—of enabling a wider range of performers to achieve their potential artistically. It is perhaps born of the conviction that the qualities that mark out the exceptional performer—to whose artistry and prowess listeners instinctively respond—are innate, intuitive, and highly personal, and that any attempt to analyze these is unlikely to reveal strategies that lend themselves to replication or adaptation by others apparently less gifted.

This book does not discount the significance of this viewpoint but complements it by sharing research findings on performance enhancement, findings which suggest that performers who achieve greater control over their mental and physical states can often surpass expectations of their potential as artists. The areas singled out for attention in this book focus on matters that concern many performers throughout their careers—matters such as practice, memorizing, improvisation, and sight-reading. None of the strategies are offered as "quick fixes," but they are presented to encourage musicians to select and explore for themselves approaches to fulfilling their potential as performers and maintaining this momentum in their professional lives.

It is through sustained positive experience in individual practice, in rehearsal, and in performance itself that excellence is fostered. As this book shows, applied music research has the potential to contribute to each of these areas. I hope, therefore, that those individuals and organizations involved in the education, training, and employment of skilled performers will take account of the findings that research into performance enhancement is making available, will ensure that the information is shared and used, and will do whatever they can to foster further investigation. The music profession as a whole can only benefit if performers acquire, during their training, strategies for physical and psychological preparation which complement and support their musical preparation and which they can continue to apply and refine as part of their ongoing career development.

In the introduction to her autobiographical journal, *Full Circle*, which recounts her final year on the operatic stage, Janet Baker speaks of help she received that enabled her "to understand and participate in the joy of performing"—help that focused on the need to prepare "musically, physically and psychologically for a performance and then stand aside to allow the music to speak for itself." The relief that this gave from the fear that had dogged her for much of her professional life she describes as a miracle. *Musical Excellence* does not claim to achieve miracles, but it does offer insights into the kinds of preparation that may help performers retain the joy of performing while achieving the standards that are demanded of professional musicians today. If you are a performer, I hope that you will feel encouraged to explore some of these ideas for yourself.

Janet Ritterman
Royal College of Music
London, 2004

References

Baker, J. (1982). *Full Circle*. London: MacRae Books.

Rooley, A. (1990). *Performance: Revealing the Orpheus Within*. Shaftesbury, UK: Element Books Limited.

CONTENTS

CONTRIBUTORS

Roger Chaffin is professor of psychology at the University of Connecticut. His recent work on piano performance reflects a longstanding interest in how knowledge is represented in the mind, which previously led him to study the representation of word meaning in memory, how new words are learned, analogical problem solving, what people know of their own memory abilities, and the effects of gender on thinking. His work has appeared in journals such as *Psychological Science*; *Journal of Experimental Psychology: Learning, Memory, and Cognition*; *Cognitive Science*; and *Memory and Cognition*. His books are *Practicing Perfection: Memory and Piano Performance* (Erlbaum, 2002), *Cognitive and Psychometric Analysis of Analogical Problem Solving* (Springer-Verlag, 1991), and *Memory in Historical Perspective: The Literature before Ebbinghaus* (Springer-Verlag, 1988). He is an amateur flute player who has performed in public exactly once.

Christopher Connolly is co-founder of SyCon: The Sporting Bodymind Group, a London-based consultancy that has pioneered applied sports psychology in mental training since 1979. He trained with Moshe Feldenkrais in the Israeli scientist's revolutionary movement education system, which he then taught throughout Europe before establishing the first professional training program in this method in the UK. Since, Connolly has worked as coach and mental trainer with professional, national, and Olympic teams in Britain, Europe, and the United States, as well as with several diverse organizations within the business community. He has co-authored numerous books with John Syer, including *Think to Win* (Simon and Schuster, 1991), *How Teamwork Works* (McGraw-Hill, 1996), and *Sporting Body, Sporting Mind* (Simon and Schuster, 1998). In 1999, he helped launch "Zoning In: Motivating the Musical Mind," a performance enhancement research project based at the Royal College of Music, London.

Jane W. Davidson is reader in music at the University of Sheffield. She has a background in psychology, music, drama, and contemporary dance, and teaches areas of the curriculum related to the social psychology of music and performance, including masters courses in psychology of music and music theater studies. Her extensive publication record reflects a strong interest in bodily expression, performance, communication, and also the therapeutic and developmental aspects of artistic creativity and performance. Davidson performs as a singer/dancer, but her main artistic output is in the direction of operas. She has worked with companies such as Complicite and Drama per Musica and forthcoming projects include the medieval music drama *Ludus Danielis* with Andrew Lawrence-King.

Tobias Egner is a research fellow in the fMRI Research Center at Columbia University. He studied psychology at Goldsmiths College, University of London, and undertook his PhD research at Imperial College London, involving a collaboration with the Royal

College of Music, London. He has worked extensively in the field of physiological self-regulation of the electroencephalogram (EEG) and its relation to event-related brain potentials and attention, as well as music performance measures. Other research interests encompass the investigation of central executive processes in normal and altered states of consciousness (e.g. hypnosis), particularly by integrating various neuroimaging techniques, such as functional magnetic resonance imaging and EEG measurements. His personal musical development has been limited to a short-lived career as a singer with a punk rock band.

Anders Friberg is a researcher in the Department of Speech, Music, and Hearing at the Royal Institute of Technology in Stockholm. He has been working mainly with the synthesis and analysis of music performance, leading to a patented rule system translating the score to a performance, modeling common principles used by musicians concerning phrasing, metrical patterns, intonation, etc. Recently, Friberg has been focusing on automatic extraction of music parameters from audio and its relation to the emotional/motional qualities of performance, as well as recognition of emotional qualities in dancing. This has resulted in the development of an interactive collaborative game, in which the players interact using singing and dancing. He teaches a course on musical communication and music technology and is an active pianist with a degree from Berklee College of Music, playing mostly salsa and jazz with groups in the Stockholm area.

Jane Ginsborg is a lecturer in psychology in the School of Health and Human Sciences at Leeds Metropolitan University. She is also an associate lecturer with the Open University. She has a BA in music from the University of York, an advanced diploma in singing from the Guildhall School of Music and Drama, and a BA in psychology from the Open University; she gained her PhD at Keele University. Her research and teaching interests include music psychology (particularly in relation to practice and performance), as well as cognitive, developmental, and lifespan psychology. In 2002, Ginsborg won the British Voice Association's Van Lawrence Award for her research on song memorization. In her first career as a professional singer, she performed and recorded a wide range of music as a recitalist, chamber musician, and soloist with a variety of ensembles and choirs, specializing in twentieth century and contemporary music. She continues to sing and enjoys giving concerts whenever the opportunity arises.

John H. Gruzelier is professor of psychology in the Faculty of Medicine at Imperial College London. His main research interests concern the relation between psychology and brain function, as well as the mind–body connection in health and illness. He has published over 250 scientific articles in journals and books on topics such as schizophrenia and psychosis-proneness, hypnosis, stress, immune enhancement, self-regulation of brain rhythms, and individual differences. Gruzelier has also been co-editor of the *International Journal of Psychophysiology* since its inception in 1984 and editor of *Contemporary Hypnosis* since 2001. His research in music began with the project "Zoning In: Motivating the Musical Mind" in conjunction with the Royal College of Music, London, and has focused on self-regulation of brain electrical activity and stress reduction with a view to strengthening musical performance.

Harald Jørgensen is professor of education at the Norwegian Academy of Music in Oslo. Within music education and psychology of music, he has published books on theories of musicality, the experience of music, and the history of school music education in Norway, as well as journal articles (in both Norwegian and international journals) on the same topics. He has also published several reports and presented papers on time perspectives and planning in practice (mostly related to practice among students in higher music education) and has co-edited *Does Practice Make Perfect?* (Norwegian Academy of Music, 1997) and *Musical Imagery* (Swets and Zeitlinger, 2001). In addition, he has been engaged in research in schools in sparsely populated areas and has published books and articles about general research methodology. Jørgensen has served as rector of the Academy from both 1983–1989 and 2002 onwards and was head of research there from 1995 to 2002. He studied flute at the Oslo Conservatory of Music in the 1960s.

Patrik N. Juslin is associate professor of psychology at Uppsala University, where he teaches courses on emotion, perception, and music psychology and is the director of the interdisciplinary research project "Feedback-learning of Musical Expressivity." He is a member of the International Society for Research on Emotions and, in 1996, received the Young Researcher Award by the European Society for the Cognitive Sciences of Music. He has published numerous articles in journals that include *Psychological Bulletin*; *Emotion*; *Journal of Experimental Psychology: Human Perception and Performance*; and *Music Perception*. Juslin also edited the book *Music and Emotion: Theory and Research* for Oxford University Press (2001) together with John Sloboda. Research interests include music performance, music and emotion, music education, and nonverbal communication. Alongside his work as a researcher, Juslin has worked professionally as a guitar player and toured internationally with blues/jazz bands.

Jessika Karlsson is a PhD candidate in the Department of Psychology at Uppsala University. She holds a masters degree in cognitive science (human–computer interaction) from Linköping University and a candidate degree in psychology (specializing in music psychology) from Uppsala University. In addition, she has previously worked as research assistant in developmental psychology with Professor Claes von Hofsten at Uppsala University. Her doctoral work is part of the research project "Feedback-learning of Musical Expressivity," and it combines her experience in human–computer interaction with investigations of new methods of teaching expressivity in music (i.e. computer-based feedback learning). Her musical background encompasses, among other things, being a guitarist and singer in several punk rock bands.

Elaine C. King is a lecturer in music at the University of Hull. She completed her doctoral work on ensemble rehearsal and performance in 2000 at Royal Holloway, University of London. Her research interests include music analysis, psychology of music, performance studies, and popular music, and her publications include "Ensemble performance" in John Rink's edited book *Musical Performance: A Guide to Understanding* (Cambridge University Press, 2002). King intends to continue developing her research activity on aspects of performance, specifically on gestures and breathing in piano and ensemble playing. She is an active cellist, pianist, and conductor, performing regularly in regional chamber and orchestral ensembles.

Andreas C. Lehmann is professor of systematic musicology at the Würzburg Academy of Music in Germany. After a degree in music education and doctoral work in musicology at the Hanover University of Music and Drama, he spent several years as a postdoctoral fellow in the Department of Psychology at the Florida State University. His areas of teaching relate mainly to the psychology and sociology of music, and he also teaches music education. His research interests are in skill acquisition, practice, and perform-ance. Lehmann was awarded a Young Researcher Merit Award from the European Society for the Cognitive Sciences of Music and is associate editor of the society's jour-nal *Musicæ Scientiæ*. Among other instruments, he plays the piano and likes listening to any type of music, including non-Western genres.

Anthony F. Lemieux is currently a PhD candidate in social psychology and a research fellow in the Center for Health/HIV Intervention and Prevention at the University of Connecticut. His main research area is the development and testing of music-based HIV prevention interventions for urban adolescents in a program of research funded by the US National Institute of Mental Health. Lemieux has an extensive background in music engineering and production, as well as in his primary instrument, guitar. He has performed widely and recorded five CDs with several of his bands.

Gary E. McPherson studied music education at the Sydney Conservatorium of Music before completing a master of music education at Indiana University and a doctorate of philosophy at the University of Sydney. He is an associate professor of music educa-tion at the University of New South Wales and from 2004–2006 will serve as President of the International Society for Music Education. His published research addresses visual, aural, and creative aspects of musical performance, and he has conducted two major longitudinal studies with young developing musicians. As an experienced adjudicator of solo and ensemble performances and examiner for the Australian Music Examinations Board, he has a special interest in the measurement and evaluation of musical performance. McPherson is currently on the editorial boards of all flagship jour-nals in music education, as well as being editor for *Research Studies in Music Education*. As a trumpeter, he has performed with several of Australia's leading ensembles.

Erwin Schoonderwaldt is currently a PhD candidate in the Department of Speech, Music, and Hearing at the Royal Institute of Technology (KTH) in Stockholm. He has a degree in physics, and in 1999, he became involved in research on vibrato production in cello playing in a collaborative project of the music, mind, machine group at the University of Nijmegen and the faculty of Human Movement Sciences at Vrije Universiteit Amsterdam. In 2001, he traveled to KTH as a young researcher in the EU-funded MOSART IHP network, where he developed a rule-based model for violin vibrato. He is also involved in two projects for developing software for music edu-cational purposes: "Feedback-learning of Musical Expressivity," in cooperation with the Department of Psychology at Uppsala University, and "Interactive Music Tuition System," a project within the information society technologies program of the European Commission. He also plays the violin.

Emery Schubert holds the Vice-Chancellor's postdoctoral fellowship in the School of Music and Music Education at the University of New South Wales. His formal qualifi-cations are in music, electrical engineering, psychology, and education. His music research has included studies in perception, statistics, software for recording responses, continuous measurement, and expressive devices used by performers. These studies have been published in *Musicæ Scientiæ, Psychology of Music,* several book chapters, and other journals. Much of his research is connected with the fundamental questions of measurement and assessment of performances and of musical structure. The impetus for addressing these kinds of questions stems in part from his practical involvement in administration (including organization and adjudication) at school band festivals, eisteddfods, and concerts. As an active musician, he plays the French horn and has conducted and taught numerous orchestras and bands.

Adrian H. Taylor is reader in exercise and health psychology in the School of Sport and Health Sciences at the University of Exeter. As a fellow of the British Association of Sport and Exercise Sciences, he has worked with various government agencies on policies and reviews of evidence for the effects of exercise on health. His research has focused on facilitating more physically active lifestyles among older people, smokers, drivers, and musicians, all with an aim to enhance psychological well-being and as a therapy for stress management and self-enhancement. Taylor is associate editor for the international journal *Psychology of Sport and Exercise* and has published in a variety of leading exercise and health journals, including *Cochrane Reviews, Addiction, Health Psychology, Epidemiology and Community Health,* and the *Journal of Sport Science.* His involvement in the research project "Zoning In: Motivating the Musical Mind" at the Royal College of Music, London, has enabled him to critically extend his interests to the potentially pressured context of a musical performance.

Sam Thompson is a researcher in the Centre for the Study of Music Performance at the Royal College of Music, London. He read music at the University of Cambridge and subsequently completed a masters degree in psychology of music at the University of Sheffield. His research interests include the theory and practice of musical performance evaluation (the major focus of his doctoral work, based at Royal Holloway, University of London) and the breakdown of musical abilities in performance situations, as well as various philosophical issues in music and psychology. Intermittently active as a composer and arranger, Thompson has re-scored operas for professional touring productions and had his own works performed in venues including London's Wigmore Hall. He is also a clarinetist and, recently, uilleann piper.

Elizabeth Valentine is professor of psychology at Royal Holloway, University of London, where she is director of the Psychology of Music Research Group. She is also an advisor to the Centre for the Study of Music Performance at the Royal College of Music, London. She is a member of the European Society for the Cognitive Sciences of Music as well as the Society for Education, Music, and Psychology Research. Valentine has published widely on theoretical and experimental psychology. Her publications in the psychology of music include articles on performance anxiety, Alexander technique, musical responsiveness in relation to blocked capacity for intimacy, the effect of singing on mood, relations between reading and musical ability, cognitive structures in music practice for memorized performance, and background music as an aid to autobiographical recall in dementia. She is an amateur singer and woodwind player.

David Wasley is a lecturer in exercise and health psychology at the University of Wales Institute, Cardiff. He completed a masters degree in sport and exercise behavior at

Southern Illinois University in 1999 and is currently working toward his PhD. He has published a number of papers on the psychophysiology of exercise and has over a decade of experience working at both practical and professional levels within the health and exercise industry.

Robert West is professor of health psychology in the Cancer Research UK Health Behaviour Unit at University College London. He specializes in substance dependence and particularly tobacco use. He is deputy editor-in-chief of the journal *Addiction* and co-author of national guidelines that have led to the development of comprehensive treatment services to aid smoking cessation in the UK's National Health Service. West also has an interest in the psychology of music and has co-edited texts on music comprehension and music therapy. He enjoys all types of music but particularly jazz, rock, and blues. He plays guitar and occasionally gigs with his sons Jamie and Daniel.

Aaron Williamon is the research fellow in psychology of music at the Royal College of Music, London, where he heads the Centre for the Study of Music Performance. He also holds a research fellowship in the Faculty of Medicine at Imperial College London. His research focuses on music cognition, expert performance, and (in particular) applied psychological and health-related initiatives that enable musicians to perform at their peak. He has led a number of research projects across these areas, including "Zoning In: Motivating the Musical Mind." In addition, Williamon is interested in how audiences perceive and evaluate musical performances and, in 1998, was awarded the Hickman Prize by the Society for Education, Music, and Psychology Research for his work on this topic. He has performed as a trumpeter in chamber and symphony orchestras, brass bands, and brass quintets in both Europe and North America.

Christopher B. Wynn Parry is a senior consultant physician and trustee to the British Association for Performing Arts Medicine, a charity that provides free advisory service to performing artists. Previously, he has held posts as a consultant adviser in rheumatology and rehabilitation to the Royal Air Force and as the director of rehabilitation at the Royal National Orthopaedic Hospital and at King Edward VII Hospital, Midhurst. He was co-founder and first president of the International Rehabilitation Medicine Association and is a past president of the British Society for Surgery of the Hand. His book *Rehabilitation of the Hand* (Butterworth, 1981) is now in its fourth edition, and he is co-editor of *The Musician's Hand* (Martin Dunitz, 1998) with Ian Winspur. His professional interests in the medical and psychological problems of performing artists is informed by both his past performing experience as a bass trombonist and his current involvement as a tenor.

PART I

PROSPECTS AND LIMITS

CHAPTER 1

A GUIDE TO ENHANCING MUSICAL PERFORMANCE

AARON WILLIAMON

Musicians routinely encounter an elaborate array of mental and physical demands during practice and performance, having to process and execute complex musical information with novel artistic insight, technical facility, and a keen awareness of audiences' expectations. One of the most exciting challenges facing music researchers is to develop ways of assisting performers to meet those demands efficiently and effectively. For various methodological and technological reasons, progress has been disappointingly slow—at least compared with other performance domains such as sports, where applied research has long informed the training of practitioners. Increasingly, however, researchers are forging cross-disciplinary collaborations and generating innovative methods for investigating how exceptional musical performances can be produced.

These collaborations serve as the inspiration for this volume, which brings together their emergent findings for the first time in a single collection. It does so in three parts. Part I details the prospects and limits of performance enhancement research and sets out ground rules for achieving musical excellence. What roles do innate talent, environmental influences, and sheer hard work play in attaining eminence (Chapter 2)? How can musicians best manage the physical demands of a profession that is intrinsically arduous, throughout a career that can literally span a lifetime (Chapter 3)? How can performers, teachers, and researchers effectively assess and reflect on performance enhancement for themselves, their colleagues, and their students (Chapter 4)?

Part II presents strategies for increasing the effectiveness and efficiency of practice. These are examined generally for the individual (Chapter 5) and ensembles (Chapter 6), and specifically for the tasks of memorizing (Chapter 7), sight-reading, and improvising music (Chapter 8). Musicians inevitably spend vast amounts of time and energy acquiring and refining their skills, but are there particular rehearsal strategies that they can employ to produce better performance results or to achieve the same results more quickly? What implication does existing knowledge of human information processing and physical functioning have for musical learning and practice?

Part III introduces readers to pioneering techniques and interventions from fields including exercise science, psychophysiology, sports psychology, cognitive science, and medicine that have been used to enhance performance in music. The selection of techniques is limited to those that have been evaluated scientifically, the goal of this being to provide an objective critique of the rationale and practical efficacy of each. They include research on physical fitness (Chapter 9), Alexander technique (Chapter 10), biofeedback and neurofeedback (Chapter 11), mental skills training (Chapter 12), musical expressivity and communication (Chapter 13), and the effects of drugs on performance (Chapter 14). While some of these interventions may already be well known to musicians, many have only recently been applied and tested in the musical domain.

This first chapter provides a concise introduction to each part of the book, previewing the chapters contained therein and placing them in the broader context of performance enhancement research. It then considers the extent to which the physical and psychological skills required of today's performers are amenable to improvement through scientifically tested, systematic training procedures. Finally, it discusses how one may begin to embark on a personal course of enhancement using the pragmatic advice offered in this volume. The chapters in Parts II and III describe particular strategies and techniques and their effects on musical performance; this chapter takes a contrasting approach, exploring how enhancement techniques may be selectively applied to yield specific outcomes.

1.1   Introduction to Parts I, II, and III

1.1.1   Part I: Prospects and limits

Throughout this book, recommendations are drawn from findings of empirical research so that the practitioner can reflect on how (or whether) to implement certain training approaches in search of his or her own musical fulfillment. Part I lays down explicitly, in four chapters, some of the fundamental principles of performance that musicians should consider before moving on to the practical advice offered in Parts II and III.

Chapter 2, "General perspectives on achieving musical excellence," considers the source of exceptional performance abilities. The debate as to whether these abilities arise from innate gifts or environmental influences has long been fuelled by anecdote and personal conviction. Chapter 2 gives a balanced appraisal of the scientific debate and, in doing so, elucidates salient characteristics of cognition (or mental activity) common to all expert musicians. By removing the ambiguity and mystique that often surround high-level musical achievement, performers should be in a better position to know how best to direct their efforts and those of their students.

Inevitably, achieving high performance standards is an extremely effortful endeavor. It is not uncommon for musicians to experience physical challenges that result from that effort. Chapter 3, therefore, offers musicians guidance for "Managing the physical demands of musical performance." Based on decades of medical experience, it provides an account of common physical problems that befall performers, an analysis of the source of those problems (e.g. specific instruments and practicing habits), and frank advice for how they can best be avoided. Although performance success very often hinges upon mental agility and acuity, musical ideas are ultimately expressed through physical skill. To do this effectively—and to maintain this skill over the course of a long career—the preventive measures presented in Chapter 3 are vital.

For musicians to enhance their performance, it is instructive to understand how performances are perceived and evaluated by others. Chapter 4, "Measuring performance enhancement in music," sets out some of the musical and psychological factors that influence the assessment of performance quality. It distinguishes among those factors that are under the performer's control, those that are determined by listeners, and those typically beyond the command of both. Of course, the extent to which a performer will let audience opinion influence his or her musical decisions is highly individual-specific; nevertheless, greater knowledge of how to communicate those decisions and the impact they will have on the audience can be distinctly advantageous.

Musicians can follow any number of possible routes in order to perform at the peak of their ability. Regardless of the exact path, the principles established in Part I provide indispensable starting points.

1.1.2   Part II: Practice strategies

The direction and quality of one's practice are integral to performance enhancement, whether for the fulfillment of short-term goals (e.g. performing well in an upcoming concert) or the realization of long-term ambitions. Part II explores the characteristics of quality practice for a variety of performance circumstances and relates them to core psychological mechanisms upon which they rely.

Chapter 5, "Strategies for individual practice," sets the tone for Part II by reviewing research on strategies for planning practice, executing rehearsal plans, evaluating the success of that execution, and (perhaps most importantly) reflecting on one's ability to exploit strategies for optimal benefit. The overt recognition of the processes that underlie performance skills, as promoted in Chapter 5, can be fundamental to performance enhancement and can lead to a clearer understanding of which strategies actually work and why. Indeed, self-reflection and self-evaluation are prerequisites for making the most of any strategy and technique discussed in this volume or encountered through any other source.

The ability to work with others to produce cohesive, well-coordinated performances is a hallmark of musical expertise. In such situations, verbal, aural, and visual cues are often established and shared between coperformers. Chapter 6, "Strategies for ensemble practice," weighs up the importance of these cues in driving successful rehearsals and performances. It examines a variety of ensemble types (from cello-piano duos to symphony orchestras) and the functions of members within those ensembles.

Chapter 7 explores "Strategies for memorizing music." The memorization of music is commonplace within virtually all performance traditions—although the extent to which precise recall is compared against established standards varies immensely between genres. A substantial body of evidence has been accumulated within the wider psychological literature that informs the process of committing music to memory, as well as its subsequent retrieval. Chapter 7 reviews that evidence alongside findings from interview, observational, and experimental studies specifically with musicians.

Finally, Chapter 8 focuses on "Strategies for sight-reading and improvising music." The abilities to read fluently at sight and improvise convincingly hold a curious and somewhat paradoxical status. On one hand, they are highly prized and seen as indicators of great musical ability. On the other, they are often regarded as natural gifts that one either possesses or does not. Chapter 8 considers how these two skills share a common etiology, both in their use of similar mental processes (e.g. pattern recognition) and their generative, "online" nature. In addition, it explores how these two tasks can be systematically enhanced through structured training and how the augmentation of generative musical abilities as such could actually provide new insight for improving other musical skills.

Within the research reviews provided throughout Part II, specific recommendations for enhancing practice efficacy are bulleted in close proximity to the research from which they are drawn. In this way, their derivation is intended to be transparent for the reader. In some cases, the practice-strategies presented may be the same as those that musicians would employ automatically or as a matter of course. This is not surprising, since much of the research in this area has arisen directly from practitioners' intuitions; in fact, it is encouraging when the findings of empirical research and common practice correspond. However, not all musicians have (or follow) the same intuitions. By highlighting what research has shown, the chapters in Part II aim to supply a greater number of musicians with *explicit* access to verified strategies. Moreover, by organizing these strategies according to the psychological mechanisms to which they relate, it is hoped that practitioners will find new and useful ways of thinking about them.

1.1.3   Part III: Techniques and interventions

The performance enhancement methods presented in Part III represent the first collection of extramusical, scientifically validated techniques for enhancing musicians' achievement. They originate from a wide range of disciplines and, naturally, impact on performance in different ways. Each chapter provides a review of the theory behind the presented findings so that readers will understand why these interventions were first applied and are relevant to music. The techniques and interventions are ordered from the more physical (Chapters 9–10) to the psychological (Chapters 11–13) to the pharmacological (Chapter 14); however, they *all* address issues of both mental and physical significance for the musician.

It is well documented that keeping physically fit can be an effective strategy for managing stress. This includes the anxiety experienced in conjunction with specific events and the more general anxiety that can accumulate from working in a demanding, high-profile profession. Chapter 9, "Physical fitness," explores how musicians can integrate physical activity into their lifestyles in ways that can optimize their musical performance. In particular, both regular and single sessions of aerobic-type exercise have been shown to enable musicians to control physical and psychological responses to stress.

Chapter 10, "Alexander technique," provides a critique of this popular method of kinesthetic re-education, which is aimed at eliminating unnecessary tension and developing efficient use of the body. Since its development by F. M. Alexander in the first half of the twentieth century, an increasing number of studies have provided scientific evidence for both its anatomical and physiological benefits. They have shown positive effects of Alexander technique training on breathing, heart rate and blood pressure, posture and bodily use, quality of musical performance, and mental attitude.

Chapter 11, "Physiological self-regulation: Biofeedback and neurofeedback," details techniques that have been designed to empower individuals to control physiological processes through mental activity. The general rationale behind biofeedback is that physiological responses (such as heart rate, blood pressure, and in the case of *neuro*feedback, the electrical activity of the brain) can be recorded and fed back to an individual so that he or she can eventually gain voluntary control over those responses. Such physiological self-regulation holds great potential for enhancing musical performance. Notably, biofeedback of electric muscle activity has been used successfully to reduce muscular tension in certain types of instrumentalists. Also, neurofeedback training of "slow wave" activity has been shown to facilitate remarkable improvements in musicians' performance skills.

Being able to achieve conscious control over one's mental and physical states can prompt successful performance. One route to such control is through the acquisition and refinement of mental skills aimed at relaxing and reducing tension, realizing one's artistic possibilities, and optimizing the time spent working toward goals. Chapter 12, "Mental skills training," surveys fundamental skills that are common to elite performance across disciplines and describes how they can be propagated through select relaxation and visualization techniques.

Chapter 13, "Feedback learning of musical expressivity," explores the very nature of musical expression and evaluates a novel method for teaching expressivity based on recent advances in musical science, psychology, technology, and acoustics. The empirically based approach presented here purports to grant musicians greater control over the expression of their own musical ideas and, importantly, the tools for conveying those ideas to listeners. The chapter also assesses the potential for implementing this novel method within music education contexts.

Finally, Chapter 14, "Drugs and musical performance," focuses on the multifarious effects of "lifestyle," "prescription," and "illicit" drugs on performance and general well-being. Regardless of their possible benefits or hazards, drugs do factor into many musicians' pre-performance routines and lives generally. A number of studies have examined the scope of such drugs as alcohol, sedatives, and beta-blockers in controlling symptoms of anxiety and improving performance quality. Here, a forthright and comprehensive appraisal is offered of these substances' impact on the demands of performance.

Collectively, the chapters in Part III stand as clear evidence that applied research can facilitate musicians' strive for performance excellence. The strength of this evidence lies in the fact that results have been obtained in real-world performing contexts and in relation to outcome variables that musicians themselves deem important (e.g. performance quality, anxiety reduction, and respiratory efficiency). In some cases, the extent to which the practitioner can directly implement a given intervention for his or her own benefit will vary, depending on access to technology and expert assistance. Nevertheless, these research initiatives represent a positive step toward establishing suitable educational and professional environments where artists are supported in their acquisition of secure, holistic strategies for maintaining and enhancing their performance skills.

1.2   The potential for enhancement

1.2.1   Physical and psychological enhancement

Musical performance, at its best, is indicative of the upper limits of human physical and mental achievement. The training required to reach such lofty heights can be substantial, and invariably, the acquisition and refinement of requisite musical skills develop through the implementation of high-quality practice and the accrual of high-quality training and experience (see Chapter 2 for an extended discussion). Although there is no ideal performance standard that pervades all music, either within or across genres, the prospects for using specifically targeted training methods (even if adopted from domains other than music) to enhance the physical and mental skills needed for performance seem good. The chapters of this book set out to highlight ways for performers to make the most of their existing practice, training, and experience and to give them additional tools for acquiring and developing new skills.

In relation to long-term engagement in music, it is possible for musicians to experience both anatomical and broader psychological changes that permit the effective implementation of their abilities. As a consequence of repeated exposure to the physical demands of extensive practice, musicians are susceptible to changes in musculature, bone structure, circulation, and respiration to the same degree as expert performers in other domains (see Allard & Starkes, 1991; Ericsson *et al.*, 1993; Ericsson, 1996; Williamon & Valentine, 2000). For example, it will come as no great surprise that focused training can instill greater precision, speed, and stamina in specific muscle groups that contribute to music making; after all, countless generations of musicians have practiced scales, études, and the like for precisely that purpose.

Furthermore, extended training can also instigate performance-related refinements in the body's nervous system. Since the nervous system lies at the center of all skilled endeavor, its most fundamental characteristics are set out here as a precursor to discussion in subsequent chapters. As a matter of routine, the nervous system controls and monitors our basic support systems (e.g. respiration and circulation); directs movements; maintains balance and posture; receives, records, and interprets information from the outside world; and enables the generation of new ideas, communication, and emotional responses. It is a set of interrelated divisions that, at the most global level, is partitioned into the *central* and *peripheral* nervous systems (see Figure 1.1). The central nervous system (CNS) is composed of the brain and spinal cord and is connected to the rest of the body through nerve cells of the peripheral nervous system (PNS). The PNS is divided into the *somatic* and *autonomic* systems. The somatic system contains sensory neurons that carry impulses to the CNS and motor neurons that carry impulses from the CNS to the skeletal muscles. It allows for the production of voluntary movements such as walking, running, or throwing, as well as involuntary movements such as the adjustment of balance and posture. The autonomic system is responsible for the functioning of vital internal organs and glands (e.g. the heart, lungs, and stomach). Neurons within this system link these organs to the CNS and allow the brain to regulate life-supporting processes without the need for voluntary or conscious involvement. The autonomic system is divided further still into the *sympathetic* and *parasympathetic* systems. The former enables "fight or flight" responses that prepare the body physically for action during periods of high excitement or stress (e.g. adrenalin is secreted, glucose is released, heart rate accelerates, the bronchi dilate, and salivary flow decreases). The latter operates to conserve resources during periods of calm (i.e. heart rate is slowed, the bronchi constrict, and salivary flow is stimulated; for further discussion, see Rosenzweig & Leiman, 1989).

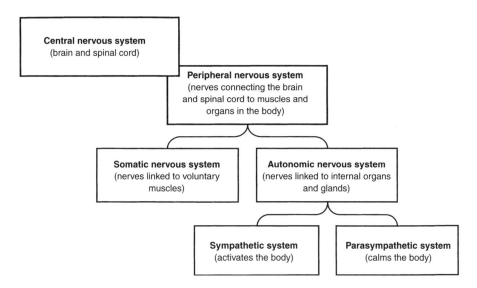

Figure 1.1 Major divisions of the human nervous system.

For musicians, the range and extent of refinements that are possible at all levels of the nervous system are extraordinary, from the higher-order functioning of the CNS to the primitive "fight or flight" responses of the autonomic system (see Halpern & Bower, 1982; Salthouse, 1991; Ericsson *et al.*, 1993; Fyk, 1995; Gabrielsson, 1999, 2003; Altenmüller & Gruhn, 2002; Williamon & Valentine, 2002). Evidence for the advancement of mental and physical skills within music has been so great over time that some authors have claimed that the violin virtuoso Paganini would indeed cut a sorry figure if placed upon the modern concert stage. Regardless of the extent to which this may be true, the wide availability of recordings and global marketing and distribution of music has meant that today's performers are increasingly held to exacting standards and required to meet a host of diverse expectations. Throughout this book, the chapters detail the existing research on and benefits of given strategies and techniques for reaching such high standards. In some cases, the professed benefits overlap between chapters; therefore, Table 1.1 offers a summary of the areas of physical, psychological, and musical improvement that emerge.

1.2.2   Managing and overcoming obstacles

The emphasis of this book is decidedly on *enhancing* performance rather than simply surviving the demands of it. One area, however, that has received considerable attention from researchers and practitioners alike is the management of performance anxiety. "Stage fright" has been documented as a problem for many performers, with one study indicating that 24% of orchestral musicians are regularly affected by it and 15% finding it a severe limitation to their performance (Fishbein *et al.*, 1988). Likewise, distinguished and veteran soloists such as Maria Callas, Enrico Caruso, Pablo Casals,

Table 1.1 A summary of the (a) physical, (b) psychological, and (c) general musical skills addressed in *Musical Excellence*. As musical performance ultimately relies on the overarching coordination of multifaceted skills, the delineation of physical, psychological, and musical areas for enhancement provided here is approximate and is intended only as a general guide

Area for enchancement	Chapter												
	2	3	4	5	6	7	8	9	10	11	12	13	14
(a) Physical skills													
General physical fitness; health		×						×					×
Relaxation; tension reduction		×						×	×	×	×		×
Musculoskeletal function		×							×	×			×
Cardiovascular function								×	×				
Respiratory function									×				
Movement generation; coordination		×	×		×		×		×				×
(b) Psychological skills													
General psychological well-being								×	×				×
General stress reduction								×	×	×	×		×
Management of stage fright								×	×	×	×		×
Concentration; attention	×						×	×	×	×	×		
Memory						×				×			
Sensory awareness; perception				×	×	×	×		×		×	×	
Motivation; attribution	×												
Self-efficacy; confidence	×		×							×	×		
(c) General musical skills													
General practice efficacy	×	×		×	×						×	×	
Goal setting	×			×							×		
Time management	×		×								×		
Problem identification	×			×			×					×	
Self-evaluation of skill	×		×	×								×	
Evaluation of others' skill	.		×										
Memorizing music						×	×				×		
Sight-reading							×						
Improvisation							×						
Analytical music skills						×	×						
Expressive range			×							×	×	×	×
Expression of emotions											×		×
Teaching expressivity													×
Communication within the ensemble			×		×								
Communication with the audience			×								×	×	×

Vladimir Horowitz, and Ignacy Paderewski have been noted as sufferers (Valentine, 2002; see also Schonberg, 1963).

To make the most of any technique for managing stage fright, it is often constructive first to understand its symptoms and causes. Salmon (1990) defines performance anxiety as "the experience of persisting, distressful apprehension about and/or actual impairment of performance skills in a public context, to a degree unwarranted given the individual's musical aptitude, training, and level of preparation" (p. 3). This apprehension can manifest itself in three general types of interrelated symptoms. *Physiological* symptoms are natural, sympathetic responses of autonomic nervous system. They include increased heart rate and palpitations, hyperventilation, dry mouth, sweating, nausea, diarrhea, and dizziness. Valentine (2002) describes these symptoms as follows:

This fight-flight response, which assisted our hunter-gatherer forebears in fleeing large animals, is highly detrimental to musicians requiring dexterity and fine muscular control over their instruments. Trembling limbs and slippery fingers are likely to hinder rather than help the performer. In addition, this autonomic arousal may have become associated with fear as a result of past experience. Increased arousal generally leads to a narrowing of the focus of attention, which may also be deleterious (p. 168).

Behavioral symptoms include shaking, trembling, fidgeting, stiffness, and dead-pan expression. Unfortunately, these symptoms can exude clear signals to others that the performer is nervous (thus potentially undermining his or her effort to communicate effectively with the audience) or actually impair performance itself (e.g. through the shaking of a violinist's bow arm). *Cognitive* (or mental) symptoms consist of subjective feelings of anxiety and negative thoughts about performing. These are often associated with the overidentification of self-esteem and self-worth with performance success. As a result, such worry can lead "to poor concentration, diverting attention and wasting valuable resources, possibly also acting as a cue to increase anxiety further" (Valentine, 2002, p. 169).

Wilson (2002) has identified three underlying causes to these symptoms. First, *trait anxiety* is a person's disposition to become anxious in response to situations of social stress. It may stem from an overreactive autonomic nervous system or low self-esteem and is generally related to neuroticism and social phobias (Steptoe & Fidler, 1987; Cox & Kenardy, 1993). Second, the degree of task mastery can impact greatly on one's subjective feelings of stress. Anxiety is likely to be lower when the person is well prepared or finds the task simple, than when he or she is under-rehearsed or when the task is complex. Adequate preparation and realistic appraisal of task requirements, therefore, are essential for eliminating this source of worry. Finally, situational stress is a pervasive determinant of stage fright (Leglar, 1978; Abel & Larkin, 1990; Brotons, 1994; LeBlanc et al., 1997), and factors such as the size and make-up of the audience and whether a performance is from memory are classic examples.

Trait anxiety, task difficulty, and situational stress interact in multifarious ways to contribute to one's perception of threat in social settings (see Hamann & Sobaje, 1983; Cox & Kenardy, 1993), which in turn can trigger basic survival instincts. Unfortunately, as Wilson and Roland (2002) point out, "running from or attacking the audience is seldom appropriate" (p. 47). Beck and Emery (1985) posit that the perception of threat is usually linked to an overestimation of the severity of the feared event, an underestimation of coping resources (i.e. what can be done about it), or an underestimation of rescue factors (i.e. what other people can do to help). Therefore, it is reasonable to conclude that musicians can profitably employ techniques to reduce their fear of performance. Steptoe (1989) lists the following strategies used by professional musicians to reduce anxiety (some of whom reported more than one strategy): 38% deep breathing, 28% distraction, 23% muscle relaxation, 22% alcohol, and 12% sedatives. In a survey of almost 200 musicians, Wolfe (1989) reports a total of 478 strategies used, of which approximately two-thirds were "emotion-focused" (e.g. "I try to sit quietly and pray for calmness before I sing") and about one third "problem-focused" (e.g. "Much like an athlete I stay in shape and have a regular warm-up routine, so that I can rely on my body to do what it has to do to operate my instrument" (Wolfe, 1990, p. 34).

Despite the debilitating nature of physiological, behavioral, and cognitive symptoms of anxiety, performers should be aware that arousal can, in fact, *benefit* performance. The Yerkes–Dodson law (Yerkes & Dodson, 1908) states that performance is best when arousal is at moderate levels—that is, when the performer is neither too relaxed nor too anxious. Unusually low arousal can result in dull or lifeless performances, whereas very high arousal can lead to physical and psychological impairment of ability. This long established relationship is commonly referred to as the *inverted U function*, as shown in Figure 1.2 (see Steptoe, 1983, for confirmation of the Yerkes–Dodson law within music). Undeniably, many musicians do claim that the thrill or "buzz" of the performance situation fosters spontaneity and encourages new musical insight. Some researchers, however, caution that the relationship between arousal and performance quality is often not so straightforward. Fazey and Hardy (1988) make a useful distinction between the effects of physiological and cognitive components on performance quality. They argue that when cognitive anxiety is low (i.e. when there is little fear of failure and its consequences), the Yerkes–Dodson law holds; however, when cognitive anxiety is high, performance quality is susceptible to a catastrophic drop, from which immediate recovery is difficult to achieve (see Figure 1.3). The basic idea, based on data from performance in sports, is that excessive apprehension and rumination can lead to a vicious spiral of negative thoughts and, hence, can cause performance to collapse.

Several chapters of this book offer advice on reducing unnecessary physiological, behavioral, and cognitive symptoms of performance anxiety (commonly measured and labeled as *state anxiety*, i.e. a person's level of anxiety at a given moment), as well as how those symptoms interact with a musician's general disposition for becoming anxious (i.e. *trait anxiety*; Spielberger *et al.*, 1983). Table 1.1 offers a synopsis of where this advice appears in this volume (for comprehensive critiques of methods specifically designed to manage anxiety, see reviews by Brodsky & Sloboda, 1997; Steptoe, 2001; Valentine, 2002; Wilson, 2002; Wilson & Roland, 2002).

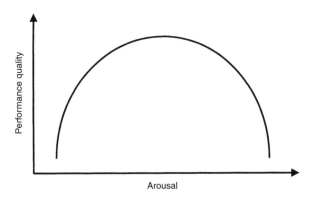

Figure 1.2 The Yerkes–Dodson inverted-U curve, depicting the relationship between arousal level and performance quality.

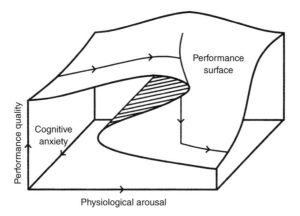

Figure 1.3 The catastrophe model of the relationship between anxiety and performance. (From Fazey & Hardy, 1988. © Sports Coach UK, used by permission.)

1.3   Selecting a personal program for enhancement

Performance enhancement in music can take various forms, operating at different levels and on different timescales. The practical recommendations offered here are ultimately aimed at skilled performers (i.e. those approaching entry into higher music education and above), in that certain performance enhancement interventions may not, for instance, benefit novice musicians who have yet to acquire elementary performance proficiency. Even so, the contributors have prepared their chapters with educational implications in mind. Thus, it is hoped that this volume will serve as a stimulus for in-depth student–teacher discussions of a range of possibilities for exploiting physical and mental skills in practice and performance.

But how exactly might performers or teachers identify the most efficacious route for their own personal enhancement or that of their students? A helpful first step is to carry out a realistic assessment of individual strengths and weaknesses in skill. The number of differences that can exist between musicians in this respect, even those at the highest levels of performance, is tremendous. This is to be expected, given that individual differences pervade so many aspects of human functioning, including such well-documented factors as personality (Eysenck, 1981), attention (Hunt, 1980), reasoning (Sternberg, 1977), and intelligence (Sternberg, 1985; for discussions on the evolutionary roots of individual differences, see Lancaster, 1975; Baer & McEachron, 1982). Also, individual differences in artistic insight are commonly seen as positive characteristics and are features by which audiences of all types make their decisions about which concerts to attend and what records to buy. Hence, a candid evaluation of personal skills can open up a clear path for the musician to accentuate strengths and eliminate weaknesses, as well as to gain greater control over shaping and developing a unique musical persona. Classical musicians typically spend years working privately with teachers who, with expert knowledge, assist them in reflecting on how best to improve their skills. For professional players (who inevitably have less time to pursue further private study) or for other performers from nonclassical traditions where extended tuition is not the norm, the ability to evaluate oneself and to make astute decisions about personal improvement is essential for artistic longevity. The development of this ability can be bolstered by learning about constituent physical and psychological skills that support musical performance (as detailed throughout this book) and by generally working to expand one's *metacognitive knowledge* (i.e. knowledge about learning itself, or simply put, thinking about thinking; see Nielsen, 1999; Barry & Hallam, 2002; and Chapter 5 of this volume).

After identifying strengths and weaknesses, careful attention should then be given to the selection of appropriate methods for achieving desired outcomes. Table 1.1 is provided as an aid for this in relation to the outcomes presented here. Although the empirical evidence for these has been obtained through controlled scientific investigations (which suggests that the benefits are potentially generalizable to the entire population of musicians), not every strategy or technique will be suitable or have the exact same impact for every musician. This could be determined by the performer's individual preferences for how to practice and learn, open-mindedness toward using a particular strategy or technique, and access to adequate training resources and facilities. Although a performance enhancement intervention may have scientific validation, this does not mean that it will necessarily work for a person who is unwilling to engage it.

Granted, it may be difficult to decide whether an enhancement method is entirely appropriate until hands-on experience can be obtained. As a natural next step, therefore, performers should use trial-and-error wherever possible in order to grasp how particular interventions can be used in specific performance situations and for more long-term gains. Furthermore, some techniques may have immediate and dramatic effects on one's physical and mental state; consequently, performers are advised to experiment with interventions conservatively, at a pace where the effects will be easily predictable and in situations where there is flexibility for experimentation (e.g. before rehearsals or leading up to low-pressure performances).

Finally, it is important to stress that this book does not supply a series of quick-fix solutions to musical problems. Rather, it provides a broad review of techniques that have been shown to optimize performance through careful and deliberate training. In many cases, the full potential of a performance enhancement method can only be realized through patience, concerted effort, and attention to subtle detail. Thus, performers should be aware of the timescale on which an intervention has been shown to deliver benefits and be willing to persevere for as long as is necessary. Indeed, readers should note that the benefits displayed throughout this book have been documented over different time periods and measured in diverse ways. Chapters 9–12, for instance, all stem from related investigations carried out by one research team and, to some extent, afford comparisons between techniques. Figure 11.4 shows the extent to which conservatory students receiving instruction in exercise, mental skills, three types of neurofeedback, and Alexander technique improved their scores on performance examinations from before to after training (which spanned approximately 16 weeks). In this case, the students receiving "alpha/theta" neurofeedback training improved their performances far more than those in any other group. At first glance, one could easily conclude that this type of neurofeedback is in everyway superior to the other interventions; however, it should be noted that the 16-week period between the two performances was ideally suited to the timescale needed to administer the designated 10 alpha/theta neurofeedback sessions. The other techniques, conversely, may feasibly require a longer period of involvement and may also present different challenges for the musician to overcome (e.g. exploiting mental skills training to enhance performance is not easy and can take years of deliberate use, and some argue that Alexander technique should be viewed more as a way of life than as a temporary intervention). In addition, it is worth noting that not every technique is directly concerned with enhancing quality judgments of performance. As is shown in Chapter 9, being physically fit can offer a range of physical and psychological advantages for the musician without directly changing his or her ability to give higher-quality performances. In time, this benefit may come as either a direct or an indirect consequence of exercising, but this will depend largely on how the individual integrates it into his or her own routine for performance preparation.

1.4   Conclusions

The basic precept of this book is that the findings of applied music research can be used to inform the training and teaching of performers. A range of strategies and techniques is presented so that practitioners can select an enhancement approach that they feel is best for themselves or for those who rely on their informed counsel. This is not to say, however, that the methods presented in this book are exhaustive of the full range of holistic body–mind approaches for enhancing musical performance. Ostensibly, there could be countless additional interventions capable of sharpening physical and mental skills but which have yet to be validated through systematic research or which are not currently supported by adequate theoretical frameworks. Certainly, musicians have been enhancing their performance for centuries without the aid of applied research—the Tchaikovsky Violin Concerto, for instance, once considered unplayable, is now one of the standard works in the instrument's repertory.

So why should performers and teachers concern themselves with the findings of research? By knowing that the benefits of a given approach have been rigorously tested and empirically demonstrated, practitioners are offered a certain level of quality assurance, with greater transparency as to how the technique works, an unbiased assessment of how it can improve musical skill, and a realistic appraisal of how quickly such improvement can be expected. In addition, for those musicians who have developed a unique pedagogical and/or performance enhancement method themselves, the scientific investigation of its effects can provide an excellent means for demonstrating reliability and validity.

It seems that much of the future for exploiting applied research to enhance musical performance lies in the direct collaboration of performers, teachers, and researchers, all working toward an agenda of addressing musically relevant issues through methods that are scientifically sound. One of the limitations with the extant research in this field is that, for the most part, it has been conducted within the confines of the Western classical tradition; hence, further research is needed to establish the breadth and applicability of existing findings across the whole of music. Where appropriate, the chapters in this volume examine the relevance of research results for nonclassical performance genres and consider possible benefits for all types of musicians: instrumentalists, vocalists, and conductors. Nevertheless, given that each chapter is underpinned by physical and psychological principles relevant to *all* of human performance, it is reasonable to argue that the recommendations offered here are pertinent to any performance tradition that demands extensive dedication and resilience, unique artistic vision, and effective communication.

Acknowledgments

I am grateful to Elizabeth Valentine, Roger Chaffin, Tobias Egner, and Sam Thompson for very helpful comments and suggestions on an earlier version of this chapter.

Further information and reading

Gabrielsson, A. (1999). The performance of music. In D. Deutsch (Ed.), *The Psychology of Music* (2nd ed., pp. 501–602). London: Academic Press.

Parncutt, R., & McPherson, G. E. (Eds.). (2002). *The Science and Psychology of Music Performance: Creative Strategies for Teaching and Learning.* Oxford: Oxford University Press.

Rink, J. (Ed.). (2002). *Musical Performance: A Guide to Understanding.* Cambridge: Cambridge University Press.

Wilson, G. D. (2002). *Psychology for Performing Artists: Butterflies and Bouquets* (2nd ed.). London: Whurr.

References

Abel, J. L., & Larkin, K. T. (1990). Anticipation of performance among musicians: Physiological arousal, confidence, and state anxiety. *Psychology of Music, 18,* 171–182.

Allard, F., & Starkes, J. L. (1991). Motor-skill experts in sports and other domains. In K. A. Ericsson & J. Smith (Eds.), *Toward a General Theory of Expertise: Prospects and Limits* (pp. 126–152). Cambridge: Cambridge University Press.

Altenmüller, E., & Gruhn, W. (2002). Brain mechanisms. In R. Parncutt & G. E. McPherson (Eds.), *The Science and Psychology of Music Performance: Creative Strategies for Teaching and Learning* (pp. 63–81). Oxford: Oxford University Press.

Baer, D., & McEachron, D. L. (1982). A review of selected sociobiological principles: Application to hominid evolution I. The development of group social structure. *Journal of Social and Biological Structures, 5,* 69–90.

Barry, N. H., & Hallam, S. (2002). Practice. In R. Parncutt & G. E. McPherson (Eds.), *The Science and Psychology of Music Performance: Creative Strategies for Teaching and Learning* (pp. 151–165). Oxford: Oxford University Press.

Beck, A., & Emery, G. (1985). *Anxiety Disorders and Phobias: A Cognitive Perspective.* New York: Basic Books.

Brodsky, W., & Sloboda, J. A. (1997). Clinical trial of a music generated vibrotactile therapeutic environment for musicians: Main effects and outcome differences between therapy subgroups. *Journal of Music Therapy, 34,* 2–32.

Brotons, M. (1994). Effect of performing conditions on music performance, anxiety, and performance quality. *Journal of Music Therapy, 31*, 63–81.

Cox, W. J., & Kenardy, J. (1993). Performance anxiety, social phobia, and setting effects in instrumental music students. *Journal of Anxiety Disorders, 7*, 49–60.

Ericsson, K. A. (Ed.). (1996). *The Road to Excellence: The Acquisition of Expert Performance in the Arts and Sciences, Sports, and Games.* Mahwah, NJ: Erlbaum.

Ericsson, K. A., Krampe, R. T., & Tesch-Römer, C. (1993). The role of deliberate practice in the acquisition of expert performance. *Psychological Review, 100*, 363–406.

Eysenck, H. J. (1981). *A Model for Personality.* Berlin: Springer-Verlag.

Fazey, J. A., & Hardy, L. (1988). *The Inverted-U Hypothesis: A Catastrophe for Sport Psychology* (British Association for Sports Sciences Monograph No. 1). Leeds: The National Coaching Foundation.

Fishbein, M., Middelstadt, S. E., Ottati, V., Strauss, S., & Ellis, A. (1988). Medical problems among ICSOM musicians: Overview of a national survey. *Medical Problems of Performing Artists, 3*, 1–8.

Fyk, J. (1995). *Melodic Intonation, Psychoacoustics, and the Violin.* Zielona Góra, Poland: Organon.

Gabrielsson, A. (1999). The performance of music. In D. Deutsch (Ed.), *The Psychology of Music* (2nd ed., pp. 501–602). London: Academic Press.

Gabrielsson, A. (2003). Music performance research at the millennium. *Psychology of Music, 31*, 221–272.

Halpern, A. R., & Bower, G. H. (1982). Musical expertise and melodic structure in memory for musical notation. *American Journal of Psychology, 95*, 31–50.

Hamann, D. L., & Sobaje, M. (1983). Anxiety and college musicians: Study of performance conditions and subject variables. *Psychology of Music, 11*, 37–50.

Hunt, E. (1980). Intelligence as an information processing concept. *British Journal of Psychology, 71*, 449–474.

Lancaster, J. B. (1975). *Primitive Behavior and the Emergence of Human Culture.* New York: Holt, Rinehart, and Winston.

LeBlanc, A., Jin, Y. C., Obert, M., & Siivola, C. (1997). Effect of audience on music performance anxiety. *Journal of Research in Music Education, 45*, 480–506.

Leglar, M. A. (1978). *Measurement of Indicators of Anxiety Levels Under Varying Conditions of Musical Performance.* Unpublished doctoral dissertation, Indiana University, Bloomington, IN.

Nielsen, S. G. (1999). Learning strategies in instrumental music practice. *British Journal of Music Education, 16*, 275–291.

Rosenzweig, M. R., & Leiman, A. L. (1989). *Physiological Psychology* (2nd ed.). New York: Random House.

Salmon, P. G. (1990). A psychological perspective on music performance anxiety: A review of the literature. *Medical Problems of Performing Artists, 5*, 2–11.

Salthouse, T. A. (1991). Expertise as the circumvention of human processing limitations. In K. A. Ericsson & J. Smith (Eds.), *Toward a General Theory of Expertise: Prospects and Limits* (pp. 286–300). Cambridge: Cambridge University Press.

Schonberg, H. C. (1963). *The Great Pianists.* New York: Simon and Schuster.

Spielberger, C. D., Gorsuch, R. L., Lushene, R., Vagg, P. R., & Jacobs, G. A. (1983). *Manual for the State-Trait Anxiety Inventory (Form Y1)*. Palo Alto, CA: Consulting Psychologists Press.

Steptoe, A. (1983). The relationship between tension and the quality of musical performance. *Journal of the International Society for the Study of Tension in Performance, 1*, 12–22.

Steptoe, A. (1989). Stress, coping and stage fright in professional musicians. *Psychology of Music, 17*, 3–11.

Steptoe, A. (2001). Negative emotions in music making: The problem of performance anxiety. In P. N. Juslin & J. A. Sloboda (Eds.), *Music and Emotion: Theory and Research* (pp. 291–307). Oxford: Oxford University Press.

Steptoe, A., & Fidler, H. (1987). Stage fright in musicians: A study of cognitive and behavioural strategies in performance anxiety. *British Journal of Psychology, 78*, 241–249.

Sternberg, R. J. (1977). *Intelligence, Information Processing, and Analytical Reasoning*. Mahwah, NJ: Erlbaum.

Sternberg, R. J. (1985). *Beyond IQ: A Triarchic Theory of Human Intelligence*. Cambridge: Cambridge University Press.

Valentine, E. R. (2002). The fear of performance. In J. Rink (Ed.), *Musical Performance: A Guide to Understanding* (pp. 168–182). Cambridge: Cambridge University Press.

Williamon, A., & Valentine, E. (2000). Quantity and quality of musical practice as predictors of performance quality. *British Journal of Psychology, 91*, 353–376.

Williamon, A., & Valentine, E. (2002). The role of retrieval structures in memorizing music. *Cognitive Psychology, 44*, 1–32.

Wilson, G. D. (2002). *Psychology for Performing Artists: Butterflies and Bouquets* (2nd ed.). London: Whurr.

Wilson, G. D., & Roland, D. (2002). Performance anxiety. In R. Parncutt & G. E. McPherson (Eds.), *The Science and Psychology of Music Performance: Creative Strategies for Teaching and Learning* (pp. 47–61). Oxford: Oxford University Press.

Wolfe, M. L. (1989). Correlates of adaptive and maladaptive musical performance anxiety. *Medical Problems of Performing Artists, 4*, 49–56.

Wolfe, M. L. (1990). Coping with musical performance anxiety: Problem-focused and emotion-focused strategies. *Medical Problems of Performing Artists, 5*, 33–36.

Yerkes, R. M., & Dodson, J. D. (1908). The relation of strength of stimulus to rapidity of habit-formation. *Journal of Comparative and Neurological Psychology, 18*, 459–482.

CHAPTER 2

GENERAL PERSPECTIVES ON ACHIEVING MUSICAL EXCELLENCE

ROGER CHAFFIN AND ANTHONY F. LEMIEUX

Are exceptional musicians born or made? The everyday explanation for outstanding accomplishment—whether it be a virtuoso performance by a concert soloist, the triple axel jump of an ice skater, or a kayaker shooting a class 6 rapid—is to attribute it to an innate gift or talent. The idea of "talent" reflects the feeling of awe that such displays of virtuosity induce in us: the sense that these abilities lie outside the range of normal mortals. It has been one of the goals of psychology, since its earliest days, to understand the nature of outstanding talent. Galton framed the issues in his book *Hereditary Genius* (1869/1979), in which he attributed outstanding achievement to natural, inherited gifts, combined with a capacity for hard work and the ability to focus one's skills on a particular goal. In support of this analysis, he offered the genealogies of eminent men to show that eminence runs in families.

While there are clear limitations in his evidence—which overlooks the roles of inherited wealth, social position, and gender—Galton's views are still widely espoused today (Ericsson & Charness, 1994). Talent is regularly invoked whenever outstanding achievement needs to be explained, and often seems to be the only plausible explanation for the dramatic differences commonly observed in musical accomplishment. The idea that extraordinary abilities are an inborn gift of nature flatters the talented, while relieving the rest of us of the expectation that our own efforts should be measured on the same scale. A great deal of scientific effort has been directed at pinning down the genetically based traits and abilities of which talent is composed. Many likely candidates have been identified (see Coon & Carey, 1989). Success in predicting outstanding achievement from such components has, however, been relatively meager (Winner, 1996a; Simonton, 1999, 2001). Good evidence of a genetic basis for intellectual ability is still lacking. This may be the result of overly simplistic assumptions about how traits combine to produce extraordinary talent (Simonton, 1999), and more sophisticated approaches may eventually succeed in demonstrating the biological basis for talent so widely taken for granted. Meanwhile, the jury is still out.

More progress has been made in understanding the other two components of Galton's analysis: a capacity for hard work and the ability to concentrate on a particular goal. These provide the main focus of the discussion here. In every field that has been examined, those who attain eminence do so only after prolonged hard work over a period of years. This is as true of music as of any other field and suggests that, whatever the role of heredity, the aspiring performer must be willing to work for success. This chapter, therefore, begins by examining the amount of work involved in achieving musical excellence. As in the joke about the visitor to New York who asked, "How do I get to Carnegie Hall?", the answer is "Practice, practice, practice."

Accumulating hours of practice, however, is not enough. High levels of accomplishment also require that practice time be well spent. Given the vast amounts of practice required to reach the highest levels in any field, even small improvements in effectiveness may yield very large differences in achievement. The second section of this chapter describes the evidence for this claim, setting the stage for the more specific, practical suggestions about how to achieve specific musical goals that are described in Chapters 5–8 of this book. The third section of the chapter identifies five general characteristics of effective practice—concentration, goal setting, self-evaluation, strategy selection, and "the big picture"—that constitute, in Galton's terms, the ability to focus and hone one's skills. These are the characteristics that allow the kinds of strategies described in Chapters 5–8 to be implemented effectively.

But where does the drive to excel come from? Is the temperament needed to devote oneself intensively to music born or made? The evidence for genetically based traits of temperament is stronger than for talent, but as with talent, there is clear evidence that environment also plays an important role. This chapter concludes, therefore, by considering the social psychological antecedents of the motive to succeed. It is intended that, by laying out the general precursors to musical excellence, performers and teachers will be better able to recognize and assess their own skills (as well as those of their students and colleagues) and make the most effective use of strategies for enhancing performance.

2.1   Quantity of practice: The 10-year rule

There is now a compelling body of evidence for the "10-year rule": a minimum of 10 years of dedicated work and practice are required to become an expert in any field. The 10-year minimum has been documented in every field of human endeavor that has been examined—from those that are largely physical in nature (like running), to those that are predominantly mental (like chess), to those requiring a combination of both (like musical performance). Indeed, this rule holds for musicians, novelists, poets, mathematicians, chess players, tennis players, swimmers, long distance runners, livestock judges, radiologists, and doctors, with the only possible exceptions being in the visual arts (Ericsson *et al.*, 1993; Winner, 1996b). And 10 years is a minimum, not the norm; for most, the path to eminence is much longer. And this is just the beginning. At least in music, the skills acquired during the long years of training must be continuously maintained and developed through practice (Krampe & Ericsson, 1996; Krampe, 1997).

While the idea that practice is integral to success is not likely to surprise anyone, the amount of training involved is striking. It is estimated that more than 10 000 hours of practice is required before a performer is ready to begin a professional career (Ericsson *et al.*, 1993). The young pianists in a study by Sosniak (1985) started their careers as concert soloists after an average of 17 years of training. For composers, the period of preparation is even longer: 20 years from first exposure to music to first notable composition for the 76 major composers whose careers were reviewed by Hayes (1981). After a lifetime of practice, the experienced pianists in Krampe's (1997) study had put in 60 000 hours of practice. Such prolonged training has profound effects on physical and mental characteristics of the sort that have been generally thought of as determined by heredity, such as the proportion of fast and slow twitch muscle fibers and the area of cortex devoted to particular motor and sensory functions (Ericsson et al., 1993; Altenmüller & Gruhn, 2002; Chapter 3 of this volume reviews the effects of prolonged training on health and offers suggestions for how they may be managed over the course of one's career).

To those familiar with the field of music, apparent counterexamples to the 10-year rule spring readily to mind. Music has provided its share of the geniuses and prodigies whose histories appear to make the case for inborn talent. Closer examination, however, suggests that these cases support rather than demolish the 10-year rule. Even with the best of intentions, early achievements tend to be exaggerated, and given the market value of child prodigies, deliberate misrepresentation is not uncommon. For these reasons, the early achievements of prodigies tend to be obscured by myth and distortion (Hayes, 1981; Howe, 1990, 1996; Ericsson & Charness, 1994; Sloboda, 1996; Howe et al., 1998). Among composers, the most striking cases of early achievement (e.g. Alban Berg, Liszt, Mozart, and Shostakovich) all turn out to have put in the requisite 10 years before producing their first masterwork, shaving off just a year in the case of Berg and Shostakovich. These extraordinary cases "prove" the 10-year rule by demonstrating how well it marks the outer limit for even the most extreme examples of early accomplishment. In this company, the paragon of childhood genius, Mozart, was a late developer, not producing his first masterwork until he had been composing for 13 years, at the tender age of 17 (Schonberg, 1970, cited in Hayes, 1981, p. 211).

Close examination of that other class of apparent exceptions to the 10-year rule, musical savants, points to the same conclusion. Savants are people with a special ability that contrasts with their generally low level of functioning in other areas. Often their abilities appear to emerge very suddenly and without the opportunity for practice. The cases that have been studied, however, suggest that savants learn their skills in the same way as other people and that it is the recognition of their skills that occurs suddenly (Sloboda et al., 1985; Ericsson & Faivre, 1988; Howe, 1996). Studies of musical savants and geniuses, thus, both point to the same conclusion: there are no clear exceptions to the 10-year rule in the field of music. Even the most exceptional talents put in 9 or 10 years of prolonged, dedicated work to develop the skills that allowed them to make their mark. For most people, a great deal more time and work is needed.

In summary, the development and maintenance of musical skills require a tremendous amount of practice. To reach the finals of international piano competitions, for instance, young pianists must practice regularly from childhood, increasingly dedicating their lives to music. Estimates of the amount of practice required for high achievement are remarkably uniform: about 2500 hours by age 13, 6500 by age 17, and approaching 10 000 by age 21 (Ericsson et al., 1993; Sloboda et al., 1996). Those who practice less generally achieve less. This is true for students, and it is true for professionals, even after a lifetime of performing. Once a person has put in the 10 000 or more hours of practice needed to acquire the skills of a concert soloist, additional practice is needed to maintain those skills. The relationship between amount of practice and level of skill continues to hold, even among professional pianists (Krampe & Ericsson, 1996; Krampe, 1997).

This is not to say that achievement is solely determined by the amount of practice. It is almost certainly not the case that anyone who puts in the required number of hours would achieve the same high level of skill. More accomplished musicians may simply be more motivated to engage in musical activities and, as a result, practice more; in turn, their abilities may make practice itself more rewarding. Regardless, the relationship between practice and achievement suggests that practice is an important, indeed essential, part of the road to high achievement.

2.2   Quality of practice

Simply putting in hours of practice, however, is not enough. Practice time must be managed effectively. The same amount of practice can produce very different levels of achievement in different people. In a study by Sloboda *et al.* (1996), there were considerable differences in the amount of reported practice *within* each of four groups of music students, with the groups representing different levels of musical achievement. Among the "elite" group (i.e. students enrolled in a selective, specialist high school for music), there was "a small handful of outliers who [did] vastly greater amounts of practice than anyone else" (p. 301), and there was a handful of students in all groups who managed on very little practice, less than 20% of the group average. In preparing for Associated Board examinations (a system of standardized music exams), there were students in each group who passed with one fifth as much practice as the other students, and there were others who did four times more practice. Similarly, there were large differences in the amount of practice reported by the pianists in Sosniak's (1985) study. In their early years, some spent "every free minute" at the piano, while others practiced as little as possible—although with practice enforced by parents, this was still a substantial amount (p. 34). These differences narrowed as the pianists became more serious about their practice in their middle years, but still ranged from 2 to 4 hours per day. Williamon and Valentine (2000, 2002) also found a wide range in the amount of practice student pianists required to learn a new piece, with some students taking two or three times as much time as others. Moreover, these differences in quantity of practice were not related to the quality of the final performance; rather, quality of performance was predicted by how practice was organized. As learning progressed, practice was increasingly organized in terms of the structure of the music (as identified by each pianist), and those who started doing this earlier gave the best performances at the end of the learning process. Musical achievement in this case was predicted by the ability to discern the musical shape of the piece and thus to form an "artistic image" of how it should be performed (Neuhaus, 1973), rather than by the amount of practice.

Similar differences in the effectiveness of practice also occur in beginning students. O'Neill (1997) found that, during their first year of music lessons, children who exhibited a "helpless" orientation to practice put in twice as much time to reach the same level of achievement as those exhibiting a "mastery" orientation. McPherson and

Zimmerman (2002) found that achievement during the first 9 months of music lessons was determined less by the amount of practice than by commitment to the instrument. Regardless of how much practice they did, students who felt they would be playing their instrument throughout their schooling made more progress than those who felt they would play for only a few years.

What is the source of these enormous differences in the amount of time needed to reach similar levels of accomplishment? One possibility is that the differences are due to raw, native talent. It may be that those who practice less are simply more talented and need to put in less work to achieve the same end. As noted above, however, psychologists have so far been unsuccessful in providing the evidence needed to substantiate this explanation. The contribution to achievement made by native talent has yet to be determined. Native talent is, in any case, not something that anyone can do anything about. Meanwhile, it is clear that enormous amounts of practice are needed, even for the most talented, and it seems very likely that at least some of the large differences in musical achievement that can be observed at every level of training are due to differences in how effectively practice time is spent.

Preparing a musical performance is a complex task and the necessary skills develop over many years. Musicians learn to practice more effectively as their skills develop. The pianist Misha Dichter noted, "I hate to think of the time I wasted as a student. Now it's just so easy to see certain shortcuts that would have saved thousands of hours" (Noyle, 1987, p. 57). Psychological studies of practice in fields other than music indicate that Dichter was probably right. Effective practice depends on finding strategies that work (Seashore, 1939; Chase & Ericsson, 1982; Ericsson & Faivre, 1988; Ericsson et al., 1993). Without an effective strategy, practice does not lead to improvement (Chase & Ericsson, 1981). Within the field of music, there is ample evidence that use of more effective practice strategies results in faster and better learning. Details of this evidence with regard to individual and ensemble practice and in terms of achieving specific musical goals—such as memorizing, sight-reading, and improvising—are provided in Chapters 5–8 of this volume.

The characteristics of effective practice have been the subject of investigation in a variety of domains for over a century (e.g. Bryan & Harter, 1899; see reviews by Ericsson & Lehmann, 1996; Ericsson et al., 1993; Ericsson, 1996, 1997). Effective practice is not simply a matter of going through the motions. The repeated exercise of a skill, even for professional purposes, does not necessarily lead to improvement. In most fields, skill development stops at a stable plateau when performance reaches the level required to get the job done, and further improvement occurs only when there is some new incentive, like a pay raise or opportunity for promotion, to motivate the hard work required (Bryan & Harter, 1899). Ericsson and colleagues have characterized the work needed to produce improvement as "deliberate" practice. Whether the skill involved is cognitive (such as solving algebra problems), physical (such as typing), or perceptual (such as wine-tasting), improvement requires setting goals that are attainable from the current skill level and which lead to the development of effective strategies (Chase & Ericsson, 1981). Progress must be constantly monitored and new routes to improvement continually explored. For those with the necessary skills, self-evaluation and self-directed exploration may be sufficient, but for students and for the less skilled, the help of a teacher or coach is essential to provide the necessary feedback and to suggest productive strategies for overcoming problems. Although it is the everyday grind of practice that often seems most salient, effective practice is anything but routine. Rather, it is a matter of continuous, creative problem solving, self-evaluation, and striving.

2.3   Fundamental characteristics of musical excellence

In this section, five fundamental characteristics of effective practice are outlined. They are based on the literature on expertise and skill learning reviewed in the previous section and are general characteristics of effective practice, not limited to music. Evidence that these characteristics of effective practice also apply to the field of music can be found in the writings of noted piano pedagogues (e.g. Gieseking & Leimer, 1932/1972; Neuhaus, 1973; Sandor, 1981), in published interviews with eminent pianists (see Chaffin *et al.*, 2002, for a summary), and in interview studies that have investigated how accomplished musicians practice and perform (Wicinski, 1950, cited in Miklaszewski, 1989; Hallam, 1995a, 1995b, 1997a, 1997b; Aiello, 2001). In order to provide performers and teachers with useful examples, the discussion here has been restricted to characteristics that can be drawn from the limited number of empirical studies of the practice of expert musicians.

2.3.1   Concentration

The ability to concentrate fully on the task at hand is probably the most important characteristic of effective practice for musicians (Auer, 1921; Hallam, 1998). Heinrich Neuhaus, the eminent Russian pianist and teacher notes "The greater the . . . concentration, the better the result" (1973, p. 4). The eminent pianists whose comments about practice were collected by Chaffin *et al.* (2002) appear to agree. Misha Dichter warns,

In practicing, never daydream. Never use the piano as a vehicle for simply moving the fingers and passing time. If you have only one moment when you're not aware of what you're doing musically or technically (and usually both), you're wasting your time . . . (Noyle, 1987, p. 59).

Once a piece is learned, it is easy to fall into mindless practice because the piece can be played automatically, without attention. As David Bar-Illan notes, "One can all too easily play music without actually listening to it" (Dubal, 1997, pp. 40–41). Playing without full attention is dangerous, Leon Fleischer warns, because "under the stress of public performance [motor memory is] the first thing that goes, if you are nervous" (Noyle, 1987, p. 95). Emile Sauer sums up the situation as follows:

One hour of concentrated practice with the mind fresh and the body rested is better than four hours of dissipated practice with the mind stale and the body tired. With a fatigued intellect the fingers simply dawdle over the keys and nothing is accomplished (Cooke, 1913/1999, p. 238).

What does this kind of concentration look like? To answer this question, Chaffin *et al.* (2002) observed the practice of a concert pianist as she learned the Presto of J. S. Bach's Italian Concerto. The practice sessions, which were videotaped, give a predominant impression of continuous, urgent activity as the pianist played without pause, stopping and starting continuously at top speed. When asked about the frantic pace of her work the pianist reported, "When I start on a new piece, I have such an appetite to take hold of it and make it mine" (p. 255).

In an attempt to quantify this "appetite to take hold," Chaffin *et al.* compared the *practice rate* (the number of beats actually played per minute) with the *mean target tempo* (number of beats per minute dictated by the tempo at which the pianist was trying to play). The expectation was that the two values would be nearly identical, showing that the pianist played almost continuously throughout each practice session. The reality proved very different, and much more interesting. The practice rate was less than a fourth of the target tempo; the pianist played only a quarter the number of notes expected, based on the tempo at which she was nominally playing. This might suggest that the pianist had spent three quarters of her practice time daydreaming, except that the videotapes showed otherwise. Rather, the discrepancy between the two measures reflected time spent in micro-pauses and momentary decreases in tempo, each no more than a few seconds, which occurred continually throughout every practice session. During these pauses and hesitations the pianist was thinking: evaluating what she had just done, planning what to do next, mentally previewing the upcoming passage, allowing time for what Matthay (1926, p. 5) calls "pre-listening."

The pianist was indeed engaged in nonstop practice; the impression from the videotape of continuous, unrelenting effort was not mistaken. But nonstop practice does not mean nonstop playing. Effective practice must be guided by thought; and thinking takes time. The measurements showed that only a quarter of the time was spent actually playing (moving the fingers over the keys) and that the remaining three quarters of the time was spent in thinking. These measurements suggest that a central characteristic of effective practice is the mental effort and concentration that is involved and that, at least for accomplished musicians, the level of effort may be reflected in the ratio of rate of practice to target tempo (pp. 130–135).

The need to maintain full attention is the reason that practice is most effective if done in short sessions of an hour or less, separated by breaks for recuperation (Auer, 1921; Seashore, 1938/1967; Rubin-Rabson, 1940a). As the pianist Rudolf Firkusny noted, "Concentration is very tiring . . . Sometimes one or two hours of concentrated practicing is much more tiring than playing seven or eight hours" (Noyle, 1987, p. 81). Bella Davidovich reports,

I find that a one-hour period is where I achieve the utmost in terms of concentration. I work very intensively for one hour and then take a ten, fifteen, or twenty minute break during which I will occupy myself with something completely different, whether it's to eat or something else. This method works out well so that I can continue for eight hours, in one-hour periods (Noyle, 1987, p. 43).

The same is true for the practice of all kinds of skills, not just music (see Ericsson *et al.*, 1993, for a review) and the ability to practice effectively for even this much time develops only with experience and training (Sosniak, 1985). For maximum effectiveness, the length of practice sessions must be tailored both to the task at hand and to the energy required. In Chaffin *et al.*'s (2002) account of the concert pianist learning the Presto of the Italian Concerto, the length of practice sessions decreased steadily from an hour at the beginning to half an hour towards the end of the learning process nearly a year later. Throughout, the pianist monitored her energy level, making comments like, "I definitely feel like I am running out of steam" (p. 163) and stopped when she became too tired, even when this conflicted with her goals for the practice session (e.g. "I'll stop now and take a break and come back to it later," p. 163). Ericsson *et al.* (1993) noted that, in a study of student violinists, the most accomplished student performers took more naps than less accomplished performers and students preparing for careers as music teachers. The implication is that musicians should take care to be well rested when they practice in order to practice effectively.

The need to practice attentively is also responsible for the common preference among experienced musicians to practice in the morning and to use the morning hours for their most demanding tasks. For many people, mental capacities are at their peak during the morning (May *et al.*, 1993; Hasher *et al.*, 2002; Yoon *et al.*, 2000) and this appears to be the case for many of the pianists surveyed by Chaffin *et al.* (2002). Bella Davidovich reports that, "The best hours for practice are in the morning when a person's mind is fresh and the ears are fresh" (Noyle, 1987, p. 43). Emil Sauer said, "I find in my own daily practice that it is best for me to practice two hours in the morning and then two hours later in the day" (Cooke, 1913/1999, p. 238). Janina Fialkowska confirms May *et al.*'s (1993) finding that morning practice becomes more important later in life:

For me, the best time to learn something new is in the morning. I, absolutely, at my advanced age cannot learn a new piece, I cannot memorize, in the afternoon after lunch. I don't know why, I cannot . . . (Noyle, 1987, pp. 67–68).

More systematic evidence comes from Sloboda *et al.*'s (1996) study of student musicians, in which the most accomplished students reported doing a higher proportion of their scales in the morning while less accomplished students practiced scales more in the evening. The more accomplished students were apparently devoting their most effective practice time to the type of practice that, for most people, is least rewarding and therefore harder to concentrate on (see Chapters 11 and 12 of this volume for suggestions of specific techniques for enhancing concentration).

2.3.2   Goal setting

A second general characteristic of effective practice is that it involves setting and meeting specific goals. Neuhaus (1973) describes an incident in which Sviatislav Richter reported that he had repeated one difficult passage of 10 bars over 100 times and recommends,

You have to put the kettle on the stove and not take it off until it boils. . . . Mastering the art of working, of learning compositions is characterized by an unwavering determination and an ability not to waste time. The greater the part . . . played by willpower (going straight for the goal) . . . the better the result. . . . (pp. 3–4).

This is why students are generally urged to work on a piece initially in small segments (Barry & Hallam, 2002). Limiting the number of problems to be dealt with makes it possible to focus attention on a small number of problems and solve them, mastering the passage at once instead of returning to it time and time again. By not playing through passages before they have been mastered, the musician also avoids developing bad motor habits that will later have to be laboriously unlearned.

Expert musicians appear to follow Neuhaus's advice, organizing practice into periods of *work* in which one passage of a few bars is repeated many times, separated by *runs* in which progress is evaluated and new problems are identified for work (Gruson, 1988; Miklaszewski, 1989; Chaffin *et al.*, 2002; Williamon *et al.*, 2002). Chaffin *et al.* (2002) describe an example of the effectiveness of the strategy in which the pianist they were studying worked through one eight-bar section for the first time, repeating different short segments for a total of more than 150 repetitions. In a second practice session, the same passage received another 50 repetitions and, from then on, needed no further work; it had been mastered in two focused encounters. This pattern of work interspersed by runs continued throughout the 10 months of preparation. Even when the pianist was able to perform fluently and was polishing the piece for performance, intensive work on short passages continued to account for about 5% of the music played in each session. As playing became more fluent, runs increased in length, but work did not. Instead, work segments became slightly shorter as the pianist was able to focus more narrowly on individual problems. This pattern of activity is indicative of practice that is goal-directed with problems being identified and eliminated in every session, as Neuhaus recommends (strategies for setting goals and action planning are discussed in Chapters 5 and 12 of this volume).

2.3.3 Self-evaluation

To know when a goal has been accomplished the performer needs feedback about success and failure. Ultimately, this must come from within. While teachers play an essential role in setting standards and developing discrimination in their pupils, they cannot be present during every practice session and cannot provide the continuous, moment-to-moment feedback that determines the microstructure of practice with its constant starts, stops, and repetitions. It has already been noted that the opportunity for feedback is a necessary condition for the improvement of any kind of skill (Ericsson *et al.*, 1993). Here, the suggestion is more specific—that effective practice in the field of music requires the feedback provided by self-evaluation and that without it, progress is slower. For example, McPherson and McCormick (1999) found that students who practiced more also made more evaluative judgments about the success and failure of their efforts. Similarly, the majority of the comments made by the pianist observed by Chaffin *et al.* (2002) during practice were evaluative in nature. General evaluative remarks were the most frequent topic, accounting for nearly 40% of all remarks, and most of the comments classified under other headings also contained an evaluative component, suggesting that self-evaluation was part of every decision and action. It may also be important that most of these evaluative remarks, whether positive or negative, were delivered with an air of dispassionate detachment—for example, "That needs work too. It's coming along" (p. 159). Chapter 4 of this volume offers specific suggestions for how self-evaluation can be used to enhance performance.

2.3.4   Strategies

The ability to meet goals depends on being able to come up with an effective practice strategy to meet the needs of the moment. Effective practice depends on a wide range of strategies that can be flexibly deployed. Hallam (1995a, 1995b) interviewed 22 professional musicians selected for their reputation for technical and musical excellence, asking about their practice habits and how they would go about learning a new piece. The musicians reported a wide range of strategies that they used flexibly to address every aspect of their task: learning new repertory, maintaining skills, preparing for performance, and managing the physical and emotional demands of their challenging careers. Direct observations of the practice of experienced musicians confirms these reports. Chaffin *et al.* (2002) describe strategies dealing with everything from choice of fingering, what bars to use as starting places, and the spacing of practice sessions, to the management of frustration, memorization techniques, and deployment of attention during performance (see also Miklaszewski, 1989, 1995; Hallam, 1994; Chaffin & Imreh, 1997, 2001, 2002; Lehmann & Ericsson, 1998; Nielsen, 1999, 2001; Ginsborg, 2002; and Chapters 5–8 of this book for recommended strategies for individual and ensemble rehearsal).

2.3.5   The big picture

A fifth characteristic of effective practice is the ability to keep in mind the larger musical picture, the "artistic image" of a piece (Neuhaus, 1973), at the same time as attending to details of technique and interpretation. The performer needs to have an idea of the overall expressive shape of the piece while making initial decisions about technique. If these decisions are made without the big picture in mind, many of them may have to be changed later, which greatly increases the learning time. The ability to switch attention from detail to big picture and back increases with experience (Chaffin *et al.*, 2002, p. 90; Williamon *et al.*, 2002). Most of the experienced performers interviewed by Hallam (1995a, 1995b) and the eminent Russian pianists interviewed by Wicinski (1950, cited in Miklaszewski, 1989) reported beginning work on a new piece by first looking at the big picture and thinking about how it should be performed. Similarly, the pianist studied by Chaffin *et al.* (2002) began by identifying the overall shape of a new piece and locating the main difficulties for performance, anticipating from the outset decisions that would not be made until later in the learning process (see Chaffin *et al.*, 2003, for details). The ability to anticipate in this way is characteristic of expert problem solving in many fields. For example, chess experts are able to play "lightning chess," intuitively making snap decisions that anticipate later developments in the game (Chase, 1983; Glaser & Chi, 1988; Gobet & Simon, 1996). Similarly, when accomplished performers acquaint themselves with a new work there is an "instantaneous and subconscious process of 'work at the artistic image'" (Neuhaus, 1973, p. 17).

One effect of paying attention to the larger musical picture is the use of the formal structure of a piece to organize practice, something recommended by many pedagogues (e.g. Matthay, 1926; Sandor, 1981; Shockley, 1986). Experienced musicians spontaneously do this from the outset, starting practice segments at the beginnings of sections when first learning a new piece (Miklaszewski, 1989, 1995; Nielsen, 1999, 2001; Chaffin & Imreh, 2002; Chaffin *et al.*, 2002). Later in the learning process, the use of section boundaries as starting places is abandoned, at least for a time, in order to ensure fluent transitions between sections (see Chaffin *et al.*, 2002). For less experienced musicians, in contrast, use of the structure to organize practice begins later in the learning process and increases across sessions. In Williamon and Valentine's (2002) study, the students did not initially have a good grasp of the structure and only began using it to organize practice later in the learning process as they began to appreciate its musical significance. Earlier use of the structure was associated with a more musical final performance. Students who were quicker to grasp the musical shape of the piece gave better performances.

2.3.6   Caveat

The five characteristics identified above have been noted as important by distinguished teachers, reported of their own practice by eminent musicians, and identified in empirical observations of the practice of expert or experienced musicians. The list is necessarily tentative since it remains to be shown, for any of these characteristics, that they are more common among professionals than among students. For this, further studies comparing the practice of musicians at different levels of training are needed. Eventually, experimental studies will be needed to determine which characteristics can be usefully induced in student practice by instruction (Hallam, 1997a, 1997b), and for this, the pioneering studies of Rubin-Rabson (1937, 1939, 1940a, 1940b, 1941a, 1941b, 1941c) still provide the model.

2.4   The social psychological antecedents of musical excellence

Concentration, setting clear goals, evaluating progress, using strategies flexibly, and looking for the big picture are complex skills. Developing them requires unusual motivation. Where does that motivation come from? It is likely that motivation is one of several necessary components of musical talent, and it seems to be the one most strongly constrained by biology (Ericsson *et al.*, 1993). Heredity plays a large role in determining other aspects of temperament (Kagan *et al.*, 1992, 1994), and it may be that the same is true of the motivation to master musical skills. As with the case for abilities, it is still uncertain as to the extent to which genetics contribute to the motivation to play music. Meanwhile, there is ample evidence of the powerful contribution of the social environment to both the motivation to succeed and the development of musical excellence.

Social factors involved in the development of musical excellence are summarized in Figure 2.1, which provides a conceptual model integrating the motivational and social cognitive principles discussed in the remainder of the chapter. Those who develop the deep commitment needed to master a musical instrument (1) play for their own satisfaction, rather than to please someone else or for other external reasons, (2) attribute their achievements (and failures) to their own efforts, and (3) feel that they have the capacity to improve.

2.4.1   Sources of motivation

Motivation determines what people like and what they do. Motivation to engage in an activity such as instrumental practice can come either from inside a person (intrinsic,

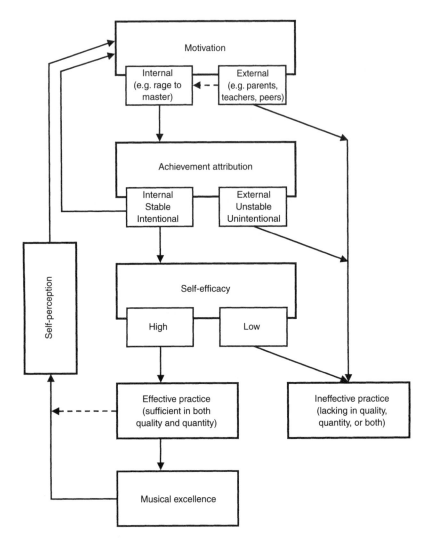

Figure 2.1 A conceptual model of the social antecedents of musical excellence.

e.g. am I doing this because I want to?) or from someone or something else (extrinsic, e.g. am I doing this because someone else—parents, teachers, or peers—wants me to?), or some combination of the two (Deci & Ryan, 1985; Ryan & Deci, 2000; see also Hallam, 1997a). Intrinsic motivation appears to be essential for the development of effective practice strategies (see Maehr *et al.*, 2002 and O'Neill & McPherson, 2002, for reviews). Studies of parental involvement in the practice of young instrumental students show that children's initial motivation to practice comes largely from their parents (Pitts *et al.*, 2000a, 2000b; McPherson & Zimmerman, 2002). Internalization of the motivation to practice represents the development of intrinsic motivation as students begin to undertake practice of their own volition. As intrinsic motivation develops, students need fewer parental reminders and are more likely to engage in goal-directed and self-regulated practice. Parents who continue to supervise or compel practice can ultimately hinder the development of the sustainable, intrinsic motivation that is essential if students are to engage in the kinds of effective practice described in the previous section (O'Neill, 1997; Pitts *et al.*, 2000a, 2000b; McPherson & Renwick, 2001; McPherson & Zimmerman, 2002).

The motivation to undertake the intense effort required to practice effectively has been identified in gifted children as the "rage to master." Winner (1996a, 1996b) describes it as a powerful motive to excel in a given behavioral or intellectual arena that emerges when children work on appropriately challenging, self-assigned tasks that they are highly motivated to accomplish. The rage to master is an unusually intense form of intrinsic motivation, and Winner's descriptions of its development provide good examples of the transition from external to internal motivation. Children need to have at least some modicum of success at a task before they develop their own internal motivation to perform it. Some initial positive experience is needed for the child to decide that he or she is "good" at a task. Children come to recognize their own talents, as well as their likes and dislikes, from observation of their own successes and failures (e.g. Bem, 1972).

Although Winner introduced the construct of rage to master to describe the motivation of gifted children, it can be usefully extended to adults. In fact, the term provides an excellent description of the kind of concentrated, goal-oriented absorption identified in the previous section as a hallmark of effective practice (Chaffin *et al.*, 2002). In adults, this state of intense creative engagement with a task has been characterized as "flow" (Csikszentmihalyi & Csikszentmihalyi, 1988; Csikszentmihalyi, 1990; Csikszentmihalyi *et al.*, 1993; O'Neill & McPherson, 2002). The trance-like state often described by musicians as occurring during their best performances is another manifestation of flow. The groundwork for these transcendent experiences during performance is laid during practice when many hours must be spent in a similar state of absorption in the task of mastering the music. When the same intense, focused attention is finally transferred from the details of practice to the expressive effects of a fluent performance, the result is the very special, transcendent experience so often reported by performers (Chaffin & Imreh, 2002).

2.4.2   Attribution

People constantly try to understand themselves and other people by identifying the causes of their behavior, a process that social psychologists refer to as "attribution" (Heider, 1958; Jones & Davis, 1965; Kelley, 1971; Dweck & Goetz, 1978). The attributions people make in explaining their own achievements have important effects on their subsequent motivation (Weiner *et al.*, 1972, 1976; Weiner, 1974, 1985, 1986).

Weiner *et al.* (1972) identified three elements in the attribution process that affect expectations for future performance and, thus, motivation. The first element is whether the causal factor has an internal or external locus (e.g. is my success due to my own efforts or abilities?). The second element is intentionality (e.g. did I try?). The third element is whether the causal factor is stable or unstable over time and across situations (e.g. can I expect to succeed again next time?). To the extent that a student feels herself to be in control of her successes or failures, engages intentionally in practice activities, and perceives the causal factors associated with her successes and failures as having stability across time and situation, she assumes a greater level of responsibility for her performance. She also assumes responsibility for her own improvement and for problem solving. On the other hand, if a student feels that her success or failure is due to someone or something else (external attributions), feels that her efforts were not important to the overall outcome (lack of intentionality), and that the results could just as well be otherwise next time (lack of stability over time or situation), she is unlikely to assume personal responsibility for addressing and remedying problems with her practice and their effects on her performances.

2.4.3   Self-efficacy

Thus far, the importance of motivation and the role of attribution have been addressed. However, a person's intense desire to excel and sense of personal responsibility must also be accompanied by feelings of competence, capability, and personal agency (e.g. Bandura, 1977, 1982, 1986, 1997). Studies by McPherson and McCormick (1999) and Pitts *et al.* (2000a) provide evidence of the importance of feelings of self-efficacy in music students. So, while students must have both the motivation to engage in effective practice and a sense of personal agency, these factors alone may not be sufficient to sustain effective practice. It is also necessary that students feel that they either have or are capable of developing the requisite skills.

As the student makes more internal attributions for his successes and failures, self-efficacy becomes increasingly important. For example, if a student makes internal attributions and feels a sense of personal responsibility for his achievement (or lack thereof), but does not have a sense of self-efficacy, he could become discouraged and ultimately stop practicing. However, if internal attributions for successes and failures are accompanied by a sense of self-efficacy, the student not only feels personally responsible for his progress, but also feels confident that he will indeed have the skills and ability necessary for further improvement.

2.5   Conclusions

Some of the variability in musical achievement can be attributed to the amount of time spent in practice. Tens of thousands of hours of practice are needed to reach and sustain a professional level of playing in the Western classical music tradition. The idea that very gifted individuals can achieve the highest levels of accomplishment in this field with minimal effort is a myth. In music, as in most fields of human endeavor, even the most exceptional prodigies put in at least 10 years of dedicated effort and practice in order to develop their skills to the point that they are capable of attaining eminence.

Another important factor determining the level of musical accomplishment is the effectiveness of those thousands of hours of practice time. Because preparation time is so long, and because so many hours must be spent in practice, even small differences in efficiency may accumulate over years, resulting in very large differences in accomplishment.

To be effective, practice must be guided by efficient strategies and continuous monitoring of their effectiveness. It seems indisputable that some of the differences between individuals in musical accomplishment are due to the effectiveness of their practice. Five characteristics of effective practice are:

- concentration
- setting and meeting specific goals
- constant self-evaluation
- flexible use of strategies
- seeing the big picture

This list of characteristics is offered in the hope that it will stimulate research on the characteristics of effective music practice. In addition, identifying the characteristics of effective practice is worthwhile because it can help to understand the basic psychological processes involved in skill acquisition and because of its pedagogical value. Knowing that practicing in a particular way systematically produces better results should be helpful to both students and teachers in their efforts toward excellence. Concentration, goal setting, self-evaluation, use of strategies, and attention to the big picture can all be seen as manifestations of an intense desire to produce music, of the "rage to master." Such motivation must be nurtured; it cannot be produced strictly by instruction. There are, however, important situational and social factors involved in the development of the motivation toward mastery, and some of the most important have been enumerated here. There is still much to learn about the long and complex process of developing musical skill. The process is, however, well worth understanding, since it is both a universal of human culture and a microcosm of cognitive development.

Acknowledgments

We would like to thank Mary Crawford for helpful comments on an earlier version of this chapter.

Further information and reading

Chaffin, R., Imreh, G., & Crawford, M. (2002). *Practicing Perfection: Memory and Piano Performance*. Mahwah, NJ: Erlbaum.

Ericsson, K. A. (Ed.). (1996). *The Road to Excellence: The Acquisition of Expert Performance in the Arts and Sciences, Sports, and Games*. Mahwah, NJ: Erlbaum.

Howe, M. J. A. (1990). *The Origins of Exceptional Abilities*. Oxford: Blackwell.

References

Aiello, R. (2001). Playing the piano by heart. *Annals of the New York Academy of Sciences, 930*, 389–393.

Altenmüller, E., & Gruhn, W. (2002). Brain mechanisms. In R. Parncutt & G. E. McPherson (Eds.), *The Science and Psychology of Music Performance: Creative Strategies for Teaching and Learning* (pp. 63–81). Oxford: Oxford University Press.

Auer, L. (1921). *Violin Playing as I Teach It.* New York: Stokes.

Bandura, A. (1977). Self-efficacy: Towards a unifying theory of behavioral change. *Psychological Review, 84,* 191–295.

Bandura, A. (1982). Self-efficacy mechanism in human agency. *American Psychologist, 37,* 122–147.

Bandura, A. (1986). *Social Foundations of Thought and Action: A Social Cognitive Theory.* Englewood Cliffs, NJ: Prentice Hall.

Bandura, A. (1997). *Self-Efficacy: The Exercise of Control.* New York: Freeman.

Barry, N. H., & Hallam, S. (2002). Practice. In R. Parncutt & G. E. McPherson (Eds.), *The Science and Psychology of Music Performance: Creative Strategies for Teaching and Learning* (pp. 151–165). Oxford: Oxford University Press.

Bem, D. J. (1972). Self-perception theory. In L. Berkowitz (Ed.), *Advances in Experimental Social Psychology* (Vol. 6, pp. 1–62). London: Academic Press.

Bryan, W. L., & Harter, N. (1899). Studies on the telegraphic language: The acquisition of a hierarchy of habits. *Psychological Review, 6,* 345–375.

Chaffin, R., & Imreh, G. (1997). "Pulling teeth and torture": musical memory and problem solving. *Thinking and Reasoning, 3,* 315–336.

Chaffin, R., & Imreh, G. (2001). A comparison of practice and self-report as sources of information about the goals of expert practice. *Psychology of Music, 29,* 39–69.

Chaffin, R., & Imreh, G. (2002). Practicing perfection: Piano performance as expert memory. *Psychological Science, 13,* 342–349.

Chaffin, R., Imreh, G., & Crawford, M. (2002). *Practicing Perfection: Memory and Piano Performance.* Mahwah, NJ: Erlbaum.

Chaffin, R., Imreh, G., Lemieux, A., & Chen, C. (2003). "Seeing the big picture": Piano practice as expert problem solving. *Music Perception, 20,* 465–490.

Chase, W. G. (1983). Spatial representation in taxi drivers. In D. R. Rogers & J. A. Sloboda (Eds.), *Acquisition of Symbolic Skills* (pp. 391–405). New York: Plenum.

Chase, W. G., & Ericsson, K. A. (1981). Skilled memory. In J. R. Anderson (Ed.), *Cognitive Skills and Their Acquisition* (pp. 141–189). Hillsdale, NJ: Erlbaum.

Chase, W. G., & Ericsson, K. A. (1982). Skill and working memory. In G. H. Bower (Ed.), *The Psychology of Learning and Motivation* (Vol. 16, pp. 1–58). London: Academic Press.

Cooke, J. F. (1913/1999). *Great Pianists on Piano Playing: Godowsky, Hofmann, Lhévinne, Paderewski and 24 Other Legendary Performers.* New York: Dover. (Original work published in 1913; expanded edition published in 1917).

Coon, H., & Carey, G. (1989). Genetic and environmental determinants of musical ability in twins. *Behavior Genetics, 19,* 183–193.

Csikszentmihalyi, M. (1990). *Flow: The Psychology of Optimal Experience.* New York: Harper and Row.

Csikszentmihalyi, M., & Csikszentmihalyi, I. S. (Eds.). (1988). *Optimal Experience: Psychological Studies of Flow in Consciousness.* Cambridge: Cambridge University Press.

Csikszentmihalyi, M., Rathunde, K. R., Whalen, S., & Wong, M. (1993). *Talented Teenagers: The Roots of Success and Failure.* Cambridge: Cambridge University Press.

Deci, E. L., & Ryan, R. M. (1985). *Intrinsic Motivation and Self-Determination in Human Behavior.* New York: Plenum.

Dubal, D. (1997). *Reflections from the Keyboard: The World of the Concert Pianist* (2nd ed.). New York: Schirmer.

Dweck, C. S., & Goetz, T. E. (1978). Attributions and learned helplessness. In J. H. Harvey & W. Ickes & R. F. Kidd (Eds.), *New Directions in Attribution Research* (Vol. 2). Hillsdale, NJ: Erlbaum.

Ericsson, K. A. (Ed.). (1996). *The Road to Excellence: The Acquisition of Expert Performance in the Arts and Sciences, Sports, and Games.* Mahwah, NJ: Erlbaum.

Ericsson, K. A. (1997). Deliberate practice and the acquisition of expert performance: An overview. In H. Jørgensen & A. C. Lehmann (Eds.), *Does Practice Make Perfect? Current Theory and Research on Instrumental Music Practice* (pp. 9–51). Oslo: Norwegian Academy of Music.

Ericsson, K. A., & Charness, N. (1994). Expert performance: Its structure and acquisition. *American Psychologist, 49,* 725–747.

Ericsson, K. A., & Faivre, I. A. (1988). What's exceptional about exceptional abilities? In L. K. Obler & D. Fein (Eds.), *The Exceptional Brain: Neuropsychology of Talent and Special Abilities* (pp. 436–473). London: Guildford.

Ericsson, K. A., Krampe, R. T., & Tesch-Römer, C. (1993). The role of deliberate practice in the acquisition of expert performance. *Psychological Review, 100,* 363–406.

Ericsson, K. A., & Lehmann, A. C. (1996). Expert and exceptional performance: Evidence of maximal adaptation to task constraints. *Annual Review of Psychology, 47,* 273–305.

Galton, F. (1869/1979). *Hereditary Genius.* London: Julian Friedman. (Original work published in 1869).

Gieseking, W., & Leimer, K. (1932/1972). *Piano Technique.* New York: Dover. (Original work published in 1932).

Ginsborg, J. (2002). Classical singers learning and memorising a new song: An observational study. *Psychology of Music, 30,* 58–101.

Glaser, R., & Chi, M. T. H. (1988). Overview. In M. T. H. Chi, R. Glaser & M. J. Farr (Eds.), *The Nature of Expertise* (pp. xv–xxviii). Hillsdale, NJ: Erlbaum.

Gobet, F., & Simon, H. A. (1996). The roles of recognition processes and look ahead search in time-constrained expert problem solving: Evidence from grand-master-level chess. *Psychological Science, 7,* 52–55.

Gruson, L. M. (1988). Rehearsal skill and musical competence: Does practice make perfect? In J. A. Sloboda (Ed.), *Generative Processes in Music: The Psychology of Performance, Improvisation, and Composition* (pp. 91–112). Oxford: Clarendon Press.

Hallam, S. (1994). Novice musicians' approaches to practice and performance: Learning new music. *Newsletter of the European Society for the Cognitive Sciences of Music, 6,* 2–10.

Hallam, S. (1995a). Professional musicians' approaches to the learning and interpretation of music. *Psychology of Music, 23,* 111–128.

Hallam, S. (1995b). Professional musicians' orientations to practice: Implications for teaching. *British Journal of Educational Psychology, 12,* 3–19.

Hallam, S. (1997a). Approaches to instrumental music practice of experts and novices: Implications for education. In H. Jørgensen & A. C. Lehmann (Eds.), *Does Practice Make*

Perfect? Current Theory and Research on Instrumental Music Practice (pp. 89–107). Oslo: Norwegian Academy of Music.

Hallam, S. (1997b). What do we know about music practising? Towards a model synthesising the research literature. In H. Jørgensen & A. C. Lehmann (Eds.), *Does Practice Make Perfect? Current Theory and Research on Instrumental Music Practice* (pp. 179–231). Oslo: Norwegian Academy of Music.

Hallam, S. (1998). The predictors of achievement and dropout in instrumental tuition. *Psychology of Music, 26,* 116–132.

Hasher, L., Chung, C., May, C. P., & Foong, N. (2002). Age, time of testing, and proactive interference. *Canadian Journal of Experimental Psychology, 56,* 200–207.

Hayes, J. R. (1981). *The Complete Problem Solver.* Philadelphia: Franklin Institute Press.

Heider, F. (1958). *The Psychology of Interpersonal Relations.* New York: Wiley.

Howe, M. J. A. (1990). *The Origins of Exceptional Abilities.* Oxford: Blackwell.

Howe, M. J. A. (1996). The childhoods and early lives of geniuses: Combining psychological and biographical evidence. In K. A. Ericsson (Ed.), *The Road to Excellence: The Acquisition of Expert Performance in the Arts and Sciences, Sports, and Games* (pp. 255–270). Mahwah, NJ: Erlbaum.

Howe, M. J. A., Davidson, J. W., & Sloboda, J. A. (1998). Innate talents: Reality or myth? *Behavioral and Brain Sciences, 21,* 399–442.

Jones, E. E., & Davis, K. E. (1965). From acts to dispositions: The attribution process in person perception. In L. Berkowitz (Ed.), *Advances in Experimental Social Psychology* (Vol. 16, pp. 219–266). London: Academic Press.

Kagan, J., Arcus, D., Snidman, N., Feng, W. Y., Hendler, J., & Greene, S. (1994). Reactivity in infants: A cross-national comparison. *Developmental Psychology, 30,* 342–345.

Kagan, J., Snidman, N., & Arcus, D. M. (1992). Initial reactions to unfamiliarity. *Current Directions in Psychological Science, 1,* 171–174.

Kelley, H. H. (1971). *Attribution in Social Interaction.* Morristown, NJ: General Learning Press.

Krampe, R. T. (1997). Age-related changes in practice activities and their relation to musical performance skills. In H. Jørgensen & A. C. Lehmann (Eds.), *Does Practice Make Perfect? Current Theory and Research on Instrumental Music Practice* (pp. 165–178). Oslo: Norwegian Academy of Music.

Krampe, R. T., & Ericsson, K. A. (1996). Maintaining excellence: Deliberate practice and elite performance in young and older pianists. *Journal of Experimental Psychology: General, 125,* 331–359.

Lehmann, A. C., & Ericsson, K. A. (1998). Preparation of a public piano performance: The relation between practice and performance. *Musicæ Scientiæ, 2,* 67–94.

Maehr, M. L., Pintrich, P. R., & Linnenbrink, E. A. (2002). Motivation and achievement. In R. Colwell & C. Richardson (Eds.), *The New Handbook of Research on Music Teaching and Learning* (pp. 348–372). Oxford: Oxford University Press.

Matthay, T. (1926). *On Memorizing and Playing from Memory and on the Laws of Practice Generally.* Oxford: Oxford University Press.

May, C. P., Hasher, L., & Stoltzfus, E. R. (1993). Optimal time of day and the magnitude of age differences in memory. *Psychological Science, 4,* 326–330.

McPherson, G. E., & McCormick, J. (1999). Motivational and self-regulated learning components of musical practice. *Bulletin of the Council for Research in Music Education, 141,* 98–102.

McPherson, G. E., & Renwick, J. M. (2001). A longitudinal study of self-regulation in children's musical practice. *Music Education Research, 3*, 169–186.

McPherson, G. E., & Zimmerman, B. J. (2002). Self-regulation of musical learning: A social cognitive perspective. In R. Colwell & C. Richardson (Eds.), *The New Handbook of Research on Music Teaching and Learning* (pp. 327–347). Oxford: Oxford University Press.

Miklaszewski, K. (1989). A case study of a pianist preparing a musical performance. *Psychology of Music, 17*, 95–109.

Miklaszewski, K. (1995). Individual differences in preparing a musical composition for public performance. In M. Manturzewska, K. Miklaszewski & A. Bialkowski (Eds.), *Psychology of Music Today: Proceedings of the International Seminar of Researchers and Lecturers in the Psychology of Music* (pp. 138–147). Warsaw: Fryderyk Chopin Academy of Music.

Neuhaus, H. (1973). *The Art of Piano Playing.* New York: Praeger.

Nielsen, S. G. (1999). Learning strategies in instrumental music practice. *British Journal of Music Education, 16*, 275–291.

Nielsen, S. G. (2001). Self-regulating learning strategies in instrumental music practice. *Music Education Research, 3*, 155–167.

Noyle, L. J. (1987). *Pianists on Playing: Interviews with Twelve Concert Pianists.* London: Scarecrow Press.

O'Neill, S. A. (1997). The role of practice in children's early musical performance achievement. In H. Jørgensen & A. C. Lehmann (Eds.), *Does Practice Make Perfect? Current Theory and Research on Instrumental Music Practice* (pp. 53–70). Oslo: Norwegian Academy of Music.

O'Neill, S. A., & McPherson, G. E. (2002). Motivation. In R. Parncutt & G. E. McPherson (Eds.), *The Science and Psychology of Music Performance: Creative Strategies for Teaching and Learning* (pp. 31–46). Oxford: Oxford University Press.

Pitts, S. E., Davidson, J. W., & McPherson, G. E. (2000a). Models of success and failure in instrumental learning: Case studies of young players in the first 20 months of learning. *Bulletin of the Council for Research in Music Education, 146*, 51–69.

Pitts, S. E., Davidson, J. W., & McPherson, G. E. (2000b). Developing effective practice strategies: Case studies of three young instrumentalists. *Music Education Research, 2*, 45–56.

Rubin-Rabson, G. (1937). *The Influence of Analytical Pre-Study in Memorizing Piano Music.* New York: Archives of Psychology.

Rubin-Rabson, G. (1939). Studies in the psychology of memorizing piano music: I. A comparison of the unilateral and the coordinated approaches. *Journal of Educational Psychology, 30*, 321–345.

Rubin-Rabson, G. (1940a). Studies in the psychology of memorizing piano music: II. A comparison of massed and distributed practice. *Journal of Educational Psychology, 31*, 270–284.

Rubin-Rabson, G. (1940b). Studies in the psychology of memorizing piano music: III. A comparison of the whole and part approach. *Journal of Educational Psychology, 31*, 460–476.

Rubin-Rabson, G. (1941a). Studies in the psychology of memorizing piano music: IV. The effect of incentive. *Journal of Educational Psychology, 32*, 45–54.

Rubin-Rabson, G. (1941b). Studies in the psychology of memorizing piano music: V. A comparison of pre-study periods of varied length. *Journal of Educational Psychology, 32*, 101–112.

Rubin-Rabson, G. (1941c). Studies in the psychology of memorizing piano music: VI. A comparison of two forms of mental rehearsal and keyboard overlearning. *Journal of Educational Psychology, 32,* 593–602.

Ryan, R. M., & Deci, E. L. (2000). Self-determination theory and the facilitation of intrinsic motivation, social development, and well-being. *American Psychologist, 55,* 68–78.

Sandor, G. (1981). *On Piano Playing: Motion, Sound, Expression.* New York: Schirmer.

Seashore, C. E. (1938/1967). *Psychology of Music.* New York: Dover. (Original work published in 1938.)

Seashore, R. H. (1939). Work methods: An often neglected factor underlying individual differences. *Psychological Review, 46,* 123–141.

Shockley, R. (1986). A new approach to memorization. *Clavier, July–August,* 20–23.

Simonton, D. K. (1999). Talent and its development: An emergenic and epigenetic model. *Psychological Review, 106,* 435–457.

Simonton, D. K. (2001). Talent development as a multidimensional, multiplicative, and dynamic process. *Current Directions in Psychological Science, 10,* 39–43.

Sloboda, J. A. (1996). The acquisition of musical performance expertise: Deconstructing the "talent" account of individual differences in musical expressivity. In K. A. Ericsson (Ed.), *The Road to Excellence: The Acquisition of Expert Performance in the Arts and Sciences, Sports, and Games* (pp. 107–126). Mahwah, NJ: Erlbaum.

Sloboda, J. A., Hermelin, B., & O'Connor, N. (1985). An exceptional musical memory. *Music Perception, 3,* 155–170.

Sloboda, J. A., Davidson, J. W., Howe, M. J. A., & Moore, D. G. (1996). The role of practice in the development of performing musicians. *British Journal of Psychology, 87,* 287–309.

Sosniak, L. A. (1985). Learning to be a concert pianist. In B. S. Bloom (Ed.), *Developing Talent in Young People* (pp. 19–67). New York: Ballantine Books.

Weiner, B. (1974). An attributional interpretation of expectancy-value theory. In B. Weiner (Ed.), *Cognitive Views of Human Motivation* (pp. 51–70). London: Academic Press.

Weiner, B. (1985). An attributional theory of achievement motivation and emotion. *Psychological Review, 92,* 548–573.

Weiner, B. (1986). *An Attributional Theory of Motivation and Emotion.* New York: Springer-Verlag.

Weiner, B., Russell, D., & Lerman, D. (1976). The cognition-emotion process in achievement-related contexts. *Journal of Personality and Social Psychology, 20,* 82–92.

Weiner, B., Frieze, I., Kukla, A., Reed, L., Rest, S., & Rosenbaum, R. M. (1972). Perceiving the causes of success and failure. In E. E. Jones, D. E. Kanouse, H. H. Kelley, R. E. Nisbett, S. Valins & B. Weiner (Eds.), *Attribution: Perceiving the Causes of Behavior* (pp. 95–120). Morristown, NJ: General Learning Press.

Williamon, A., & Valentine, E. (2000). Quantity and quality of musical practice as predictors of performance quality. *British Journal of Psychology, 91,* 353–376.

Williamon, A., & Valentine, E. (2002). The role of retrieval structures in memorizing music. *Cognitive Psychology, 44,* 1–32.

Williamon, A., Valentine, E., & Valentine, J. (2002). Shifting the focus of attention between levels of musical structure. *European Journal of Cognitive Psychology, 14,* 493–520.

Winner, E. (1996a). *Gifted Children: Myths and Realities.* New York: Basic Books.

Winner, E. (1996b). The rage to master: The decisive role of talent in the visual arts. In K. A. Ericsson (Ed.), *The Road to Excellence: The Acquisition of Expert Performance in the Arts and Sciences, Sports, and Games* (pp. 271–301). Mahwah, NJ: Erlbaum.

Yoon, C., May, C. P., & Hasher, L. (2000). Aging, circadian arousal patterns, and cognition. In D. C. Park & N. Schwarz (Eds.), *Cognitive Aging: A Primer* (pp. 151–171). Hove, UK: Psychology Press.

CHAPTER 3

MANAGING THE PHYSICAL DEMANDS OF MUSICAL PERFORMANCE

CHRISTOPHER B. WYNN PARRY

In order to achieve the highest levels of performance, a musician needs to be physically, emotionally, and mentally fit, for what is a hugely demanding profession. Sadly, the education and training of performers very often fail to incorporate advice to students on care of the body and prevention of injury. Until quite recently, in fact, it seems to have been accepted that pain is an inevitable accompaniment of a life in music. The pernicious exhortation "no pain, no gain" has been accepted without challenge. However, provided that technique is sound, body fit, mind and spirit calm, the musician can spend a lifetime in music, with only occasional aches and pains, such as affect most people.

Until 1986, there was little understanding of the scope and nature of the medical problems confronting musicians. There were sporadic reports in the literature that musicians suffered cramps, fatigue, and neuritic symptoms (e.g. Singer, 1932), but there were no indications of their incidence and effect on a playing career. It took the publicity of an article in the *New York Times* on Gary Graffman's "dystonia" to reveal the true magnitude of the predicament. Graffman (1986) records that, following the appearance of this article, he was inundated by calls from musicians recounting a wide variety of physical ills.

The medical profession has responded by setting up specialist clinics and instigating surveys into the scope of the problem. From this, one point has emerged as certain: many musicians suffer seriously, yet unnecessarily, for their art. Clearly, the act of practicing and performing intensely over several years can bear profound effects on human anatomy, including musculature, bone structure, circulation, and the respiratory system. Adopting a healthy approach to engaging in music, especially early on in one's career, can have substantial impacts on achieving and maintaining peak performance and, therefore, on one's ability to exploit the practice strategies and performance enhancement interventions included in this book.

The underlying theme of this chapter is that the majority of medical problems facing the musician are preventable. Relatively few medical investigations have been carried out on the physical demands of performance, partly because the music profession is quite naturally secretive about ailments. For example, the incidence of damage to joints or muscles from a professional lifetime of repetitive movements is not known—nor will it be known without further longitudinal research. Nonetheless, this chapter reviews the existing scientific literature on music and physical health and offers a clinical perspective on some of the more common medical conditions that affect musicians—namely, musculoskeletal structural disorders and focal dystonia. Moreover, it explores some of the more general, nonstructural problems that typically arise in conjunction with certain types of music making (playing the piano, violin, cello, guitar, flute, and conducting) and provides advice on how to prevent such problems before they become career threatening (the equally pertinent and closely related issue of psychological well-being and health is discussed in detail in Chapter 9).

3.1   Surveys

The first large-scale surveys on the physical and mental demands of performance have revealed some disturbing facts. Of the 2212 musicians in a survey by Fishbein *et al.* (1988), 76% reported at least one serious medical condition that affected their playing. Brandfonbrener (1990) surveyed 22 000 music teachers, of whom 19% reported performance-related medical problems. Caldron *et al.* (1986) found that, of 250 musicians studied, 57% suffered musculoskeletal symptoms, and 37% had to seek medical help. Newmark and Lederman (1987) studied a group of 79 amateur musicians who normally practiced for an hour a day; when on an intensive course playing seven hours per day, 72% reported musculoskeletal symptoms. A consensus among these and many other reports ascribe performance-related symptoms to a variety of causes, the most common being excess practice, change of instrument, difficult repertory, and stress of a demanding lifestyle. Among students, these include overpractice, change of teacher, stressful conditions, and examinations.

In 1997, the Fédération Internationale des Musiciens (FIM) surveyed 57 orchestras worldwide (James, 2000). This was the most comprehensive survey to date and enquired into a host of factors that might affect the performer—physical, psychological, and pedagogical. Throughout the world, the results were consistent: 56% had suffered pain when playing within the last year and 34% experienced pain more than once a week. The most common sites of pain were the neck, shoulder, and back. In 19%, pain was severe enough to stop performance. To the question "do you think your training college or academy gave you sufficient help in preparing for the stresses and strains of being an orchestral musician," the answer in 83% was "no." It is, thus, clear that musicians can suffer for their art and that their education should be sufficiently geared toward identifying and preventing these problems.

3.2   Specific medical diagnoses

The author has run specialist clinics for musicians over the last 40 years and in the last 12 years as a founding member of the British Association for Performing Arts Medicine (BAPAM). A detailed analysis has been carried out on 1046 musicians personally seen at these clinics (see Figure 3.1). Half (just over 48%) had a clear-cut pathology, in which a specific diagnosis could be made. In the remaining 52%, few

(a) Specific medical diagnoses

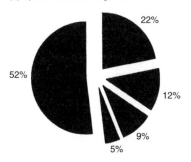

22%

22% old injuries (111 of 507)
12% tenosynovitis (62 of 507)
9% hypermobility (48 of 507)
5% focal dystonia (23 of 507)
52% various other (263 of 507)

52%

12%

9%

5%

(b) Nonspecific musculoskeletal problems

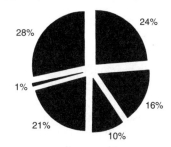

24%

28%

24% piano (129 of 539)
16% violin (88 of 539)
10% cello (54 of 539)
21% guitar (111 of 539)
1% conducting (5 of 539)
28% various other (152 of 539)

1%

16%

21%

10%

Figure 3.1 Musicians seen at the British Association for Performing Arts Medicine (BAPAM). A total of 1046, including (a) 507 with specific medical diagnoses and (b) 539 with nonstructural problems resulting, generally, from poor posture, tense neck and shoulder muscles, inappropriate practice regimes, lack of fitness, and stress.

(if any) physical signs could be found. Symptoms were often vague and general, and the musicians themselves attributed these to "doing it wrong" (e.g. poor posture, bad practice technique, lack of fitness, and stress). The fact that such a high proportion of patients were suffering from nonstructural, performance-related problems is a major challenge to the profession, for many of these problems are preventable (see "Nonstructural musculoskeletal problems" below for further discussion).

3.2.1   Structural disorders

The structural disorders observed resulted from three broad sources: old injuries, tenosynovitis, and hypermobility. The most common of these was the result of an old injury (22%), which had left the musician with residual stiffness of joints, weak muscles, and a lack of confidence that was impairing performance. The moral from this is clear: full rehabilitation to 100% capacity is vital after injury.

Tenosynovitis (or inflammation of tendons) was relatively rare (12%). The label "tenosynovitis" is often too liberally used to describe any ache or pain in a specific area. True tenosynovitis is associated with redness, swelling, crepitus, and severe pain or restricted movement. This is rare in musicians and usually follows extramusical activities, such as household chores and gardening. The exception is De Quervain syndrome, which affects the long abductor and extensors of the thumb and can occur in percussionists as a result of repetitive, high-pressure activity and in cellists who grip the neck of the cello too tightly.

Just over 9% of the musicians with structural disorders were hypermobile. The term hypermobility refers to the increased range of movement beyond the accepted norm, often described in lay terms as "double jointed." The joints most commonly affected are the fingers, thumb, elbow, shoulder, spine, and knee. To be classified as hypermobile, for example, the knuckle should be passively hyper-extendable to more than 90°; the thumb can be opposed to the volar (front) aspect of the forearm; the elbow and knee can be extended 10° beyond 180°; the hands can be placed flat on the floor without bending the knees; the hand can be placed behind the back as high as the seventh cervical vertebra. There is undoubtedly a genetic element to hypermobility, and its expression is at its height during youth, peaking at 12–15 years and tending to decline slowly thereafter.

It seems that there is a higher incidence of hypermobility among musicians than in the population at large. An increased range of movement can, in fact, be of benefit to the musician (e.g. Liszt's hands could together span three octaves—i.e. about 20 inches or 50 cm). Larsson *et al.* (1987) studied 660 musicians and concluded that hypermobility of the thumb, wrist, and fingers can be an asset in playing instruments such as the flute, violin, and piano for passages requiring repetitive motions, but that it can be a liability in situations where joints are required to be used as stabilizers (e.g. knees and spine for timpanists and others who stand to play).

In general, hypermobile musicians are more liable to strains and sprains of the affected joints. There is evidence to suggest that hypermobile joints are less sensitive to relaying information about position and rate of change of joint movement (i.e. proprioception; see Hall *et al.*, 1995). This can result in greater pressure being exerted by fingers on keys or strings, with the possibility of chronic strain. In addition, hypermobile individuals can suffer generalized rheumatic symptoms. The "full house" of multiple joints being affected is rare; it is, in fact, more common to see only one or two joints affected. At BAPAM, every patient is examined for hypermobility. If the muscles of hypermobile joints are found to be weak, either from repeated or previous injury or from general poor muscle tone, an exercise program to restore full power and improve proprioception is normally recommended. Often a musician's "nonspecific pains" can relate to this, and even if there is a clear cause of symptoms unrelated to hypermobility, guidance for general care of the joints is always given. Advice from a therapist on joint protection and general lifestyle is strongly recommended in those with persistent symptoms.

3.2.2   Focal dystonia

Focal dystonia (literally meaning, localized abnormal muscle tone) refers to the incoordination of movement—often with cramps—that can affect fingers or embouchure. It is perhaps the most devastating medical condition that can affect the musician, and of the 507 patients with a clear-cut pathology seen by the author, 5% were diagnosed with dystonia. The problem usually arises in mid-career, although it may affect musicians sooner, particularly if they began playing in early childhood. Several reports have suggested that dystonia can follow trauma or a particularly stressful situation, such as significant increase in work or the tackling of particularly difficult repertory. Brandfonbrener (1995) reviewed the cases of 58 musicians with dystonia and found that 10 had suddenly increased their playing/practice, 8 had recently undergone an extensive change in technique or a change in instrument, and 7 had engaged in intensive playing/practice after a long repose. In 19, however, no antecedent factor could be implicated. Gary Graffman (1986) described the condition as it affected him:

To begin with, I had no pain. No numbness, either; nor any such symptom that one could possibly explain to a doctor. For all normal purposes—opening jars, tying shoelaces, manipulating chopsticks, and even at the piano 99.9% of the time, my hand operated as always. It was only in certain extended positions—playing a series of octaves, for example—that my trouble surfaced. I was able to play the first octave normally, but striking each subsequent one caused my fourth finger to draw in more and more, dragging the fifth along with it as the hand contracted, and, of course, hitting wrong notes. This behavior was in no way affected by fatigue, warming up, or "good" or "bad" days. Either I could play a certain pattern, or I could not. Every time it was exactly the same. An octave span of eight notes on the keyboard is about seven inches. A child can deal with that. But I, at fifty, was no longer capable of doing so (p. 3).

The condition is a form of "occupational cramp," and the characteristic sudden loss of coordination has been observed in conjunction with a number of motor skills, including telegraphy, typing, watchmaking, tailoring, snooker playing, and golf (the "yips"). The condition is usually highly task-specific and depends on sensory input. The musician notices the problem only when playing his or her instrument, not when playing other instruments or in any of the usual activities of daily living, such as using a computer. The amount of practice seems to be an important factor in the development of dystonic symptoms. Soloists are much more often affected than orchestral musicians. Furthermore, orchestral musicians can cope by resting or avoiding difficult passages and, thus, abort its development; soloists have nowhere to hide and often must keep playing with ever-increasing symptoms. The condition is often made worse by practicing passages that trigger the dystonic movements.

There even seem to be specific patterns of symptoms for different instruments. Wind players, for instance, may find that they split notes or blur a run (e.g. in clarinetists, it often results in an inability to extend the middle finger but can also interfere with the little finger flexing and the index finger extending). Jazz drummers may not be able to control their foot on the pedal. In guitarists, it is commonly the third or middle finger that is affected (see Hayes, 1987). In piano playing, as in the case of Gary Graffman, the ring and little fingers flex into the palm. The task specificity might be so distinct that symptoms occur only when playing particular passages, or playing scales upward and not downward, or vice versa. Therefore, in some cases, it is not possible to track the appearance of symptoms to one single finger rather than to a complex movement pattern. Another interesting phenomenon is that, in most pianists, the dystonic movement pattern appears only when playing on an actual piano keyboard, rather than when "playing" on the wooden cover of the piano or on plastic keys. This clearly highlights that focal dystonia is not simply a motor disorder but a disorder of sensorimotor integration, which requires transforming incoming sensory input from an ongoing movement into an adequate motor output, as is necessary for the guidance of skilled motor acts.

The salient feature for diagnosis is that the condition is quite painless, unlike other local disorders that can interfere with playing. The course is variable, but it may be months or years before the musician finally realizes that the situation is unacceptable. The clinician can carry out tests for any local or central neurological disorder that might have precipitated or caused the dystonia, but in most cases, full examination reveals normal functioning—all the tendons, joints, and nerves being in full working order.

It is still not fully understood as to how musicians at the top of their profession (whose technique is seemingly faultless) can be so affected, but in recent years, the knowledge about the underlying complex pathophysiology has increased alongside the development of research. Byl *et al.* (1996) described a primate model for focal hand dystonia. They trained primates to perform a gripping task 300 times a day for several weeks. The primates developed incoordination and cramps similar to symptoms of focal hand dystonia. Topographical mapping of the primates' sensory cortex revealed that the receptive fields of single fingers were remarkably enlarged and overlapping. Their conclusion was that this degradation of sensory representations of single fingers might have caused the observed motor disturbance. Elbert *et al.* (1998), in measuring cortical finger representations in the somatosensory cortex with magnetencephalography (MEG), described a smaller distance (i.e. fusion) between the representations of the digits in the somatosensory cortex for the affected hand of dystonic musicians than for the hands of nonmusicians. They suggested that use-dependent susceptibility to digital representation fusion in the cortex may be involved in the etiology of focal dystonia.

Similar to these findings in the somatosensory cortex, enlargements and blurring of motor cortical representations of single hand muscles have been described in focal hand dystonia patients (Byrnes *et al.*, 1998). These changes in the motor cortical representation may be secondary to altered afferent inputs from both clinically affected and unaffected muscles, which underlines the strong link between the alterations in the sensory and motor system forming a kind of "dysfunctional network" in focal hand dystonia. Part of this network is formed by the basal ganglia, deep-lying structures in the forebrain that are involved in motor control in terms of filtering and focusing sensory input to respective pre-motor and motor cortical areas. "Blurred" sensory input certainly leads to imprecise output, which in turn can lead to an unfocused input to motor cortical areas.

In the FIM survey (James, 2000), one of the questions asked was "do you ever suffer from clumsiness or incoordination of your fingers." Surprisingly, 39.5% answered "yes," and 21% admitted to loss of lip seal or coordination. This highlights that incipient dystonia may be more common than is realized, but on the other hand, it shows that the symptoms are often very unspecific in the beginning. Focal hand dystonia should really only be diagnosed after ruling out any incoordination or painless playing problems that may result from other sources or simply from bad playing habits.

Treatment of this condition remains a difficult task. Improvement of the symptoms can be attained in most cases, but it is understandable that for many patients this is not enough. Complete recovery is rare and some restrictions may remain with respect to particular pieces, or to the speed and power required in certain motor movements.

Drugs can help in some cases, but of course, possible side effects have to be considered. Botulinum toxin (Botox), which temporarily paralyses the nerve endings in muscles, can relieve symptoms for a while, but when the drug wears off, they reappear. It can also cause muscle weakness; therefore, injections of botulinum toxin should only be administered by an experienced neurophysiologist in order to avoid any unwanted widespread weakening effect. There have not, as of yet, been long-term follow up studies, so it is not entirely clear whether the repeated application of this drug has negative effects itself. Its use in cases with musicians has now been restricted to those where nothing else has worked.

Recently, a very promising therapeutic approach has been developed that is based on the assumption that use-dependent re-organization of cortical networks (as described above) contribute to the fundamental abnormalities seen in focal dystonia. It has used a method of sensory motor retuning that involves the immobilization of different unaffected fingers and the training of sequential finger movements (including the affected one). Through this procedure, a re-differentiation of the finger representation in the somatosensory cortex has been achieved, which has also been accompanied by an amelioration of dystonic symptoms (Candia *et al.*, 2003).

Rehabilitation is slow and relapses not uncommon; therefore, the musician must show great patience. Naturally, dystonic patients can be deeply distressed and tense and may benefit from a general muscular relaxation program, such as Feldenkrais technique (which teaches whole body control over a progressive period) or basic yoga. At the same time, any postural or musculoskeletal dysfunction must be tackled. All authorities agree that the earlier the patient is treated, the more likely a cure is possible. Musicians who present themselves to physicians in late stages of the disorder, with inability to play even quite simple runs without mistakes, rarely improve. This is a difficult area, and much research still is needed to identify the causes of dystonia and to determine an adequate course for rehabilitation and management. It is imperative, however, that affected players seek expert advice as early as possible—indeed, as soon as it is clear that a painless incoordination of hand or embouchure is affecting performance.

3.3   Nonstructural musculoskeletal problems

3.3.1   General remarks

This section deals with the 52% of musicians seen at BAPAM whose musculoskeletal symptoms were adjudged to be due to technical faults (i.e. improper technique, poor posture, misuse of the body, or inappropriate practicing procedures). These musicians spanned all instruments and styles of music, but the vast majority were pianists (129), violinists (88), cellists (54), and guitarists (111). Common faults and symptoms have been analyzed and studied according to instrument, and a selection of these are discussed below.

Every instrument presents problems in terms of physical interface, some being notoriously user-unfriendly (e.g. the violin, viola, and flute). It is particularly important that performers are aware of these problems early on in their careers and take steps to prevent injury. Generally speaking, one can alter either the player's approach or the instrument itself. The latter is occasionally possible, but it is the player in virtually all cases who has to make allowances for the instrument. Unlike other performers, the singer *is* the instrument and needs especial care to keep body and mind in first-class order. To that end, regular sessions with a voice coach and, if necessary, joint discussions with a sympathetic laryngologist should be part of a singer's life (despite the common association between body size and the tradition of monumental Wagnerian opera, singers should not be overweight, as obesity reduces vital capacity and physical endurance and is associated with reflux laryngitis).

Common to all the musicians seen at BAPAM were the following faults: poor posture, tense neck and shoulder muscles, inappropriate practice regimes, lack of fitness, and stress.

Posture

Postural deficits are common, but as Dommerholt *et al.* (1998) point out, musicians are usually not aware of their own misalignments. When shown their playing position on video, performers are often stunned to see how inappropriate their posture is. The relationship of head to neck and neck to trunk is all-important, as F. M. Alexander discovered when analysing the neck and shoulder symptoms associated with his own loss of function as an actor (Rosenthal, 1987; see also Chapter 10 of this volume). In addition, pelvic and spinal alignment is equally important for trunk and pelvic stability and is essential—whether standing or sitting to play—for muscle control, as well as awareness of body position and rate at which movement occurs.

The most common fault is the forward head posture. Haughie *et al.* (1995) showed a statistically significant relationship between the degree of forward head posture and pain. A typical example in music is the need for string players sitting at the front desks in orchestras to look up and to the side to see the conductor. Similarly, musicians may need to crane forward—and, thus, be susceptible to neck pain—when reading from poorly photocopied scores or if their sight is not properly corrected. A hunched position at the keyboard and forward stoop with the cello are common and also highly likely to cause chronic pain. Furthermore, excessive lordosis and kyphosis (i.e. rounded shoulders and excessive arching of the lower back, respectively) inevitably lead to pain.

Singing teachers have long known of the vital importance of good balanced posture, which is at the heart of comfortable and effective singing. As Davies and Jahn (1998) point out, singing involves vocal athletics, and a fit body and mind are essential. Indeed, performers and teachers of all types could benefit tremendously from a similarly healthy approach to postural awareness. It is encouraging to see that Alexander technique has been incorporated so widely into performance education (see Chapter 10), but more could be done in terms of bringing posture and bodily awareness to the forefront of musical training—be it through the Alexander technique or other methods. Doing so could dramatically decrease the number of *unnecessary* strains on the musician's body. Given the amount of time that musicians spend (and are expected to spend) practicing—as documented in the preceding chapter—it is vital that those hours are spent ergonomically correctly.

Practice, tension, and fitness

The human body is not designed to remain in one position for hours at a time; prolonged muscle tension causes fiber shortening and restriction of circulation, which results in inadequate dispersal of muscle metabolites and chronic pain. In response to this, the musician may unknowingly adjust the hold of the instrument, causing stresses elsewhere. To relieve stress in the neck and shoulder, for example, string players frequently alter the grip of the left hand and cause wrist strain; they then complain of wrist pain when the source of the mischief is actually higher up.

Rigid advice on how many hours to practice per day cannot be given, as much depends on the individual capacity for prolonged concentration and level of fitness (see Chapters 9, 11, and 12 for suggestions on how to enhance concentration and fitness). Learning new repertory in a hurry may mean putting in an excessive amount of practice (say, over 5 hours per day), but painful symptoms and damage can be minimized by regular breaks and short spells of physical activity, involving stretching the contracted muscles and freeing up stiffened joints. John Williams, a professional guitarist whose father was a distinguished musician and taught him care of the body from an early age, never practices for more than 20 minutes at a time. He stretches, walks around, carries out deep breathing, and then resumes play. He has said that it takes him 4 hours to do 2.5 hours of good practice, which includes warming up, cooling down, breaks, and taking notes of his performance (Williams, 1998).

Insistence on many hours of practice a day by some music schools and conservatories has led to a culture of work intensity (a recent brochure of one academy has stated that violin pupils are expected to practice 6 hours per day). An excessive workload on tired muscles—compounded by lack of instruction in correct posture, practice regime, and care of the body in general—is the most common cause of injuries with students. While 52% of all musicians seen at BAPAM were suffering because of technical faults, the figure was 70% in students. Warrington *et al.* (2002) found that nonspecific causes of pain (clearly resulting from technical faults) were present in 4% of patients over 40 years old, 19% in the 25–40 age range, and 48% in those under 25.

There are several general recommendations that clinicians can make in this area. Firstly, Spaulding (1988) points out that a child's early teachers and family should emphasize prevention of injury. After the mid-twenties, preventive techniques can be difficult to learn and perhaps even more difficult to incorporate into everyday musical life. There are many aspects to effective prevention—correct technique, good posture, general attitude, and emotional set, as well as a sensible perspective on appropriate quantity of practice. Young students should be regularly encouraged to think about these issues so that the process of self-reflection becomes automatic. This is a serious responsibility for music educators and one that is far too frequently neglected, either from exigencies of time or ignorance. Redmond and Tiermond (2001) carried out a survey of music teachers and found that less than half had received any education on preventive measures. In a pilot study, Spahn *et al.* (2001) found that musculoskeletal symptoms were significantly reduced in students who received a weekly 2-hour instruction on anatomy and physiology relevant to music making, along with specific exercises for the particular instrument.

Secondly, all athletes warm up before and cool down after practice and performance. Coaches have known for years that injuries are common if muscles are not slowly exercised to maximum output. A surprising number of musicians admit that they neglect these precautions. The body dislikes sudden exertion, particularly in an unheated environment. Zaza and Farewell (1997) showed that warming up before and taking breaks during practice can protect musicians from performance-related musculoskeletal disorders.

Thirdly, the intensity of practice advisable can vary with different degrees of fitness. In general, the more physically fit one is—with strength, stamina, flexibility, and good cardiovascular reserve—the more one can play without harm. It has been suggested that the prolonged periods of practice required for musical performance at the highest levels is all that is necessary for fitness. This may be true to a limited extent, in that no specific extra exercises are required for strength and dexterity in the wrists or hands other than playing and practice (except in the case of weakness from old injuries or hypermobility). However, other physical parameters are required, including strong postural muscles to maintain neck and back position (particularly for keyboard and string players). It is equally important to develop stamina, the ability to sustain repeated stress to the musculoskeletal system over a period of time. This is achieved by a program of high-repetition, low-load exercises (conversely, increased strength is achieved through high-load, low-repetition exercises). In all cases, it is wise for musicians to consult an expert physiotherapist or trainer for advice on a particular regime suited to their starting fitness level, physique, and specific instrumental requirements. Also, it is as much the demands of long-distance traveling, adjusting to new countries, irregular meals, change in climate, and anxiety about arrangements that cause fatigue as the actual physical demands of music performance. An extensive discussion of physical fitness, psychological well-being, and stress management is provided in Chapter 9 of this volume.

Fourthly, it has been recognized of late that much good practice can be performed in the mind. Mental rehearsal has been shown to be highly effective (Freymuth, 1993; Stanton, 1994), and electrophysiological studies have revealed that the same neural pathways are excited when musical imaging occurs as when the instrument is actually played. Serious professional musicians are increasingly making mental rehearsal a significant part of their practice, and sports psychologists have shown how such techniques can be used to improve subsequent performance. Chapter 12 reviews and assesses specific mental skills training techniques.

Finally, Zaza and Farewell (1997) insist that other repetitive tasks, such as computing and knitting, should be avoided or limited by the musician. It is not uncommon to find that symptoms develop in musicians who spend 2–3 hours on a computer, on top of their music making.

3.3.2   Individual instruments

Piano

Of the 129 pianists whose symptoms were adjudged to be due to technical faults, 58 felt pain in the wrists and hands and 26 in the neck and shoulders. Common sources of pain were stiff wrists, a hunched posture, excessive pressure on the keys, and overpracticing without adequate breaks and thorough warm up. There can be a number of antecedent factors that lead to symptoms from technical faults, including individual differences in basic anatomy and in how pianists engage physically with the instrument.

In terms of anatomy, Charles Rosen (1999), in an article in the *New York Review of Books*, surveyed a number of great pianists and found that size and dimensions of the hands varied considerably. Richter, for instance, could play intervals as large as a twelfth, but Hofmann, one of Rosen's heroes, could only span an octave. Denison (2000) has argued that manufacturers should make keyboards smaller, so as to accommodate those with small hands. It seems that practicing parallel octaves is a typical cause of trouble (Rosen cites Schubert's *Erlkonig* as a particularly vicious example). Sakai (1997) analyzed the physical problems of 40 professional pianists and found that octaves and chords were the most common cause of pain. Pianists would therefore be wise to monitor (and possibly limit) the amount of time given to repetitive practice in this area. Rosen notes that Steinway built a piano in which the ivories were slightly narrower, so that he could manage a ninth. Thus, it is possible that, in time, the instrument may conform to the player's anatomy, but for the moment, pianists with small hands must vary technique in order to master certain physical challenges.

Similarly, problems can emerge as a result of anomalous tendon linkages. Richard Beauchamp, Head of Piano at St. Mary's Music School (Edinburgh), has made a special study of these (see Beauchamp, 1996, 1997, 1999, 2001, 2003). The most common is the absence of the sublimus flexor tendon in the little finger (i.e. the tendon that allows independent bending at the middle joint of the finger). This can be determined by holding the hand flat on a table—palm upwards, with the index, middle, and ring fingers held by the other hand—and trying to bend the little finger at the middle joint without bending the end joint. An inability to do this can present problems, for example, when attempting to use fingerings such as those indicated in bars 415–416 of Figure 3.2. A number of other anomalous linkages can be problematic, including the presence of a connecting tendon between the profundus tendons used in bending the end joints of the little, ring, and middle fingers. These can be closely joined as far up as the wrist, which can interfere with achieving independence of the third, fourth, and fifth fingers. Beauchamp (2003) has recommended several practical solutions—ranging from alternative fingerings to rearrangement of passages between the hands—to avoid

Figure 3.2 Chopin's Scherzo No. 2 in B-flat minor, Op. 31. Rather than using the indicated fingering, Beauchamp (2003) recommends two possible solutions: (1) playing the E with the third finger and rapidly changing to the fifth or (2) not actually trying to join the F# to the E physically, as the sustaining pedal will almost certainly be down at that point.

strain caused by these anomalies (see also Winspur & Wynn Parry, 1998, for further information on the musician's hand).

In terms of differences in how individuals engage physically with the piano, Rosen (1999) notes that Horowitz played with his fingers flat, Iturbi held his wrist below the level of the keyboard, Gould used a very low piano stool, and Richter preferred a very high stool. It seems that many approaches have been proposed as to the ideal curvature of the hand when playing. Matthay (1903/1950) stressed the importance of a curved hand, using wrist and forearm rotation, and moving the body rather than the wrist for major stretches (certainly, from a medical viewpoint, playing with stiff wrists and too flat hands can cause problems). Bejjani et al. (1989) compared three types of hand—flat, arched, and flexed—using video and sound recording to study the finger, wrist, elbow, and shoulder joints. The flexed-finger approach involved more ulnar deviation (i.e. rotating the wrist in the direction of the little finger), which is a potent cause of injury. Until a long-term study is mounted with state-of-the-art electronic recording of the muscles used in playing (comparing different techniques over many years and the incidence of musculoskeletal symptoms that result from each), pianists can only be guided by traditional teaching methods that obey the laws of human ergonomics. Grindea (2001) strongly emphasizes the importance of a relaxed wrist and the position of the piano—upright posture, head level, shoulders relaxed, and wrists in line with the fifth finger and elbow. Brown (2000) has reviewed her own experience from master-classes over many years and found a direct correlation between injury and tense or awkward hand and finger positions. She counsels against a down-flexed wrist, and keeping the elbows too close to the body.

In general, the pianist must think of the upper limb as a single connected unit and make full use of the shoulders for power—not the hand. Excessive lifting of the fingers off the keys is dangerous. Many players attempt to overcome the natural weakness of extension of the ring finger (which has less independence in this movement than the other fingers) by resistance exercise, which can be a major cause of pain. It is better to use the excursion of the wrist "dropping" on to the key.

Violin and viola

Among the 88 violinists seen at BAPAM, symptoms were equally divided between the neck and shoulder and the forearm and hand/wrist. Common faults were poor posture, overpractice, unsatisfactory chin/shoulder rest, and too tight pressure on the bow—and in students, a change of teacher and re-jigging of technique.

Filling the gap between chin and chest is a major problem. A common fault among violinists, typically due to an ill-fitting shoulder rest, is to hunch up the left shoulder, which can cause excess tension in the neck and shoulder muscles. Using electrical recordings, Levy et al. (1992) analyzed the activity in the shoulder and neck muscles in 15 professional violinists with and without shoulder rests. There was a highly significant reduction in muscle activity with the rest. Also, violinists should ideally not be too tall because additional height makes the gap between chin and chest difficult to fill comfortably. Of course, one option for players with long or unusually shaped necks is to obtain a custom-built chin/shoulder rest. Weilerstein and Neal (2000) strongly recommend all players not to have the instrument always under the chin and never to practice for more than 5 hours per day. They also note that injuries can arise from stubborn tuning pegs.

Fischer (1998) has written extensively on technique and musculoskeletal problems. He points to a multitude of interrelated factors, many subtle and invisible, that can set off a chain reaction of tension. Some important factors are speed of dropping the finger in relation to tempo, speed of bow related to pressure and distance from the bridge, and different speeds and widths in vibrato. Fischer points out that problems arise when players point the violin too far forward or use too much clockwise rotation of the left hand or finger pressure. Drop release, not drop press, avoids locking the hand, which is a common cause of pain, as is too strong a grip on the bow with counter pressure of the thumb. Raising the fingers too high off the string in fast passages triples the energy required. Also, postural errors are common, with the hip joint collapsing forward, pulling down from the diaphragm causing the upper back to bend forward and the shoulders to pull up. Fischer concludes that, in almost every example of a player suffering from debilitating tension, there are simple technical/physical causes that can quickly be rectified. "It is really never too late, and players of any age and stage can continue to polish and refine their overall technique, and move ever closer to truly effortless playing" (p. 22).

Similar problems are seen in viola players, and with the instrument being heavier, it can be more disabling. Violas vary surprisingly in size and weight, and symptoms may arise after a change of instrument. Donald Ehrich of the San Francisco Symphony Orchestra had severe problems with his bowing arm. The Rivinus viola provided a deeper cut away on the bowing side and angled the fingerboard towards the right hand, thus "untwisting" his left arm with excellent results (Markison, 1998). Gelberman *et al.* (1981) have cut away the body on the right side of the instrument to allow reduction in wrist flexion in higher positions, particularly useful for musicians with incipient median nerve compression (i.e. carpal tunnel syndrome).

Cello

With the 54 cellists, symptoms were equally divided between shoulder/neck and wrist/hand. Causes were excessive playing, poor posture, weak shoulder and arm muscles, and poor bow hold. Extended thumb with excess pressure in the bow hand was a common cause of pain and loss of sonorous tone, particularly in students.

It seems that cellists suffer some degree of backache as part of their life as a result of the playing position. Most take great trouble to ensure satisfactory seating with back cushions and front blocks, and many employ back exercises to avoid chronic pain. The cellist Bernard Gregor-Smith (1998) advises that the torso should incline towards the cello, counteracting the tendency for the weight of the cello to push back on the torso. One should lean forward from the base of the spine—not halfway up the back, which is a common cause of back pain.

Joan Dixon, a professional cellist whose masterclasses were legendary, noted that symptoms frequently arise when the cellist's area of motion is too restricted. If movements are free and full, the posture balanced, and there is no tension in back or neck, playing should be pain free.

Cellists would be wise to adopt a program of exercises to maintain strength in the spinal extensor muscles and abdominal muscles, in addition to the fitness and warm up procedures recommended for all musicians (see Chapter 9).

Guitar

A relatively large number of guitarists (111) seen at BAPAM had technical faults. This was principally because most of the guitarists were self-taught and had no formal instruction in care of the body or posture while playing. Pain was felt predominantly in the fingers, wrist, and hand (twice as common as in the neck and shoulders), and common faults were poor posture, tense neck/shoulders leading to painful adjustments of the wrist, poor practice regime, change of teacher, and many hours spent on the computer (as most of the guitarists had jobs outside of music).

In the classical guitar, the wrist and thumb tends to be hyperflexed, and resting the inner arm near the elbow against the instrument can irritate the ulnar nerve where it runs superfically at the inner elbow. This results in pins and needles in the fourth and fifth fingers and weakness of the small hand muscles. As John Williams (1998) has pointed out, unlike piano and violin, little large-scale movement is required of the guitarist. Indeed, apart from movement of the fingers of the left hand along the strings and (to some extent) the fingers of the right hand up and down the strings, no natural movements of the upper limb are necessitated by the physical production of music.

The inevitable slight twisting of the torso consequent on the left foot being on a stool is likely to lead to neck and back pain, and it is essential that players move their bodies and stretch frequently during practice. Kember (1995a, 1995b, 1996a, 1996b, 1996c, 1996d, 1996e), a senior physiotherapist, has made a special study of guitarists' problems and, in a series of articles in *Classical Guitar*, has summarized good practice to avoid injury: (1) the choice of guitar should relate to body shape (a broad, wide palm with long fingers needs a wider neck than with stout fingers); (2) posture must allow for no rotation of the pelvis, shoulders must be level, and head central (a slumped position with a twisted pelvis is all too common); (3) if the guitar is held too high, there will be pain in the neck and shoulder; (4) the seat should not slope too far forward (a wedge shaped cushion of firm foam on a poorly shaped chair can avoid back strain); and (5) warm-up should include uncurling of the spine from a flexed position, general postural alignment, breathing exercises, and attention to balance of the shoulders (too early movement of the shoulder blades may follow imbalance and cause stress in the trapezii).

Adequately broad straps are vital for rock guitarists who stand with a heavy instrument suspended from the neck. These musicians, more than any, must pay strict attention to posture and build up powerful neck and shoulder muscles. Commonly, they experience forearm and wrist pain and a painful neck and back as a result of balancing too large a guitar in a lifted playing posture. This tempts the player to suspend the guitar too low to enable the hand to get on to the strings. Perrin (1997) has written at length on problems of student guitarists, illustrating good and bad hand, wrist, and trunk positions.

Flute

It is difficult to imagine a more diabolically designed instrument than the flute, which demands contorted positions of both arms. The left forearm has to be hyperextended, and the left wrist deviated radially. Hyperextending the left index finger provides a sort of shelf and, together with the radial deviator of the wrist, can compress the posterior interosseous nerve, causing pain and weakness in the fingers. Pain is not uncommon in the right thumb, particularly if excessive tension is used. Norris (2000) advocates an orthosis (the "Stedirest"), which uses a nonslip cork-lined metal grip to handle the instrument. It distributes the pressure over a wider area of the thumb and directs the weight of the rods through the base of support preventing the flute from rolling inwards.

Katherine Butler, a hand therapist and professional flute player, finds that muscle pain in the forearm is not uncommon among musicians she has treated. This can require re-education of technique, for which a finger block over the flute keys can be of great value. Also, she finds that neck pain can result from inadequate power in the shoulder and neck muscles with inability to maintain the playing position for extended periods, particularly when the arms are held too high.

Failure to take adequate breaks in practice is particularly likely to lead to musculoskeletal problems in the upper limb in flute players, owing to the "strained" position that players need to adopt. In cases where musculoskeletal symptoms persist, the Markison angled flute has an 88° bend that allows untwisting of both arms. If the player has very small muscles of the hand and wrist, extensions can be added to keys and a program of hand exercises instituted.

Conductors

Conductors are notoriously long lived and seem relatively free of musculoskeletal problems (Simons, 1986). This is probably due to the regular movements they make of arms and trunk. Simons studied 153 choral conductors, few of whom reported any significant musculoskeletal problems, other than backache.

At BAPAM, five international-level conductors have been seen who developed disabling damage to the tendon mechanisms of the shoulder. Repeated friction of these tendons against the end of the collarbone can cause severe inflammation and, ultimately, rupture. This results from the restricted arc of movement when the shoulder is held at about 70–90°. The shoulder is put under particular stress when conducting opera and chorus, when the arm has to be lifted up well above 90° for the baton to be seen. Physiotherapy and the judicious use of a steroid injection (a maximum of three in one year) usually solve this problem; however, there have been conductors who have submitted to overfrequent use of steroid injections and have subsequently ruptured tendons, necessitating major surgery and prolonged rehabilitation.

3.3.3   General advice to prevent injury

Musculoskeletal symptoms and injuries can be greatly reduced on all instruments and within all performance genres by the following precautions:

- Warming-up: this does not mean playing scales and specific exercises for the instrument; rather, it means stretching the arms above the head, stretching the neck in all directions, arm circling, elbow rotation, wrist shaking, knee bends, trunk rotation, and deep breathing. Even 5 minutes can be beneficial (see Chapter 9).
- Cooling down in a similar manner.

- Good posture throughout playing (see Chapter 10).
- Regular breaks every 20–30 minutes, with arm stretching, walking about, and deep breathing.
- Practicing a relaxation technique, using it before performance and auditions in order to control the body and not let the body control one's performance (see Chapter 12).
- Maintaining a good diet.
- Taking time to relax and pursue general cultural and sporting activities.

3.4   Conclusions

Life as a musician is fraught with physical, emotional, and mental demands. When injury or illness strikes, the show has to go on, often to the detriment of the player's future health. In the FIM survey (James, 2000), respondents were asked to list the top 10 stressors in orchestra life. The order and nature were virtually universal throughout the world:

- a conductor who saps confidence
- an incompetent conductor
- experiencing problems with the instrument
- playing an orchestral solo
- illegible music
- disorganized rehearsal time
- an incompatible desk partner
- having medical problems that affect work
- making a mistake when performing
- inadequate financial reward.

Clearly, musicians lead a demanding life. In Britain, for example, performers must hasten between rehearsals, concerts, recording sessions, and teaching (with many musicians having to seek work outside of music to make ends meet). In addition, they need to practice, and on tour, schedules are inordinately demanding with practically no respite on return. A top London orchestra recently toured the USA for 6 weeks, with almost nightly concerts, and was back in the concert hall the day after returning to London. In Britain, musicians are underpaid, overworked, and undervalued, yet Danziger (1997), who interviewed over 50 members of a leading orchestra about their hugely demanding lifestyle, reported that only 3 would not enter a career in music if given their time again.

It is difficult to say whether the situation will improve. Increasingly, more demands are being made on musicians, both to cram in more concerts and to take their art into the community. This is entirely laudable but has obvious implications for health. BAPAM advocates that musicians take every opportunity to improve their physical and mental condition. There is a need for a continuing dialogue with administrators to minimize stress and to ensure proper travel arrangements, satisfactory seating and lighting, more attention to the hazards of noise, regular time off (tours are *not* holidays), and a better career structure.

The whole question of damage to hearing from playing music has been opened up with the publication of *A Sound Ear* by the Association of British Orchestras (Wright Reid, 2001). There is no question that hearing suffers from playing and is not only related to the proximity of loud instruments (e.g. woodwind in front of brass) but may be due to sensitivity of the player to the high frequencies of his or her own instrument. The right answer has yet to be made clear, but it is likely to be a matter of compromise, with use of protective shields, planning repertory to avoid too many loud pieces in one concert, and improved earplugs. It is generally agreed that something has to be done to minimize this potent source of harm to orchestral players.

The implications of this discussion on physical health for students are obvious. There must be an overhaul of the curricula of music schools and conservatories. Students should be given thorough instruction on care of the body—one lecture in 4 years is inadequate. This must include posture, general and specific fitness of their musculoskeletal system, good breathing techniques, satisfactory compromise with problems of the instrumental interface, sensible practice regimes (including warming up and cooling down), coping strategies for performance anxiety and stage fright, the need for appropriate sport and recreation, and relaxation techniques. There is ample evidence to show that it is possible for students to perfect their techniques and live a fulfilling social and cultural life. When asked by one of his best pupils how he could improve his playing, Brahms reportedly replied "practice an hour less a day, and read a book."

Further information and reading

The British Association for Performing Arts Medicine offers free guidance at its London headquarters and its Manchester regional clinic (see *www.bapam.org.uk* or write to BAPAM, Fourth Floor, Totara Park House, 34–36 Grays Inn Road, London WC1X, UK, for further information). Details of similar such clinics around the world can be obtained through the websites of the following organizations: the Performing Arts Medicine Association (*www.artsmed.org*), the International Foundation for Performing Arts Medicine (*www.ifpam.org*), Médecine des Arts (*www.arts-medicine.com*), and the International Association for Dance, Medicine, and Science (*www.iadms.org*). For further reading on music and health, see:

Brandfonbrener, A. G., & Kjelland, J. M. (2002). Music medicine. In R. Parncutt & G. E. McPherson (Eds.), *The Science and Psychology of Music Performance: Creative Strategies for Teaching and Learning* (pp. 83–96). Oxford: Oxford University Press.

Grindea, C. (Ed.). (1995). *Tensions in the Performance of Music: A Symposium* (6th ed.). London: Kahn and Averill.

Tubiana, R., & Amadio, P. C. (Eds.). (2000). *Medical Problems of the Instrumentalist Musician*. London: Martin Dunitz.

Winspur, I., & Wynn Parry, C. B. (Eds.). (1998). *The Musician's Hand: A Clinical Guide*. London: Martin Dunitz.

References

Bejjani, F. J., Ferrara, L., Xu, N., Tomaino, C. M., Pavlidis, L., Wu, J., & Dommerholt, J. (1989). Comparison of three piano techniques as an implementation of a proposed experimental design. *Medical Problems of Performing Artists, 4,* 109–113.

Beauchamp, R. (1996). *Curved Fingers and Tension?* Retrieved August 28, 2003, from the Music and Health website: *www.musicandhealth.co.uk/tension.html.*

Beauchamp, R. (1997). Curved fingers and tension? *Classical Piano Magazine, March/April,* 27.

Beauchamp, R. (1999). *Our Anatomical Differences.* Retrieved August 28, 2003, from the Music and Health website: *www.musicandhealth.co.uk/differences.html.*

Beauchamp, R. (2001). *The Ergonomics of Piano Playing.* Retrieved August 28, 2003, from the Music and Health website: *www.musicandhealth.co.uk/ergonomics.htm.*

Beauchamp, R. (2003). *Examples of Passages Which May Cause Problems due to Tendon Linkages or Absences.* Retrieved August 28, 2003, from the Music and Health website: *www.musicand health.co.uk/linkages.htm.*

Brandfonbrener, A. G. (1990). The epidemiology and prevention of hand and wrist injuries in performing artists. *Hand Clinics, 6,* 365–378.

Brandfonbrener, A. G. (1995). Musicians with focal dystonia: A report of 58 cases seen during a ten-year period at a performing arts clinic. *Medical Problems of Performing Artists, 10,* 115–120.

Brown, S. (2000). Promoting a healthy keyboard technique. In R. Tubiana & P. C. Amadio (Eds.), *Medical Problems of the Instrumentalist Musician* (pp. 559–571). London: Martin Dunitz.

Byl, N. N., Merzenich, M. M., & Jenkins, W. M. (1996). A primate genesis model of focal dystonia and repetitive strain injury: I. Learning-induced dedifferentiation of the representation of the hand in the primary somatosensory cortex in adult monkeys. *Neurology, 47,* 508–520.

Byrnes, M. L., Thickbroom, G. W., Wilson, S. A., Sacco, P., Shipman, J. M., Stell, R., & Mastaglia, F. L. (1998). The corticomotor representation of upper limb muscles in writer's cramp and changes following botulinum toxin injection. *Brain, 121,* 977–988.

Caldron, P. H., Calabrese, L. H., Clough, J. D., Lederman, R. J., Williams, G., & Leatherman, J. (1986). A survey of musculoskeletal problems encountered in high-level musicians. *Medical Problems of Performing Artists, 1,* 136–139.

Candia, V., Wienbruch, C., Elbert, T., Rockstroh, B., & Ray, W. (2003). Effective behavioral treatment of focal hand dystonia in musicians alters somatosensory cortical organization. *Proceedings of the National Academy of Science, 100,* 7942–7946.

Danziger, D. (1997). *The Orchestra: The Lives Behind the Music.* London: Harper Collins.

Davies, D. G., & Jahn, A. F. (1998). *Care of the Professional Voice: A Management Guide For Singers, Actors, and Professional Voice Users.* Oxford: Oxford University Press.

Denison, C. (2000). Performer's perspective: Hand size versus the standard piano keyboard. *Medical Problems of Performing Artists, 15,* 111–114.

Dommerholt, J., Norris, R. N., & Shaheen, M. (1998). Therapeutic management of the instrumental musician. In R. T. Sataloff, A. G. Brandfonbrener, & R. J. Lederman (Eds.), *Performing Arts Medicine* (pp. 277–290). San Diego: Singular Publishing.

Elbert, T., Candia, V., Altenmuller, E., Rau, H., Sterr, A., Rockstroh, B., Pantev, C., & Taub, E. (1998). Alteration of digital representations in somatosensory cortex in focal hand dystonia. *Neuroreport, 9,* 3571–3575.

Fischer, S. (1998). The interface: Violin. In I. Winspur & C. B. Wynn Parry (Eds.), *The Musician's Hand: A Clinical Guide* (pp. 16–22). London: Martin Dunitz.

Fishbein, M., Middelstadt, S. E., Ottati, V., Strauss, S., & Ellis, A. (1988). Medical problems among ICSOM musicians: Overview of a national survey. *Medical Problems of Performing Artists, 3*, 1–8.

Freymuth, M. (1993). Mental practice for musicians: Theory and applications. *Medical Problems of Performing Artists, 8*, 141–143.

Gelberman, R. H., Hergenroeder, P. T., Hargens, A. R., Lundborg, G. N., & Akeson, W. H. (1981). The carpal tunnel syndrome: A study of carpal canal pressures. *Journal of Bone & Joint Surgery, 63*, 380–383.

Graffman, G. (1986). Doctor can you lend an ear? *Medical Problems of Performing Artists, 1*, 3–4.

Gregor-Smith, B. (1998). The interface: Cello. In I. Winspur & C. B. Wynn Parry (Eds.), *The Musician's Hand: A Clinical Guide* (pp. 24–25). London: Martin Dunitz.

Grindea, C. (2001). *Healthy Piano Technique*. London: Richard Schauer.

Hall, M. G., Ferrell, W. R., Sturrock, R. D., Hamblen, D. L., & Baxendale, R. H. (1995). The effect of the hypermobility syndrome on knee joint proprioception. *Rheumatology, 34*, 121–125.

Haughie, L. J., Fiebert, I. M., & Roach, K. E. (1995). Relationship of forward head posture and cervical backward bending to neck pain. *Journal of Manual and Manipulative Therapy, 3*, 91–97.

Hayes, B. (1987). Painless hand problems of string pluckers. *Medical Problems of Performing Artists, 2*, 39–40.

James, I. M. (2000). Survey of orchestras. In R. Tubiana & P. C. Amadio (Eds.), *Medical Problems of the Instrumentalist Musician* (pp. 195–201). London: Martin Dunitz.

Kember, J. (1995a). You and your guitar: 1. *Classical Guitar, November*, 24–25.

Kember, J. (1995b). You and your guitar: 2. *Classical Guitar, December*, 16–18.

Kember, J. (1996a). You and your guitar: 3. *Classical Guitar, January*, 16–18.

Kember, J. (1996b). You and your guitar: 4. *Classical Guitar, February*, 26–27.

Kember, J. (1996c). You and your guitar: 5. *Classical Guitar, March*, 31–32.

Kember, J. (1996d). You and your guitar: 6. *Classical Guitar, April*, 26–27.

Kember, J. (1996e). You and your guitar: 7. *Classical Guitar, August*, 26–27.

Larsson, L.-G., Baum, J., & Mudholkar, G. S. (1987). Hypermobility: features and differential incidence between the sexes. *Arthritis & Rheumatism, 30*, 1426–1430.

Levy, C. E., Lee, W. A., Brandfonbrener, A. G., Press, J., & Levy, A. E. (1992). Electromyographic analysis of muscular activity in the upper extremity generated by supporting a violin with and without a shoulder rest. *Medical Problems of Performing Artists, 7*, 103–109.

Markison, R. E. (1998). Adjustment of the musical interface. In I. Winspur & C. B. Wynn Parry (Eds.), *The Musician's Hand: A Clinical Guide* (pp. 149–159). London: Martin Dunitz.

Matthay, T. (1903/1950). *The Act of Touch in All its Diversity: An Analysis and Synthesis of Pianoforte Tone-Production*. London: Bosworth and Co. (Original work published in 1903).

Newmark, J., & Lederman, R. J. (1987). Practice doesn't necessarily make perfect: Incidence of overuse syndrome in amateur instrumentalists. *Medical Problems of Performing Artists, 2*, 93–97.

Norris, R. (2000). Applied ergonomics. In R. Tubiana & P. C. Amadio (Eds.), *Medical Problems of the Instrumentalist Musician* (pp. 595–613). London: Martin Dunitz.

Perrin, P. (1997). Réflexion autour du schéma postural des guitaristes. *Médecine des Arts, 22,* 13–19.

Redmond, M., & Tiermond, A. M. (2001). Knowledge and practice of piano teachers in preventable playing-related injuries in high school students. *Medical Problems of Performing Artists, 16,* 32–38.

Rosen, C. (1999). Playing the piano. *New York Review of Books,* October 21, pp. 49–52.

Rosenthal, E. (1987). The Alexander technique. What it is and how it works: Work with three musicians. *Medical Problems of Performing Artists, 2,* 53–57.

Sakai, N. (1992). Hand pain related to keyboard techniques in pianists. *Medical Problems of Performing Artists, 7,* 63–65.

Simons, H. (1986). Health and the choral conductor. *Medical Problems of Performing Artists, 1,* 56–57.

Singer, K. (1932). *Diseases of the Musical Profession: A Systematic Presentation of Their Causes, Symptoms, and Methods of Treatment* (W. Lakond, Trans.). New York: Greenberg.

Spahn, C., Hildebrandt, H., & Seidendanz, K. (2001). Effectivess of a prophylactic course to prevent playing-related health problems of music students. *Medical Problems of Performing Artists, 16,* 24–31.

Spaulding, C. (1988). Before pathology: Prevention for performing artists. *Medical Problems of Performing Artists, 3,* 135–139.

Stanton, H. E. (1994). Reduction of performance anxiety in music students. *Australian Psychologist, 29,* 124–127.

Warrington, J., Winspur, I., & Steinwede, D. (2002). Upper extremity problems in musicians related to age. *Medical Problems of Performing Artists, 17,* 131–134.

Weilerstein, D., & Neal, C. (2000). Violin technique. In R. Tubiana & P. C. Amadio (Eds.), *Medical Problems of the Instrumentalist Musician* (pp. 573–594). London: Martin Dunitz.

Williams, J. (1998). The interface: Guitar. In I. Winspur & C. B. Wynn Parry (Eds.), *The Musician's Hand: A Clinical Guide* (pp. 22–24). London: Martin Dunitz.

Winspur, I., & Wynn Parry, C. B. (Eds.). (1998). *The Musician's Hand: A Clinical Guide.* London: Martin Dunitz.

Wright Reid, A. (2001). *A Sound Ear.* London: Association of British Orchestras.

Zaza, C., & Farewell, V. T. (1997). Musicians' playing-related musculoskeletal disorders: An examination of risk factors. *American Journal of Industrial Medicine, 32,* 292–300.

CHAPTER 4

MEASURING PERFORMANCE ENHANCEMENT IN MUSIC

GARY E. McPHERSON AND EMERY SCHUBERT

Musical performance incorporates many facets—hours of laborious practice, mental preparation, and physical well-being—and for many, it is the performance itself that is the ultimate goal of all this preparation. However, once the performance is complete (and sometimes even before), listeners will cast judgment upon it. The assessment may be in the form of a rapturous ovation or a cool murmur of unconvincing applause, a grade or report that provides an evaluation of how well the musician has satisfied certain criteria, or alternatively, a critic writing polemical or glowing reports in the next day's paper. Regardless of the assessment process, it is an integral part of the performance.

The first part of this chapter attempts to deconstruct some of the (often unwritten) assumptions of assessment, so that readers are aware of the flaws and limitations that are inherent in any form of evaluation made by humans. This leads to the central question addressed in the final part of the chapter, which details what performers can do, in addition to performing at their peak, to enhance how their performance is received and evaluated by an audience. While most of this book focuses on how musicians can improve specific aspects of their performance, the current chapter examines performance from a different perspective, by exploring how musicians might enhance their own performance *assessment*.

4.1 The process of assessing musical performances

Typical forms of music assessment seek either to determine the ranking of a performance in comparison with others (*norm referenced*), or how well a performance satisfies predetermined examination criteria (*criterion based*). Norm-referenced procedures are common in competitions, eisteddfods, and music festivals, where the intention is to rank the musicians or ensembles from most to least accomplished, or to determine a winner and runners up. Criterion-based methods are more common in institutions that seek to determine how much progress or learning has been achieved and whether the musician or ensemble can demonstrate mastery of certain predetermined skills. The work of a music critic in some ways bridges both purposes in that the critique will often compare the musician to other performances that have taken place in the same venue or city, in addition to commenting on how well the performance satisfies generally agreed principles about how the work should be and was performed.

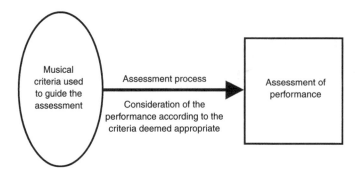

Figure 4.1 Assumed assessment process.

In both the norm referenced and criterion based forms of assessment, it is typical for judges to focus their assessment on a series of *musical* parameters to guide their evaluation—be they the personal criteria that result from their previous work as evaluators and musicians, or the type of criteria that have been identified by authorities assigned with the task of defining the most appropriate parameters to guide an evaluation. Figure 4.1 depicts this process.

This perspective has several limitations because any music evaluation will be influenced by a number of additional factors that impact on the quality of the evaluation. Thus, a more complete understanding of the music assessment process only comes with an expanded view that includes—along with the musical criteria—extramusical and nonmusical parameters in addition to errors in measurement that influence all forms of evaluation. So, while adjudicators may *think* they are evaluating the "musical value" of a performance, they are also necessarily including other factors in their judgment. Figure 4.2 depicts this broader perspective. In this figure, the three areas indicated by dashed lines on the left side of the diagram refer to factors that may be beyond the assessor's control. The lines flowing from left to right indicate that the adjudication is not simply an assessment of musical value. Instead, it is masked by other factors that can, for ease of interpretation here, be categorized as measurement errors, as well as other extramusical and nonmusical factors. Extramusical factors overlap musical value because it is a fuzzy component, with some aspects of it lying outside the boundary of the assessor's aim of recording musical value. Each component of this model is explicated in the four sections which follow.

4.2   Musical value

Much assessment literature tacitly assumes that it is possible to access the true value of a behavior, a view that is also evident when inspecting the criteria traditionally used to assess musical performances. Undoubtedly, aiming to enhance the value of a musical performance is an essential, though not singular, goal of achieving successful assessment, but musical evaluation in all practical terms is far more complicated.

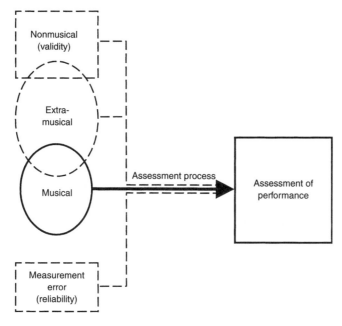

Figure 4.2 Expanded model of music assessment process.

The published literature on the criteria used to assess performances suggests that there are at least four types of competencies that are typically used by music institutions, from which appropriate performance assessment criteria are devised (see, for example, Hollis, 2001a, 2001b; Hunter & Russ, 1996; Hunter, 1999; Palatine Report, 2000; Stanley *et al.*, 2002). These can be summarized as follows:

- Technique

  Physiological

  —breathing

  —posture

  —relaxation—tension

  —balance

  —coordination

  Physical

  —sound: production, projection, and control of instrument/voice and consistency, clarity, and focus of tone across all registers and dynamic levels

  —range

  —intonation

  —physical control (e.g. stamina, endurance)

—bodily coordination

Instrumental

—ensemble coordination, balance, and cohesion

—accuracy, assuredness, and facility of rhythm, pitch, articulations, dynamics, timing, as well as the degree to which errors undermine and detract from the overall quality of the performance

—pacing of performance

—sensitivity to intonation, both individual and ensemble

- Interpretation

  —authenticity: understanding of the style/genre and established performance practice (e.g. use of a reliable edition)

  —accuracy: based on faithful reading and/or memorization of the score, and realization and exploration of the composer's intentions

  —musical coherence: perceptive choice of tempo, phrase shaping, dynamic shadings, sense of line, and understanding of overall structure

- Expression

  —understanding of the emotional character of the work

  —projection of mood and character of the work

  —communication of the structural high points and turning points of the work

  —sensitivity to the relationship between parts within a texture

  —appropriate use of tone and color, light and shade, and/or drama

- Communication

  —among the members of the ensemble (e.g. listening and leadership)

  —confidence, as demonstrated in performances that are both convincing and purposeful

  —interest, in terms of the degree to which the performer holds the audience's attention, maintains a sense of direction, creates a sense of occasion, and ends the work convincingly

  —projection of expressive, interpretative, and structural features of the composition performed

The above assessment criteria contain a mixture of categories that could be classed as either skill or artistry. A commonly discussed difficulty in assessment is the issue of marking interpretation. If it is subjective, then any assessment of interpretation can be no more than unreliable speculation. However, over the past decade, music psychologists have begun to clarify the microstructural changes that affect expressive playing, and there now exists a substantial set of "rules" of expression that performers can incorporate into their playing that help them convey their expressive intentions to their audiences (see Chapter 13 of this volume). Another difficulty is the inevitable overlap between constituent elements of technique, interpretation, expression, and communication. For example, as an evaluative dimension, the "projection of mood and character of the work," classified above as expressive, could be seen to overlap with the "projection of expressive, stylistic, and structural features of the composition performed," as in the communication category.

4.3   Measurement error

The process of assessing musical performances is often based on several implicit and often flawed assumptions. One is that the musical value of a performance can be assessed accurately and reliably. A second is that experienced listeners are able to make consistently accurate judgments. This leads to a third assumption, that expert judges possess the ability to make finer discriminations than average listeners due to their more refined abilities to determine which of the components of a performance were effective and which were not. This situation is analogous with using a microscope to examine a chemical sample. Most people have access to a basic microscope, but the adjudicator has an especially powerful one and can, therefore, see more (see Thompson & Williamon, 2003, for further discussion of these assumptions). However, in all fields of human pursuit where fine esthetic discriminations are made, we can never know everything about the thing we wish to measure. Hence, all measurement is subject to some kind of coloration by error, which leads to the serious implication that it is impossible to judge with perfect accuracy and, even worse, fairness.

The most common kind of error found in assessment is measurement error. In a statistical sense, measurement errors do not produce a systematic bias, but consist of more or less random fluctuation that cannot be easily controlled. Measurement error has important implications in music assessment; it means that a judge cannot be expected to behave in an idealized, machine-like way because there is always likely to be some kind of unbiased, random fluctuation. For example, Fiske (1978, 1983) and Manturzewska (cited in Davidson & Coimbra, 2001) both asked evaluators to judge performances, some of which were the same, and found very low correlations between scores. For this reason, statistical measurement error corresponds to what psychometric researchers call *reliability*, or the consistency and accuracy of a measurement. In this chapter, little attention is given to the manipulation of measurement error for the purpose of enhancing performance assessment because, by definition, measurement error cannot be manipulated to favor one performance over another in a systematic manner. Measurement error could be minimized, but this would lead to fairer assessment across all performances, regardless of the strategies used.

4.4   Extramusical factors

Extramusical factors are an unclearly defined, fuzzy set that may belong to true musical value or to nonmusical aspects of performance assessment. The location of these factors are largely subjective or dependent on circumstances. Some selected extramusical factors are reviewed below. Although this is not a definitive list, the labeling of factors as such is useful in parsing the assessment process into smaller, more manageable units. This area is complex and controversial, however, because the many items that could be grouped in this category are considered by some as essential parts of musical value and by others as something that only produces messiness in the evaluation, as it introduces biases that are not related to the essential formal properties of a musical performance. In some cases, the issues mentioned may seem more relevant to measurement error. The decision to include such items under extramusical factors was guided by the criterion that the performer might be able to use some knowledge about the factor to systematically enhance their performance assessment.

While there are clearly marked boundaries between such aspects as interpretation and technique, which are part of the performance, it is often less clear whether stage presence, individuality, and flair of the performer should have an influence on evaluation. It is these underlying factors that are included in the definition of extramusical used here. The existing literature suggests that categories related to the performer, the context in which the performance takes place, and the evaluator help explain the types of extramusical factors that can potentially impact on the evaluation of a musical performance. The following sections are, therefore, divided into three sources of extramusical assessment enhancement:

- those that the player can directly control (including less obvious issues such as self-efficacy and cognitive mediation)
- those that depend on the playing context
- those that require research about the adjudicator.

Understanding these can be useful in knowing how to maximize one's performance assessment.

4.4.1 Performer-related aspects

The following factors are those over which the performer can exercise direct control to enhance their performance assessment. The internal thoughts and mechanisms related to a musician's preparation for the performance are examined first, followed by an explanation of research on expressive variations from the norm, attractiveness, flair, and movement.

Self-efficacy

How individuals control and monitor their own cognition before, during, and after engaging in a challenging activity provides a powerful insight into how well they are able to perform. One of the most important cognitive processes is self-efficacy, which refers to the perception or judgments a person holds for being able to perform a certain task successfully (Bandura, 1997; see also Chapter 2 of this volume). As an example, opera singers will "differ in their perceived efficacy to fulfill the vocal, emotive, and theatrical aspects of their artistic craft and to fuse them into dramatic performances" (Bandura, 1997, p. 36), because their self-beliefs are linked to distinct realms of functioning that influence not only how they perform, but their thought processes, motivation, and affective and physiological states as well.

Self-efficacy has been shown to be the strongest predictor of a musician's perform-ance in assessment situations, such as a graded music examination (McCormick & McPherson, 2003). The extensive literature on this topic in academic areas demon-strates that students who display slightly higher perceptions of their own ability to accomplish a task than is justified by their actual ability, are more likely to choose more challenging tasks, exert more effort, persist longer, and be less likely to experience debilitating anxiety (Bandura, 1986; Pajares, 1996; Zimmerman, 2000). In contrast, even accurate self-perceptions can lower optimism, which then affects effort, persist-ence, and perseverance (Pajares, 1996). All of this reinforces the importance of training the mind, as well as the body, because how musicians feel about their own ability and level of performance has a powerful effect on how they project themselves to their audience and, as a result, how their audience reacts to their performance.

Expressive variations

Expressive variation in performance is an extramusical factor directly related to inter-pretation, and here it is referred to as deviations from the expressive norm. Contrary to common belief, it is possible to measure expression empirically (see Chapter 13), and also to establish an expressive norm that relates to the typical amount of deviation from a musical score that is considered necessary for expressive playing. Layered upon this norm are deviations from it to obtain greater expression, and this deviation from the norm is classified here as extramusical. The music expression literature has identified some of these deviations (e.g. Repp, 1997; Woody, 2000), but there is controversy as to how and when to apply them. For example, Repp (1997, 1999) reports that student per-formers tend to exhibit fewer deviations from the expressive norm for a given piece than famous performers: "expert pianists' performances are much more diverse in timing than student performances, which tend to stay close to the norm" (Repp, 1999, p. 1983). In line with Woody's (2000) report regarding the locations at which musically appropri-ate deviations are noticeable, Schubert (2002) argues that there exists a quantifiable boundary of acceptable deviation in expression, where deviations too far beyond these hypothetical limits produce dull, awkward, inappropriate, or even comical-sounding effects. This boundary theory suggests that students can maximize the impact of their performances by deliberately varying expressive content from the norm, even though culturally specific performance conventions, expectations, and standards may dictate that they need to stay within well-defined boundaries.

Attractiveness and flair

Social psychologists have known for some time that a person's physical appearance affects the impression they project to others (Myers, 1999), and so it is of no surprise that performers' physical *projections* of themselves influence how their audiences per-ceive them and their performance. For example, audiences who are asked to provide written comments on a performance will often start by referring to the attractiveness of the performer (Wapnick *et al.*, 1997; Davidson & Coimbra, 2001; Stanley *et al.*, 2002). This seems especially true for singers, with studies showing that maintaining eye contact and smiling at appropriate times in the performance influence how they are rated by judges (Bermingham, 2000; Wapnick *et al.*, 1997, 1998, 2000). But it is important to note that this dimension acts along a continuum, such that the stage presence required to bring off a performance of a solemn piece will be quite different from that required to perform a piece that is joyful and lively. Expert performers know that it is all a matter of degree and appropriateness to the repertory being performed and the type of audience that is listening.

Movement

Some estimates suggest that vision accounts for more than 75% of all information learned (Gladney, 1997; Long, 1997), and as the dominant sense, it can inhibit the processing of information from other modalities (Posner *et al.*, 1976; Smyth, 1984). In terms of the visual component of a musical performance, physical movements and gestures provide important expressive information about a musician's intentions and, thereby, help an audience to judge the interpretation and "musicality" of a performance (Davidson, 1993, 1994, 1995, 2001). This is not surprising, given how closely physical movements are linked to and driven by the mental representations of the music being performed (Lehmann & Davidson, 2002).

The types of visual cues that influence an audience include the actual quantity of the performer's movements, as well as specific gestures that are an integral part of a performer's way of expressing specific musical intentions (Davidson, 2002). A key point is that the context is all-important; better performers are able to achieve a "balance in the articulation of musical expression, coordination, and virtuosic display within the social convention" (Lehmann & Davidson, 2002, p. 554). In this way, communication is a two-way process in which performers:

are just as likely to pick up information from the audience as audiences are likely to pick up information from the performer. Not only do general behaviors such as applause provide the performer with feedback about their performance, but moment by moment, smiles, frowns, laughs, coughs, etc. can all have an effect on the performer (Davidson, 1997, p. 224).

4.4.2 Context related aspects

While not directly under the control of the performer, there are several aspects of the performer's environment that can be used to enhance one's assessment. The communication of players within an ensemble, the acoustics, social elements, and the audience response are included in this subcategory as examples of extramusical factors.

Communication within the ensemble

An extension to the processes involved in attending to and concentrating on the music being performed is the way the performer communicates with the other musicians. Again, evidence suggests that these social interactions are extremely important. The way performers maintain eye contact and use nonverbal information such as gestures and body movement to converse "musically" helps their coperformers and their audience discern finely grained cues about their musical and expressive intentions (Davidson, 1993, 2001; Williamon & Davidson, 2002). This is especially evident for nonmusicians, who are more reliant on visual rather than aural cues to discern the extent to which a musician is playing with or without expression (Davidson, 2001).

Highly competent accompanying musicians affect an audience's overall impression of a performance, not only because they are more likely to provide an accurate reading of their own part and interact at a higher level with the soloist, but because the presence of superior coperformers acts to heighten or "lift" a musician to perform closer to his or her peak. This type of enhancement has been reported by psychologists for the past few decades: from Zajonc (1965) who proposed that the presence of others raises a person's general arousal level and can affect task performance, to investigations by Seta (1982), who explains that feedback from a superior co-actor can alter an individual's performance because it serves as a cue for competition and as a source of motivation to achieve at higher levels (see also Bryant & Driskell, 1997).

Some of the more illuminating research on this topic has been undertaken by Williamon and Davidson (2002) who, in one of their studies, explored social and non-verbal communication between two expert pianists who prepared and then presented a recital of duet music. Results show that the pianists used a rich variety of visually based information—such as eye-contact, facial expressions, physical gestures, and swaying movements—to communicate specific musical ideas while they performed. These forms of visually based feedback help performers coordinate their playing (Clayton, 1985) and are, therefore, an integral part of effective interaction between musicians (Yarbrough, 1975). They enable musicians to converse musically (see Chapter 6 for further discussion of ensemble communication).

Acoustics

There is a significant literature on how room acoustics affect sound quality (e.g. Naylor, 1988; Gade, 1989a, 1989b; Meyer, 1993) but virtually no mention of it in performance assessment literature. It is self-evident that room acoustics may serve one instrument over another, and perhaps even one performance technique over another. Moreover, the size, shape, and design of a room all have a bearing on the sound an instrument can produce, in addition to the position at which the assessor sits (Ando, 1988). Wolfe (2003), an expert in acoustics, makes suggestions of which many musicians are aware, such as playing softer in an auditorium with little background noise and playing slower with more separation between the notes in a larger, reverberant auditorium. While a performer may not necessarily be interested in becoming an expert in acoustics, there are some commonsense practices that may benefit the well prepared performer:

- attending other performances in the concert venue, especially those performances featuring the same instrument or ensemble combination and taking notes on tone quality and how sitting in different parts of the auditorium affect the sound
- practicing in the venue beforehand if possible, remembering that the acoustics of an auditorium are dramatically altered when there is a shift of people and equipment
- being prepared to compensate and adjust for any weaknesses caused by the acoustic during the performance (see Ando, 1988).

Working on this extramusical aspect of performance can potentially enhance the assessment one receives under a musical category such as tonal production, and as such, the contribution made to tone quality by the acoustic environment is an important consideration.

Social factors

The context in which a performance will take place can be thought of as representing yet another facet of extramusical influences. First, the *purpose of the assessment*—a music competition, concert, festival, end of semester recital/examination, audition, or public concert—can influence the way an evaluator or music critic will listen to, and therefore, evaluate a performance (McPherson & Thompson, 1998). Second, the *type of performance*—whether the musician is performing from memory, with music, by ear, or by improvising—can affect not only the criteria relevant to how the performance should be assessed but also how judgments will be formed. Some instruments are considered harder to play than others, or may have different technical skills and repertory, all of which can potentially impact on the assessment process.

Clearly, the way a performance will be perceived by an audience depends on a number of complex social factors (Davidson, 1997). Social etiquette in performances of all types of music operates via a two-way process between what the audience expects from the performer, and what the performer expects from the audience. So, actively integrating the cultural values—such as dress codes and stage manner—is an important means of maximizing one's performance assessment. For example, in art music, performances from memory have been shown to allow players to perform more freely and expressively, as well as to communicate their expressive intentions more effectively to their audience (Aiello & Williamon, 2002; see also Chapter 7 of this volume).

Audience support

Another interesting factor in assessment is the audience support for the performer. This may appear to be a nonmusical factor, but audience response can enhance the perception of a performance, especially in situations where greater audience support creates a sense of excitement that encourages us to believe that a performance is better than its true musical value. It is for this reason that the factor of audience support is positioned in the extramusical category. While no studies have been cited in the empirical music assessment literature, crowd noise has been shown to have a significant effect on judges' decisions in various sports, where distinct advantages have been found in favor of the home team. Nevill and Holder (1999) argue that referees make decisions that are influenced by the audience. So, the more "noise" and auditory support (clapping, cheering, etc.) the audience gives a performance, the more positive the adjudication may be. As with many extramusical factors, adjudicators may require training and experience to minimize the unfair influence this may have, but as mentioned, it is conceivable that audience support may enhance a performance in this extramusical way.

4.4.3 Evaluator characteristics

The ways in which individuals draw a conclusion based on available evidence can be quite different, depending on a number of personal factors. For this reason, additional extramusical factors relevant to the evaluator (or listener) need to be recognized. Below, a selection of evaluator-related aspects of assessment are discussed that can be understood and controlled by obtaining reliable information about the characteristics of the assessor(s). If it is possible and ethical, collecting such information may help the performer to enhance his or her performance. Several factors seem to be relevant here, which follow the path from knowledge about the performer before the performance, to first impressions of the performance, to the mood of the adjudicator at the time of the assessment, and finally, to the adjudicator's overall familiarity with and preferences for the literature being performed.

Memory influences

Memory-influenced biases occur when individuals are primed with information or have expectations about someone that subsequently color their expectations about how that person will react or perform (Fyock & Stangor, 1994). In music, Radocy (1976) provides clear evidence that listeners' impressions are influenced by what they expect to hear from a performer and that prior knowledge or expectations can exert a major influence on their assessment of a performance. He assigned undergraduate students to one of five conditions where bias was manipulated by introducing false information about performers before the students made their evaluations. Students in the moderate bias conditions were given misleading information, such as being told that the performer was a "former symphony player" or "young graduate assistant." Students in the strong bias conditions were given misleading information about the player and reasons why the performances by the professional performer were supposedly preferred by prior listeners. Results showed overall biases in the undergraduate students' evaluations, in that they preferred the performances by musicians they thought were professionals or more experienced. Interestingly, however, Radocy reports that some instruments (e.g. piano) were more susceptible to these biases than others (e.g. trumpet). Unfortunately, there is very little research on how susceptible highly experienced adjudicators are to such memory priming effects.

First impressions

First impressions are often more lasting than we might think. In music, evidence shows that rankings of performers are not markedly different when evaluators hear entire performances as compared to only the first sections of the performances (Vasil, 1973) and that expert musicians are able to form a relatively quick global assessment very early in a performance (Stanley *et al.*, 2002). For example, in a study at the Sydney Conservatorium of Music, one member of the staff stated: "I look at them and I say 'Distinction, high Credit'. I have bands in my own mind and then the number is immaterial—to me the number is way more negotiable than the actual range" (Stanley *et al.*, p. 47). This examiner then moved to a process of justifying his immediate reaction, by stating

This is why I feel this way. . . . I may find out that all that appealed to me was the person looked smart or behaved in a good way and then I would say: "Well the presentation was so spectacular that I forgot to listen to the playing, but now when I come to think of it the playing was not all that really good" (p. 47).

Studies in social cognition provide an explanation for this fairly typical, though complex, response. According to this line of research, strong first impressions we have of a person persevere and color our subsequent judgments about that person. Initial opinions affect how we will draw in (i.e. adapt) or resist drawing in (i.e. isolate) subsequent information to form an extant impression (Ybarra, 2001). Initial *positive* impressions tend to exert a different influence on subsequent judgments than initial *negative* impressions. For example, if a performer creates a good initial impression at the start of his or her program but fails to sustain this level of performance in subsequent parts of the performance, a judge will be more capable of integrating new information (in this case, a poorer level of performance) into his or her final judgment. In contrast, an initial *negative* impression appears to exert a more stable, long-term influence, in that a judge will be less inclined to include new information (e.g. better playing) as the basis of changing his or her overall impression. This asymmetry emerges because people find it easier to infer dispositional characteristics from negative behavior rather than positive behavior. Negative information about a person is more likely to result in a more stable evaluation over time than positive information (Carston, 1980), because negative first impressions make it harder for a person to *isolate* their initial impressions from information that occurs subsequently.

Mood of the assessor

The mood of the assessor probably has some effect on his or her adjudication, and if it does, there exists ample literature demonstrating how different kinds of music can evoke different moods that vary in degrees of valence (happiness and sadness) and arousal (activity and sleepiness; Gorn *et al.*, 2001), as well as how a listener's mood can be altered by listening to a particular piece of music (Västfjäll, 2001–2002). An important part of this dimension for performers to consider is the principal of habituation, which suggests that listeners will become bored when hearing a series of pieces that do not vary sufficiently in interpretative or expressive intent (Schubert, 1996). It is, therefore, of paramount importance for musicians to strike a balance between the *intensity* and *variety* of emotions expressed in the repertory they are performing, in order to optimize the pleasure their listeners derive from it, thereby enhancing their own assessment.

Familiarity and preference

Judges often find it more difficult to assess a work that they have never heard before than a work that is highly familiar to them. Flores and Ginsburgh (1996) studied whether judges are more severe in adjudications of works heard for the first time by analysing results over a number of decades from the Queen Elisabeth music competition in Belgium. Their study provides convincing evidence that judges tend to be more severe for the first few performances of a new commissioned work than for later performances after they have had a chance to form an impression of how difficult the work is to perform and are, consequently, more forgiving of problems in the performance. In this way, memories of literature being performed—whether formed immediately before the performance such as in a music competition with a newly commissioned work or long-term as a result of previous exposure—have the potential to exert a major influence on a judge's assessment of the performer's efforts.

From another perspective, this can be explained by applying theories from the literature on preference, of which the most well known is the inverted-U curve that relates preference to massed exposure. Massed exposure is equivalent to a listener hearing the same piece many times in sequence (see Martindale, 1988; North & Hargreaves, 2000).

The inverted-U theory suggests that preference for the new work will start to rise with familiarity and then decay as the listener becomes bored from overexposure. In this way, a preference peak will occur after the first performance, which confirms the type of bias reported in the study by Flores and Ginsburgh (1996).

Halo effect

The halo effect arises from a tendency of a judge to be unduly influenced by a single factor, such as a particular strength or weakness in a person's performance, their physical appearance, or another aspect of their behavior (Anastasi & Urbina, 1997). This often occurs in situations where a person's performance is particularly high on a factor that an assessor personally feels is important, which then unduly influences them to inflate their assessment on other attributes of the person's performance. The phenomenon has received much attention in areas such as marketing (e.g. Leuthesser *et al.*, 1995), gymnastics (Ansorge & Scheer, 1988), and management (e.g. Wirtz & Bateson, 1995), but little is understood about its influence and how it might be controlled in music performance.

The most obvious type of halo effect in music is where a judge will draw on previous knowledge of a performer as being a very good or very poor musician, and incorrectly or unjustly inflate or decrease their assessment rating, even though a particular performance may be better or worse than would normally be achieved. There is evidence that knowing the performer can lead to "in group" and "out group" biases, such that assessors give more generous marks to performers they know (Manturzewska, 1970, cited in Davidson & Coimbra, 2001). For example, Hunter and Russ (1996) found that unrealistic marks were sometimes awarded for musicians based on reputation, particularly in situations "when a performer has a high reputation and there is a buzz of expectancy when they enter the hall" (p. 71; see also Hunter, 1999). In such instances, this type of bias can occur at different levels, from knowing the performer personally to having heard the performer play on previous occasions. A professional relationship of this sort does not necessarily mean a bias will occur on all occasions—only that the likelihood increases.

In other areas, techniques are used to reduce the effect (Bagozzi, 1996), and there is evidence that training might be essential to alert the adjudicator of this subconscious bias. Given that the halo effect can influence many aspects of a performance and that the aim in adjudications should be to minimize this, it is perhaps better to view it as a measurement error rather than an extramusical factor. It is treated as an extramusical factor here as it could conceivably be used to enhance one's own performance assessment. For example, a musician who has a noticeable strong point (especially one that an adjudicator is known to appreciate), should consider how to maintain and exploit this aspect of performance, and perhaps develop it through the repertory he or she performs.

4.5   Nonmusical factors

Nonmusical factors are defined as those related to *validity*—that is, whether evaluators are actually assessing what they think they are assessing. Because nonmusical factors produce unfair biases, it is important that educators, adjudicators, and researchers work toward understanding them. However, from the performer's perspective, apart from being aware of their existence, there is little they can, or should have to do to manipulate these factors in order to enhance their performance assessment. Only two kinds of nonmusical factors are discussed here, but several issues raised in the extramusical section could also be listed as nonmusical, such as attractiveness and audience support.

4.5.1   Stereotyping

Stereotyping based on gender or race has the potential to impact on assessment in subtle ways (McCrary, 1993; Green, 1997; O'Neill, 1997; Morrison, 1998; Bermingham, 2000; Dibben, 2002). This was shown most convincingly in a study by Elliott (1995), who used videotaped performances of four trumpet players and four flute players. Each instrument had a male/female and black/white performer. Elliott's master videotape of the eight performances controlled the soundtracks for each of the four trumpet and flute performances so that the musicians pretended to coordinate their playing over the same sound recording for each instrument. Undergraduate and graduate music specialists who rated the performances were unaware that the soundtrack for each instrument was identical, but still consistently rated the performances according to both dimensions. Black performers scored significantly lower than their white peers, with the female trumpeters scoring lower than female flautists. Other studies have shown that people sharing the race of the judge tend to be awarded higher marks (Green, 1997), and that the higher percentage of women now playing in professional orchestras is a direct result of the introduction of "blind" auditions where the auditioning panel sits behind a screen and cannot see the performer (Goldin & Rouse, 2000).

4.5.2   Order of performance

Order is known to affect judgments. In wine tasting, there is a bias that favors the first sample tasted (Filipello, 1956), and in gymnastics, the fourth position within a team tends to receive the more advantageous adjudication (Scheer & Ansorge, 1975; Plessner, 1999). In international music competitions, order biases have also been observed. For example, Flores and Ginsburgh (1996) report that rankings of performers in the Queen Elisabeth competition were significantly related to the order in which they performed. Performers near the beginning had a statistically lower chance of being ranked highly in comparison with those who performed near the final day, who tended to be ranked in the top category by the adjudicators. For international competitions, Flores and Ginsburgh suggest that repeated hearings of the same piece may nurture a greater appreciation, which in turn casts a more positive light on the performance itself (see also "Familiarity and preference of repertory" above). Another explanation is that adjudicators tend to start with "higher expectations and more strict rules, and then progressively adapt them to the reality of the actual performance" (Flores & Ginsburgh, p. 102; see also McPherson & Thompson, 1998).

4.6   A model with practical implications: The Johari window

So far, a variety of issues have been presented that can or do affect performance assessment. Each issue varies in relevance to different performers, depending on their age, expertise, mood, self-efficacy, and so on. Furthermore, several adjudicator factors, such as experience, training, and mood will determine how much these issues influence assessment. This final section draws together the various elements of the assessment model as a means of helping musicians understand which aspects of assessment most concern them and, consequently, which aspects can be improved to maximize their chances of enhancing their own assessment.

The "Johari window" is the framework for this new model. The Johari window is a model of awareness of behavior and motivation (Luft, 1969), used primarily in psychodynamic therapy, but it has received a wide variety of applications and continues to attract interest (e.g. Afolabi, 1993; Sole, 1997). The model proposes that, when interacting with others, "awareness" can be divided into four areas:

- *public area*: an individual will be aware of some behaviors and motivations that are also noticeable to others.

- *blind area*: some behaviors and motivations will be inaccessible to the individual but accessible to others (hence, this is like a blind spot for the individual).

- *secret area*: the individual will hide certain motivations and behaviors, and therefore this is the secret part of the model.

- *hidden area*: there is a part of behavior and motivation of which neither the individual, nor others, are aware.

The model is represented as a window with four quadrants. In this application of the Johari window, "others" are the person (or persons) who makes the assessment, such as an adjudicator or an audience. Consequently, it is suggested that performers organize their personal windows according to what they are aware of themselves, and to what they believe the adjudicator to be aware of that is relevant to their performance. An example of some of the issues discussed above could be sorted into a typical, but hypothetical, individual's Johari window (see Figure 4.3).

From the example shown, it becomes clear how the general principles of our model apply to individuals. The leitmotif of the present review is the questioning of the assumption that musical value can be measured. From the Johari window perspective, this translates to musical value being in the top left quadrant, where this is known by both the performer and the assessor. However, it has been argued that the assessor may not be able to access the musical value of a performance, and so only certain aspects may reveal themselves in this quadrant. Measurement error, on the other hand, falls into the bottom right quadrant where assessment factors are hidden from both assessor and performer. This hidden region appears to be a general location where *reliability* of assessment is threatened. The secret and blind areas appear to mark regions where assessment *validity* is threatened. Various other factors in performance can be sorted into the four panes. No two individuals will have identical windows. For the hypothetical relationship shown, several factors have been added that are not mentioned in this chapter because literature could not be cited that specifically describes how they can be used to enhance a player's assessment. For instance, preparation and effort have been added, speculatively, to the secret pane. As an exercise, performers should attempt to produce their own personal Johari window and sort the various factors discussed in this chapter, and elsewhere in the book, into the appropriate panes.

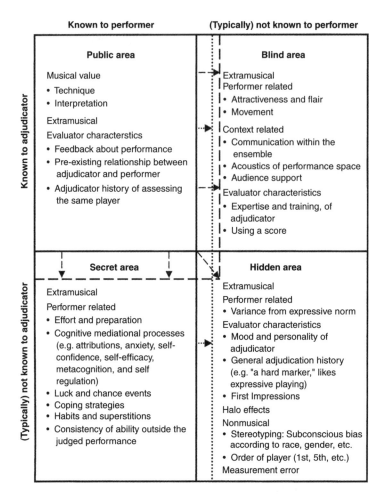

Figure 4.3 Example of the Johari window applied to an imaginary individual and adjudicator awareness relationship. The dotted line and arrows indicate the direction in which the individual should aim the quadrant shapes—that is, to increase the left side and reduce the right side. The dashed line and arrows indicate the traditional direction in which the Johari window should be changed—that is, to make the public quadrant larger and all other quadrants smaller.

Apart from organizing assessment and performance related issues, the window has an important application. In general, performers should strive to reduce the area of the right quadrants of the window, and widen the left quadrants. That is, individuals will be more likely to enhance their performance if they know as much about their performance-controlling factors as possible. For example, if the adjudicator is not aware of the halo effect, and the performer becomes aware of how a particular extramusical factor might enhance his or her performance (of which he or she was not previously aware), then an item from the right side of the window will shift to the bottom left pane, in effect expanding the left side of the window: the aim of the model from the performer's perspective. Furthermore, suppose the hypothetical performer plays with insufficient expressive movement and is penalized as a result. If the adjudicator, teacher, or colleague alerts the performer that this is a performance problem, the player can then work on developing this extramusical factor and hence shift it into the top left (public) quadrant. The window also explains how an adjudicator may vary the criterion for individuality and expression by deducting marks for an overly expressive, though appropriate, performance. In this case, the performer's blind window-pane has been enlarged, because the adjudicator knows that the criterion has been changed but the performer does not.

The window also helps to allow recognition that some things might never be moved from the right to the left, particularly some items in the bottom right (hidden) quadrant, because no one has access to these factors. The main example is measurement error. It may be possible, however, for the performer to develop some insights into the bottom right corner of the window and to be able to shift these into one of the left panes. For instance, it is vital that stereotyping issues are brought to the adjudicator's awareness so that the impact of such unfair biases can be minimized or eliminated. Importantly, researchers and educators need to provide ways of enabling adjudicators to shift the bottom two panes up to the top two, so that the adjudicator's reliability and validity can improve via appropriate assessment recording techniques.

4.7   Conclusions

The present chapter has presented a framework to explain the complexities of the assessment process that are not commonly understood or considered by musicians. In the sampling of literature discussed, it is evident that extramusical factors of a performance are a largely untapped source for performance enhancement because performers, adjudicators, and in many cases even music researchers are unaware of the major impact these could and do have upon the assessment of a performance. This does not suggest that performers do not need to work on the traditional elements associated with musical value. The chapters that follow provide methods for developing these features, but for players of a very high standard, this approach may give them an edge. By the same token, apart from measurement error, it is not implied that all adjudicators are prone to making the various kinds of errors that allow performers to use some less traditional means of enhancing their assessment. However, it does need to be acknowledged that an "evaluation of a performer does not mean anything until we know how reliable the judge was who evaluated that performance" (Fiske, 1994, p. 76). Like learning how to play proficiently, learning how to provide reliable and accurate assessments of musical performance is an acquired skill that requires reflection and practice for any degree of success. While more research is needed, it is acknowledged that there will be some adjudicators who have a very deep understanding of the process of adjudication. The wider adjudicating community could be well served by discovering and applying the knowledge such individuals possess.

Understanding the process of assessment is a key to enhancing one's performance beyond the traditional mantra of "practice makes perfect." The expanded theory outlined here, therefore, presents a perspective that crystallizes many of the problems that have previously been hidden beneath the general guise of assessment. While many issues await investigation by researchers to ensure that fair, unbiased, and reliable assessment regimes are provided, performers can maximize their reception by applying the theory to their own personal Johari window; as research develops, so will the nature and shape of the window. The main point, however, is that performers should organize their window in such a way as to enhance their assessment, and therefore further enhance their performance. Such reflective practices have considerable potential in the area of performance enhancement.

Acknowledgments

We thank James Renwick and two anonymous referees who provided very helpful suggestions and insightful comments on an earlier version of this chapter, plus Aaron Williamon, whose attention to detail and critical mind helped at all stages of the process.

Further information and reading

Hollis, E. (2001a). *The Guildhall School's* clear *Performance Assessment System: How* clear *Works*. London: Guildhall School of Music and Drama Publications.

Hollis, E. (2001b). *The Guildhall School's* clear *Performance Assessment System: Marking Schemes for the Assessment Categories*. London: Guildhall School of Music and Drama Publications.

Luft, J. (1969). *Group Processes: An Introduction to Group Dynamics*. Bethesda, MD: National Press Books.

McPherson, G. E., & Thompson, W. F. (1998). Assessing music performances: Issues and influences. *Research Studies in Music Education, 10,* 12–24.

Palatine Report (2000). *Palatine Learning and Teaching Support Network*. Retrieved August 28, 2003, from Palatine website: *www.lancs.ac.uk/users/palatine/report8nov.htm*.

References

Afolabi, M. (1993). Application of JOHARI Communication Awareness Model to special libraries management. *Library Management, 14,* 24–27.

Aiello, R., & Williamon, A. (2002). Memory. In R. Parncutt & G. E. McPherson (Eds.), *The Science and Psychology of Music Performance: Creative Strategies for Teaching and Learning* (pp. 167–181). Oxford: Oxford University Press.

Anastasi, A., & Urbina, S. (1997). *Psychological Testing* (7th ed.). Englewood Cliffs, NJ: Prentice Hall.

Ando, Y. (1988). *Architectural Acoustics: Blending Sound Sources, Sound Fields, and Listeners*. New York: Springer.

Ansorge, C. J., & Scheer, J. K. (1988). International bias detected in judging gymnastic competition at the 1984 Olympic Games. *Research Quarterly for Exercise and Sport, 59,* 103–107.

Bagozzi, R. P. (1996). The role of arousal in the creation and control of the halo effect in attitude models. *Psychology & Marketing, 13,* 235–264.

Bandura, A. (1986). *Social Foundations of Thought and Action: A Social Cognitive Theory.* Englewood Cliffs, NJ: Prentice Hall.

Bandura, A. (1997). *Self-Efficacy: The Exercise of Control.* New York: Freeman.

Bermingham, G. A. (2000). Effects of performers' external characteristics on performance evaluations. *Update: Applications of Research in Music Education, 18,* 3–7.

Bryant, B. M., & Driskell, J. E. (1997). Presence of others and arousal: An integration. *Group Dynamics: Theory, Research, and Practice, 1,* 52–64.

Carston, D. E. (1980). The recall and use of traits and events in social inference processes. *Journal of Experimental Social Psychology, 16,* 303–328.

Clayton, A. M. H. (1985). *Coordination between Players in Musical Performance.* Unpublished doctoral dissertation, University of Edinburgh, Edinburgh, UK.

Davidson, J. W. (1993). Visual perception of performance manner in the movements of solo musicians. *Psychology of Music, 21,* 103–113.

Davidson, J. W. (1994). Which areas of a pianist's body convey information about expressive intention to an audience? *Journal of Human Movement Studies, 26,* 279–301.

Davidson, J. W. (1995). What does the visual information contained in music performances offer the observer? Some preliminary thoughts. In R. Steinberg (Ed.), *The Music Machine: Psychophysiology and Psychopathology of the Sense of Music* (pp. 105–113). Berlin: Springer-Verlag.

Davidson, J. W. (1997). The social in musical performance. In D. J. Hargreaves & A. C. North (Eds.), *The Social Psychology of Music* (pp. 209–228). Oxford: Oxford University Press.

Davidson, J. W. (2001). The role of the body in the production and perception of solo vocal performance: A case study of Annie Lennox. *Musicæ Scientiæ, 5,* 235–256.

Davidson, J. W. (2002). Understanding the expressive movements of a solo pianist. *Deutsches Jahrbuch für Musikpsychölogie, 16,* 9–31.

Davidson, J. W., & Coimbra, D. D. C. (2001). Investigating performance evaluation by assessors of singers in a music college setting. *Musicæ Scientiæ, 5,* 33–53.

Dibben, N. (2002). Gender identity and music. In R. R. MacDonald, D. Hargreaves, & D. Miell (Eds.), *Musical Identities* (pp. 117–133). Oxford: Oxford University Press.

Elliott, C. A. (1995). Race and gender as factors in judgments of musical performance. *Bulletin of the Council for Research in Music Education, 127,* 50–56.

Filipello, F. (1956). Factors in the analysis of mass panel wine-preference data. *Food Technology, July,* 321–326.

Fiske, H. E. (1978). *The Effect of a Training Procedure in Music Performance Evaluation on Judge Reliability.* Toronto, Canada: Ontario Educational Research Council.

Fiske, H. E. (1983). Judging musical performances: Method or madness? *Update: Applications of Research in Music Education, 1,* 7–10.

Fiske, H. E. (1994). Evaluation of vocal performances: Experimental research evidence. In G. Welch & T. Murao (Eds.), *Onchi and Singing Development* (pp. 74–103). London: David Fulton Publishers.

Flores, R. G., & Ginsburgh, V. A. (1996). The Queen Elisabeth musical competition: How fair is the final ranking? *The Statistician, 45,* 97–104.

Fyock, J., & Stangor, C. (1994). The role of memory biases in stereotype maintenance. *British Journal of Social Psychology, 33,* 331–343.

Gade, A. C. (1989a). Investigations of musicians' room acoustic conditions in concert halls: I. Methods and laboratory experiments. *Acustica, 69,* 193–203.

Gade, A. C. (1989b). Investigations of musicians' room acoustic conditions in concert halls: II. Field experiments and synthesis of results. *Acustica, 69,* 249–262.

Gladney, G. A. (1997). Impact of visuals in selecting NNA General Excellence winners. *Newspaper Research Journal, 18,* 157–168.

Goldin, C., & Rouse, C. (2000). Orchestrating impartiality: The impact of "blind" auditions on female musicians. *American Economic Association, 90,* 715–741.

Gorn, G., Pham, M. T., & Sin, L. Y. (2001). When arousal influences evaluation and valence does not (and vice versa). *Journal of Consumer Psychology, 11,* 43–55.

Green, L. (1997). *Music, Gender, Education.* Cambridge: Cambridge University Press.

Hollis, E. (2001a). *The Guildhall School's* clear *Performance Assessment System: How* clear *Works.* London: Guildhall School of Music and Drama Publications.

Hollis, E. (2001b). *The Guildhall School's* clear *Performance Assessment System: Marking Schemes for the Assessment Categories.* London: Guildhall School of Music and Drama Publications.

Hunter, D. (1999). Developing peer-learning programmes in music: Group presentations and peer assessment. *British Journal of Music Education, 16,* 51–63.

Hunter, D., & Russ, M. (1996). Peer assessment in performance studies. *British Journal of Music Education, 13,* 67–78.

Lehmann, A. C., & Davidson, J. W. (2002). Taking an acquired skills perspective on music performance. In R. Colwell & C. Richardson (Eds.), *The New Handbook of Research on Music Teaching and Learning* (pp. 542–560). Oxford: Oxford University Press.

Leuthesser, L., Kohli, C. S., & Harich, K. R. (1995). Brand equity: The halo effect measure. *European Journal of Marketing: Bradford, 29,* 57–66.

Long, K. (1997). *Visual-Aids and Learning.* Retrieved August 28, 2003, from the University of Portsmouth, Department of Mechanical and Manufacturing Engineering website: *www.mech.port.ac.uk/av/AVALearn.htm.*

Luft, J. (1969). *Group Processes: An Introduction to Group Dynamics.* Bethesda, MD: National Press Books.

Martindale, C. (1988). Cognition, psychobiology, and aesthetics. In H. F. Farley & R. W. Neperud (Eds.), *The Foundations of Aesthetics, Art, and Education* (pp. 7–42). New York: Praeger.

McCormick, J., & McPherson, G. E. (2003). The role of self-efficacy in a musical performance examination: An exploratory structural equation analysis. *Psychology of Music, 31,* 37–51.

McCrary, J. (1993). Effects of listeners' and performers' race on music preferences. *Journal of Research in Music Education, 41,* 200–211.

McPherson, G. E., & Thompson, W. F. (1998). Assessing music performances: Issues and influences. *Research Studies in Music Education, 10,* 12–24.

Meyer, J. (1993). The sound of the orchestra. *Journal of the Audio Engineering Society, 41,* 203–213.

Morrison, S. J. (1998). A comparison of preference responses of white and African-American students to musical versus musical/visual stimuli. *Journal of Research in Music Education, 46,* 208–222.

Myers, G. (1999). *Social Psychology* (6th ed.). New York: McGraw-Hill.

Naylor, G. (1988). Modulation transfer and ensemble music performance. *Acustica, 65*, 127–137.

Nevill, A. M., & Holder, R. L. (1999). Home advantage in sport: An overview of studies on the advantage of playing at home. *Sports Medicine, 28*, 221–236.

North, A. C., & Hargreaves, D. J. (2000). Musical preferences during and after relaxation and exercise. *American Journal of Psychology, 113*, 43–67.

O'Neill, S. A. (1997). Gender and music. In D. J. Hargreaves & A. C. North (Eds.), *The Social Psychology of Music* (pp. 46–60). Oxford: Oxford University Press.

Pajares, F. (1996). Self-efficacy beliefs in academic settings. *Review of Educational Research, 66*, 543–578.

Palatine Report (2000). *Palatine Learning and Teaching Support Network*. Retrieved August 28, 2003, from Palatine website: *www.lancs.ac.uk/users/palatine/report8nov.htm*.

Plessner, H. (1999). Expectation biases in gymnastics judging. *Journal of Sport & Exercise Psychology, 21*, 131–144.

Posner, M. I., Nissen, M. J., & Klein, R. M. (1976). Visual dominance: An information-processing account of its origins and significance. *Psychological Review, 83*, 157–171.

Radocy, R. E. (1976). Effects of authority figure biases on changing judgments of musical events. *Journal of Research in Music Education, 24*, 119–128.

Repp, B. H. (1997). Expressive timing in a Debussy Prelude: A comparison of student and expert pianists. *Musicæ Scientiæ, 1*, 257–268.

Repp, B. H. (1999). A microcosm of musical expression: II. Quantitative analysis of pianists' dynamics in the initial measures of Chopin's Etude in E major. *Journal of the Acoustical Society of America, 105*, 1972–1988.

Scheer, J. K., & Ansorge, C. J. (1975). Effects of naturally induced judges' expectations on the ratings of physical performances. *Research Quarterly, 46*, 463–470.

Schubert, E. (1996). Enjoyment of negative emotions in music: An associative network explanation. *Psychology of Music, 24*, 18–28.

Schubert, E. (2002). Continuous response methodology applied to expressive performance. In C. Stevens, D. Burnham, G. McPherson, E. Schubert, & J. Renwick (Eds.), *Proceedings of the Seventh International Conference on Music Perception and Cognition* (pp. 83–86). Adelaide, Australia: Causal Productions.

Seta, J. J. (1982). The impact of comparison processes on coactors' task performance. *Journal of Personality and Social Psychology, 42*, 281–291.

Smyth, M. M. (1984). Perception and action. In M. M. Smyth & A. M. Wing (Eds.), *The Psychology of Human Movement* (pp. 119–152). London: Academic Press.

Sole, D. (1997). Johari's window for generating questions. *Journal of Adolescent & Adult Literacy, 40*, 481–483.

Stanley, M., Brooker, R., & Gilbert, R. (2002). Examiner perceptions of using criteria in music performance assessment. *Research Studies in Music Education, 18*, 43–52.

Thompson, S., & Williamon, A. (2003). Evaluating evaluation: Musical performance assessment as a research tool. *Music Perception, 21*, 21–41.

Vasil, T. (1973). *The Effects of Systematically Varying Selected Factors on Music Performing Adjudication*. Unpublished doctoral dissertation, University of Connecticut, Storrs, CT.

Västfjäll, D. (2001–2002). A review of the musical mood induction procedure. *Musicæ Scientiæ, Special Issue*, 173–211.

Wapnick, J., Darrow, A. A., Kovacs, J., & Dalrymple, L. (1997). Effects of physical attractiveness on evaluation of vocal performance. *Journal of Research in Music Education, 45,* 470–479.

Wapnick, J., Mazza, J. K., & Darrow, A. A. (1998). Effects of performer attractiveness, stage behavior, and dress on violin performance evaluation. *Journal of Research in Music Education, 46,* 510–521.

Wapnick, J., Mazza, J. K., & Darrow, A. A. (2000). Effects of performer attractiveness, stage behavior, and dress on evaluation of children's piano performances. *Journal of Research in Music Education, 48,* 323–335.

Williamon, A., & Davidson, J. W. (2002). Exploring co-performer communication. *Musicæ Scientiæ, 6,* 53–72.

Wirtz, J., & Bateson, J. E. G. (1995). An experimental investigation of halo effects in satisfaction measures of service attributes. *International Journal of Service Industry Management, 6,* 84–102.

Wolfe, J. (2003). From idea to acoustics and back again: The creation and analysis of information in music. Paper presented at the Seventh Western Pacific Regional Acoustics Conference, Melbourne, Australia.

Woody, R. H. (2000). Learning expressivity in music: An exploratory study. *Research Studies in Music Education, 14,* 14–23.

Yarbrough, C. (1975). Effect of magnitude of conductor behaviour on students in mixed choruses. *Journal of Research in Music Education, 23,* 134–146.

Ybarra, O. (2001). When first impressions don't last: The role of isolation and adaptation processes in the revision of evaluative impressions. *Social Cognition, 19,* 491–520.

Zajonc, R. B. (1965). Social facilitation. *Science, 149,* 269–274.

Zimmerman, B. J. (2000). Self-efficacy: An essential motive to learn. *Contemporary Educational Psychology, 25,* 82–91.

Part II

PRACTICE STRATEGIES

CHAPTER 5

STRATEGIES FOR INDIVIDUAL PRACTICE

HARALD JØRGENSEN

For the most part, individual practicing is a solitary activity. The performer is alone, with his or her instrument, and must rely on personal skill to achieve progress throughout the practice session. What musicians strive for, and what this chapter is about, is achieving *effective* individual practice. Hallam (1998) describes effective practice as "that which achieves the desired end product, in as short a time as possible, without interfering with long term goals" (p. 142).

By selecting and implementing appropriate practice *strategies*, a performer can acquire necessary tools to accomplish this. For the sake of clarity, practice strategies can be defined as thoughts and behaviors that musicians engage in during practice that are intended to influence their motivational or affective state, or the way in which they select, organize, integrate, and rehearse new knowledge and skills (adapted from Weinstein & Mayer, 1986). For instance, when a musician makes plans for a practice session, this is a "thought" strategy, and when a musician gradually increases the tempo of a performance, this is a "behavior" strategy. Strategies are (usually) consciously applied but may become automatic with repetition.

Most strategies are neither functional nor dysfunctional in and of themselves. Practicing a piece of music by playing it over and over again from beginning to end without interruption may be beneficial for some, but ineffective for others. Indeed, advanced students and professional musicians often hold idiosyncratic views as to what constitutes effective practice. Such differences in approach are to be expected, as performers work to accentuate their individual strengths and eliminate their weaknesses. In spite of this diversity, however, there are common strategies that musicians can employ to produce better performance results or to achieve the same results more quickly.

A number of music teachers have suggested that it is convenient for students to view practicing as a means of "self-teaching", where in the absence of the teacher, students must act as the teacher's deputy, assigning themselves definite tasks and supervising their own work (Galamian, 1964). Based on this view, one can emphasize that effective practice (both within a single session and across longer periods of time) should include three self-teaching phases:

- planning and preparation of practice
- execution of practice
- observation and evaluation of practice.

An alternative view, offered by educational psychologists, is the metaphor of "self-regulated learning" (i.e. how students acquire the tools necessary to take control of their own learning and, thereby, learn effectively). In this approach, the practitioner should engage in three self-regulating phases:

- *forethought*: the thought processes and personal beliefs that precede efforts to engage in a task
- *performance/volitional control*: processes that occur during learning that affect concentration and performance
- *self-reflection*: the learner's reaction and subsequent response to the experience (see McPherson & Zimmerman, 2002; Zimmerman, 1998).

The three phases identified in this approach can easily be mapped onto those of self-teaching described above. Moreover, both approaches view the respective phases of practice as interwoven, or cyclical.

This chapter presents and classifies practice strategies in terms of the self-teaching phases of planning, execution, and observation and evaluation, as these terms tend to be more commonly used by performers and teachers (see Figure 5.1 for a model of strategies based on self-teaching). Nevertheless, within a larger frame of reference, theory

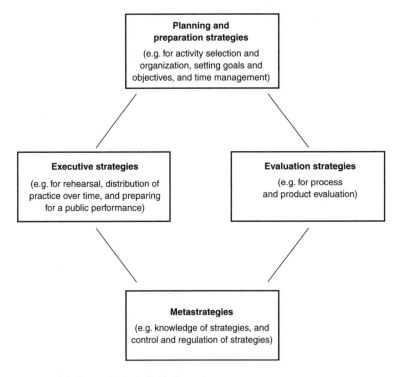

Figure 5.1   A model of strategies for individual practice.

and research on self-regulation of learning form an important basis for this chapter. Directing the practitioner's attention to three phases to be employed within practice is not, however, sufficient for optimal use of individual strategies. Every practitioner—from the student to the professional musician—must have a thorough knowledge of his or her *repertory* of strategies and must be able to control, regulate, and exploit this repertory. Therefore, the issue of metastrategies (i.e. knowing about and controlling one's strategies) is addressed toward the end of the chapter.

5.1   Individual practice: A historical perspective

Since roughly 1700, an abundance of books have been written about instrumental methods or approaches, each containing material for individual practice (e.g. Quantz, 1752/1985; Tosi, 1723/1987; Türk, 1789/1982). Most of these works are based on the personal experience and opinions of the authors, and their views are often contradictory.

Empirical research on individual practice has a much shorter history. The Hungarian pianist, Sandor Kovacs, published the first empirical study in 1916. He was puzzled by the problems his students had in performing difficult pieces from memory. His conclusion was that musicians should engage in mental practice, especially when initially learning a new piece. During the subsequent 20 years, only three research studies were published. Two of these (Brown, 1928; Eberly, 1921) examined the issue of the "whole" versus "part" approaches to practicing (see Section 5.3.1), while the third dealt with the coordination of hands in piano playing (Brown, 1933). Then, in 1937, Grace Rubin-Rabson, an American psychologist and educationist, published the first of a series of 10 research studies on piano practicing. The last of her studies appeared in 1947. After that, there was a period of silence for almost 30 years.

Since 1975, the number of published studies on individual practice strategies has gradually increased with each decade, and approximately two thirds of the published works from 1916 to present are dated 1990 or later. All in all, this research has explored the efficacy of a wide range of practice strategies, as well as the psychological and pedagogical principals that underpin learning and teaching in music. Although some conflicting results have emerged within the body of empirical work since 1916, the strategies offered below are drawn from a selection of the most salient and robust findings.

5.2   Planning and preparation strategies

5.2.1   Strategies for activity selection and organization

The quality of a practice session is characterized and defined by the specific activities in which the practitioner engages. Some activities are *not* related to learning, such as daydreaming or avoidance behaviors that include taking a long time to set up a music stand or perform maintenance on an instrument (see Pitts *et al.*, 2000a; McPherson & Renwick, 2001). It almost goes without saying that these strategies are to be avoided.

Practice activities *with* learning objectives can be divided into "playing practice" and "nonplaying practice" (e.g. studying the score, writing in the score or in a notebook, silent fingering, etc.). Research suggests that playing activities tend to dominate the practice session, and within those, musicians most commonly engage in repertory work, followed by practice on technical issues (Geringer & Kostka, 1984; Hallam, 1995; Sloboda *et al.*, 1996; Jørgensen, 1998; McPherson & Renwick, 2001). From this, the following suggestions emerge:

◆ Reduce the nonlearning time in practice sessions by enhancing concentration and motivation (see Chapters 11 and 12).

◆ Balance "playing practice" with "nonplaying practice" in a single session or over a period of time. Focused, nonplaying practice will give more time for mental rehearsal and reflection and prevent overuse of muscles (as discussed in Chapter 3). In the long run, this is not a waste of time, but in fact, quite the opposite (see Section 5.3.1).

There appears to be a wide range of strategies used by practitioners to select and organize practice activities, from those who do as they "usually do" to those who change practice activities from session to session (Jørgensen, 1998).

◆ If you have a specific routine, try to introduce new elements into your practice sessions or practice schedule. For instance, you can reserve one session a day for "unexpected demands" (e.g. a sight-reading task) or use a whole session for technical work.

◆ If you vary practice content and sequence of activities from session to session, reflect on the benefits of a more regular regime that touches on all the immediately relevant aspects of performance before you turn to something else.

Warm-up exercises are used by most musicians and are included in most sessions. These exercises are so closely related to the instrument's peculiarities and physical demands (as well as to the individual's muscular and technical proficiency) that it is difficult to offer specific recommendations. However:

◆ Ask yourself: why is this particular warm-up exercise necessary for me in this session? Are other exercises better suited for this particular practice situation? For my short-term needs? For my long-term needs?

These same questions can be applied to practice on exercises and etudes that are intended to prepare particular technical and musical aspects of performance. Of course, such exercises can benefit the general advancement toward performance excellence, but exercises should be well focused and carefully selected if they are to address specific challenges within a given composition (Harvey *et al.*, 1987; Pacey, 1993; Pierce, 1992).

Finally, research has shown that, within practice sessions, musicians normally begin with technical exercises and then move on to repertory work (Duke *et al.*, 1997; Jørgensen, 1998). Within this repertory work, however, there is evidence to suggest that many students practice only new pieces and do not have a strategy for systematically reviewing "old" pieces (Jørgensen, 1998).

◆ Include deliberate work on formerly rehearsed music in your practice schedule to keep your core repertory active.

5.2.2   Strategies for setting goals and objectives

Goals are necessary to achieve learning and improvement (as shown in Chapters 2 and 12 of this volume). However, in a study of conservatory students, Jørgensen (1998) found that many practice sessions were started without efforts to plan and establish goals. Nevertheless, there seems to be a tendency to focus on two types of goals for the practice of a specific piece of music: goals for technical performance quality and goals for expressive performance quality.

The expressive intentions for a piece should be regarded as part of a *performance plan*, which is comprised of more or less conscious musical ideas or communicative messages to be developed and incorporated into performance. Some musicians let their expressive ideas guide their technical work. Others develop their performance with no preconceived plan, allowing it to evolve as practice progresses. Still others use a combination of a preconceived plan and intuitive processes in working toward a performance (Hallam, 1997a). Another approach is to develop a performance plan after mastering most of the technical challenges in a piece (Nielsen, 2001). There is no research indicating that one approach is more efficient than the others independent of circumstances. This is certainly one of the strategies where effectiveness depends on individual-specific preferences for learning and particular characteristics of the performer, in addition to the nature of the music. However, one general recommendation is:

◆ At the beginning of the session, formulate some of your overall intentions for the practice session (whatever these may be) as clearly and precisely as possible. What do you specifically want to develop? To master?

Goals come and go, and they will change during a long rehearsal process. Individuals who plan what to do—and know why they do something and what they wish to accomplish—can make their practice sessions more efficient. Practitioners must not refrain from formulating specific plans just because they know that unexpected events and frustrating moments will inevitably pop up and may alter any planning efforts. Goals and related issues are dealt with further in several sections of this chapter, as well as in Chapter 12.

5.2.3   Time management strategies

Time management is integral to effective practice. For novice students, the two most frequently asked questions are "how much time do I have to practice" and "how often do I have to practice." Both of these questions concern the management of practice quantity, and the general answer to all practitioners is that there is a positive relationship between quantity of practice and overall musical achievement (Jørgensen, 2002).

As expertise develops, both the length and frequency of practice sessions tend to increase (Sloboda *et al.*, 1996). During the formative years of childhood and youth, increasing practice quantity is typically more the result of longer sessions than of more frequent sessions or more practice days (Hallam, 2001a). Also, Hallam noted, not surprisingly, that 95% of the novices and advanced students in her study reported an increase in practice during the weeks preceding examinations. Another event that seems to generate more practice activity is an upcoming or recently concluded private lesson (Lehmann & Ericsson, 1998), while school holidays usually result in a decrease in practice activity (Sloboda *et al.*, 1996).

The notion of what constitutes a "normal" frequency and volume of practice for students across the performance programs in higher music education seems to be fairly consistent. First of all, students are expected to practice regularly—that is, every day or most of the days in a week. This means that they have to manage the distribution of practice sessions throughout the week and during a practice day within the context of a busy study schedule. Several management strategies have been observed in relation to this. Some students practice at the same time every day (Duke *et al.*, 1997), and some integrate practice into a daily or weekly plan (Jørgensen, 1997b). Most students, however, try to fit in practice sessions between other activities without any preconceived plan. There may be many sound reasons for this, but some crucial questions to ask are:

◆ Do you give practice sessions the highest priority among your study activities throughout a study day?

◆ Do you say "no" to other activities that interfere with your planned sessions, or do you look at practice sessions as something that can easily be subordinated to other demands, cancelled, or postponed?

The answers to these questions can offer an important indicator of practicing behavior and may help trigger a new way of thinking about study habits.

Is there an optimal time of day for practicing? Certainly, common sense tells us that we need to be awake and alert. Thus, one strategy is to practice those pieces that are considered to be most difficult in the morning (Lehmann & Ericsson, 1998). Ericsson *et al.* (1993) found that the students at the highest skill level in one conservatory practiced in the morning, took naps in the afternoon, and then put in more practice in the evening. Although this may be a strategy that can be adopted by only a select few, its general relevance is clear:

◆ Attack what you regard as your day's most challenging practice task at a time when you feel most alert and ready for serious work.

There is no universally applicable answer to the question of how much to practice. For students in higher education, however, an unwritten norm for the amount of individual practice seems to average around 20–25 hours per week. There are pronounced variations in both directions from this average, primarily depending on the nature of the instrument. In general, keyboard players have a higher quantity of individual practice than string players, who practice more than wind players (Jørgensen, 1997a). There are also differences between specific instruments within these groups. Violinists, for instance, tend to practice more than double bass players, and flute players practice more than tuba players. These differences are partly related to the restrictions posed by the instrument's physical and technical demands and partly on the aspirations and motivation of the performer, which is why such large differences can be observed in the amount of individual practice among students who play the same instrument. While one trumpet player may practice 10 hours in a week, another may practice for 20 or more. Similarly, a violin student practicing 20 hours in a week may have a friend who practices for 35 or 40 hours.

Looking at these differences, and keeping in mind that there is a positive relationship between the amount of practice and rise in general proficiency, it is reasonable to conclude that different levels of musical accomplishment may be demonstrated between those who practice less versus those who practice more during the 4–6-year duration of higher music education. Suppose there are two students of the same instrument, one of whom has practiced 1500 hours in 4 years of study, while the other has practiced in excess of 4500 hours. Assuming that they started their studies at the same general level of proficiency and engaged in the same quality of practice, it is highly probable that they will exhibit a clear difference in proficiency after those 4 years.

In order to manage the amount of time spent in practice successfully, you should observe and reflect upon the relationship between the time you invest in individual practice, and the progress you witness in your playing. Do you invest too little time to make progress? Do you invest just enough time to progress slowly and manage your short-term demands and goals?

Are there strategies that a practitioner can use to help increase practice volume? Individuals who are not sure of how much time they actually invest in individual practice should start by systematically observing and registering their individual practice time.

♦ If you realize that you ought to practice more, you can formulate a contract (strictly for yourself) of how much time you intend to invest in individual practice for the next week, month, etc. Then, it is up to you to comply with the contract.

♦ The term "invest" has been consciously used in relation to practice time as a potentially helpful metaphor. View the practice you do over days, weeks, and years as an investment in a "practice amount account," and plan your investment accordingly.

Quantity, however, must not be the only concern of the practitioner. In their study of three young wind students in their first year of practice, Pitts *et al.* (2000a) observed that both the mother of one of the students and her practicing daughter were exclusively concerned with quantity, with the mother insisting on "more" without addressing the quality of the playing and practice. In this respect, there is reason to wonder how many students have only one time management strategy: the dysfunctional "filling time" strategy. Effective practice is not a question of "filling time," but of filling the optimal amount of time with the optimal quality of practice, which means employing carefully selected strategies.

It is intended that, by using appropriate practice strategies to enhance *practice* quality, *performance* quality will, in turn, be enhanced. It is important to note that focusing on practice quality (initially through adequate planning and preparation) will most probably reduce the need for quantity.

5.3   Executive strategies

5.3.1   Rehearsal strategies

Mental versus playing rehearsal strategies

Mental rehearsal is a type of nonplaying practice (see Section 5.2.1) that has been championed by a number of pedagogues and psychologists. It is usually defined as the cognitive or imaginary rehearsal of a physical skill without overt muscular movement and is often presented as an alternative or a supplement to the playing approach. However, it is important to remember that there is virtually no playing without cognitive activity, which means that the playing approach is inevitably a combination of mental and physical effort.

No specific mental strategy can be identified as the "right" one. There are a myriad of different techniques that can be applied; particular suggestions are offered in Chapter 12 of this volume. The basic purpose of mental strategies is to establish and activate visual, aural, and kinesthetic images of the music for use in both practice and performance.

◆ Regard the score as a wellspring of information for cognitive activity. Respond to it as a source of information about signs, keys, structures, sounds, movements, touch, etc.

In order to exploit all the possible cues inherent in a score, performers should activate their analysis and ear training skills, as well as their ability to develop images of movements and touch, their knowledge of style and history of music, and their powers of reflection and memorization. There are marked differences between musicians in the breadth and quality of images that they receive and process from the score (Grøndahl, 1987), and only the individual's personal effort can expand and differentiate the repertory of mental strategies.

The relative merits of mental strategies, as compared with playing strategies, have been addressed in a number of studies (see Jones, 1990; Kopiez, 1990; Ross, 1985; Rubin-Rabson, 1937), with some conflicting results and recommendations. Trying to determine which of these strategies function best in a practice situation is not, however, the most important issue because mental and playing strategies are not inseparable. The most important point to consider is how to combine these two approaches in the most constructive fashion during practice.

◆ Always reflect on how you can combine mental strategies with playing strategies to ensure that they support and enhance each other. For instance, when is it convenient to bring in mental strategies: before you start playing, used as an interruption in playing practice, or after playing as a mental reminder? How do the style and complexity of the music (including the length and familiarity of the piece) influence your choice of strategy?

Strategies to master the whole piece versus smaller parts

Every piece of music can be broken down into smaller sections or parts. How can this be applied in practice? Three main approaches have emerged in recent research. One strategy is to play through the entire piece several times, not stopping for special treatment of parts of the piece. A second strategy is to concentrate only on parts of the music before attempting to master the whole; going through each part several times before going on to the next is a characteristic of this approach. The third strategy combines the whole and the part approaches. One could, for instance, play through the music and stop to practice larger parts *en route* (Hallam, 1997b; Miklaszewski, 1989); alternatively, one could start with the whole to gain sufficient knowledge of the piece (either by studying the entire score or by playing through the piece as well as possible) in order to select and relate parts to larger sections or to the whole piece (Chaffin & Imreh, 1997; Nielsen, 1997, 1999b; Williamon & Valentine, 2002; Williamon *et al.*, 2002).

Although the first strategy is more common among novices than professionals, each of the three strategies has its own merits, depending on the circumstances that define the practice situation. These include the time available for the rehearsal of the piece, the style and complexity of the music, the individual's familiarity with the music, the goal of the practice, and the individual's skill at evaluating and correcting performances on repeated rehearsals.

◆ Make use of all three major strategies to master both the whole and its parts; do not stick to a single strategy regardless of circumstances.

How is a "part" to be selected? The formal structure of the piece has been shown in some studies to be a good starting point. Even so, there may be technical difficulties within a formal part that forces the practitioner to subdivide it further (Chaffin & Imreh, 1997; Miklaszewski, 1989; Miklaszewski & Sawicki, 1992). Parts may also be selected because of their visual layout and harmonic progressions (Williamon & Valentine, 2002). One study of organ students found that some chose parts that had a musical or technical content that was either new or vaguely related to other sections, rather than sections that were identical (Nielsen, 1999b).

◆ You are not bound to partition a piece into formal parts in accordance with the composer's view; however, the parts you select ought to be musically meaningful to you.

◆ Adopt a procedure that combines overview and care for the "whole," with special treatment of difficult or challenging parts that are connected to the whole.

The parts on which one focuses are likely to become longer as practice progresses, and this process has been linked to the production of higher quality musical, communicative, and technical performances (Williamon & Valentine, 2000, 2002). Nevertheless, it is not unusual for attention to be focused on small parts and details throughout the duration of practice on a piece, even in sessions just before a performance (Williamon *et al.*, 2002). Further consideration of the part approach is offered in Chapter 7 in relation to memorizing music.

Strategies for difficult and challenging parts

An issue that is closely tied to the above involves practicing difficult or challenging parts. Clearly, "difficulty" depends on each musician's skill and experience, as well as instrument-specific challenges (e.g. double stops, triple tonguing, etc.). One strategy is to use general exercises and etudes that simplify the problem and gradually bring one toward a solution that is applicable to the specific piece. When this happens, it is called positive "transfer of learning" (Nielsen, 1999b).

Another strategy is to practice the difficult part within the given piece repeatedly until it is mastered. For example, choral singers in one study relied on this approach when practicing specific intervals, rather than using exercises to train them to master these intervals (Harvey *et al.*, 1987). Research on this issue is scant, but the crucial question for the practitioner is:

◆ Are these exercises really bringing you toward mastery of the specific problem? If you use exercises to master a difficult passage, make sure there is positive transfer between the exercises and the passage itself, with the conditions for learning and performance being as similar as possible (Hallam, 1997a).

Strategies concerned with tempo of performance

Research has shown that there are three primary strategies used when a practitioner encounters a composition that he or she is unable to play immediately at the required tempo. The first, starting slowly and then gradually increasing tempo, is the most frequently recommended (see Barry, 1992). Interestingly, however, slower performances may contain more errors than those that are faster (Drake & Palmer, 2000). This is not necessarily an argument against the strategy, as the piece will no doubt grow more familiar and contain fewer errors as practice progresses. A more important objection, though, is that starting out using arm, finger, or mouth movements that are far from the physical and muscular demands of the final movements can cause the initial learning not only to be a waste of time, but also counterproductive in developing the "correct" muscular responses. The reason for this is that qualitatively different movements activate different muscles (Winold *et al.*, 1994). Another strategy is to alternate, if possible, between a slow tempo and the faster performance tempo (Donald, 1997). This may bring the piece up to the performance tempo more quickly, since it entails regular tests of one's ability to play at that tempo. A third strategy is to practice at the performance tempo from start to finish.

The general rule of thumb here is that a tempo strategy should be chosen only after careful consideration of what it can accomplish. There is one issue, however, that is often overlooked by students who restrict their use of alternative tempo strategies. This involves the ability to identify and classify errors that are and are not acceptable during practice. It seems that most students are willing to accept rhythmic and dynamic deviations from the "target" performance, as they are extremely anxious to play the "right notes" (and to play them in tune). The issue of errors will be dealt with further in Section 5.4.2; as for now:

◆ Decide the types and number of performance errors you are willing to accept to bring the tempo up to speed as quickly as possible, and choose a tempo strategy in accordance with this decision.

Practicing tempo variations can also be useful for trying out different expressive renderings of the music (see Oura & Hatano, 2001).

5.3.2   Strategies for the distribution of practice over time

Imagine a situation in which there is one week to rehearse a new piece and that this rehearsal, in total, will take approximately 10–12 hours. In such a situation, one could spread practice over the entire week (the "distributed" approach) or cluster it together in just a few sessions (the "massed" approach). There are, of course, many available options for deciding on the length and distribution of practice sessions, but one must consider what is going on in the period between sessions. Does this comprise rest, practice on other pieces, or activities unrelated to practicing? In light of an almost complete lack of research in this area and the complexity of the issue, the best recommendation may still be from Fleischman and Parker (1962):

◆ Use distributed practice when the practice sessions are long enough to bring about improvement and when the time between sessions is long enough to overcome fatigue, but not so long that forgetting occurs.

5.3.3   Strategies for preparing for a public performance

There are several issues that influence public performance that could benefit from close attention during practice. Performance is often accompanied by worries regarding memory lapses, anxiety, and stage fright, and these issues are addressed in detail elsewhere in this book (see Chapters 7, 9, 10, 12, and 14). In addition, it is important to consider the audience's perspective during practice. For example, experienced performers have reported taking the audience's perspective into account when developing their expressive ideas (Oura & Hatano, 2001) and working deliberately on the communication of musical ideas in the final stages of practice on a piece (Williamon *et al.*, 2003). Many have also reported imagining how the audience will perceive the performance in a range of different acoustical environments (Edlund, 2000). These considerations lead to questions such as:

◆ Who is your audience and what type of concert venue are you going to perform in? When you practice, imagine how the audience will perceive and react to the soundscape you create.

In performance, many students seem preoccupied solely with the music and forget to prepare their stage behavior adequately. Understanding the role of body movement in performance, for instance, may help harmonize musical and bodily messages to the audience (Davidson, 1993; see also Chapter 4 of this volume for a discussion of factors that influence audiences' evaluations of performance).

◆ Observe your body movements and ask whether they are supporting your musical intentions? Are they counterproductive? Viewing videos of previous concerts, combined with written self-evaluations of your stage behavior, is recommended for improvement (Daniel, 2001).

5.4   Evaluation strategies

5.4.1   The necessity of evaluation

Knowledge of results, or informative feedback, is essential to the learning process. This means that a practitioner should explicitly diagnose his or her strengths and weaknesses in prescribing solutions to problems. Practicing requires constant vigilance and attention to all kinds of feedback, as well as a repertoire of knowledge and skills to remedy problems. This is an area in which many practitioners could improve. For instance, the end of a practice session is an important time for evaluation. However, only 21% of conservatory students in one study regularly evaluated and made subsequent plans after practice (Jørgensen, 1998). Thus, sessions may be ended rather haphazardly, with no reflection on progress and how to continue practicing.

♦ Do you use evaluation as a regular strategy in your efforts to improve?

5.4.2   Strategies for process evaluation

Aural and visual models

In process evaluation, evaluative thoughts and behaviors are interwoven with ongoing practice. One approach to this type of evaluation is for the individual to have a model performance in mind during practice (see also Chapters 7 and 12). Accomplished performers are expected to develop their own models as mental images, while less experienced performers may need to use others' performances as models (e.g. from a recording of a piece). With unfamiliar and complex music, research suggests that experts, too, can benefit from studying others' performances as models (see Lisboa *et al.*, in press, for discussion).

♦ Develop a performance plan or use a recording to guide your evaluation of your performance.

Viewing videos of your own previous performances is also recommended, especially if this is combined with written self-evaluations (Daniel, 2001). This has the additional advantage of enhancing student independence in assessing performance, since students usually rely on comments from teachers to improve.

Strategies to detect and correct errors

Detecting and correcting errors is a major task during practice. The musician must have a notion of what errors are and the ability to recognize them when they occur, including errors in pitch, rhythmic accuracy, dynamics, intonation, steadiness of pulse, and tonality (see Drake & Palmer, 2000; Palmer & van de Sande, 1995). Some of these are closely related to the specific demands of the instrument, but the question each practitioner must ask is:

♦ Do you have a preoccupation with some errors and ignore others? Develop a broad knowledge of error types. Write out the most important types of errors related to your instrument or your own most recurring errors, and keep a watchful eye on them.

The German cellist, Gerhard Mantel (1984), recommends that the practitioner direct his or her attention to different aspects of the music studied in a systematic and planned manner. This will aid concentration and also aid in detecting and correcting errors. In many cases, errors are made but go unobserved because the performer has not studied or grasped essential features of the score.

♦ Use a thorough study of the score to identify important aspects of the music and thus prevent unnecessary errors.

How can errors be corrected? One strategy is to ignore errors and play on, hoping that they will disappear on replaying. Another is for the musician to stop and correct errors whenever they occur. Both approaches have certain advantages, as long as the practitioner remains aware of major pitfalls of each. Regarding the first of these, errors once made tend to be practiced in, instead of removed (Hallam, 1997a). As for the second strategy, "stopping" may also be learned, prompting small pauses at the location of errors in subsequent performances. A third approach is probably the most generally useful:

◆ Practice whole sections followed by specific attention to errors and error-correction within these sections.

Self-guiding strategies

Self-guidance involves covertly or overtly describing how to proceed, giving comments on progress, and reminding oneself of concentration lapses and motivational aspects of the situation (Nielsen, 2001). There are warning strategies ("Oh, here comes that tricky bit, I have to play it slower"), comments as strategies ("No, not so fast!"), supportive verbalizations as strategies ("One, two, three, one, two, three"), and reminder strategies ("Remember the melody in the left hand"). Guidance strategies also involve singing along with playing.

◆ Regardless of which approach is used, it is important to give constructive messages to yourself when practicing.

5.5   Metastrategies

5.5.1   Knowledge about strategies

The importance of having a repertory of strategies, ready for use, has been mentioned several times, and by reading this chapter, it is intended that the practitioner will learn more about the strategies that best suit his or her needs. Such knowledge about strategies is commonly referred to within psychology as "metacognitive knowledge." Borkowski and Turner (1990) have proposed three different areas of metacognitive knowledge.

● *Specific knowledge* is comprised of the strategies that the individual actually knows.

● *Relational knowledge* covers the knowledge of how different strategies may contribute toward satisfying different tasks and goals.

● *General knowledge* has to do with an understanding of how much effort is required when employing practice strategies; for instance, concentrated practice on problem areas in a piece is typically regarded by students as requiring greater effort than playing familiar repertory (Lehmann, 2002).

A distinction may also be made between *knowledge about personal variables* and *task knowledge* (Flavell, 1987). The first offers insight into individual learning processes and the individual's personal thoughts about these processes. The second is knowledge about how tasks differ from each other (e.g. in complexity) and how an individual's goals influence the ways in which tasks will be addressed (e.g. different strategies for sight-reading and memorizing music).

Several studies have observed that practitioners have a restricted knowledge of specific strategies and that there are considerable differences between beginners, novices, and experts (e.g., Hallam, 2001b; Pitts *et al.*, 2000a, 2000b; Renwick & McPherson, 2002; Sloboda *et al.*, 1996), as well as individual differences among musicians at the same level of accomplishment (Nielsen, 1997, 1999a, 1999b, 2001). The same applies to relational and general knowledge and personal and task knowledge. Developing a repertory of strategies and acquiring knowledge about these, as well as one's own cognitive functioning, is certainly one of the most important objectives for any practitioner and should be emphasized by teachers in students' lessons and rehearsal time.

◆ Observe your practice behavior, and try to register the strategies you use. Do you have strategies for all issues covered in this chapter? Doing this, you will probably find that you have a broader range of strategies than expected.

5.5.2   Control and regulation of strategies

A second metacognitive area is the control and regulation of strategies. Control of strategies is, first of all, dependent on knowledge and classification of strategies as described above. Based on this knowledge, one can then proceed with *checking, evaluation*, and *prediction* (Kluwe, 1987).

◆ What strategies are being used? (*knowledge and classification*).

◆ How well is your practice proceeding? (*checking and evaluation*).

◆ What type of result will occur if . . . ? (*prediction*).

The regulation of strategies involves deliberate *effort, task* selection, *speed*, and *intensity* (see Nielsen, 1999b). Questions such as the following may be helpful in regulating strategy use in specific practice situations:

◆ How much effort are you willing to invest in this problem, and consequently, what strategies will you use? (*effort*).

◆ Where will you start? (*task selection*).

◆ How many strategies are you willing to use to solve this problem? (*speed*).

◆ How long will you persist with a strategy if it does not give results? (*intensity*).

5.6   Conclusions

This chapter has addressed a number of strategies for individual practice. The development from beginner and novice to higher levels of accomplishment and expertise is accompanied by a broadening of one's repertory of strategies and skills in using them. At all levels of accomplishment, however, research indicates that there may be a range of individual differences in the extent to which strategies are appropriate, applicable, and effective. This is a reminder that the person, task, and context must always be kept in mind when reflecting on strategy use. There is, as Hallam (1995) observes, no simple correspondence between a particular practice strategy and success as a performer.

Developing a thorough knowledge of strategies and strategy use is not necessarily straightforward. Many instrumental teachers are of the opinion that they teach their students how to practice. When Barry and McArthur (1994) asked teachers if they included specific instructions on how to practice in their lessons, 84% answered "always" or "almost always." However, what the student perceives and remembers may not correspond to what the teacher thinks he or she is communicating. For three consecutive years, Jørgensen (2000) asked students entering a music conservatory how much their former instrumental teachers had emphasized practice. Approximately 40% reported that their teachers had put "very little" or "no" emphasis on practice behavior. This discrepancy, therefore, presents a challenge to all teachers to include instruction on practice strategies in their lessons in a way that directly captures the interest of the student, and then to follow that up with appropriate learning and performance assignments.

Barry (1992) has demonstrated that strategies can, indeed, be successfully taught. She found, for example, that wind instrument students, when instructed, were able to examine the music visually, to "finger through" the music silently, and to tap the rhythm of an entire étude before playing it. These strategies were generally not observed among students who were simply asked to "practice in any way you think best." Similarly, Kenny (1992) reported positive results from a study in which beginning band students were instructed in strategies such as problem identification, practice planning, goal selection, monitoring, and evaluation. This study lasted for only 18 weeks, and there was no difference in technical proficiency and sight-reading ability between the students that were instructed in practice strategies and those who were not. However, the instructed students expressed stronger favorable opinions about practicing, were more likely to engage in practice planning and problem identification, were better able to select appropriate performance goals, and were able to formulate goals that were more cognitively complex than their control group counterparts. These results remind us that:

◆ Practice must be practiced! Observe your practice sessions regularly, and concentrate your observation on one or two specific features at a time. For example, try to register how much time you spend on specific tasks during a practice session, what types of errors you produce, how you include repetition of previously rehearsed repertory into your practice schedule, etc. The number and range of issues are limitless. The main point is that practicing must be taken seriously, as the *professional* musician is dependent on a *professional* level of practicing.

At the beginning of this chapter, it is stated that books about instrumental methods and approaches are primarily based on personal experience and on the opinions of the respective author. Thus, the views put forth are often contradictory at a very profound level. What is called for now is for teachers and practitioners to employ their personal experience, the experience of others, as well as research findings, in order to reflect on and experiment with practice, while remaining open to both traditional and nontraditional strategies.

Further information and reading

Bernstein, S. (1981). *With Your Own Two Hands: Self-Discovery Through Music.* New York: Schirmer. [See Chapter 1 "Why do your practice?" and Chapter 2 "Why don't you practice?" for a discussion of the relationship between practicing and personal self-integration.]

Hallam, S. (1997). What do we know about music practising? Towards a model synthesising the research literature. In H. Jørgensen & A. C. Lehmann (Eds.), *Does Practice Make Perfect? Current Theory and Research on Instrumental Music Practice* (pp. 179–231). Oslo: Norwegian Academy of Music. [Gives an overview of research up to 1997.]

Lehmann, A. C. (1997). The acquisition of expertise in music: Efficiency of deliberate practice as a moderating variable in accounting for sub-expert performance. In I. Deliège & J. Sloboda (Eds.), *Perception and Cognition of Music* (pp. 161–187). Hove, UK: Psychology Press. [Relates a discussion of deliberate practice to research on expertise and development of practice throughout the life-span.]

McPherson, G. E., & Zimmerman, B. J. (2002). Self-regulation of musical learning: A social cognitive perspective. In R. Colwell & C. Richardson (Eds.), *The New Handbook of Research on Music Teaching and Learning* (pp. 327–347). Oxford: Oxford University Press. [Contains a thorough review of the self-regulation phases of forethought, performance/volitional control, and self-reflection.]

References

Barry, N. H. (1992). The effects of practice strategies, individual differences in cognitive style, and gender upon technical accuracy and musicality of student instrumental performance. *Psychology of Music, 20,* 112–123.

Barry, N. H., & McArthur, V. (1994). Teaching practice strategies in the music studio: A survey of applied music teachers. *Psychology of Music, 22,* 44–55.

Brown, R. W. (1928). A comparison of the "whole," "part" and "combination" methods of learning piano music. *Journal of Experimental Psychology, 11,* 235–247.

Brown, R. W. (1933). The relation between two methods of learning piano music. *Journal of Experimental Psychology, 16,* 435–441.

Borkowski, J. G., & Turner, L. A. (1990). Transsituational characteristics of metacognition. In W. Schneider & F. E. Weinert (Eds.), *Interactions Among Aptitudes, Strategies, and Knowledge in Cognitive Performance* (pp. 159–176). New York: Springer.

Chaffin, R., & Imreh, G. (1997). "Pulling teeth and torture": musical memory and problem solving. *Thinking and Reasoning, 3,* 315–336.

Daniel, R. (2001). Self-assessment in performance. *British Journal of Music Education, 18,* 215–226.

Davidson, J. W. (1993). Visual perception of performance manner in the movements of solo musicians. *Psychology of Music, 21,* 103–113.

Donald, L. S. (1997). *The Organization of Rehearsal Tempos and Efficiency of Motor Skill Acquisition in Piano Performance.* Unpublished doctoral dissertation, University of Texas, Austin, TX.

Drake, C., & Palmer, C. (2000). Skill acquisition in music performance: Relations between planning and temporal control. *Cognition, 74,* 1–32.

Duke, R. A., Flowers, P. J., & Wolfe, D. E. (1997). Children who study piano with excellent teachers in the United States. *Bulletin of the Council for Research in Music Education, 132,* 51–84.

Eberly, L. E. (1921). *Part versus Whole Method in Memorizing Music.* Unpublished masters dissertation, Columbia University, New York.

Edlund, B. (2000). Listening to oneself at a distance. In C. Woods, G. Luck, R. Brochard, F. Seddon, & J. A. Sloboda (Eds.), *Proceedings of the Sixth International Conference on Music Perception and Cognition*. Keele, UK: Keele University.

Ericsson, K. A., Krampe, R. T., & Tesch-Römer, C. (1993). The role of deliberate practice in the acquisition of expert performance. *Psychological Review, 100*, 363–406.

Flavell, J. H. (1987). Speculations about the nature and development of metacognition. In F. E. Weinert & R. H. Kluwe (Eds.), *Metacognition, Motivation, and Understanding* (pp. 21–29). Hillsdale, NJ: Erlbaum.

Fleischman, E. A., & Parker, J. F. (1962). Factors in the retention and relearning of perceptual-motor skill. *Journal of Experimental Psychology, 64*, 215–226.

Galamian, I. (1964). *Principles of Violin Playing and Teaching*. London: Faber & Faber.

Geringer, J. M., & Kostka, M. J. (1984). An analysis of practice room behavior of college music students. *Contributions to Music Education, 11*, 24–27.

Grøndahl, D. (1987). *Thinking Processes and Structures Used by Professional Pianists in Keyboard Learning*. Unpublished masters dissertation, Norwegian Academy of Music, Oslo.

Hallam, S. (1995). Professional musicians' approaches to the learning and interpretation of music. *Psychology of Music, 23*, 111–128.

Hallam, S. (1997a). What do we know about practising? Towards a model synthesising the research literature. In H. Jørgensen & A. C. Lehmann (Eds.), *Does Practice Make Perfect? Current Theory and Research on Instrumental Music Practice* (pp. 179–231). Oslo: Norwegian Academy of Music.

Hallam, S. (1997b). Approaches to instrumental music practice of experts and novices: Implications for education. In H. Jørgensen & A. C. Lehmann (Eds.), *Does Practice Make Perfect? Current Theory and Research on Instrumental Music Practice* (pp. 89–107). Oslo: Norwegian Academy of Music.

Hallam, S. (1998). *Instrumental Teaching: A Practical Guide to Better Teaching and Learning*. Oxford, UK: Heinemann.

Hallam, S. (2001a). The development of expertise in young musicians: Strategy use, knowledge acquisition and individual diversity. *Music Education Research, 3*, 7–23.

Hallam, S. (2001b). The development of metacognition in musicians: Implications for education. *British Journal of Music Education, 18*, 27–39.

Harvey, N., Garwood, J., & Palencia, M. (1987). Vocal matching of pitch intervals: Learning and transfer effects. *Psychology of Music, 15*, 90–106.

Jones, A. R. (1990). *The Role of Analytical Prestudy in the Memorization and Retention of Piano Music with Subjects of Varied Aural/Kinesthetic Ability*. Unpublished doctoral dissertation, University of Illinois, Urbana-Champaign, IL.

Jørgensen, H. (1997a). Time for practising? Higher level music students' use of time for instrumental practising. In H. Jørgensen & A. C. Lehmann (Eds.), *Does Practice Make Perfect? Current Theory and Research on Instrumental Music Practice* (pp. 123–139). Oslo: Norwegian Academy of Music.

Jørgensen, H. (1997b). Higher instrumental students' planning of practice. In A. Gabrielsson (Ed.), *Proceedings of the Third Triennial ESCOM Conference* (pp. 171–176). Uppsala, Sweden: University of Uppsala.

Jørgensen, H. (1998). *Planlegges øving? [Is Practice Planned?]*. Oslo: Norwegian Academy of Music.

Jørgensen, H. (2000). Student learning in higher instrumental education: Who is responsible? *British Journal of Music Education, 17*, 67–77.

Jørgensen, H. (2002). Instrumental performance expertise and amount of practice among instrumental students in a conservatoire. *Music Education Research, 4,* 105–119.

Kenny, W. E. (1992). *The Effect of Metacognitive Strategy Instruction on the Performance Proficiency and Attitude Toward Practice of Beginning Band Students.* Unpublished doctoral dissertation, University of Illinois, Urbana-Champaign, IL.

Kluwe, R. H. (1987). Executive decisions and regulation of problem solving behavior. In F. E. Weinert & R. H. Kluwe (Eds.), *Metacognition, Motivation, and Understanding* (pp. 31–64). Mahwah, NJ: Erlbaum.

Kopiez, R. (1990). *Der Einfluss kognitiver Strukturen auf das Erlernen eines Musikstücks am Instrument.* Frankfurt am Main, Germany: Peter Lang.

Kovacs, S. (1916). Untersuchungen über das musikalische Gedächtnis. *Zeitschrift für angewandte Psychologie, 11,* 113–135.

Lehmann, A. C., & Ericsson, K. A. (1998). Preparation of a public piano performance: The relation between practice and performance. *Musicæ Scientiæ, 2,* 67–94.

Lehmann, A. C. (2002). Effort and enjoyment in deliberate practice: A research note. In I. M. Hanken, S. G. Nielsen, & M. Nerland (Eds.), *Research in and for Higher Music Education: Festschrift for Harald Jørgensen* (pp. 55–67). Oslo: Norwegian Academy of Music.

Lisboa, T., Williamon, A., Zicari, M., & Eiholzer, H. (in press). Mastery through imitation. *Musicæ Scientiæ.*

Mantel, G. (1984). Üben schwerer Stellen nach dem Prinzip der rotierenden Aufmerksamkeit. *Üben und Musizieren, 3,* 147–150.

McPherson, G. E., & Renwick, J. M. (2001). A longitudinal study of self-regulation in children's musical practice. *Music Education Research, 3,* 169–186.

McPherson, G. E., & Zimmerman, B. J. (2002). Self-regulation of musical learning: A social cognitive perspective. In R. Colwell & C. Richardson (Eds.), *The New Handbook of Research on Music Teaching and Learning* (pp. 327–347). Oxford, UK: Oxford University Press.

Miklaszewski, K. (1989). A case study of a pianist preparing a musical performance. *Psychology of Music, 17,* 95–109.

Miklaszewski, K., & Sawicki, L. (1992). Segmentation of music introduced by practicing pianists preparing compositions for public performance. In R. Dalmonte & M. Baroni (Eds.), *Secundo Convegno Europeo di Analisi Musicale* [Proceedings of the Second European Conference on Musical Analysis] (pp. 113–121). Trento, Italy: University of Trento Press.

Nielsen, S. G. (1997). Self-regulation of learning strategies during practice: A case study of a church organ student preparing a musical work for performance. In H. Jørgensen & A. C. Lehmann (Eds.), *Does Practice Make Perfect? Current Theory and Research on Instrumental Music Practice* (pp. 109–122). Oslo: Norwegian Academy of Music.

Nielsen, S. G. (1999a). Learning strategies in instrumental music practice. *British Journal of Music Education, 16,* 275–291.

Nielsen, S. G. (1999b). Regulation of learning strategies during practice: A case study of a single church organ student preparing a particular work for a concert performance. *Psychology of Music, 27,* 218–229.

Nielsen, S. G. (2001). Self-regulating learning strategies in instrumental music practice. *Music Education Research, 3,* 155–167.

Oura, Y., & Hatano, G. (2001). The constitution of general and specific mental models of other people. *Human Development, 44,* 144–159.

Pacey, F. (1993). Schema theory and the effect of variable practice in string teaching. *British Journal of Music Education, 10*, 91–102.

Palmer, C., & van de Sande, C. (1995). Range of planning in music performance. *Journal of Experimental Psychology: Human Perception and Performance, 21*, 947–962.

Pierce, M. A. (1992). The effects of learning procedure, tempo, and performance condition on transfer of rhythm skills in instrumental music. *Journal of Research in Music Education, 40*, 295–315.

Pitts, S. E., Davidson, J. W., & McPherson, G. E. (2000a). Developing effective practice strategies: Case studies of three young instrumentalists. *Music Education Research, 2*, 45–56.

Pitts, S. E., Davidson, J. W., & McPherson, G. E. (2000b). Models of success and failure in instrumental learning: Case studies of young players in the first 20 months of learning. *Bulletin of the Council for Research in Music Education, 146*, 51–69.

Quantz, J. J. (1752/1985). *On Playing the Flute* (E. R. Reilly, Trans. 2nd ed.). London: Faber and Faber. (Original work published in 1752).

Renwick, J. M., & McPherson, G. E. (2002). Interest and choice: Student-selected repertoire and its effect on practising behaviour. *British Journal of Music Education, 19*, 173–188.

Ross, S. L. (1985). The effectiveness of mental practice in improving the performance of college trombonists. *Journal of Research in Music Education, 33*, 221–230.

Rubin-Rabson, G. (1937). *The Influence of Analytical Pre-Study in Memorizing Piano Music.* New York: Archives of Psychology.

Rubin-Rabson, G. (1947). Studies in the psychology of memorizing music. VIII: The inhibitory influence of the same and of different degrees of learning. *Journal of Musicology, 5*, 13–28.

Sloboda, J. A., Davidson, J. W., Howe, M. J. A., & Moore, D. G. (1996). The role of practice in the development of performing musicians. *British Journal of Psychology, 87*, 287–309.

Tosi, P. F. (1723/1987). *Observations on the Florid Song* (J. Galliard, Trans.). London: Stainer and Bell. (Original work published in 1723).

Türk, D. G. (1789/1982). *School of Clavier Playing* (R. H. Haggh, Trans.). Lincoln, NE: University of Nebraska Press. (Original work published in 1789).

Weinstein, C. E., & Mayer, R. E. (1986). The teaching of learning strategies. In M. C. Wittrock (Ed.), *Handbook of Research on Teaching* (3rd ed., pp. 315–327). New York: Macmillan.

Williamon, A., & Valentine, E. (2000). Quantity and quality of musical practice as predictors of performance quality. *British Journal of Psychology, 91*, 353–376.

Williamon, A., & Valentine, E. (2002). The role of retrieval structures in memorizing music. *Cognitive Psychology, 44*, 1–32.

Williamon, A., Valentine, E., & Valentine, J. (2002). Shifting the focus of attention between levels of musical structure. *European Journal of Cognitive Psychology, 14*, 493–520.

Williamon, A., Lehmann, A. C., & McClure, K. (2003). Studying practice quantitatively. In R. Kopiez, A. C. Lehmann, I. Wolther, & C. Wolf (Eds.), *Proceedings of the Fifth Triennial ESCOM Conference* (pp. 182–185). Hanover, Germany: Hanover University of Music and Drama.

Winold, H., Thelen, E., & Ulrich, B. D. (1994). Coordination and control in the bow arm movement of highly skilled cellists. *Ecological Psychology, 6*, 1–31.

Zimmerman, B. J. (1998). Developing self-fulfilling cycles of academic regulation: An analysis of exemplary instructional models. In D. H. Schunk & B. J. Zimmerman (Eds.), *Self-Regulated Learning: From Teaching to Self-Reflective Practice.* London: Guilford Press.

CHAPTER 6

STRATEGIES FOR ENSEMBLE PRACTICE

JANE W. DAVIDSON AND ELAINE C. KING

Within the music profession, ensemble rehearsals are commonly geared toward public performance, most typically with the focus of attention being on the achievement of musical fluency and group coordination. Ultimately, this relies on high-quality practice for motor, cognitive, and social skill development, but it is well documented that musical knowledge, even among professionals, varies in degree, with some players being for example "better" at sight-reading or manipulating the expressive features of the music. As a result, the absolute time involved in rehearsing specific pieces can differ enormously. Indeed, there are clearly no prescriptive rules for how much practice is to be done, and in this sense, the advice offered in Chapter 5 (that the person, task, and context must be considered when deciding on appropriate practice strategies) applies equally well to the ensemble situation. Nevertheless, within ensembles, it is vital that each person not only exploit his or her own individual skills, but think beyond them for the sake of the group's musical and interpersonal cohesion—at the very least, to an extent that will convince audiences. What is certain is that, for the music to be negotiated between the players and then communicated effectively to the audience, two levels of knowledge must be integrated and articulated.

The first is a general musical and social knowledge that provides performance rules and regulations based on historical, social, and cultural factors (e.g. scale systems, harmonic and melodic expressive rules, and sociocultural interaction and performance practices). Whilst this knowledge is fairly genre specific (with art music, jazz, pop, folk, etc. all emerging out of different musicohistorical traditions, and so, different knowledge bases), it has a sense of being *permanent knowledge* for both the producer and perceiver of the music. It forms, therefore, a stable base on which a musical performance is built and received. Although such knowledge is a requisite for all types of performance, be it alone or in a group, the social psychological aspects of it are of paramount importance to ensemble practice and performance.

The second is the specific moment-by-moment information that must be processed and responded to in an ongoing manner—for instance, accommodating a coperformer's sudden change of tempo or coping with a memory slip. Of course, the ability to deal with moment-by-moment novelty depends on familiarity with other similar situations and, hence, relies on knowledge of a permanent sort. Thus, although each performance is a unique confluence of new interactive elements in the moment-by-moment process, familiarity with such experiences can help prepare for likely scenarios and outcomes. Consider, for instance, any musical tradition in which improvisation takes place (e.g. jazz or Indian classical music), where the musicians learn a repertory of musical materials and stock-cultural practices about the length and style of improvised solos. When the music is being created afresh, it emerges from a context and depends on shared knowledge, so that coperformers and audience alike can experience the unfurling of musical ideas (this is akin to the long-term working memory theory of Ericsson & Kintsch, 1995; see also Chapter 7).

Working on the basis that musicians and audiences use and constantly develop the two forms of knowledge described above, the current chapter explores ways in which ensemble rehearsals operate, and how they may be facilitated for public performance. Largely because of existing research, the central focus is on classical music ensembles, ranging from piano duos through to the orchestra. Of course, all ensembles depend on the successful interaction of individual members; therefore, the chapter begins with a discussion of the dynamics of group membership. This is followed by an analysis of the rehearsal situation itself (both the general structure of rehearsals and approaches to individual pieces), as well as the functions of verbal and nonverbal communication. To close, two case studies of ensemble practice, with two very different types of group membership, are presented so as to elucidate the specific practical recommendations arising throughout the chapter.

6.1   Group dynamics

It is obvious that in ensembles the players must have a common connection to the *music*, and research suggests that this is the primary source of cohesion for the group (Davidson & Good, 2002). In small ensembles, cohesiveness can be supplemented by factors such as the potential for equal musical input and the fact that all players use essentially comparable instrumental techniques (e.g. in string quartets or flute choirs; Davidson, 1997). Even when the ensembles are comprised of quite different instruments, as in the case of a wind quintet where the French horn is juxtaposed alongside a flute, the complementarity of the instrumental timbres is often regarded by the group members as a cohesive element too (Ford & Davidson, 2003). Thus, similarity and complementarity can contribute to ensemble cohesion from a compositional/ instrumental point of view. However, is the same true in terms of the social, interpersonal relationships?

Social psychological research suggests that, in order for any group to function, the members need to have a personal sense of "affiliation" (Douglas, 1993). That is, there needs to be a connection or association between individuals and to the group as a whole. The existing music research literature suggests that this affiliation is highly dependent on an individual's sense of self within the ensemble. Young and Colman (1979), who investigated string quartets, point out that group closeness achieved through trust and respect of each individual's boundaries is absolutely vital in order for quartets to continue functioning, with leaders and followers conforming to their interactive roles, which are mirrored in their musical roles.

Previous research, however, indicates that different types of ensembles function in unique ways. Work on piano duos shows that personal friendships seem critical to the functioning of the rehearsal and performance situation (Blank & Davidson, 2003), with male–female or female–female dyads working far more successfully than male–male partnerships. They argue that this is because men in Western culture in general are not encouraged to be in working relationships with close friends, and so find the intimacy of the physical proximity of the piano duo difficult.

At the other extreme, Atik (1994) has shown that the orchestra, which itself is comprised of smaller sections, elicits very different group interactions. Atik discovered that, in this context, the players' sense of self has to be sublimated to a certain extent in order to facilitate the sense of group affiliation. Since between 50 and 100 people make up an orchestra, with section leaders and a conductor, it is evident that complex and subtle interactions are required in order for the ensemble to function successfully. An individual occupying a relatively low rank within the hierarchical structure may be asserting an inappropriately prominent voice to make his or her personal views common knowledge within the context of a whole orchestra rehearsal; here, the role of section leader—as a filter to the conductor—is the mechanism through which the player can express views.

◆ The prerequisite for effective ensemble rehearsal is that the operational principles of the ensemble are established, understood, and complied with. This depends, of course, on the nature of the ensemble itself, as well as the task.

In small ensembles, both conflict and compromise have been commonly found (see Young & Colman, 1979; Murninghan & Conlon, 1991). That is, when one person disagrees, the best solutions have been shown to come about through compromise, rather than one individual taking a dictatorial approach. Generally, in groups of four individuals, there is the potential for a three-to-one conflict, where one player can literally be overruled by the others; worse still, a two-to-two deadlock can occur. So, ironically, despite their prevalence as music groups, quartets can be problematic ensembles in terms of social dynamics and functioning. Intriguingly, although a democratic approach is generally favored, it has been found that the second violinist—above all other players—is the one who needs to feel respected and encouraged; if he or she is overwhelmed by the opinions of the others, especially that of the first violinist, the group has been shown simply to break down. It has been argued that this is because the two violinists need similar skill levels and play the same instrument, but owing to the nature of the part-writing, the first violinist is often perceived by others to be the superior player (Davidson & Good, 2002).

◆ In rehearsals, it is important that every voice is heard, or at least for every individual participant to feel that he or she can contribute as desired.

In a slightly larger ensemble—the wind quintet, for instance—members appear to be more relaxed about their roles. Perhaps this is because the ratio of disagreement is rarely four-to-one; any disagreement is more likely to feel like a group split, rather than one against the group. However, as mentioned earlier, the complementarity of the timbres and techniques of the instruments within a wind ensemble may well ensure that each person feels his or her own sense of belonging to the group.

6.2   The rehearsal situation

6.2.1   General structure of rehearsals

The existing research literature on the structure of a rehearsal has shown that approaches are widely varied (see Davidson, 1997). However, those of a professional standard share several overriding traits (see Goodman, 2000). Firstly, there is a rough plan of the material to be covered across the span of rehearsals in preparation for performance. Secondly, there is always room in the schedule for extra practice, accounting for unexpected circumstances, such as a player being unable to attend a rehearsal. Of course, very often when people come together, they are surprised that some pieces take longer to rehearse than others. Blank and Davidson (2003) discussed with a top piano duo the unexpected difficulties they faced when preparing Bartók's Sonata for Two Pianos and Percussion. One player intriguingly commented:

We could not believe how difficult it was not only to play the notes, but to coordinate that second bar of the opening movement. We spent most of our rehearsal time on that . . . but having said that, the act of concentrating on that singular difficulty seemed to facilitate the preparation of the rest of the piece. We, if you like, faced the most difficult challenge, and that put everything else into context (personal communication; taken from the interview transcript but not quoted by Blank & Davidson, 2003).

This comment is revealing, for it shows that it is often the need to find an appropriate manner for approaching the rehearsal process that takes time. The singular difficulty of the Bartók focused everyone's attention, and thus they had all developed a similar level of concentration and awareness of the difficulties involved in the piece. The comment has a flip side, which is that often ensembles do not achieve such a coordinated manner of working, with the consequence that rehearsal time may end up unfocused and unproductive. In Davidson and Good's (2002) string quartet research, there was a difficult social dynamic in the rehearsals in which one member had an obsession with tuning, while the others were more interested in working on entrances and exits of the individual lines of the pieces being rehearsed. Although the group adjusted to this individual particularity, the researchers observing the rehearsals sensed that the player who continually tuned during discussions created a distraction to the main musical activity.

♦ A key rehearsal aim is for you to establish shared musical goals within the ensemble as soon as possible (be they of a technical or expressive nature). In relation to the literature on group dynamics, it is also necessary for you to find a means of coordination that leaves room for individual needs and styles.

♦ Leave space in your practicing schedule for unexpected difficulties, such as a piece being more challenging than expected or unanticipated absences of ensemble members.

In addition to the overall context of a series of rehearsals, the content of single rehearsals is critically important. Specific strategies for effective single rehearsals have been suggested. Goodman (2000) found that a warm-up routine can provide a helpful focus for groups. Vikram Seth's (1999) novel *An Equal Music*, in which the members of a professional string quartet are described warming up, seems to capture much of the sentiment found in Goodman's data:

Every rehearsal of the Maggiore Quartet begins with a very plain, very slow three-octave scale on all four instruments in unison: sometimes major, as in our name, sometimes minor, depending on the key of the first piece we are to play. No matter how fraught our lives have been over the last couple of days, no matter how abrasive our disputes about people or politics, or how visceral our differences about what we are to play and how we are to play it, it reminds us that we are, when it comes to it, one... No one appears to lead. Even the first upbeat is merely breathed by [the first violinist], not indicated by any movement... When I play this I release myself into the spirit of the quartet. I become the music of the scale. I mute my will, I free my self (p. 12).

In addition to warming up together, Cox (1989) has stressed the role of the pace of rehearsals. In particular, there needs to be periods where players are required to concentrate intensely, such as in a very fast passage, which is then set against less intense work, such as running through for an overview of a section or the entire piece. This is what Blum (1986) considers to be the "balance" of key components of the rehearsal (e.g. sight-reading versus working on familiar pieces or parts therein). Allied to this is the fact that, according to most of the existing studies, all players need to be equally involved in the rehearsal. Durrant (1994), for instance, found that in conducting situations, the conductor could easily lose control if players and/or singers showed signs of boredom after having been neglected. Thus, sustaining the interest of all participants seems to be critically important. In summary:

◆ For the small ensemble, warming up together can bring focus and unity to the rehearsal.

◆ Balance the key components of practice, in order to achieve both technical progress and musical fluency.

◆ Make sure that each member of the ensemble is, in some way, engaged in the rehearsal musically and mentally, so as to prevent boredom or a sense of exclusion.

For the professional and advanced student, a concert appears to be an obvious key focal point for rehearsals. Indeed, Blank and Davidson (2003), Goodman (2000), and Murninghan and Conlon (1991) all found that the concrete goal of a performance on a specific date aided focus and effectiveness. However, this is where professional and amateur players differ. Blank and Davidson (2003) found that for the amateur player, it was the rehearsal itself that was the pleasurable activity and not the planning for a specific goal. Within the rehearsal time, there was an emphasis on "fun" and "chat," with the session often lasting several hours and being broken by coffee breaks. The selection of repertory covered was also less goal-oriented and included familiar pieces being played through to give a sense of "reward," alongside some time spent tackling new and difficult pieces for a smaller proportion of time. This amateur approach has been well-reported by Booth (1999) in a personal account of the joys of music-making for fun. For him, the social aspect is clearly as important as the musical. The question that each practitioner should ask when thinking about a rehearsal approach is:

◆ Are your rehearsals strictly for the pleasure of participation and for entertainment, or are they in preparation for professional-level performance? Depending on the answer to this question, the focus and structure of rehearsal may be very different; however, achieving a balance between pleasure and work is important for all ensembles, and healthy music making generally.

6.2.2   Approaches to individual pieces

The particular demands of individual pieces often mean that effective practice strategies can be as many and varied as performers themselves. Goodman (2000, 2002), Gruson (1988), Miklaszewski (1989), and Williamon *et al.* (2002) all discovered that there can be many differences in approach to a piece. Some groups only play through from beginning to end, whilst others tend to stop and start to focus on "tricky" passages. Hallam (1995, 1997) has examined these differences in strategy in detail and, although she does not favor one type of strategy above another, she comments that they are indicative of individual differences in cognitive style: either a "holist" or "serialist," respectively. Still, looking at the different approaches found to exist, ensembles can work in the following manner to achieve thorough and accurate learning:

◆ Identify and work within and up to structural boundaries in the music. This immediately highlights the form of the piece, and so can strengthen your ensemble's shared understanding of it (Chaffin *et al.*, 2002; Miklaszewski, 1989; Williamon & Valentine, 2002).

◆ Balance the focus in rehearsal between long and short segments of the piece. Doing this within a piece can help sustain concentration and involvement in the rehearsal (Goodman, 2000) and has been shown to be a salient characteristic of effective learning (Williamon *et al.*, 2002).

◆ Integrate "run-throughs" during the rehearsal process, for it is important to put expressive ideas and/or technical problems into the context of the whole. This can be important for reinforcing memory and consolidating common tempi, dynamics, and other expressive elements (see Chaffin and Imreh, 1997; Chaffin *et al.*, 2002).

◆ Consider working both sequentially and nonsequentially through an individual movement or composition. These strategies can help you place portions of the music in their chronological context and also allow common material, or sections of similar levels of difficulty, to be explored. Goodman (2000) found that different ensembles tended to use one or both of these strategies, but the former was particularly used to generate new thoughts about sub-sections of a work.

Other strategies that could be explored include:

◆ When time is short, have an "economical rehearsal approach"—that is, only work on passages that need attention, so as not to waste time going over parts that are sufficiently grasped.

- For chamber groups: you can save much time and effort if all players have access to a copy of the full score and even take time to go through the score together. Typically in chamber music, individual parts are handed out, so unless each person in the ensemble can be acquainted with the others' parts through repeated playing, it is often difficult for one instrument to know what is going on around them. This strategy has been found to be useful and a good shortcut to lengthy rehearsal processes (Goodman, 2000).

- For conductors: you need to think about potential areas of difficulty in the piece to ensure technical security and to confirm that your interpretation is robust (to know what you want from the players in each passage and for the player to understand what is required; Durrant, 1994).

From the existing literature, it is evident that despite individual differences, a clear rehearsal method can be prescribed to ensure positive outcomes. Nonetheless, these strategies are offered with some caution, since all players have to display similar levels of commitment to the rehearsal and have the same goals—whether it be for social amateur entertainment or for professional engagement.

6.3   Verbal and nonverbal communication

6.3.1   Between a conductor and ensemble

There can be various types of "talk" used in rehearsals. Directions such as "find letter 'A' in your score" or "let's try that again but at a slower tempo" are the most common types of exchanges. Typically, when there is a conductor, he or she leads the speech. Time and again, however, ensemble research indicates that too much talking, either from the conductor or in the form of questions from an individual player, disrupts the flow of the music in rehearsals (see Yarbrough, 1975; Durrant, 1994; Weeks, 1996; Price & Byo, 2002). That is, if too much questioning is permitted from one individual, it is likely to lead to interference as others may become irritated or distracted.

Obviously, talk cannot be avoided. Instructional talk, however, seems acceptable, whereas discussion is often less welcomed (although there needs to be space for this). In the larger ensemble context, discussion should be carefully managed, for it is easy for the talking to turn into confrontation. Davidson (1997) gives an example of this through an incident with Leonard Bernstein and José Carreras when making a television documentary on the CD recording of Bernstein's *West Side Story*. Carreras was singing the role of Toni and had mislearned or could not sing accurately a part of one of his songs. Beginning relatively patiently, Bernstein, who was conducting, pointed out the tenor's error. Bernstein stopped when the tenor repeatedly made the same mistake, but after several corrections in front of the whole orchestra, Bernstein became extremely vexed and asked the tenor why he could not do this simple thing. The tenor, furious and shamed by the situation, swore profusely and stormed out of the rehearsal.

- It is evident that it is best for the conductor not to allow a situation to escalate into confrontation, otherwise there can be dire consequences. By contrast, of course, the odd word of praise, especially to an individual within an entire group setting, has been found to be extremely beneficial. However, even an individual comment needs to be moderated, otherwise other group members could feel undervalued.

Verbal instructions can be necessary, but are best minimized. Talk with any sort of social dynamic context needs to be carefully monitored, as the stakes for all parties can be high (see Davidson, 1997, for a further exploration of this issue). In the light of the comments above, it is not surprising to learn that, although both verbal and nonverbal indicators to others can be employed in rehearsals, conductors are at their most efficient when using nonverbal cues (Durrant, 1994). The conductor, of course, typically controls the ensemble through the use of gestures, and the rehearsal period is the time for the players to learn the meaning behind those gestures.

The extensive literature on general nonverbal communication has demonstrated that we typically use four main categories of gesture in our interactions:

- *adaptors*: movements of self-stimulation (e.g. head-scratching and touching the finger to the bridge of the nose)
- *regulators*: movements that allow for entrances and exits to speech or movement (e.g. using a hand movement to encourage someone to make a point during a discussion, or using an open arm gesture to indicate to someone to walk ahead and pass through the door first)
- *illustrators*: self-explanatory gestures of emphasis with direct musical or speech translations (e.g. making a cradling arm movement when talking about a baby)
- *emblems*: culturally defined gestures (e.g. the "V for Victory" sign used by Churchill to the British troops during the Second World War; see Ekman & Freisen, 1969, for further discussion).

In performance where a conductor is involved, regulatory gestures and illustrators are obviously required in order to indicate when and how something should happen. Durrant (1994) has found that some conductors use emblems extensively. These, however, are often very elaborate codes, and part of the rehearsal period must then be concerned with performers learning and quickly decoding what these emblems signify. The emblems are usually complex signs intended to substitute for spoken technical and expressive instruction (e.g. using the hand at the side of the head in a rotational gesture to indicate the notion of creating "space" for the singing voice to sound, and accompanying this with a sharp downward pointed gesture to indicate the vocal attack on the sound). Although there is no formal research to date, Davidson (1997) has hypothesized that the most successful conductors on the international professional circuit are those who not only keep to nonverbal interaction, but who are also efficient in their use of illustrators and regulators and keep emblems to a minimum, given the time involved in learning their meanings. In choral music, it is more usual for a conductor to work with the same ensemble for long periods, so a common understanding of emblems can be built up over time.

◆ An overly zealous, gesticulating conductor can become a distraction (Davidson, 1997). Scrutinize your movements and consider whether these can be easily and quickly deciphered by others.

◆ Besides being able to give instructions using gestures, you need to read cues from the ensemble. Be aware of possible signals (in practice and performance) that are used by musicians in your ensemble, and determine which are consistent across the entire group and which are individual-specific. In doing so, you will be able to work toward establishing an effecting three-way communication between yourself, the ensemble, and the audience.

6.3.2   Between coperformers

Coperformers need to be able to decipher what is going on both within and between musical parts in order to achieve a fluent performance. Davidson and Good (2002) discovered that there are two major categories of interaction between string quartet members: (1) those of musical content and its coordination (e.g. achieving entrances and exits) and (2) those of a more personal nature (e.g. the first violinist making a head-nodding gesture of approval to the second violinist after a particularly well-played passage). Davidson and Good reported a power struggle going on in a rehearsal based principally on sexual politics (one flirtatious male among three compliant, admiring females), and it was noted that the flirtation worked around the use of nonverbal gestures. The male teased the first violinist about her lack of clarity, or even the sudden jerkiness of her regulatory gesture to say "start the upbeat, now." Ironically, the two researchers did not find her cue remotely ambiguous, but the example demonstrates how multifunctional the role of nonverbal communication can be on both a musical and social level in the rehearsal.

Williamon and Davidson (2002) found that in the practice of two professional pianists forming a duo, the quantity of nonverbal interaction increased significantly from first meeting through to a performance. Here, the most used movement was a slight head-and-eye indication for regulation. Also and somewhat intriguingly, through the course of the rehearsals, the movement styles of the two individuals coalesced. The player who moved the most moderated and reduced the quality of his movements somewhat, while the more conservative player produced more movement. It was as if they began to move as one, rather than two individuals. According to interviews with the pianists, this was for the sake of musical coherence. In fact, these physical expressions provided a means of understanding and sharing musical intentions, as they were most coordinated at key points in the music's structure (as identified by the pianists); for an audience, this level of coordination can give an additional access point to the music's meaning (Davidson, 1993). The musicians' movements also seemed to have a social dimension as well. Evidently, they sensed that they were performing the pieces "together," as one "unit." Davidson and Good (2002) also observed this with a string quartet playing Britten's *Rhapsody*. They found it much easier to achieve the canonical musical entries if they were all ebbing and flowing in exactly the same manner.

◆ Movement can help to bring about musical coherence and social unity. Consider the movements made within your ensemble. Are these readily recognized and shared among the group? Are they timed to correspond with certain points in the music? Will audiences consciously notice and be able to interpret them, or are the movements purposefully too subtle for this?

Goodman (2002) and Murninghan and Conlon (1991) found that nonverbal communication during playing often solved problems where talk had failed. By simply playing and sorting out coordination "on the hoof," there was often no need to discuss a particular point at all. Alternatively, when a verbal disagreement about musical interpretation emerged, playing the piece through in several different ways would often lead to a decision without verbal discussion (or at least nothing more than exchanging a few syllables).

Finally, it is important to note that nonverbal cues can be discussed in rehearsal too. Blank and Davidson (2003) interviewed one duo partnership who said that, early on in their career together, they would discuss where they were going to give such cues. As time went by and familiarity with their musical repertory grew, the cues often did not occur as they had done originally, and new ones emerged.

◆ It is important for you to think about how your ensemble is to use talk and nonverbal gestures in rehearsal. Strategies based on the regulator and illustrator can help with musical coordination, but eye contact and smiles (found in the rehearsals recorded by Goodman, 2000, and Williamon & Davidson, 2002) can be extremely important in helping you provide clarity in a message and express the degree of satisfaction between ensemble members.

6.4   Case studies

The case studies presented here are on two cello–piano duos. Both duos were asked to rehearse and perform (at the end of their rehearsal) the second movement (Minuet and Trio) of Brahms's Sonata for Piano and Cello, Op. 38. The players in both ensembles were unfamiliar with one another before the investigation and were matched together according to age, playing standard, and experience. None of the musicians had played this particular movement for at least 5 years. Neil (cello) and Matthew (piano) were grouped together as professionals, and Mary (cello) and Mikako (piano) were grouped as advanced students (i.e. they had each recently completed undergraduate studies at a conservatory). One month before the rehearsal, they were sent copies of the movement and were asked to learn the relevant part in preparation for the rehearsal. For the purposes of analysis, the rehearsals were videotaped and transcribed by documenting all verbal and pertinent nonverbal communication. Three aspects of the duo rehearsals are addressed below: rehearsal method, communication, and social interaction (the complete method and set of analyses are reported in Goodman, 2000).

6.4.1   Rehearsal method

In the first instance, the duos began the rehearsal by playing through the movement in its entirety without stopping. Thereafter, their practice proceeded in quite different ways, although in both cases this involved breaking down the music into long and short segments in order to address specific issues. Interestingly, the performers did not discuss *how* they would tackle the piece, or propose a specific agenda for the rehearsal, but simply got on with the task of playing the movement. On the one hand, Mary and Mikako rehearsed the piece in a sequential fashion by working progressively from beginning to end. On the other, Neil and Matthew maintained a nonsequential agenda, in so far as they isolated certain parts of the score throughout the rehearsal with no particular concern for the movement's chronological progression. They used their initial run-through of the movement as a benchmark or baseline for discussion, and they modified, clarified, and reshaped aspects of their playing accordingly. These different styles of rehearsing the music are illustrated in Figure 6.1.

In view of the contrasting styles of approach undertaken by the two ensembles, it is useful to speculate which of the two is the most effective. First, it is possible to suggest that a nonsequential method of practice is more economical in terms of time than a sequential approach, for Neil and Matthew's rehearsal lasted 30 minutes while Mary and Mikako's rehearsal was strikingly longer at 80 minutes. Arguably, however, the total duration of the rehearsal is not an indication of its quality, but rather a reflection on how the performers have been trained to practice and how they decided to apply their training in the context of the new partnership established in this study (cf. Krampe & Ericsson, 1995). It is plausible to suggest, however, that the professional musicians, Neil and Matthew, were used to working under time constraints and, therefore, adopted a "quick-fit solution" approach to the rehearsal, while Mary and Mikako wanted to take the time to ensure that all corners of the music were worked out in rehearsal.

Second, the sequential agenda could be regarded as more demanding or thorough because it allowed for a step-by-step approach to the movement. Mary and Mikako seemed to explore details of the piece and inspire each other to consider ideas about the piece *en route*. In effect, the sequential method allowed for the generation and confirmation of ideas in the rehearsal. By contrast, in studying select areas of the movement in relation to their initial run-through, Neil and Matthew adopted a more retrospective or reflective style. To this end, the nonsequential agenda could be regarded as more "risky," in the sense that the performers did not address every part of the movement in rehearsal and, hence, left a certain amount of passagework to the whim of the performance. As professional musicians, however, Neil and Matthew obviously felt comfortable with their preparation, and they had the confidence in one another to be able to perform the movement at the end of the rehearsal.

There is inevitably a degree of overlap between these two rehearsal methods, and it is possible that they could be combined quite successfully. Indeed, other data from Goodman's (2000) research showed that one of the duos rehearsing the Prologue from Debussy's Cello Sonata adopted a nonsequential agenda and then switched to a sequential approach midway through the rehearsal. Nevertheless, in the cases discussed here, the ensembles achieved the goal of performing the movement but adopted alternative methods of preparation, both of which can be regarded as appropriate in their own right.

6.4.2   Rehearsal communication

The performers communicated using verbal and nonverbal discourse, the latter including singing, humming, counting aloud, gesturing, and clicking the pulse. There was a relatively high amount of talking, as the musicians made many of their ideas explicit through verbal discourse either before or after playing segments of the

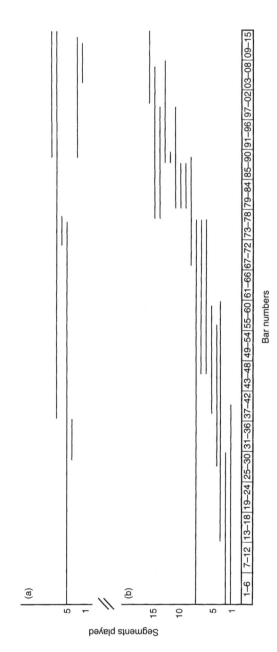

Figure 6.1 Sample transcriptions of (a) the non-sequential practice of Neil and Matthew and (b) the sequential practice of Mary and Mikako in their respective rehearsals of the second movement of Brahms's Sonata for Piano and Cello, Op. 38. Horizontal lines (read from bottom to top) represent segments of the music played, which correspond to the bar numbers listed along the x-axis (graphical method adapted from Chaffin & Imreh, 1997).

music (above all, the relatively high degree of talking seems to reflect the musicians' unfamiliarity with one another). Nonetheless, some issues were resolved "tacitly" while playing. For example, Neil and Matthew realized that they were "not together" at the end of the Trio, but the problem of coordination ironed itself out in a subsequent run-through of the section, so there was no further discussion about the point.

Of particular interest, however, are the issues that the performers addressed verbally, and the manner in which they negotiated their ideas. The musicians in both ensembles divided their rehearsal time relatively equally between the Minuet and the Trio. There were several common issues of consideration: the dynamics in the Minuet (particularly across the climactic build up in bars 50–58), the rubato in the Trio, and the tempo at the end of the Minuet. The performers discussed these issues in different ways, thus highlighting the potential variety and complexity of musical interaction manifest in chamber rehearsal. For example, the realization of the *crescendo poco a poco* in bar 50 of the Minuet caused varying problems for them (see Figure 6.2). Matthew suggested that the music should be played more softly at bar 50 in order to enhance the subsequent build-up: "start that bit quietly, then we can make more of the crescendo." Indeed, Neil confessed that he found the cello part difficult to interpret at that point ("I've got a complex about that bit") and admitted that he originally conceived the start of the crescendo a few bars earlier (i.e. bar 48). Neil readily conformed to Matthew's sugges-tion to "play quieter" at bar 50. In this case, negotiation was achieved easily on the basis of adherence to the dynamic indication in the score, and Matthew's practical direction.

Mikako made a similar request to Mary in their rehearsal of the same passage: "I know you have a crescendo, but can you do it . . . in a softer way?" In contrast to Neil and Matthew's relatively quick resolution of the point, Mary and Mikako discussed the

Figure 6.2 Bars 50–59 of the Minuet from the second movement of Brahms's Sonata for Piano and Cello, Op. 38.

issue at length. Mikako mentioned the difficulty of exposing the melody in her right hand because of its high register. For this reason, she suggested that the cellist should delay the crescendo until bar 54 and exemplified her point by talking and playing through the passage. Essentially, she wished to use dynamic contrast to highlight the melodic repetition in the piano part: bars 50–51 are echoed by bars 52–53, which are quieter, and from bar 54, the crescendo begins with the cello. By contrast, Mary conceived a "broad flow forwards. . . not crescendoing too early, and doing it really with a very fine gradient." To this end, she claimed that Mikako's dynamic fluctuations contradicted the marking in the score, "which is. . . just to crescendo really gradually". In order to negotiate their conflicting points of view, Mary and Mikako played the passage in several different ways, hence using trial-and-error. In addition, they gave further attention to performance indications in the score, discussed the music's process (i.e. the concept of build-up across the passage), and reconsidered the nature of the melodic line in the piano part. There was a certain degree of compromise by both performers in order to reach a workable solution: Mikako conformed to Mary's notion of a broad build-up, while Mary agreed to play quietly at the beginning of bar 57 to exaggerate the hairpin dynamic marking in her part. Similarly, Mikako accepted Mary's conception of the arrival point at bar 58 as "louder than *forte*," and they both agreed that the dynamic level at bar 50 should be reduced.

The above example reflects the potential scope of communication between performers about a single issue, and the fact that there are alternative ways in which musical negotiation can arise. In this case, the two ensembles used the following strategies to negotiate their ideas:

- awareness of score indications
- personal judgment based on trial-and-error
- analytical reasoning
- consideration of the music's form as process.

Other types of negotiation are reported by Goodman (2000) in the duo rehearsals, including practical reasoning and reconciliation of emotional insights. In both ensembles, the most effective strategy for resolving the issue of dynamics in the Minuet was to follow the indications in the score. Still, the other strategies usefully supported the discussion of this issue (particularly for Mary and Mikako), which suggests that a wide range of strategies should be explored to reach a workable solution when members of an ensemble are in disagreement.

6.4.3 Social interaction

From an analysis of the performers' discourses, it is evident that the majority of social interaction in both ensembles was task-related, notably through "giving opinions" about the music. This can be regarded as quite characteristic of small-group behavior in general (see Bales, 1950, 1999). At the same time, a high level of agreement existed in the rehearsals, although phatic acknowledgements mainly consisted of "yeah." In fact, the amount of agreement expressed in the performers' discourses was tremendous (as compared with that witnessed in other, nonmusical small group scenarios; see Bales, 1999), which indicates that the performers gave mainly positive socioemotional responses. Once again, the musicians' unfamiliarity with one another is a likely explanation for this point, as they possibly felt more inclined to express positive reactions in order to establish a "friendly" group dynamic (undoubtedly, the relationship would develop in time, and it is possible that negative reactions would be expressed more frequently in ensuing rehearsals).

It is apparent that Neil dominated much of the task-related discussion in his rehearsal, for he gave more suggestions, opinions, and orientation than Matthew. Indeed, Neil initiated a majority of the points or areas of discussion (e.g. he mentioned "What I'd like to do first is actually the very end of the Trio"). By contrast, Matthew asked for more orientation, which perhaps reflects his desire, as an accompanist, to ascertain as much information from the cellist as possible. In general, however, Neil and Matthew generated a very relaxed and positive atmosphere in their rehearsal, not least because there were no signs of negative tension or antagonism; they simply got on with the rehearsal.

The interaction between Mary and Mikako appeared to be equally positive on the surface, although the relationship between them soured as the rehearsal progressed. There were several moments of disagreement, which created negative tension. Mikako offered more suggestions, opinions, and orientation in the rehearsal, and Mary produced more utterances of agreement and disagreement. In fact, Mikako appeared to lead the discussion by virtue of the fact that she did most of the talking and contributed fully to the realization of musical ideas. Mary, however, showed signs of discontent with Mikako's persistent verbal explanation of points and her constant desire to stop and start, for Mary clearly preferred to concentrate on letting the music "just play itself." There was a certain amount of conflict here between "musical" personalities (one wanting to analyze the musical detail intently and the other wanting simply to let the music happen), as well as differences in perception of each other's standard. The social dynamic was invariably strained.

Nevertheless, Mary and Mikako continued to offer supportive opinions to one another throughout the rehearsal, even if they were used as a tactic to soften critical suggestions or disagreement. For instance, Mary remarked, "[the dynamic] makes a really nice contrast, but can we try it just once where we follow exactly what it says in the copy . . . ?" and "I know that you're really playing out your tune and I think that's really good, but I think it's a little bit too much . . ." Likewise, Mikako commented, "I thought that was good, but if you could come in less . . ." These utterances reflect the performers' sensitivity toward each other, for they seemed wary of giving comments without offering solidarity first.

The performers in both of these ensembles thus maintained working relationships by sustaining a "friendly," positive group dynamic. This was primarily achieved by ensuring that the discussion was focused on the task at hand and that opinions were offered sensitively. However, the rehearsals were led by different instrumentalists, Neil (cellist) and Mikako (pianist), which indicates that the stereotypical hierarchy between a soloist and an accompanist does not necessarily dictate the social relationship between performers in rehearsal.

6.5   Conclusions

The case studies above demonstrate that there is no single "best" method or strategy for rehearsing a particular piece of music—rather, that individual ensembles will necessarily find their own "best" ways of rehearsing. Here, it has been revealed that two ensembles can effectively rehearse the same piece in contrasting ways in order to achieve the same goal, whilst adopting alternative approaches and using different strategies to negotiate musical ideas. At the same time, the rehearsal must be underpinned by a strong social framework, with musicians working hard to achieve a positive socioemotional ambience through sensitive and friendly behavior.

Undoubtedly, musical interaction in rehearsal is most effective and pleasurable when musicians "click" with one another at both musical and social levels, but when this is not possible, can an ensemble still be successful? Research data reveal that a social framework can be sustained in different ways, yet still enable a group to achieve its goal. In the case studies, one partnership "clicked" quite comfortably, and the musicians simply proceeded with the task at hand. The other duo experienced conflict, resulting in a much more tense rehearsal environment. Nonetheless, both ensembles achieved their goal of successfully performing Brahms's Minuet and Trio.

The crucial advice for performers—be they in small or large ensembles—is to develop a greater awareness of the social psychological principles that govern group interaction and cohesion. At the same time, players should reflect over the effectiveness of their rehearsal methods and ways of communicating. Such knowledge will invariably offer new perspectives in approaching and subsequently optimizing ensemble practice and performance.

Further information and reading

Blum, D. (1986). *The Art of Quartet Playing: The Guarneri String Quartet in Conversation with David Blum*. New York: Cornell University Press.

Cox, J. (1989). Rehearsal organisational structures used by successful high school choral directors. *Journal of Research in Music Education, 37*, 201–218.

Goodman, E. (2002). Ensemble performance. In J. Rink (Ed.), *Musical Performance: A Guide to Understanding* (pp. 153–167). Cambridge: Cambridge University Press.

Murninghan, J. K., & Conlon, D. E. (1991). The dynamics of intense work groups: A study of British string quartets. *Administrative Science Quarterly, 36*, 165–186.

Price, H. E., & Byo, J. L. (2002). Rehearsing and conducting. In R. Parncutt & G. E. McPherson (Eds.), *The Science and Psychology of Music Performance: Creative Strategies for Teaching and Learning* (pp. 335–351). Oxford: Oxford University Press.

Williamon, A., & Davidson, J. W. (2002). Exploring co-performer communication. *Musicæ Scientiæ, 6*, 53–72.

References

Atik, Y. (1994). The conductor and the orchestra: Interactive aspects of the leadership process. *Leadership and Organisation Development Journal, 13*, 22–28.

Bales, R. F. (1950). A set of categories for the analysis of small group interaction. *American Sociological Review, 15*, 257–263.

Bales, R. F. (1999). *Social Interaction Systems: Theory and Measurement.* London: Transaction Publishers.

Blank, M., & Davidson, J. W. (2003) A consideration of the effect of gender on co-performer communication in piano duos. Manuscript submitted for publication.

Blum, D. (1986). *The Art of Quartet Playing: The Guarneri String Quartet in Conversation with David Blum.* New York: Cornell University Press.

Booth, W. (1999). *For the Love of It: Amateuring and Its Rivals.* Chicago: University of Chicago Press.

Chaffin, R., & Imreh, G. (1997). "Pulling teeth and torture": Musical memory and problem solving. *Thinking and Reasoning, 3*, 315–336.

Chaffin, R., Imreh, G., & Crawford, M. (2002). *Practicing Perfection: Memory and Piano Performance.* Mahwah, NJ: Erlbaum.

Cox, J. (1989). Rehearsal organisational structures used by successful high school choral directors. *Journal of Research in Music Education, 37*, 201–218.

Davidson, J. W. (1993). Visual perception of performance manner in the movements of solo musicians. *Psychology of Music, 21*, 103–113.

Davidson, J. W. (1997). The social in musical performance. In D. J. Hargreaves & A. C. North (Eds.), *The Social Psychology of Music* (pp. 209–228). Oxford: Oxford University Press.

Davidson, J. W., & Good, J. M. M. (2002). Social and musical co-ordination between members of a string quartet: An exploratory study. *Psychology of Music, 30*, 186–201.

Douglas, T. (1993). *A Theory of Groupwork Practice.* New York: Macmillan.

Durrant, C. (1994). Towards an effective communication: A case for structured teaching of conducting. *British Journal of Music Education, 11*, 56–76.

Ekman, P., & Friesen, W. V. (1969). The repertoire of non-verbal behaviour: Categories, origins, usage and coding. *Semiotica, 1*, 49–98.

Ericsson, K. A., & Kintsch, W. (1995). Long-term working memory. *Psychological Review, 102*, 211–245.

Ford, L., & Davidson, J. W. (2003). An investigation of members' roles in wind quintets. *Psychology of Music, 31*, 53–74.

Goodman, E. (2000). *Analysing the Ensemble in Music Rehearsal and Performance: The Nature and Effects of Interaction in Cello-Piano Duos.* Unpublished doctoral dissertation, University of London.

Goodman, E. (2002). Ensemble performance. In J. Rink (Ed.), *Musical Performance: A Guide to Understanding* (pp. 153–167). Cambridge: Cambridge University Press.

Gruson, L. M. (1988). Rehearsal skill and musical competence: Does practice make perfect? In J. A. Sloboda (Ed.), *Generative Processes in Music: The Psychology of Performance, Improvisation, and Composition* (pp. 91–112). Oxford: Clarendon Press.

Hallam, S. (1995). Professional musicians' approaches to the learning and interpretation of music. *Psychology of Music, 23*, 111–128.

Hallam, S. (1997). The development of memorisation strategies in musicians. *British Journal of Music Education, 14*, 87–97.

Krampe, R. T., & Ericsson, K. A. (1995). Deliberate practice and elite musical performance. In J. Rink (Ed.), *The Practice of Performance: Studies in Musical Interpretation* (pp. 84–102). Cambridge: Cambridge University Press.

Miklaszewski, K. (1989). A case study of a pianist preparing a musical performance. *Psychology of Music, 17,* 95–109.

Murninghan, J. K., & Conlon, D. E. (1991). The dynamics of intense work groups: A study of British string quartets. *Administrative Science Quarterly, 36,* 165–186.

Price, H. E., & Byo, J. L. (2002). Rehearsing and conducting. In R. Parncutt & G. E. McPherson (Eds.), *The Science and Psychology of Music Performance: Creative Strategies for Teaching and Learning* (pp. 335–351). Oxford: Oxford University Press.

Seth, V. (1999). *An Equal Music.* London: Phoenix.

Weeks, P. (1996). A rehearsal of a Beethoven passage: An analysis of correction talk. *Research on Language and Social Interaction, 29,* 247–290.

Williamon, A., & Davidson, J. W. (2002). Exploring co-performer communication. *Musicæ Scientiæ, 6,* 53–72.

Williamon, A., & Valentine, E. (2002). The role of retrieval structures in memorizing music. *Cognitive Psychology, 44,* 1–32.

Williamon, A., Valentine, E., & Valentine, J. (2002). Shifting the focus of attention between levels of musical structure. *European Journal of Cognitive Psychology, 14,* 493–520.

Yarbrough, C. (1975). Effect of magnitude of conductor behaviour on students in mixed choruses. *Journal of Research in Music Education, 23,* 134–146.

Young, V. M., & Colman, A. M. (1979). Some psychological processes in string quartets. *Psychology of Music, 7,* 12–16.

CHAPTER 7

STRATEGIES FOR MEMORIZING MUSIC

JANE GINSBORG

It is common in many kinds of music for artists to perform from memory. Within certain musical genres, in fact, social convention and audience expectation are such that performing with a notated score would be inconceivable. Rarely does one see a folk, rock, or pop musician reading from the printed page during performance; within the Western art music tradition (where audiences have come to expect almost note-perfect renditions of well-known pieces), memorized performances are customary for concert soloists. Why is this the case? Clearly, there are a number of practical advantages to playing or singing without a score. These include not having to turn pages, being able to monitor the physical aspects of a performance (e.g. looking at the hands or at other ensemble members), and in the case of concert pianists, avoiding the need to share the platform with a page-turner.

More importantly, perhaps, performing from memory is often seen to have the effect of enhancing musicality and musical communication. It is commonly argued that the very act of memorizing can guarantee a more thorough knowledge of and intimate connection with the music (see Plunkett Greene, 1912; Hughes, 1915; Matthay, 1926). In addition, memorization can enable the use of direct eye contact with an audience (and gaze, in other ways, for expressive purposes) that is more convincing than when referring to the score. Those who "possess" the music in this way often convey the impression that they are spontaneously and sincerely communicating from the heart, and indeed, contemporary evidence suggests that musicians who achieve this are likely to find their audiences more responsive (see Davidson, 1993, 1994; Williamon, 1999). Moreover, when performers receive and react to visual feedback from the audience, a performance can become truly interactive, involving genuine communication between all involved.

While performing from memory may have benefits for the performer and audience alike, the task of memorizing music and giving a memorized performance can be arduous. Memory failure—however momentary—can have catastrophic consequences for a performer's self-confidence. The musician does not, in fact, need to have experienced such failure to be frightened of forgetting, and this may well contribute to a more generalized performance anxiety. Furthermore, the fear of memory lapses is as common among experienced professional musicians as with novices—perhaps more so, as they feel they have more to lose. Artur Rubinstein, for example, "abandoned the concert stage mainly on account of the fact that he could no longer depend on his memory in public performance" (Hughes, 1915, p. 603).

This chapter reviews a range of memorization strategies that are available to musicians. An analysis of their efficacy is based on a critique of existing observational and empirical research, most of which stems from studies carried out within the context of Western classical music. Nevertheless, the benefits of each are presented so that they may be applied equally well to performance in other musical styles. The chapter is in three main sections. It begins by setting out basic principles of human memory, including a discussion of the psychological structures thought to be involved in memorization and some recommendations for improving memory generally. The second section explores musical memory specifically and offers a selection of strategies commonly used by musicians and tested through systematic research. These include rote memorization, methods for memorizing visual and auditory information, methods for developing and exploiting "conceptual" memory, and memorization for words and music. Finally, the chapter closes with a discussion of how these strategies can be used in conjunction with one another and how individual differences in learning styles may impact on one's capacity to memorize.

7.1   Memory: Structure and general recommendations

7.1.1   Structure

Before considering strategies that musicians can use to exploit their memory effectively and efficiently, it is important to place musical memory into a broader theoretical context. Memory can be conceptualized in a variety of ways. In Atkinson and Shiffrin's (1968) modal model, for example, memory consists of three stores, as depicted in Figure 7.1. The first is the *sensory store*, which has sub-stores for the different kinds of environmental information we receive via our senses: visual, auditory, tactile, and so on. Much of this incoming information is not attended to and, consequently, remains only briefly in memory. Information that does capture attention, however, is transferred into *short-term memory* (subsequent researchers have proposed that short-term memory has a *working memory* component that is used to manipulate different kinds of information in conscious awareness; see Baddeley & Hitch, 1974). Memory storage at this level plays a vital role in basic, everyday functioning (e.g. remembering phone numbers and keeping track of an ongoing conversation). In terms of musical performance, this type of memory is integral to tasks such as sight-reading and improvisation, where new information must be retained and related to past, present, and predicted future events (see Chapter 8 for further details on sight-reading and improvisation, Chapter 11 for research on working memory enhancement, and Chapter 14 for sources of memory impairment).

Once in short-term memory, information can be rehearsed and elaborated in such a way that it is stored alongside or assimilated into existing knowledge. Unlike short-term memory, which has a capacity limited to around seven "chunks" of information (Miller, 1956), *long-term memory* seems to be of unlimited capacity and duration. It holds different kinds of information, including procedural knowledge ("knowing how" to do something), semantic knowledge (facts, i.e. "knowing that"), and episodic memories (details of events or episodes in one's life). These memories are organized

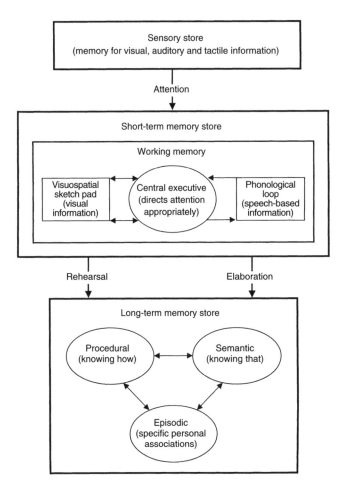

Figure 7.1 A graphical representation of the components of memory, consisting of (1) the sensory store, which temporarily holds environmental information received via the senses; (2) short-term memory, which contains information that captures attention and enables the manipulation of that information through working memory; and (3) long-term memory, which stores information that has been rehearsed and elaborated in such a way that it becomes integrated into one's knowledge. The last of these is particularly vital to the memorization of music and houses procedural and semantic knowledge ("knowing how" and "knowing that," respectively), as well as episodic memories about events in one's life (diagram adapted from Baddeley, 1990; Eysenck & Keane, 2000).

hierarchically, enabling us to make associations both within and between different categories of information. Procedural knowledge underlies the performer's ability to make music, in terms of coordinating his or her movements to produce sequences of notes, such as scales and arpeggios, on an instrument. However, the knowledge that a particular sequence of notes represents certain patterns (a scale of D major, say, or a favorite melody) depends on semantic memory. Meanwhile, the specific associations the melody has for the individual (e.g. where it was first heard, events going on at the same time as first hearing, others who were present) are held in episodic memory.

Of course, one of the primary objectives of storing information in long-term memory is to be able to retrieve that information accurately and on demand. Explicit retrieval of stored information takes place through the processes of recognition and recall. Recognition involves matching new, incoming information with information already stored in long-term memory. Recall involves actively (re-) producing that information. Both processes can occur spontaneously (the same cue can trigger recognition or recall), but recall makes greater demands on our ability to remember. The focus of this chapter is on the rehearsal and elaboration strategies that contribute to deliberate memorization in music: recall from long-term memory.

7.1.2 General recommendations

While all people possess the same memory structures and use the same basic cognitive mechanisms, some people seem to have "better" memories than others. To a limited extent, this may be due to differences in "natural" general memory ability. However, Wilding and Valentine (1997) conclude from their research with exceptional memorizers that most superior memory performance can be attributed to the use of highly effective strategies for learning (or "encoding") and, independently, for retaining information in memory.

There are many accounts of professional musicians exhibiting extraordinary feats of memory (Revesz, 1925/1999; Marcus, 1979; Marek, 1982; Charness et al., 1988). The notion of individual differences in the ability to memorize music, even among those who achieve such feats, is supported by research with musicians memorizing music in the laboratory (Lehmann & Ericsson, 1995; Ginsborg, 2000) and under more naturalistic circumstances in the studio (Ginsborg, 2002). Meanwhile, everyone who plays or sings, no matter what their level of natural ability, can benefit from learning and practicing effective strategies for memorizing music.

Before considering the strategies that have been found to be particularly useful for memorizing music, there are general recommendations for encoding information and storing it in long-term memory for easy retrieval that can aid the musician. These can be categorized in four ways: (1) improving memory in its most general sense; (2) staving off or remediating age-related memory deterioration; (3) enhancing study skills; and (4) using mnemonics by associating meaningless information with the material to be remembered. Firstly, recommendations for improving memory in its most general sense include understanding how memory works and having the motivation to try to remember (Arden, 2002). Secondly, those who fear age-related memory deterioration are advised to reduce stress, eat a balanced diet, take vitamin supplements, avoid alcohol and drugs, keep an active mind, and do "brain exercises" (Small, 2003; see also Chapters 3, 9, 10, 12, and 14 of this volume). Thirdly, students can improve their learning, and specifically their performance in examinations, by using memory strategies such as attending to the material to be remembered (e.g. in lectures) before organizing, interpreting, and understanding it, and also by visualizing, reciting, and reviewing it (Pauk, 1994). Different techniques focus on enhancing different aspects of memory. For example, "mind-mapping" (Buzan, 1989) involves organizing and making appropriate links between chunks of information. The end-product (the "mind-map") provides an elaborated set of notes; more importantly, the process of devising an idiosyncratic visual representation serves to reinforce memory. Finally, mnemonics include "peg-words," such as rhyming words and numbers (one = bun, two = shoe); the method of *loci*, dating from classical times, whereby objects or concepts are associated with familiar locations such as landmarks on a regular journey, or different rooms in one's home; and linking unrelated items by weaving them into a story (Arden, 2002).

Many of these recommendations, such as those relating to health and well-being, are supported by continuing research into the functioning of the brain (Small, 2003). Understanding how memory works may seem an ambitious aspiration, yet it is well known that metacognition, or "knowing about knowing," is essential to learning (see Chapter 5 for specific recommendations for individual practice). When students are advised to attend to and later review what has been said in lectures, this is based on the notion of transferring information from the sensory store into short-term memory and thence into long-term memory. Interpreting new information in order to understand it, and linking it with information already stored in long-term memory is a highly effective way of extending the storage capacity of short-term memory by increasing the size of information chunks. This was shown dramatically in a study carried out by Ericsson *et al.* (1980), in which one of the authors, a keen amateur runner, learned to encode up to 82 digits by thinking of them as combinations of running times (e.g. 3594 was stored as 3 minutes 59.4 seconds for a mile run, which was meaningfully classified as "fast"). Visualization and recitation are forms of elaboration and rehearsal, drawing on visual, kinesthetic, and auditory processes; reviewing involves reorganization of the material to be remembered in long-term memory. Similarly, mind-mapping combines the creative use of visual and associative memory. As for the mnemonics outlined above, they all rely on forming associations between items, using visual and/or auditory memory, in order to create new meanings and links between the new information to be remembered and existing information stored in long-term memory. Still, how do these recommendations relate to memorizing music?

◆ You are well advised to take care of your general health for sharp and long-lasting memory performance.

◆ One of the main aims of this chapter is to help you find out what is currently known about how memory works and how musicians go about memorizing music so that you can learn to use effective memorizing strategies yourself. These are based on similar principles to those that underpin most study skills.

◆ However, while study skills usually relate to the learning and memorization of semantic knowledge, you need procedural knowledge as well to sing or play. This is gained through practice involving some inevitable repetition, in order to "automatize" performance.

◆ As for mnemonics, they may not at first glance seem relevant to music memorization. Yet, they can be useful for encoding sequences of musical events within a piece, or the words of songs that do not seem to make sense otherwise.

7.2   Musical memory

One way of describing a memory for a specific piece of music—whether acquired through repeated hearings or deliberate memorization—is a "mental representation," stored in long-term memory, on which the musician can draw when performing. Lehmann (1997) suggests a structure for expert musicians' mental representations with three facets: (1) the desired performance goal, (2) the knowledge of how to produce that goal, and (3) the actual performance. The desired performance goal represents an ideal performance: a rehearsed, highly detailed interpretation of the music. This interpretation can be conceptualized at different levels, forming a hierarchy (Williamon *et al.*, 2002). At the most global level, the music is represented mentally as a whole piece, from beginning to end; at the most local level, it is represented by the notes forming each musical sequence. Of course, there are numerous possible hierarchical levels in between. In a classical sonata movement, these might be the exposition, development, and recapitulation; in a song they might be introduction, verse, chorus, and so on. The desired performance goal is achieved (to a greater or lesser extent) via the second and third facets of the mental representation suggested by Lehmann—that is, the production aspects and the actual performance. The representation of production aspects is constructed from repeated rehearsals of musical sequences that become fully automated but which must continually be monitored. The representation of the actual performance—the interpretation of the music—also involves monitoring in the context of the performance situation and feedback from the audience. In terms of the different kinds of long-term memory outlined in Section 7.1.1, musicians' semantic and episodic memories for the music they perform inform the desired performance goal. Meanwhile, actually playing, singing, or conducting music requires procedural memory.

Different kinds of memorizing strategies can contribute to the formation of mental representations at their different levels and enable attention to be shifted, during practice, from one level to another (Williamon *et al.*, 2002). Whether the information coming into the sensory store is tactile, auditory, and/or visual (e.g. the feel of the fingers on the keys of the instrument, the sound of the music, and the look of the musical score, respectively), sensory information is essential for mental representations of music at the local level. It is also essential for producing and monitoring the desired performance goal. Sequences of musical events are usually memorized—and automated—via rote repetition using "kinesthetic" memory. However, they could not be learned in the first place without the use of "visual" memory of the notated music and of the way the music is created, and "aural" memory of sounds that are imagined, heard, or produced by the performer for the first time. Depending on the learning preferences of the musicians, music can thus be rehearsed and elaborated kinesthetically, visually, and aurally for representation in long-term memory.

However, in order to represent music mentally at global and local levels and to move between the different levels of representation during practice, analytic or conceptual strategies are required. These strategies have already been introduced in relation to study skills; they enable us to understand and organize the material (in this case, the music) to be remembered. Unlike kinesthetic, visual, and aural representations, conceptual memory for music can be thought of as a form of semantic knowledge (as well as procedural), which facilitates performance.

So how do musicians go about memorizing using these different strategies? Some memorize, apparently, almost without conscious awareness. When asked how they memorize they cannot—or will not—say. Many musicians, on the other hand, have shared their experiences of memorizing, in published books and interviews, passing on the techniques they have found useful to their students. The list that follows is based on these, as well as on a growing body of research in psychology of music. Of course, no single strategy is guaranteed for all musicians and individual differences in learning styles are discussed in Section 7.3.

7.2.1   Memorizing by rote

Rote memorization is perhaps the most common form of rehearsal, particularly for novice musicians attempting to commit a piece of music to memory. Essentially, it uses kinesthetic memory (otherwise known as tactile, motor, finger or muscular memory) and consists of repetition of a bar, phrase, or page until it can be played, automatically, by "feel." For example, many pianists report memorizing with separate hands and consistently using the same fingerings so as to develop their kinesthetic memory for a piece of music (Chaffin *et al.*, 2002). In a study of singers memorizing words and music separately and together, however, the latter performed with greater accuracy and confidence, since the words and music acted as cues for each other (Ginsborg, 2000).

- If you are a keyboard player, you could memorize by rote with your hands separately as well as together; for singers, try to use it to link the words and music together.

Expert musicians use rote memorization to "overlearn" their performances, to ensure that they will be as secure as possible, but they almost always use other memorizing strategies in addition to rote memorization. This is because kinesthetic memory is vulnerable to interference. A stray thought, a cough from the audience, hearing something in the music, as it were, for the first time can "throw" the performer.

- You should use rote memorization in order to free your mind to monitor your performance, to focus on the meaning you wish to convey, and to communicate with your fellow musicians and/or your audience.

In an interview study carried out by Hallam (1997) with novice musicians and professional orchestral musicians, the majority reported memorizing—initially—without conscious awareness, as they learned their parts. When they identified passages they could not play accurately from memory, they chunked them into smaller sections and repeated each section until it was secure. Then, they grouped the small sections into longer sections, and repeated these longer sections until they too were secure. In this way, the whole piece would eventually be successfully memorized. This technique was useful for short pieces; however, for longer, more complex works, half of the professional musicians in Hallam's sample reported using what she refers to as "cognitive analysis" (see Section 7.2.5) to construct a framework into which the memorized sections could be placed.

7.2.2   Memorizing visual information

Most classical musicians begin learning and practicing new pieces from a notated source, and this can form an important foundation for memory. Indeed, many musicians report "knowing where they are on the page" when they play or sing notated music from memory—a very useful tool for preventing or recovering from memory lapses. As early as 1800, long before it was customary for classical musicians to perform from memory, Anfossi (cited in Monahan, 1978) recommended that singers should memorize at least the turn of the page.

♦ It is not a good idea to rely simply on the visual memory you acquire in the course of learning the music. This is similar to memorizing without conscious awareness; like rote memorization, it can be an unreliable technique on its own. Rather, use memory for visual information deliberately; you could mark the score with a pencil or colored pen.

Although there is anecdotal evidence of musicians' (particularly conductors') memory for musical scores (see Marcus, 1979), empirical research on memory purely for visual information is scant. Nuki (1984) asked piano and composition students first to sight-read and then to memorize a novel piece of music. When they had memorized it, they performed it from memory. They were then asked which of four strategies they had used to memorize: kinesthetic, visual, aural, or a mixture of the three. The students who reported using a visual strategy were significantly quicker to memorize than those who used one of the other strategies or a mixture of the three. However, by "visual" strategy, Nuki infers the use of the "inner ear" (see Section 7.2.3), and indeed, the quickest memorizers in her sample were the students of piano and composition who were also good sight-readers and had gained high grades in solfège at their universities.

♦ Deliberate memorization of visual information, whether signals from another musician or the score itself, is linked to conceptual memory (see Section 7.2.5). You should carry out some form of analysis of the music in order to decide which information will serve as the most reliable cues and then mark those cues in the score. Each time you rehearse the piece thereafter, you are reinforcing (sometimes unknowingly) your memory of those cues.

Visual memories can also consist of visions of the position of the instrument and of the body. Where musicians play in groups they often rely on each other's visual, as well as aural, cues.

♦ If you are playing or singing with an ensemble, visual memory may be triggered by something as basic as a conductor's down-beat or a particular movement by a section leader. These are not just trivial remembrances, but rather they can play a major role in the unfolding of a performance. For maximal efficacy in practice, particularly useful cues as such should be explicitly acknowledged to ensure their consistent delivery.

7.2.3   Memorizing by ear

Many musicians—particularly musicians who are not part of the Western classical tradition—do not rely on musical notation to learn or memorize, but rather memorize through listening and imitating what they hear. For some, this is laborious and time-consuming; for others, comparatively easy. Macek (1987) reports the case of a jazz musician who developed what he called a "photographic" ear (analogous to eidetic memory for visually-presented stimuli; Haber & Haber, 1988), which enabled him to recall and reproduce complex music in detail. Aural memory is as hard as visual memory to disentangle from the formation of mental representations and conceptual memory. Two studies in particular illustrate this. First, Sloboda *et al.* (1985) studied the exceptional verbatim memory for music of an autistic savant and showed that his memory was reliable only when he listened to music in a familiar genre. Second, Sloboda and Parker (1985) asked musicians and nonmusicians to listen to short folk melodies and then sing them as accurately as possible from memory. On the whole, the versions produced were inaccurate and/or incomplete, but they preserved the metrical and— particularly in the case of the musicians—harmonic structure of the originals. This suggests that we construct memory for specific pieces of music using what we already know about and have experienced with music; every new piece of music that we hear contributes to this knowledge.

♦ While some musicians rely on the aural memories they acquire in the course of learning music, this is rarely reliable without conceptual memory to serve as a framework for monitoring "where you are" in performance and "where you are going," and to provide you with a repertory of alternative musical sequences with which to improvise, should you have a memory lapse.

♦ Once you have a conceptual framework, using aural memory as a basis for rote repetition, either playing or singing aloud, or in your imagination, is an excellent strategy.

7.2.4   Translating visual information into imaginary sound

An important tool for musicians who do use musical notation is the ability to imagine the way a performance would sound, or how it would feel to play or sing, from the score. Gieseking and Leimer (1932/1972) call this "visualization" and recommend that pianists should memorize, referring to the printed score, using their "inner ear" *before* beginning to practice at the keyboard. Gordon (1993) refers to this as "audiation": being able to hear and understand music that is no longer, or may indeed never have been, audible. Equally, it is possible for musicians who do not use musical notation to hear a piece of music and imagine the way they, or someone else, would perform it. The research by Nuki outlined in Section 7.2.2 highlights the role of the ability to read music, translating visual information into imaginary sound and thus creating a mental representation for music.

♦ The difference between reading music and playing or singing aloud, and reading music and conjuring up imaginary sound (and "feel") is like the difference between reading a piece of text aloud, as beginners do, and reading silently. If you are a musician who must learn and memorize notated music, then learning to hear it in your mind as you read it—so that you can memorize away from your instrument—is one of the most valuable skills you can develop.

7.2.5   Developing and exploiting conceptual memory

The ability to form mental representations of music at the global and local levels, particularly for extended compositions, depends on "conceptual" memory: the musician's existing semantic knowledge—held in long-term memory—of the structures that underlie the music. These structures may vary according to musical genre, and they include chord progressions in jazz, rhythmic patterns, *ragas* in Indian music, and the conventions of tonality in Western classical music.

Lehmann and Ericsson (1995) tested the hypothesis that the ability to construct and draw on a mental representation facilitates performance from memory that is both stable (i.e. the musician can reliably "keep the music the same") and flexible (i.e. variations can be made in performance, depending on the requirements of the situation). They asked advanced students of piano to memorize two short pieces of music, providing "think-aloud" verbal reports as they did so. The pianists memorized the pieces—accompaniments to an instrumental "pacing" track—in the laboratory by carrying out a number of pairs of trials, playing each piece once with the musical score and once without until they could perform it from memory without errors twice, consecutively: the fewer trials they needed, the faster they had succeeded in memorizing. Then they carried out a series of tasks designed to test their ability to "manipulate" the pieces from memory. The results of the study showed that the pianists who were quickest to memorize made the fewest errors when transposing from memory. Thus, rather than learning musical sequences by rote and reproducing them using kinesthetic memory, it is clear that efficient memorization must involve the ability to construct and draw on a detailed mental representation of the music, allowing the performer both to reproduce it reliably and to manipulate it in performance from memory.

Ginsborg (2000) carried out a similar study to investigate the nature of mental representations for the words and music of songs with 20 singers. Each singer memorized two songs, in two separate sessions, paced by a recorded accompaniment, using the Lehmann and Ericsson (1995) memorizing paradigm. Once the songs were memorized, the singers carried out a number of tasks. Transposition—the task the quickest memorizers in Lehmann and Ericsson's study performed most accurately—is relatively simple for most singers, so instead they were asked to retrieve the words and melody of the song independently, to "deconstruct" the words and melody, to show an awareness of the compositional structure of the song, to use visual memory to retrieve information about different aspects of the musical score, and to respond to cues taken from the words and music of the song.

There was no correlation between speed of memorization and performance on some of the more straightforward tasks, such as performing the song accurately with accompaniment and at the same tempo as it was originally memorized. This would suggest a role for the automatization of performance, through the rote repetition of text and melody together (see also Section 7.2.6). On the other hand, speed of memorization was significantly correlated with performance on the seven most difficult tasks: speaking the words of the whole song at speed; retrieving fragments of the text and fragments of the music, with the words and pitches in reverse order; responding to cues, both forward and reverse; singing the phrases of the song in reverse order; and singing the pitches of the melody of the song only, without rhythm, to the regular beat of a metronome. Such tasks could not have been performed successfully in the absence of a well-formed, multicode mental representation of the song including conceptual, kinesthetic, visual, and aural information. As in Lehmann and Ericsson's study, the faster the singers acquired these mental representations, the better they performed the tasks. Mental representations of music must, therefore, underlie the ability to produce performances from memory that are both stable and flexible.

◆ Once you have memorized a piece for the first time, you should test your memory in order to simulate different possibilities for recovering from lapses. You could try starting mid-section instead of at a structural boundary, for example, or by practicing jumping from one section to a previous section and to later sections. When you have done this, you will know you have created a mental representation on which you can draw to produce a stable, yet flexible, performance.

Research has focused on two main ways of developing and exploiting mental representations using conceptual memory: analysis and the use of structural boundaries to organize practice. These are discussed and recommendations are offered in turn.

Analysis

It is often suggested that musicians should analyze the music they are to memorize (e.g. Hughes, 1915; Matthay, 1926), partly so as to be able to "chunk" or to divide the music into shorter sections; once each one is memorized they can be "grouped" together. Many researchers have investigated the efficacy of analysis as a memorization strategy. For example, half the professional musicians—though none of the novice musicians—who took part in Hallam's (1997) study reported using an analytic approach to develop a framework into which they could fit the material they had memorized by rote. According to Hallam, this included noting where the music changed from one key to another, particular harmonic progressions, the length of rests, and difficult exit points.

Rubin-Rabson (1937), on the other hand, compared four groups of piano students' memorization of short pieces. One group memorized at the keyboard. Two groups analyzed the pieces before memorizing them, one independently, the other with Rubin-Rabson's guidance. The fourth group listened to a recording of the pieces and then memorized in one of the three ways already detailed. Three weeks later, the students who had either analyzed the pieces themselves or with guidance were the quickest to relearn the pieces and to perform them accurately from memory.

Ross (1964) replicated this study with the participation of competent wind players randomly divided into experimental and control groups. Following a pre-test to establish baseline memorizing ability, the experimental group undertook a weekly hour-long session with a teacher, for 6 weeks, in which they analyzed and memorized a series of training pieces, in preparation for memorizing a test piece at the end of the 6-week period. Again, the experimental group accurately memorized the test piece significantly faster than the control group.

The most detailed account of the use of analysis to develop conceptual memory for music is provided by Chaffin and Imreh who have been collaborating for almost a decade on a project exploring the cognitive processes involved in learning and memorizing music (see Chaffin *et al.*, 2002). The purpose of their first study was to produce a systematic record of the activities of an experienced professional concert pianist (i.e. Imreh) while memorizing the third movement of Bach's Italian Concerto (Chaffin & Imreh, 1994). Imreh undertook 57 practice sessions over the course of 10 months, 34 of which were recorded on videotape and 11 on audiotape. She talked aloud about her decision-making as she worked; she was interviewed and, once the piece was success-fully memorized, she commented on her videotaped practice and annotated the score to show how she organized the music conceptually. One of the findings of this study was that she identified the compositional structure of the piece and used it not only to guide her practice, through chunking and grouping, but also to ensure accuracy when she played from memory. She practiced and memorized acknowledged sections in the music separately and together. When she came to play the whole piece from memory, she would deliberately recall the particular features of each section in order to remind herself which section she was actually playing and which came next (Chaffin & Imreh, 1997).

◆ The use of conceptual memory is the crucial overarching strategy that no musician can do without.

◆ Whatever kind of music you play or sing, you need to identify how it fits together (i.e. its structure), whether this is at a highly detailed level such as that described above or at a much simpler level—remembering, for example, that you must sing two verses interspersed with three choruses, the last time in a higher key.

◆ How you go about identifying structure and using it to help you memorize will depend on the nature of your musical training as well as the nature of the music. Some musicians rely on an understanding of underlying harmony; others rely on memory for melodic sequences; others rely on identifying and being able to repro-duce rhythmic patterns. In Western classical music, all of these are useful ways of conceptualizing music, separately and together.

Structural boundaries

Williamon and Valentine (2002) explored the development of the ability to identify structure, to use it as a tool for organizing practice, and to employ it successfully for retrieval in performance. They asked 22 pianists to learn and memorize a piece by J. S. Bach appropriate to their level of expertise. All of the pianists' practice sessions were recorded on audiotape. The final performances that they gave from memory, as part of a recital, were recorded on videotape and assessed by experienced adjudicators. The pianists made verbal and written comments on their practice, annotated their musical scores and were interviewed following their final performances about the practice and memorizing process. The results of the study showed that pianists with higher levels of skill were more likely than those at lower levels to practice segments of the piece begin-ning and ending on bars at the structural boundaries (these were defined according to the structure of the piece as understood and described by the individual pianist; only three pianists' descriptions conformed to the "textbook" formal structure of the piece). The likelihood that a pianist would use structural boundaries to guide his or her choice of the part of the piece to be practiced increased over the course of practice sessions.

The earlier the pianist began to do so, however, the better his or her final performance was likely to be judged.

Research has shown that singers, too, use structural boundaries to guide their practice during the course of memorization. Ginsborg (2002) carried out an observational study in which 13 singers learned and memorized the same song over the course of up to six 15-minute practice sessions. The sessions, which included concurrent verbal commentaries made by the singers, were taped and transcribed. Finally, an assessment of the singers' speed and accuracy of memorization was made in order to determine which of the various memorizing strategies used by the singers were more and less effective. Fast, accurate memorizers were no more likely than slower, less accurate memorizers to use structural boundaries to guide their practice. Furthermore, the use of structural boundaries did not change significantly between the beginning and end of the practice sessions. However, it was used widely: more than four fifths of "attempts", the segments of the song that were practiced, began on one of its eight phrases. Nearly half of the attempts began at the start of a phrase and finished at the end of the same or a subsequent phrase. The majority of attempts were on the first phrase, followed closely by the third phrase (i.e. the beginning and middle of the first verse); a much smaller proportion of attempts was made on the fifth and seventh phrases (the beginning and middle of the second verse). An unexpectedly high proportion of attempts on the final phrase was attributable to the fact that participants found it "technically" difficult to sing (it had two large-interval "leaps") and also to memorize.

◆ You should try to divide the music into sections in a way that makes sense to you, so as to memorize the sections one at a time before re-combining them into longer sections and fitting them into your conceptual framework for the whole piece.

◆ The more you organize your practice around sections identified in the music (especially in the early stages of learning a piece), the more likely you are to remember this basic architecture in performance.

7.2.6   Memorizing strategies for singers: Combining words and music

Like instrumental musicians, singers use kinesthetic, visual, aural, and conceptual memory. Unlike instrumental musicians, however, they must also memorize words. It should be remembered that music and words are not necessarily equal partners: sometimes the voice is used instrumentally (e.g. scat singing in jazz or choral music by Bach) and sometimes the words are more important than the melody (e.g. operatic recitative, *Sprechstimme*). The relative importance of words and music in a particular musical genre will determine the memorizing strategies used, and whether the words and music are memorized separately or together. In an observational study, Ginsborg (2002) identified a variety of "modes" of attempt used in singers' practice sessions. These were: focusing on the words alone (speaking the words, while reading from the score and from memory); focusing on the music alone (playing the melody, playing the accompaniment, vocalizing the melody, and counting—the last of these while reading from the score and from memory); and singing the words and music together, while reading from the score and from memory. Fast, accurate memorizers used more modes of attempt than the slower, less accurate memorizers. They were also more likely to count aloud, but most importantly, they began memorizing earlier and sang more of the song from memory during the course of their practice sessions.

Next, the higher-level strategies of the "best" memorizer (the first of the 13 participants in the sample to sing the whole song entirely accurately from memory) and the "worst" memorizer (the one who took longest to memorize and made the most errors when she sang from memory) were compared, with reference to their verbal commentaries as well as their practice data. The "best" memorizer sang the words and music of the song together rather than separately. She started memorizing early and tested her memory throughout the practice sessions. She worked on a variety of lengths of practice unit. She made plans and implemented them, monitored and corrected her errors, and explicitly evaluated her practice. Her strategies were varied and complex; furthermore, her verbal commentary was detailed and self-guiding. In contrast, the "worst" memorizer implemented plans, monitored errors, and evaluated her practice to a much lesser extent. She preferred to sing the music only, started to memorize comparatively late and consistently went back to the beginning of the song and repeated it in its entirety, rather than dividing it into smaller sections.

Ginsborg (2000) also investigated which of two strategies is more effective for memorizing a song: memorizing the words and melody separately or memorizing them together. Sixty singers took part in this study. Each singer was categorized in two ways: by their experience of memorizing and by their level of musical expertise. Half of them were solo singers with considerable experience of memorizing and performing from memory, while the other half were choral singers with little or no experience of memorizing songs. Half of them had undertaken musical training to advanced levels, while the other half had lower levels of musical training.

They were randomly divided into three groups and asked to memorize a short, unaccompanied song in a single 20-minute practice session. The first group memorized the words first, then the melody, and finally both together; the second group memorized the melody first, then the words, and finally both together; the third group memorized the words and melody simultaneously throughout the course of the practice session. When the singers had memorized the song, they were asked to sing it from memory twice, their two performances separated by a 10-minute interview. Their second performances from memory were transcribed, coded, and analyzed. Errors and hesitations were noted and counted. Generally, the singers who memorized the words and melody of the song together gave more accurate and more confident performances from memory. They made fewer word-only errors, and fewer simultaneous word-and-music errors. They also made fewer hesitations. So, as shown in the comparison of the strategies used by the "best" and "worst" memorizer in the observational study, memorizing words and melody together appears to be a more effective strategy than memorizing them separately.

A comparison of the performances of singers with high and low levels of memorizing experience, and with high and low levels of musical expertise, was also instructive. Those singers with considerable experience of memorizing songs were no more accurate or confident in their performances from memory than those with no experience of memorizing songs. In other words, experience is no guarantee of success, at least in terms of memorizing. On the other hand, there were observable differences between those singers who had advanced levels of musical training and those who did not. The singers with high levels of musical expertise made fewer music-only errors, and fewer simultaneous word-and-music errors, than the nonexpert singers. Furthermore, while—as one might predict—they were generally more accurate in their performances from memory, this was *only* the case when they had memorized the words and melody together.

◆ Almost every memorizing strategy recommended in this chapter is as applicable to singers as it is to instrumental musicians. The only difference between them is that singers must memorize words as well as music. Think of the words as an element of the music rather than the other way round.

◆ You might think of the words in terms of the way they look on the page (visual memory), the way they sound (aural memory), or the way it feels to produce them (kinesthetic memory). If you are learning a melody using visualization/audiation, mouth the words to yourself. Once they are securely memorized, it is helpful, of course, to think about what they mean.

7.3   Conclusions

The aim of this chapter has been to report on memorizing strategies that have been shown to be effective for all musicians, both instrumentalists and singers. To reiterate: music is stored using multiple representations in long-term memory. Effective memorization strategies capitalize on this.

◆ Analyze the music you are to memorize in order to understand it and organize it, using conceptual memory as an overarching framework.

◆ Chunk the music and practice it in small sections, from one structural boundary to the next, increasing the size of chunk as you become more familiar with the music.

◆ Use rote, kinesthetic memory in conjunction with either visual or aural memory, or both.

For the most part, discussion has focused on memorization of a specific piece of music; however, some final, more general suggestions can be made:

◆ First, it has been shown in a number of domains that "little and often" is a better strategy for memorizing than trying to memorize in just one or two extended sessions. Sometimes you find that your memory for a piece of music has improved between practice sessions without conscious effort; alternatively, you can use the time between practice sessions for recalling the music you have memorized and identifying sections that may need more work.

◆ Second, there are strategies that can be used in the final stages of preparing to give a performance from memory. One is *state-dependence*: learning to control your frame of mind so that you can conjure up the same sense of exhilaration, for instance, when you are practicing as when you are actually performing. The other is *context-dependent learning*: practicing in the room or on the stage where the performance is to take place. These strategies, like so many others, can be useful whatever kind of music you are playing or singing, and whether you are a soloist or in an ensemble.

In addition, we have to remind ourselves that different tasks may require different strategies. Furthermore, we also need to remember that different individuals have different capacities for memorizing easily and successfully. While most research investigating memorization strategies has focused on the average numbers of trials required to memorize and re-learn pieces of music, these mask a wide variety of memorization speeds. For example, Lehmann and Ericsson (1995) found that their slowest memorizer needed 6–7 times as many trials to memorize as their fastest memorizer; using the same paradigm, the singers in Ginsborg's (2000) study required from 2 to 17 trials to memorize a song with a word-text, and from 3 to as many as 49 trials to memorize the song with a digit-text. Similarly, in Ginsborg (2002), in which 13 singers learned and memorized under more (although not completely) naturalistic circumstances, the fastest memorizer produced 3232 beats before her first accurate performance from memory (equivalent to just under 20 renditions of the song) while the slowest produced 5287 beats (equivalent to 32 renditions).

These findings may well reflect the extent to which the musicians who took part in these studies found that the strategies they were encouraged to use resembled or interfered with their usual, or preferred, strategies. From interview and experimental data, it is clear that musicians not only have different memorizing abilities, but also a wide variety of views on memory and preferences for using different approaches to memorization (e.g. kinesthetic, visual, and aural). These preferences have been characterized by some educationists as learning modalities or learning styles, which can be identified through the use of checklists such as the Swassing–Barbe Modality Index (SBMI; Barbe & Swassing, 1979) and the Learning Styles Index (LSI; Price & Dunn, 1997; Dunn et al., 2003). Although learning style theories have been criticized on the grounds that they lack a psychological foundation (Sternberg & Grigorenko, 2001; Renzulli & Dai, 2001), some music teachers advocate teaching their students according to their particular learning strengths (see Garcia, 2002).

While the impact of learning styles on expert musicians' memorizing abilities and strategies has not yet been explored, research has been carried out using the SBMI and LSI with children: (1) to identify "gifted" musicians and investigate the extent to which their learning styles differ from those of the general population (Kreitner, 1981); (2) to find out if memory for rhythm patterns can be enhanced by presenting them in children's preferred modalities (Persellin & Pierce, 1988); (3) to examine the relationships between the perceptual elements of learning style, musical aptitude, and attitudes to music learning (Faulkner, 1994); and (4) to examine the influence of children's preferred modalities on the way they listen to music. The findings of these studies indicate that children's preferred modalities may influence some aspects of basic music listening and learning. However, there is only anecdotal evidence, as yet, to suggest that these persist into adulthood. If individual musicians do possess particular learning strengths then they must also have complementary learning weaknesses. Future research might well seek to determine the nature of the training whereby such weaknesses in memorization can be systematically improved.

Further information and reading

Chaffin, R., Imreh, G., & Crawford, M. (2002). *Practicing Perfection: Memory and Piano Performance*. Mahwah, NJ: Erlbaum.

Gieseking, W., & Leimer, K. (1932/1972). *Piano Technique*. New York: Dover. (Original work published in 1932.)

Lehmann, A. C. (1997). Acquired mental representations in music performance: Anecdotal and preliminary empirical evidence. In H. Jørgensen & A. C. Lehmann (Eds.), *Does Practice Make Perfect? Current Theory and Research on Instrumental Music Practice* (pp. 141–163). Oslo: Norwegian Academy of Music.

Wilding, J., & Valentine, E. (1997). *Superior Memory*. Hove, UK: Psychology Press.

Williamon, A. (2002). Memorising music. In J. Rink (Ed.), *Musical Performance: A Guide to Understanding* (pp. 113–126). Cambridge: Cambridge University Press.

References

Arden, J. B. (2002). *Improving Your Memory for Dummies*. New York: Wiley.

Atkinson, R. C., & Shiffrin, R. M. (1968). Human memory: A proposed system and its control processes. In K. W. Spence & J. T. Spence (Eds.), *The Psychology of Learning and Motivation: Advances in Research and Theory* (Vol. 2, pp. 89–195). London: Academic Press.

Baddeley, A. D. (1990). *Human Memory: Theory and Practice*. Boston: Allyn and Bacon.

Baddeley, A. D., & Hitch, G. J. (1974). Working memory. In G. H. Bower (Ed.), *The Psychology of Learning and Motivation* (Vol. 8, pp. 47–90). London: Academic Press.

Barbe, W. B., & Swassing, R. H. (1979). *Teaching through Modality Strengths: Concepts and Practices*. Columbus, OH: Zaner-Bloser.

Buzan, T. (1989). *Use Your Head*. London: BBC Consumer Publishing.

Chaffin, R., & Imreh, G. (1994). *Memorizing for Performance: A Case Study of Expert Memory*. Paper presented at the Third Practical Aspects of Memory Conference, University of Maryland.

Chaffin, R., & Imreh, G. (1997). "Pulling teeth and torture": musical memory and problem solving. *Thinking and Reasoning, 3*, 315–336.

Chaffin, R., Imreh, G., & Crawford, M. (2002). *Practicing Perfection: Memory and Piano Performance*. Mahwah, NJ: Erlbaum.

Charness, N., Clifton, J., & MacDonald, L. (1988). Case study of a musical "mono-savant": A cognitive-psychological focus. In L. K. Obler & D. Fein (Eds.), *The Exceptional Brain: Neuropsychology of Talent and Special Abilities* (pp. 277–293). London: Guilford Press.

Davidson, J. W. (1993). Visual perception of performance manner in the movements of solo musicians. *Psychology of Music, 21*, 103–113.

Davidson, J. W. (1994). Which areas of a pianist's body convey information about expressive intention to an audience? *Journal of Human Movement Studies, 26*, 279–301.

Dunn, R., Dunn, K., & Price, G. E. (2003). *Learning Style Inventory (LSI) Grades 5–12*. Lawrence, KS: Price Systems.

Ericsson, K. A., Chase, W. G., & Falloon, S. (1980). Acquisition of memory skill. *Science, 208*, 1181–1182.

Eysenck, M. W., & Keane, M. T. (2000). *Cognitive Psychology: A Student's Handbook* (4th ed.). Hove, UK: Psychology Press.

Faulkner, D. L. (1994). *An Investigation of Modality Preferences, Musical Aptitude, and Attitude Toward Music at the Third-Grade Level.* Unpublished doctoral dissertation, University of Mississippi, Oxford, MS.

Garcia, S. (2002). Learning styles and piano teaching. *Piano Pedagogy Forum, 5(1).* Retrieved August 28, 2003, from *www.music.sc.edu/ea/keyboard/PPF/5.1/5.1.PPFpp.html.*

Gieseking, W., & Leimer, K. (1932/1972). *Piano Technique.* New York: Dover. (Original work published in 1932.)

Ginsborg, J. (2000). Off by heart: Expert singers' memorisation strategies and recall for the words and music of songs. In C. Woods, G. Luck, R. Brochard, F. Seddon, & J. A. Sloboda (Eds.), *Proceedings of the Sixth International Conference on Music Perception and Cognition.* Keele, UK: Keele University.

Ginsborg, J. (2002). Classical singers learning and memorising a new song: An observational study. *Psychology of Music, 30,* 58–101.

Gordon, E. E. (1993). *Learning Sequences in Music: Skills, Contents, and Patterns: A Music Learning Theory.* Chicago: GIA Publications.

Haber, R. N., & Haber, L. R. (1988). The chacteristics of eidetic imagery. In D. Fein & L. K. Obler (Eds.), *The Exceptional Brain: Neuropsychology of Talent and Special Abilities* (pp. 218–241). London: Guilford Press.

Hallam, S. (1997). The development of memorisation strategies in musicians. *British Journal of Music Education, 14,* 87–97.

Hughes, E. (1915). Musical memory in piano playing and piano study. *Musical Quarterly, 1,* 592–603.

Kreitner, K. R. (1981). *Modality Strengths and Learning Styles of Musically Talented High School Students.* Unpublished masters dissertation, Ohio State University, Columbus, OH.

Lehmann, A. C. (1997). Acquired mental representations in music performance: Anecdotal and preliminary empirical evidence. In H. Jørgensen & A. C. Lehmann (Eds.), *Does Practice Make Perfect? Current Theory and Research on Instrumental Music Practice* (pp. 141–163). Oslo: Norwegian Academy of Music.

Lehmann, A. C., & Ericsson, K. A. (1995). *Expert pianists' mental representation of memorized music.* Poster presented at the 36th Annual Meeting of the Psychonomic Society, Los Angeles.

Macek, K. (1987). The photographic ear. *Piano Quarterly, 35*(137), 46–48.

Marek, G. R. (1982). Toscanini's memory. In U. Neisser (Ed.), *Memory Observed: Remembering in Natural Contexts* (pp. 508–511). San Francisco: Freeman.

Marcus, A. (1979). *Great Pianists Speak.* Neptune City, NJ: Paganiniana Publications.

Matthay, T. (1926). *On Memorizing and Playing from Memory and on the Laws of Practice Generally.* Oxford: Oxford University Press.

Monahan, B. J. (1978). *The Art of Singing: A Compendium of Thoughts on Singing Published between 1877 and 1927.* London: Scarecrow Press.

Miller, G. A. (1956). The magic number seven, plus or minus two: Some limits on our capacity for processing information. *Psychological Review, 63,* 81–93.

Nuki, M. (1984). Memorization of piano music. *Psychologia, 27,* 157–163.

Pauk, W. (1994). *How to Study in College* (5th ed.). Boston: Houghton-Mifflin.

Persellin, D. C., & Pierce, C. (1988). Association of preference for modality to learning of rhythm patterns in music. *Perceptual and Motor Skills, 67,* 825–826.

Plunkett Greene, H. (1912). *Interpretation in Song.* London: Macmillan.

Price, G. E., & Dunn, R. (1997). *Learning Style Inventory (LSI) Manual.* Lawrence, KS: Price Systems.

Renzulli, J. S., & Dai, D. Y. (2001). Abilities, interests, and styles as aptitudes for learning: A person-situation interaction perspective. In R. J. Sternberg & L.-F. Zhang (Eds.), *Perspectives on Thinking, Learning and Cognitive Styles* (pp. 23–46). Mahwah, NJ: Erlbaum.

Revesz, G. (1925/1999). *The Psychology of a Musical Prodigy.* London: Routledge. (Original work published in 1925).

Ross, E. (1964). Improving facility in music memorization. *Journal of Research in Music Education, 12,* 269–278.

Rubin-Rabson, G. (1937). *The Influence of Analytical Pre-Study in Memorizing Piano Music.* New York: Archives of Psychology.

Sloboda, J. A., & Parker, D. H. (1985). Immediate recall of memories. In P. Howell, I. Cross, & R. West (Eds.), *Musical Structure and Cognition* (pp. 143–167). London: Academic Press.

Sloboda, J. A., Hermelin, B., & O'Connor, N. (1985). An exceptional musical memory. *Music Perception, 3,* 155–170.

Small, G. (2003). *The Memory Bible: Ten Commandments for Keeping your Brain Young.* New York: Hyperion Books.

Sternberg, R. J., & Grigorenko, E. L. (2001). A capsule history of theory and research on styles. In R. J. Sternberg & L.-F. Zhang (Eds.), *Perspectives on Thinking, Learning and Cognitive Styles* (pp. 1–21). Mahwah, NJ: Erlbaum.

Wilding, J., & Valentine, E. (1997). *Superior Memory.* Hove, UK: Psychology Press.

Williamon, A. (1999). The value of performing from memory. *Psychology of Music, 27,* 84–95.

Williamon, A., & Valentine, E. (2002). The role of retrieval structures in memorizing music. *Cognitive Psychology, 44,* 1–32.

Williamon, A., Valentine, E., & Valentine, J. (2002). Shifting the focus of attention between levels of musical structure. *European Journal of Cognitive Psychology, 14,* 493–520.

CHAPTER 8

STRATEGIES FOR SIGHT-READING AND IMPROVISING MUSIC

SAM THOMPSON AND ANDREAS C. LEHMANN

Why discuss sight-reading and improvising together in one chapter? Seeing the title, many musicians would be forgiven for wondering just what could possibly connect the two. This confusion is partially due to the fact that the two skills are normally situated in different performance practices and stylistic areas. Sight-reading has to do with the performance of notated music, mostly from the Western classical repertory, while improvisation is associated with oral traditions, chiefly jazz. Another, arguably no less important factor is that the "creative" aspect of improvisation is usually given the most emphasis in discussions. Improvisation is seen to be an art that has the potential for individuality and self-expression. Sight-reading, by contrast, is regarded as a largely mechanical task, undoubtedly worthy but essentially unimaginative. However, from a psychological perspective the two skills take place under similar constraints, both involving the performance of musical material without overt preparation. The aim of this chapter is to show how taking this kind of analytical approach can be useful in thinking about ways to enhance ability in both sight-reading and improvising. In making the comparison, it is hoped to shed light on a perplexing question: how can one perform at a level usually encountered in a rehearsed performance, *without* preparing explicitly for the particular performance?

Psychomotor skills (which can be defined, loosely, as deliberate physical movements of the body; see also Chapter 14) are often described as being "open" or "closed." A rehearsed musical performance can be said to be a closed skill in the sense that the same movement has to be performed in an essentially unchanging environment—to draw a sporting analogy, this is something akin to the task facing a competitive swimmer. Improvisation and sight-reading, on the other hand, are open skills in that they require the performer to *adapt* constantly to a changing environment—something more like the task that confronts a soccer player. While swimmers can hone their technique, endurance, and strength, and develop strategies to cope with the psychological demands of the situation, there is no uncertainty about the activity itself—successful performance in a race is a matter of executing a particular, well-practiced motor sequence as fluently as possible. Soccer players never know ahead of the game exactly what combination of motor sequences they will be required to execute, and so must have the ability to adapt their particular technical skills quickly to the situation at hand.

In sight-reading, the musician is confronted with unfamiliar music and has to play through it at first sight, imitating—as convincingly as possible—a rehearsed performance with regard to tempo and expression. Improvisation is even more adventurous in that the performer has to chart unknown territory, sometimes in the company of other musicians who are also improvising. However, unlike sight-reading, which covers a clearly delineated range of activities, improvisation is a broad category ranging from free jazz (with virtually no points of reference) to highly patterned improvisation in classical music, not to mention the many complex types of improvisation outside Western classical music traditions (see Nettl & Russell, 1998).

There are several questions that arise from the difference between an extensively rehearsed and memorized performance, and a sight-read or improvised performance:

- What are the psychological mechanisms that underpin the ability to perform music without rehearsal?
- How are such abilities acquired?
- How can performance in sight-reading and improvising be enhanced?

These questions guide the present survey of the two skills, as they are investigated from two perspectives: (1) the underlying psychological processes and (2) practical strategies for skill acquisition and enhancement. Throughout the chapter, a number of hints are given to the practitioner; some of these are proposals for actual activities, while others offer wider suggestions for increasing knowledge and understanding of the task at hand.

Two general observations should be made at this point. Firstly, research on sight-reading has tended to focus almost exclusively on music of the Western classical tradition. Similarly, the greater part of research in improvisation has focused on American jazz styles. In the case of sight-reading, this is less of a deficit than it might appear since, as discussed below, the classical tradition is more or less unique in identifying and prizing the skill at all (or, indeed, in having a notation system capable of supporting it). With improvisation, the focus on jazz has tended to obscure the many other musical practices that involve a strong improvisational element. Despite these limitations, the intention in this chapter is to make suggestions that are broadly applicable across styles. The second observation is that in both domains the great majority of research has been conducted using keyboard instruments. This is little more than a function of the available technology; clearly it is not just keyboard players who sight-read and improvise. Again, therefore, the suggestions made are intended to have wide, cross-instrument relevance.

8.1   Comparing sight-reading and improvisation

For the purposes of this chapter, it is interesting to note that there is a historical link between improvisation and sight-reading. Sight-reading became more common at roughly the same point that improvisation, as a concert spectacle, began to lose popularity. Although sight-reading was always important in ensemble situations, be it in church choirs or various orchestras associated with the nobility, solo performances were generally given by composers who would perform their own works and then improvise in various ways (there are many reports, for example, of J. S. Bach's renowned ability to improvise a fugue on themes suggested by the audience). Toward the middle of the eighteenth century, however, emerged the virtuoso—a solo performer who was not (primarily, or at all) a composer but was instead heralded for his or her skilled and insightful performances of music by others. In some cases, feats of difficult sight-reading replaced improvisation as the performer's favorite "party trick." These days, of course, classical musicians rarely sight-read in public at all, and certainly do not advertise the fact if they are doing so. Sections 8.1.1 and 8.1.2 consider the two skills separately, in terms of the psychological processes that underpin them.

8.1.1   Task analysis: Sight-reading

Any performance of music in which the player reads from a written score could be construed as "sight-reading" in a literal sense. However, in its most common usage the term refers to the practice of playing a piece of music directly from the score on first encounter or after brief rehearsal (see Lehmann & McArthur, 2002, and Lehmann, in press, for reviews of the sight-reading literature). Defined thus, sight-reading is a normal part of the musical experience of classically trained musicians, especially pianists who work as accompanists. Ability at sight-reading involves the capacity to play the music accurately and fluently (i.e. without pauses or breaks in the musical flow) at an acceptable tempo and with adequate musical expression.

Examination systems such as the graded syllabi of the Associated Board of the Royal Schools of Music have traditionally included a statutory test of sight-reading at all levels. Rigorous assessments of sight-reading ability at the keyboard (such as reading an orchestral score at sight or sight-reading vocal scores in multiple clefs) are commonly found in higher education music courses and are usually compulsory for all students, irrespective of whether or not keyboard is their favored instrument. It is not hard to see how the ability to sight-read competently is likely to be useful in a number of common musical environments; professional musicians, for example, particularly those whose work involves recording sessions, frequently find themselves required to sight-read a new score.

Because of the dominance of notation in the Western classical tradition, sight-reading remains an almost exclusively Western classical skill, although music notation is also used in other musical styles and cultures for didactic purposes. Music in the classical tradition is learned and passed-down through notated sources, whereas many other musics are preserved aurally or, increasingly, in the form of sound recordings. While it is the case that, for example, rock music can be described in Western notation (with limitations), rock musicians do not typically learn through notation or perform from it, and so often have little need to sight-read even if the music is available to them in a notated form.

The most immediate psychological observation about sight-reading is that it is an "online" activity, which is to say it requires that a sequence of movements be produced in response to a succession of visual stimuli presented in real-time. The speed of stimulus presentation is a function of the chosen tempo and the relative density of musical events. Although any musician could read anything given enough time and a slow enough tempo, an effective minimum speed for a particular piece is generally dictated by stylistic convention. Moreover, to maintain fluency it is not possible to pause without interrupting the musical stream—and this is one important way in which musical sight-reading differs from superficially similar skills such as typing from copy or reading aloud. The sequence of events is thus, (1) perceiving notation, (2) processing it, and finally (3) executing the resulting motor program.

Perceiving notation

Perceiving notation is an intricate process involving low-level perception routines as well as higher-level cognitive functioning. The lower-level routines are most likely acquired in the same way that we learn to read, namely by slowly deciphering individual symbols at first and gradually increasing fluency (although, it is worth noting that sight-reading music and reading text involve different neurological processes; see Sargent *et al.*, 1992.) It is only after these initial routines have been developed that sight-reading—in the sense considered here—really begins.

Our eyes do not function like a photo camera, but rather more like a flashlight searching around in the dark. Gaze is directed at the page of printed material and only a small circular portion in the middle of our field of vision is in focus at any one time. This area is called the fovea, and around it lays a blurry circle called the parafovea (see Raynor & Pollatsek, 1989, for a description in the context of reading). What we experience as a continuous and coherent picture is actually the result of piecemeal information gathering by our visual system combined with a good deal of cognitive processing to fit it all together. The individual gazes, of which there are roughly five per second, and the connecting intermediate trajectories constitute what is known generically as occulomotor behavior. In sight-reading, this means that the score has to be assembled by jumping to different places on the page trying to find the relevant information.

A number of studies have investigated the movement of the eyes during sight-reading (see Lehmann, in press, for a review). From this research, it has become clearly established that unskilled readers differ markedly from experienced readers with regard to their looking behavior. In particular, better readers tend to look further ahead of the point where they are currently playing and do not fixate on every note as beginners tend to. There are many variables that could account for these differences, some physiological, but since looking behavior is not under conscious control, it is probably safe to assume that the effects of training and expertise play a major role.

♦ Perception is an interactive process of gathering information from the environment and responding to it. As such, "practicing" looking by, for example, rolling your eyes with the head still will do little to change the behavior of the occulomotor system during sight-reading. You can train the system to be more efficient, but only by performing realistic, interactive tasks.

♦ How far do you look ahead while sight-reading? A number of studies have shown that accomplished sight-readers consistently read around six or seven notes ahead (in a single-line melody), while novices read only two or three notes ahead. Try closing your eyes at random when reading and carrying on as far as you can—how many notes did you manage to play successfully?

♦ Think carefully about phrase boundaries and bar lines. Sloboda (1984) has suggested that the perceptual span of better sight-readers changes adaptively with the music. If the distance to the end of a phrase is shorter than six or seven notes, then the perceptual span decreases. In other words, skilled sight-readers are not just reading the music ahead of them note by note, but *interpreting* aspects of the musical structure first and changing their perception routines accordingly. Do you know where the end of the phrase is before you arrive at it?

♦ Novice sight-readers often find the ends of lines problematic, due to having to make large eye movements across the page. If you find that you frequently lose fluency while moving down a line, spend time practicing these moments particularly.

Cognitive processing of visual information

Research established early on that, in sight-reading tasks where a brief musical stimulus is presented, better and more experienced sight-readers remember longer sequences than less skilled players (Bean, 1938). This effect has been replicated several times since (e.g. W. B. Thompson, 1985). Integrating these results with the findings from research in eye movement implies that experts make eye movements that allow for a more efficient encoding of note sequences. This in turn leads to better memory for presented note sequences and a longer eye–hand span, since a longer lasting memory will facilitate encoding of a motor program.

These findings point toward a theoretical framework known as *long-term working memory* (Ericsson & Kintsch, 1995), which was developed as a general model of memory expertise in domains of skill such as chess playing and has more recently been applied to music (e.g. Williamon & Valentine, 2002). The long-term working memory concept proposes that during performance, experts are able to access the contents of their long-term memory (analogous to a computer hard drive) with an ease that is typically possible only for the contents of working memory (analogous to RAM in computers; see Chapter 7). In brief, experts acquire a kind of high-speed connection to long-term memory through extensive training, where previously only slower transmission rates existed. However, this high-speed connection is restricted to the domain in which the expert works (e.g. baroque music for a baroque specialist). This facilitating process has been shown to be a direct function of extensive training.

Related to memory is pattern recognition. Combinations of notes that occur frequently within a style are, over time, stored in memory as discrete entities rather than sets of individual events. They can then be easily retrieved from memory and used in novel contexts. An expert musician may see a certain familiar scale and immediately recognize what to play without further looking or thinking (see Waters *et al.*, 1997). More than this, though, different musical styles have their own characteristic patterns of notes and rhythms that recur and that are instantly recognizable from the page. This essentially means that highly familiar stimuli "stick out" more and attract attention immediately without the performer having to do much. Expert sight-readers can identify familiar patterns (e.g. a series of diminished seventh arpeggios) extremely quickly and with minimal cues.

Experienced sight-readers do not just take in larger chunks of visual information than those less experienced, they also generate more accurate predictions about what may be coming up next. This process encompasses mechanisms of inference, anticipation, and guessing. Evidence for these mechanisms comes from at least three different sources. Firstly, sight-readers can be misled into making so-called *proof-reader's errors* (Sloboda, 1976), whereby they play notes that are not really there becuase they identify a familiar pattern without looking at the individual notes. (Did you spot a misspelling in the previous sentence? If not, that is a proofreader's error.) Secondly, experts are relatively more distracted by unexpected information (Waters *et al.*, 1997), suggesting that they rely on the context (e.g. harmonies) more in planning ahead. Finally, good sight-readers perform better on tasks where they are required to fill in blank spaces in a score with an appropriate note (Lehmann & Ericsson, 1996).

◆ The ability to recognize and infer patterns is based on a profound knowledge of the style in question. Listen often to the styles you have to sight-read, so that your anticipations become informed. With people in whom this is well entrenched, it is often interpreted as "intuition."

◆ Sometimes a scale or familiar pattern may contain unusual notes. Here, errors may occur in seemingly "easy" passages. If you are experienced, do not let yourself be completely guided by what you expect. Often you are correct, but sometimes you may not be. Beginners should try the opposite, namely to let the musical context help them anticipate what is coming up. Nobody can see everything on the page, and sometimes a "best guess" is all there is time for.

Generation of movements

While sight-reading does require the online generation of movements, clearly much of the material actually played will not be totally novel to the player. As musicians become familiar with a musical style they acquire a large body of knowledge in the form of common patterns, allowing them to draw on a storehouse of previously established motor sequences; for example, scale and arpeggio patterns are easy to play at sight because most musicians already know how to play them. However, sight-reading is more than simply a chaining together of predetermined motor sequences—as argued above, it is an open skill. It seems that some sort of plan must be formed *before* the action is actually executed.

In fact, performance on a musical instrument is an example of a task that implies the so-called *motor program* account of action control (Lashley, 1951). In this account, complex movements are specified by cognitive representations of individual actions, arranged hierarchically into programs. These programs are assembled before the actual execution phase and are best thought of as cognitive "maps" of the actions that are required.

Debate in motor programming research from the musical perspective has centered largely on how the timing of movement sequences is controlled. After all, one of the distinctive things about musical performance as opposed to other, outwardly similar skills is that the timing of actions is paramount (in typing, for example, the relative timing of keystrokes is irrelevant). By contrast, playing the right notes of a piece in the right order is not enough to give a musical result. But how are motor sequences timed? There are several possibilities, of which the most popular is the "internal timekeeper" model, which proposes that individual components of the motor program are triggered at the correct moment by comparison with an imagined beat (see Palmer, 1997).

◆ When practicing sight-reading, choose a tempo at which you think you will be able to play the most difficult parts, and go no faster.

The precise mechanisms by which complex motor programs are constructed and converted into movements remain to be fully explicated. For the purposes of this chapter, however, it is enough to note that while musicians' knowledge of a musical style is primarily acquired through playing, factors unrelated to the musical material itself may impact on the motor program requirements. On woodwind and brass instruments, there is generally only one way of playing a particular note, and thus there are no alternatives open to the performer regarding which finger to use or where to position themselves in relation to the instrument. By contrast, keyboard and string instruments have a significantly greater freedom. This means that motor programs on these instruments must take account of ergonomic considerations. Sloboda *et al.* (1998) have provided evidence that expert sight-readers tend to select the most efficient, ergonomically viable fingering when sight-reading, enabling them to play faster and more fluently. For pianists, then, fingering choice may indeed be a determining factor of sight-reading expertise. In some cases, of course, there may be several alternative ways to play a given passage, all of them feasible.

◆ If applicable to your instrument, practice common patterns using as many different fingerings as you can.

8.1.2   Task analysis: Improvisation

Improvisation is most commonly discussed in the context of jazz, although many other musical styles incorporate a greater or lesser degree of improvisation (e.g. rock guitar solos and Indian art music; see Pressing, 1984). As with sight-reading, there is no one single concept of improvisation, but rather a spectrum of activities that involve improvisational elements. However, the range of cultures in whose music improvisation plays a part is significantly wider than sight-reading, since non-notated musics are the norm in our world rather than the exception (as we sometimes tend to assume).

Despite the popular cliché, improvisation is anything but "making it up as you go along." Genuinely free improvisation, in which the music has absolutely no externally observable point of reference (or *referent*; Pressing, 1984) is rare and has never become especially popular (the jazz saxophonist Ornette Coleman being perhaps the best-known exponent). Instead, improvised music is typically based around some predetermined structure or form: the chord sequence in jazz, the tune in Celtic folk music, the *maqam* in Islamic and the *raga* in Indian musical traditions, and so on. In each of these styles, some aspect of the music is left undetermined or unrealized—often the lead melodic line—and the performer is expected to improvise an acceptable solution. The acceptability of the improvisation lies in its relation to stylistic conventions and, consequently, appreciation of the improvisation often requires that the listener have an understanding of the stylistic boundaries within which the performer is working.

Good improvising is thus, in one sense, the production of novelty within identifiable constraints.

◆ Have you ever tried improvising? Because improvisation is now so strongly associated with jazz, many classical musicians never even attempt it; however, it is quite possible to improvise in any style. Many of the more obviously improvisational elements in classical music have become less common these days (e.g. improvised cadenzas), but this does not mean that they cannot be revived, even if only for use in practice rather than performance.

◆ Good improvising in any musical genre relies on a thorough knowledge and understanding of the style. The improvisation is successful because of the way it relates to established stylistic norms. It is, therefore, essential for performers to be well-versed with the style in which they wish to improvise.

Pattern chaining versus more complex models

Judging from method books on jazz improvisation, and from hearing amateurs play, one may think that improvising consists simply of chaining together pre-learned patterns. However, the process seems to be more complex than it appears at first sight. Johnson-Laird (1991) was the first to develop a cognitive theory that contradicts the "motif" notion of improvisation. This model assumes the operation of a generative process, somewhat akin to that proposed for speech production. More recently, Johnson-Laird (2002) has developed a model that entails the procedural production of possible patterns according to certain rules. For experts, this process is more or less automatic. The resulting patterns are then subjected to conscious, deliberate evaluation that allows the musician to pick the most successful of the produced patterns. This procedure can account for situational aspects, such as the mood of the audience ("they seemed to like that phrase; I'll do it again"), broader aesthetic considerations ("with these cats, I have to be a lot more sophisticated"), or the response to music just played by another musician in the group. Taking on Johnson-Laird's view means having to rethink the idea of improvisation as simply pulling patterns from a storehouse.

◆ Try to be aware of your thought processes while improvising—what kind of things go through your mind? Do you make conscious decisions about what to play? While some experienced improvisers report achieving so-called "flow" states, in which they are not aware of exerting deliberate control, it seems likely that conscious decision-making is a normal part of skilled improvisation.

Previous knowledge in a secondary function

While successful improvisation is clearly not just a matter of pattern-chaining, it certainly does require a large amount of previous knowledge. This is simply because of lack of time at the moment of production. Having to produce everything during performance would be impossible; therefore, the musician needs to buy time. Here, knowledge can be viewed as having the primary function of serving as a building block during skill acquisition, when production rules and patterns have to be learned. Later, however, this application may serve simply as a subordinate process to the more important goal of making good music. This can be done by either retrieving patterns from memory or by generating adequate patterns using entrenched algorithms (experienced public speakers such as politicians seem to do this quite well). The remaining cognitive resources can then be used to address artistic issues.

◆ Do you have your routines sufficiently well practiced that you could do something else at the same time? Perhaps test yourself by conversing with someone while playing.

Motor programming

As in sight-reading, the improvising musician must be able to generate and execute motor programs "online." However, while the number of variables open to manipulation by the performer seems to be greater in the case of improvised music than sight-reading, their solutions are inevitably expected to be style-specific. Therefore, successful improvising, like sight-reading, relies on the player having access to a large stock of style-specific knowledge, in the form of common patterns and sequences, from which to compile a suitable motor program.

Improvisers tend to program what Schramowski (1973, p. 239) calls "movement images;" they anticipate entire movement sequences that hinge on particularly salient notes. Improvisers are also subject to constraints determined by the physical characteristics of the instrument, which can be obvious (e.g. pianists cannot "bend" notes) or rather more subtle. Furthermore, individual performers will have anatomically or biographically determined typical movement patterns that factor into the equation. A pianist with large hands will be able to play chords and patterns that would not be available to others. The great jazz guitarist Django Reinhard suffered severe burns to his left hand and was forced to adopt a novel technique that used only two fingers on the fretboard; jazz guitarists have subsequently found his style of playing very difficult to imitate.

◆ Observe yourself in a mirror as you improvise; are there distinctive patterns of movement that occur in your playing? Try using particular types of movement as the basis for your improvisation and see what effect this has.

◆ What are the characteristics of your instrument? Spend some time identifying the patterns that "sit under the fingers," and then try improvising without using any of them. Another idea is to attempt to copy improvisations from other instrument. If you are a saxophone player, try playing improvised lines by, say, pianists or trumpet players.

◆ What are your own physical characteristics? Are there capabilities that you have which you do not exploit, or perhaps that you overexploit?

8.1.3   Two sides of the same coin?

From the analyses developed above, it should be clear that sight-reading and improvising have a good deal more in common than might have been initially predicted, and certainly more than their popular descriptions would suggest. To recap: both sight-reading and improvising require the "online" creation and execution of motor program sequences in response to a stimulus. This essentially breaks down into two component

External referent
(e.g. 'strict' sight-reading)

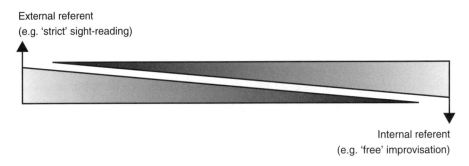

Internal referent
(e.g. 'free' improvisation)

Figure 8.1 Schematic diagram illustrating the difference between sight-reading and improvising in terms of the internal/external nature of their referents. Most real musical tasks fall somewhere between the two extremes.

skills: (1) *planning*, the ability to encode and process information from some stimuli quickly and fluently, and (2) *execution*, the ability to translate those plans into controlled, accurate motor movements.

In this analysis, the key difference between improvisation and sight-reading seems to lie in the nature and extent of the referents that specify what is to be played. Specifically, referents could be characterized as falling between the two extremes of *external* and *internal*. Completely external stimuli would be those with sufficient referents to specify the desired outcome in its entirety, without any freedom available to the player (e.g. in a "strict" sight-reading task the score details every aspect of the music to be performed). Conversely, wholly internal stimuli would be those for which no referent exists other than the performer's own intention.

This relationship can be encapsulated schematically, as illustrated in Figure 8.1. Both extremes are hypothetical. Even the most complex modern notation is not sufficiently specific as to detail every aspect of the musical outcome. As for "free" improvisation, it is certainly debatable whether this is even possible in principle, given the highly accultured experience of most musicians). Nonetheless, typical sight-reading tasks lie toward the "external" end of the scale; similarly, the most commonly discussed improvisation practices lie toward the "internal" end. Taking this perspective on sight-reading and improvising implies at least one provocative hypothesis, namely that a player who is skilled at sight-reading within a given musical style should feasibly be able to improvise within that style after some practice (see McPherson, 1995, for supporting empirical evidence).

8.2   Acquiring and enhancing sight-reading and improvising skills

Research has been slow in answering the practitioner's most pressing question, namely how sight-reading and improvising skills are best learned and improved. The reason may be that common practices seem to suffice in producing satisfactory results on the whole and that, consequently, no one is eager to invest time in researching new ways to improve the acquisition process. Such differences as exist between individuals' sight-reading and improvising abilities are often ascribed to variations in innate disposition.

This somewhat apathetic view is regrettable because it is clear from the relatively little research that does exist that both sight-reading and improvising are amenable to enhancement through structured training (see e.g. Sudnow, 1978; Kornicke, 1995; Lehmann & Ericsson, 1996; Kenny & Gellrich, 2002; Souter, 2002; Hoffmann & Lehmann, 2003). Unfortunately, these findings have barely filtered into music education systems.

8.2.1   Skill acquisition and development

Improving sight-reading is commonly presented as a matter of trial and error, the methodology being simply to practice slowly and gradually build up to the desired speed and complexity. If improvisation is deliberately taught at all, the emphasis is usually on the need to listen to skilled improvisers and copy them; a "mastery through imitation" approach rather similar to the manner in which painting skills were traditionally acquired (see Lisboa *et al.*, in press). In both cases, the mode of learning— and thus the knowledge gained—tends toward being *implicit* rather than *explicit* (i.e. when the individual has conscious access to, and is able to articulate, constituent parts of the skill). While much is known about the differences between good and bad sight-readers, the acquisition of ability in improvisation is still largely uncharted territory, which is probably due to the difficult methodological problems that beset researchers trying to study it.

It is likely that all musical skills (playing by ear, sight-reading, improvisation, playing rehearsed music) improve with time, if the student keeps playing the instrument and rehearses new pieces of music. This prediction is based on the assumption that some transfer occurs from rehearsed music to the other skills. This is hardly surprising, given that all the skills share so many basic requirements. No study has explicitly tested the claim, although McPherson's work (1994, 1995) suggests moderate to large correlations between ability in all these skills. However, despite this transfer it seems likely that significant progress can be made in performance of the individual skills when they are trained separately.

Individual differences among piano sight-readers have been related to varying amounts of sight-reading experience (Kornicke, 1995) and to more rigorous measures of sight-reading training (Lehmann & Ericsson, 1993, 1996). Better sight-readers on the piano tend to have accumulated many hours as accompanists and have a larger repertory of pieces they can use for accompanying. It might seem that one follows from the other, but the effects of the two factors (experience accompanying and repertory size) have been shown to be statistically independent. Most pianists start accompanying about 3 years after beginning piano lessons and work with instrumentalists and singers that they can technically accommodate at the piano. Gradually, their accompanying becomes more demanding. As this cycle continues, sight-reading skills improve, as do general pianist skills.

Not a great deal is known from a scientific standpoint about how to acquire improvisation skills. Hargreaves *et al.* (1991) found that novices tended to be much more detail-oriented than experts, who had a plan before they started playing. Also interesting is Sudnow's (1978) account, which documents how the tedious and effortful process of improvisation becomes quasi-automatic, and how eventually the performer (in this case Sudnow himself) merely watches his hands do surprising things while concentrating on aspects that may or may not bear relation to them (see Kenny & Gellrich, 2002). As discussed above, successful improvising in jazz is highly contingent upon a large knowledge base of style-specific patterns. At this point, however, it is not really known how learning to use these patterns ultimately results in innovative and fluent performance, and not merely a stringing together of overlearned patterns (see Johnson-Laird, 2002). Kenny and Gellrich (2002) call for *deliberate practice* and *transcendence*, whereby the first is a process of amassing a large knowledge base through systematic practice routines, and the second is "understood as a heightened state of consciousness that moves beyond the confines of (thereby often jettisoning) the accumulated knowledge base itself" (p. 124). What is not clear is precisely how to get from one stage to the other.

The relative paucity of applied pedagogical research in either area makes it difficult to recommend specific practice strategies with confidence. The following suggestions, then, are intended as ideas to stimulate practice rather than tried-and-tested methods for improving.

Acquiring the knowledge base

♦ This has been noted above, but is so important it merits repetition—*know the style of music in which you wish to play.* Successful performance on both skills depends absolutely and utterly on having a wide knowledge of the style in question.

♦ You can acquire knowledge of a style without having to play it. Both listening to recordings and looking at scores are excellent ways of becoming acquainted with a range of music. Try to ask yourself questions about what you hear. How is it put together? What are its characteristic features and patterns?

♦ Devise your own exercises. While there are many books of technical exercises available, it can be more beneficial to create your own. This requires not only playing the exercise(s) until you achieve a high level of competence, but also analyzing the music to extract the most relevant aspects from it. This, again, is a good way to expand the knowledge base.

♦ Sing, hum, or whistle. A common frustration of learning to improvise or sight-read is having a strong idea of what you wish to play, but being unable physically to find the notes. Ultimately, of course, perceptual and cognitive skills will have to meet with motor skills in order to produce a successful improvisation or sight-read performance. However, research suggests that the two areas can develop independently, especially at early stages. Try sight-singing, or singing an improvised melody line.

Things to consider when practicing

♦ McPherson (1994) has suggested that better sight-readers are able to assimilate more information about the score *before* beginning to play than those who are less skilled. In other words, they scan the music and quickly notice features such as time and key signature, phrase structure, passages likely to be problematic, and so on. Try scanning a new piece for a few seconds and then writing down what you remember about it. How much information did you gather on first glance?

♦ The illusion of a well thought-out interpretation in sight-reading comes from applying rules of musical expression, and arguably these "performance rules" can be deliberately learned in much the same way that we learn the more fundamental parameters of music like the meaning of pitch and rhythm symbols (see Chapter 13 of this volume). Think about what some of these rules could be by analyzing a rehearsed performance. For example, what usually happens to the tempo at major cadence points in classical music?

♦ Be aware of what your referents are. When improvising, think carefully about what requirements your improvisation needs to meet. Do you need to arrive and finish on a particular beat or highlight a particular chord change? If you are sight-reading, it can be useful to reflect on the information that is *not* provided—what alternatives are open to you in your interpretation?

Some general thoughts

♦ Do not be put off if things are difficult at first. Initially, sight-reading and improvising take a great deal of cognitive effort, but by practicing, you are gradually making automatic many of the processes that at first seem to require a lot of thinking.

♦ Both improvising and sight-reading require a certain degree of nerve and (at least at the beginning) self-confidence. Because of this, both are also good ways of learning to take artistic risks, making you rely on your own abilities and technical facilities. The confidence to take risks at the right moment can be learned, like anything else.

♦ There is little evidence to suggest that "talent" has anything much to do with proficiency in sight-reading or improvising. Rather, it is a case of diligent and inventive practice.

8.2.2   Identifying problems

After the initial stages of improvement, it is common for skills to reach a plateau where the same problems seem to recur, and it is difficult to make further progress. If this happens, it can be useful to try to understand the nature and causes of these problems; examining errors provides a means for players to make explicit the implicit knowledge they possess. By identifying the types of error to which they are prone, players can become aware of weaknesses in their technical ability and develop strategies that focus on these specific areas.

General theories of failure in human performance (e.g. Reason, 1990) posit that errors can arise from one of two sources. Either the action itself can be incorrectly performed (this is often labeled an *execution failure* or a *slip*), or the action can prove to have been insufficiently specified to achieve its intended outcome, correct execution notwithstanding (this is a *planning failure* or *mistake*). This distinction accords well with the analyses of sight-reading and improvising given above. Note also that in both cases the *intention* of the person performing the action is critical to determining whether an error has taken place.

The types of errors that can be made in sight-reading may be usefully thought of as arising from either misreading (where the error occurs during the processing stage) or misexecution (where the error occurs during the execution stage). In terms of the distinction between mistakes and slips, a wrong note caused by misreading seems to be a mistake in that it reflects the correct execution of a flawed plan. By contrast, the case of a correct note being misstruck (e.g. on a piano keyboard) is a slip, as it reflects not a failure of planning but of execution (see Thompson *et al.*, 2002, for further discussion of this distinction).

This system can provide a useful method of self-diagnosis. By making careful note of the types of error that they commit most frequently, players may be able to identify the particular aspects of sight-reading that are causing problems and in most need of work. This in turn could prompt the development of appropriate exercises focusing on that particular aspect, perhaps along the lines suggested earlier in this chapter.

◆ There is more to errors than just wrong notes. Record yourself sight-reading and then listen to the mistakes you made. Try dividing them into categories; for example, incorrect rhythm, incorrect note, note misstruck, and so on. Then, in each case, try to decide whether the error occurred due to misreading (e.g. the number of leger lines), forgetting (e.g. an accidental from earlier in the bar), or failed execution (e.g. missing the key). Does a pattern emerge?

The issue of making errors in improvised music is at once the same and rather more complex than in sight-reading. While there are "no wrong notes in jazz, just possibilities," conceptually speaking there is not much difference between errors in sight-reading and errors in improvising. It is perfectly possible to claim that an error has occurred in an improvised performance when a player either fails to execute a passage in the way he or she intended, or else deliberately plays a passage in such a way that he or she later regards to be unsuccessful (e.g. due to an incorrect anticipation of the harmonic progression). The difficulty arises in trying to identify precisely what the intention was in the first place, and at what stage in the process a failure occurred that led to it being unsatisfactorily realized. Unlike in the sight-reading situation, there may be little or no outward clue as to what was actually intended, and this is something about which players themselves often find it difficult or even impossible to be explicit. Some educated guesswork may help but necessarily relies on *a priori* knowledge of the player's personal style and musical habits. To those only familiar with "traditional" jazz, the modal improvisations of Miles Davis over otherwise functional tonal harmony might sound like a succession of wrong notes played with haphazard rhythm. The kind of self-analysis recommended for improving sight-reading may be a profitable exercise for those concerned with enhancing their improvisational skills; however, individual instances of error may be hard to identify.

◆ There need be no contradiction between improvising with originality and having conscious awareness of what you want to play. Much colloquial discussion of improvising speaks as if it is a mystical process by which notes come "from within"—this is just a function of conscious and deliberate processes becoming automated over time. Do not be afraid of thinking about what you play.

◆ As with sight-reading, using recordings is often the best way to analyze your own playing. When listening to yourself improvise, highlight the areas of the improvisation that you are unhappy with and try to work out precisely what you played, and what you were intending to play.

◆ Sometimes when improvising you do not make errors as such, but feel that what you are playing is unoriginal or otherwise unsatisfying. If this happens, try imposing artificial constraints on your playing (for example, only allowing yourself to play within a certain range, or deliberately avoiding certain notes). This can force you to take your improvisation in different directions by breaking your so-called "mental set."

8.3   Conclusions

The most crucial challenge in the mastery of either sight-reading or improvisation is to maximize the use of the knowledge base, both by becoming as familiar as possible with the musical style in question and by mastering the motor sequences that are required to execute the patterns that typically occur. The more stylistically relevant patterns are "under the fingers," the more one's limited cognitive resources will be free for use in artistic decision-making or for dealing with unexpected performance problems. A dividing factor between sight-reading and improvising is that the ultimate goal of the improviser is to become a uniquely recognizable artist with a distinct personal voice, whereas the goal of sight-reading is to create the perfect illusion of a rehearsed performance despite the lack of rehearsal. A common factor is the necessary ability to adapt skills to a changing environment.

It seems likely that many musicians would benefit from spending more time engaged in both sight-reading and improvising, and within a range of musical styles. They are not mysterious and extraordinary feats of skill, out on their own in terms of requirements. On the contrary, they are heavily reliant on the same knowledge and psychomotor skills that underpin successful performance, memorization, and (to an extent) ensemble playing. Certainly, they are both useful abilities for the musician to possess, and in some cases they are essential ones. More than this, however, they are skills that—if properly and diligently practiced—can develop intuition and bring new levels of musical awareness. Even for the musician who does not need, or dare, to engage in sight-reading or improvising outside the practice room, the potential benefits to their overall musical ability are clear. One could regard them as enhancement strategies in themselves.

Further information and reading

Kenny, B. J., & Gellrich, M. (2002). Improvisation. In R. Parncutt & G. E. McPherson (Eds.), *The Science and Psychology of Music Performance: Creative Strategies for Teaching and Learning* (pp. 117–134). Oxford: Oxford University Press.

Hill, P. (2002). From score to sound. In J. Rink (Ed.), *Musical Performance: A Guide to Understanding* (pp. 129–143). Cambridge: Cambridge University Press.

Lehmann, A. C., & McArthur, V. (2002). Sight-reading. In R. Parncutt & G. E. McPherson (Eds.), *The Science and Psychology of Music Performance: Creative Strategies for Teaching and Learning* (pp. 135–150). Oxford: Oxford University Press.

Rayner, K., & Pollatsek, A. (1989). *The Psychology of Reading*. Hillsdale, NJ: Erlbaum.

References

Bean, K. L. (1938). An experimental approach to the reading of music. *Psychological Monographs, 50*, 1–80.

Ericsson, K. A., & Kintsch, W. (1995). Long-term working memory. *Psychological Review, 102*, 211–245.

Hargreaves, D. J., Cork, C. A., & Setton, T. (1991). Cognitive strategies in jazz improvisation: An exploratory study. *Canadian Journal of Research in Music Education, 33*, 47–54.

Hoffmann, A., & Lehmann, A. C. (2003). Anfänger und Profis bei der Improvisation: Unterschiede als Wegweiser für Übung und Unterricht [Experts and novices in improvisation: Differences as a guide for practice and teaching]. *Üben & Musizieren, 20*, 35–42.

Johnson-Laird, P. N. (1991). Jazz improvisation: A theory at the computational level. In P. Howell & R. West & I. Cross (Eds.), *Representing Musical Structure* (pp. 291–325). London: Academic Press.

Johnson-Laird, P. N. (2002). How jazz musicians improvise. *Music Perception, 19*, 415–442.

Kenny, B. J., & Gellrich, M. (2002). Improvisation. In R. Parncutt & G. E. McPherson (Eds.), *The Science and Psychology of Music Performance: Creative Strategies for Teaching and Learning* (pp. 117–134). Oxford: Oxford University Press.

Kornicke, L. E. (1995). An exploratory study of individual difference variables in piano sight-reading achievement. *Quarterly Journal of Music Teaching and Learning, 6*, 56–79.

Lashley, K. S. (1951). The problem of serial order in behavior. In L. A. Jeffress (Ed.), *Cerebral Mechanisms in Behavior: The Hixon Symposium* (pp. 112–136). New York: Wiley.

Lehmann, A. C. (in press). Vomblattspiel und Notenlesen [Sight-reading and note reading]. In H. Stoffer & R. Oerter (Eds.), *Enzyklopädie der Psychologie*: Vol. D/VII/1. *Allgemeine Musikpsychologie*. Göttingen, Germany: Hogrefe.

Lehmann, A. C., & Ericsson, K. A. (1993). Sight-reading ability of expert pianists in the context of piano accompanying. *Psychomusicology, 12*, 182–195.

Lehmann, A. C., & Ericsson, K. A. (1996). Structure and acquisition of expert accompanying and sight-reading performance. *Psychomusicology, 15*, 1–29.

Lehmann, A. C., & McArthur, V. (2002). Sight-reading. In R. Parncutt & G. E. McPherson (Eds.), *The Science and Psychology of Music Performance: Creative Strategies for Teaching and Learning* (pp. 135–150). Oxford: Oxford University Press.

Lisboa, T., Williamon, A., Zicari, M., & Eiholzer, H. (in press). Mastery through imitation. *Musicæ Scientiæ*.

McPherson, G. E. (1994). Factors and abilities influencing sightreading skill in music. *Journal of Research in Music Education, 42*, 217–231.

McPherson, G. E. (1995). The assessment of musical performance: Development and validation of five new measures. *Psychology of Music, 23*, 142–161.

Nettl, B., & Russell, M. (Eds.). (1998). *In the Course of Performance: Studies in the World of Musical Improvisation*. Chicago: University of Chicago Press.

Palmer, C. (1997). Music performance. *Annual Review of Psychology, 48*, 115–138.

Pressing, J. (1984). Cognitive processes in improvisation. In W. R. Crozier & A. J. Chapman (Eds.), *Cognitive Processes in the Perception of Art* (pp. 345–363). Amsterdam: Elsevier.

Rayner, K., & Pollatsek, A. (1989). *The Psychology of Reading*. Hillsdale, NJ: Erlbaum.

Reason, J. (1990). *Human Error.* Cambridge: Cambridge University Press.

Sargent, J., Zuck, E., Terriah, S., & MacDonald, B. (1992). Distributed neural network underlying musical sight-reading and keyboard performance. *Science, 257,* 106–109.

Schramowski, H. (1973). Schaffenspsychologische Untersuchungen zur instrumentalen Improvisation [Psychology of creative behavior regarding instrumental improvisation]. *Beiträge zur Musikwissenschaft, 15,* 235–251.

Sloboda, J. A. (1976). The effect of item position on the likelihood of identification by inference in prose reading and music reading. *Canadian Journal of Psychology, 30,* 228–236.

Sloboda, J. A. (1984). Experimental studies of music reading: A review. *Music Perception, 2,* 222–236.

Sloboda, J. A., Clarke, E. F., Parncutt, R., & Raekallio, M. (1998). Determinants of fingering choice in piano sight-reading. *Journal of Experimental Psychology: Human Perception and Performance, 24,* 185–203.

Souter, T. (2002). Manipulating working memory to improve sight-reading skills. In C. Stevens, D. Burnham, G. McPherson, E. Schubert, & J. Renwick (Eds.), *Proceedings of the Seventh International Conference on Music Perception and Cognition* (pp. 639–642). Adelaide, Australia: Causal Productions.

Sudnow, D. (1978). *Ways of the Hand: The Organisation of Improvised Conduct.* London: Routledge and Kegan Paul.

Thompson, S., Valentine, E., & Williamon, A. (2002). Error patterns in piano sight-reading. In C. Stevens, D. Burnham, G. McPherson, E. Schubert, & J. Renwick (Eds.), *Proceedings of the Seventh International Conference on Music Perception and Cognition* (pp. 643–646). Adelaide, Australia: Causal Productions.

Thompson, W. B. (1985). *Sources of Individual Differences in Music Sight-Reading Skill.* Unpublished doctoral dissertation, University of Missouri, Columbia, MO.

Waters, A. J., Underwood, G., & Findlay, J. M. (1997). Studying expertise in music reading: Use of a pattern-matching paradigm. *Perception and Psychophysics, 59,* 477–488. .

Williamon, A., & Valentine, E. (2002). The role of retrieval structures in memorizing music. *Cognitive Psychology, 44,* 1–32.

PART III

TECHNIQUES AND INTERVENTIONS

CHAPTER 9

PHYSICAL FITNESS

ADRIAN H. TAYLOR AND DAVID WASLEY

The link between a healthy body and healthy mind is not a new concept for optimizing performance and general functioning in life. Recent acknowledgment of this has come from violinist Maxim Vengerov in a television documentary, who noted: "I try to work out regularly. Keeping fit as a musician is important" (NVC Arts, 1998). Indeed, physical *inactivity* is not something for which the human body was designed; however, in modern life, it is all too easy to become enticed by technological and social change that can remove opportunities to be physically active. As a result, sedentary (or "hypo-kinetic") related health problems seem to be dramatically on the rise (Sallis & Owen, 1999; US DHHS, 1996).

Across the broad spectrum of educational and professional music performance contexts, general physical fitness is an area that receives surprisingly little formal emphasis. Admittedly, the connections between physical exercise, personal well-being, and performance are easy to overlook. Until recently, in fact, this link has been largely ignored by researchers, with only scant evidence in the current literature on how physical and psychological well-being can interact for the betterment of the musician.

This chapter is broadly about these links and is written for performers and anyone else responsible for enhancing the well-being and performance of musicians. Its aim is to introduce applications of physical activity to music and to explore how practitioners can integrate exercise into their lifestyle in ways that can optimize their skills. It considers how different aspects of physical activity—including frequency, intensity, duration, and type—impact on physiological and psychological responses to performance, focusing primarily on the well-documented health benefits of moderate intensity, aerobic-type exercise (see Table 9.1 for typical examples of vigorous, moderate, and low-intensity activities). However, because of the absence of literature directly applied to musicians, much of the initial evidence and rationale behind the music-specific benefits are drawn from other fields. Nevertheless, research findings from recent studies with musicians are presented in which the effects of both regular and single sessions of exercise (just before performance) have been examined. The results confirm Vengerov's observation and support the notion that exercise can give the musician valuable insight and tools for managing the demands of being a performing artist.

9.1 Background

Exercise scientists and epidemiologists have, in the past 50 years, systematically accumulated a considerable body of knowledge about the benefits of physical activity, to

Table 9.1 Examples of vigorous, moderate, and light exercise, sports, and general physical activity (adapted from Blair *et al.*, 1985)

Vigorous	Moderate	Light
Exercise and sports	*Exercise and sports*	*Exercise and sports*
(if out of breath or sweaty)	(if not out of breath or sweaty)	(if not out of breath or sweaty)
Aerobics	Aerobics	Bowls
Cycling	Cycling	Darts
Racquetball/squash	Golf	Fishing
Running	Swimming	Golf
Soccer	Soccer	Pool/snooker
Swimming	Table Tennis	Table tennis
Tennis	Tennis	Long walks (average pace)
	Long walks (brisk or fast pace)	
General physical activity	*General physical activity*	*General physical activity*
Occupations that involve	Occupations that are active but	Occupations that are not
frequent climbing, lifting,	not vigorous	entirely sedentary
or carrying heavy loads	Heavy "do it yourself"	Light "do it yourself"
	activities (e.g. mixing cement)	activities (e.g. decorating)
	Heavy gardening (e.g. digging)	Light gardening (e.g.
	Heavy housework (e.g. spring	weeding)
	cleaning)	Social dancing
	Social dancing	

the point where a consensus now exists on its impact on many facets of health and well-being. Expected health gains from specific increases in physical activity intensity, duration, frequency, and type have partly been established for:

- cardiovascular disease and associated risk factors, such as obesity, hypertension, and type 2 diabetes
- cancer (Batty & Thune, 2000)
- musculoskeletal problems (Videman *et al.*, 1995; Vuori, 2001)
- osteoporosis (Bonaiuti *et al.*, 2003).
- Dimensions of psychological well-being and mental health, such as reduced anxiety and depression, and enhanced cognitive functioning and self-perceptions (Steptoe & Cox, 1988; Moses *et al.*, 1989; Kubitz *et al.*, 1996; Morgan, 1997; Biddle *et al.*, 2000; Lawlor & Hopker, 2001).

Being overly sedentary can, for instance, triple the risk of cancer and diabetes. At the other end of the continuum of physical activity, it is equally important to consider how physical inactivity impacts on our emotions, mood, and affect; inactivity may lead to negative moods (e.g. restlessness, irritability, fatigue, and depression) and a negative affective state (low activation and high tension or "bottled-up energy"). Guidelines for the amount of physical activity that people should do—musicians included—to prevent health problems associated with an inactive lifestyle have been produced according to the above evidence base (see Pate *et al.*, 1995). The internationally recommended minimum amount for cardiovascular health is to accumulate at least 30 minutes of moderate intensity exercise (e.g. brisk walking) on five or more days per week

(Murphy *et al.*, 2002). A debate still exists about whether it is the number of sessions or total energy expenditure that is more important.

What is evident, however, is that lasting changes take time and are rarely as rapid as people want. Take weight management, for example. It is now accepted that calorie restriction alone is insufficient to bring about long-term, positive weight alterations and body change. Achieving such change requires both increased physical activity as well as a balanced diet, roughly according to the following relationships:

- Weight gain occurs when "energy in" is more than "energy out".
- Weight loss occurs when "energy in" is less than "energy out".
- Weight stability is achieved when "energy in" equals "energy out".

Here, "energy in" is the food and drink one consumes; "energy out" is the physical activity and daily living energy (i.e. metabolic rate) of the individual. Importantly, in comparison to diet restriction, physical activity positively stimulates muscular development in a number of ways to deal with the demands placed on the body. Firstly, a change in the balance between fat and lean muscle can be realized. Muscle is denser than fat and takes up less space for an equal amount of weight; thus, individuals who become physically active over a prolonged period experience positive changes in body shape (e.g. tone and firmness, as well as possible reductions in overall weight). Secondly, more muscle is beneficial because it increases metabolism, which in turn impacts on the energy relationships mentioned above. Specifically, a person with more muscle mass is able to eat more than an equivalently weighted person and can still maintain weight stability.

It is worth noting that the general evidence for the health-related benefits of increased physical activity is based on statistical relationships and provides no guarantee for any one individual. Genetics and other environmental factors may limit or refine the predictive power of these statistical relationships. For example, it is possible to find a healthy older person—or a top performer, for that matter—who has never been particularly active. It is therefore common for an individual's vicarious experience to determine levels of motivation for changing lifestyle, rather than relying on health information based on statistics and probability. Nevertheless, the fields of preventive and public health medicine are now beginning to employ strategies for changing the motivations of populations and individuals for adopting a healthy lifestyle.

But how exactly can physical activity offer a positive impact on musical performance? As shown above, there are a number of benefits that can be derived from being physically fit, and certainly, any of these may have a direct or indirect effect on an individual's performance ability. This chapter focuses on what is commonly described as stress or performance anxiety (see also Chapter 1). Individual performers will prepare for a performance in different ways, with each method consciously or subconsciously designed to facilitate the "right" mental and physical state for optimum performance. Performance stress can arise from cognitive appraisal and an imbalance between the perceived demands of the situation and the perceived ability of the performer (Lazarus & Folkman, 1984). In addition, other events outside of the musical setting may cause stress, which can then bear on one's performance state. The challenge of achieving optimum performance is to replicate one's own ideal performance state consistently.

To do this, it is necessary to be calm—yet energized—and confident, and not to be distracted by negative emotions and thoughts. It is typically recommended, therefore, that a pre-performance routine (i.e. the hours just before a performance) be designed to provide consistency in building one's mental and physical state for performance (also see Chapter 12).

Research on the effects of physical fitness on responses to stress has generally focused on two broad types of exercise programs: (1) *chronic exercise*, which is regular exercise participation, and (2) *acute exercise*, which is a single session of exercise (lasting at least 20 minutes) that can be embedded into a pre-performance routine. Firstly, the "cross-stressor hypothesis" suggests that fitter people will show less cardiovascular response to physical and psychological stressors (Sothmann *et al.*, 1996). Chronic exercise improves fitness and, thereby, reduces cardiovascular (e.g. heart rate and blood pressure) and neuroendocrine (e.g. cortisol) response to both physical and psychological stressors. Awareness of reduced physiological arousal may, consequently, result in lower perceived physical symptoms (somatic anxiety) and tension. Secondly, within a pre-performance routine, acute exercise has been shown to impact positively on arousal, anxiety, and other dimensions of affect and mood. Exercise physiologists have long known about post-exercise hypotension (i.e. reduced blood pressure) that can last for several hours after moderate intensity aerobic exercise. Given that some musicians and other performing artists turn to beta-blockers, alcohol, and tranquilizers to cope with the stress from performing (Steptoe & Fidler, 1987; Steptoe, 1989; also see Chapter 14 of this volume), it seems reasonable to ask whether a behavioral approach might be equally effective. From the existing research literature on physical activity and well-being, several key questions emerge in relation to music:

- Is physical activity particularly common among musicians?
- Can physical activity impact on the psychological well-being of musicians (which may, in turn, impact on musical performance), in what are clearly occupationally demanding circumstances?
- Do fitter musicians respond differently to the psychological stress of a musical performance?
- Does engaging in regular exercise change how musicians physiologically and psychologically respond to a performance?
- Can a single session of exercise (within a pre-performance routine) influence physiological and psychological responses to a musical performance?

A top musical performer, like an athlete, should be a finely tuned individual. To date, however, more is known about tuning an athlete than a musician. Nevertheless, the following sections consider the questions raised above, and evidence is presented that weighs up the musical relevance of chronic and acute exercise.

9.2   Chronic exercise

Fitness is usually used to describe an ability to perform a particular task. Being fit as a musician will imply having the necessary endurance, strength, and coordination to function effectively on a specific musical instrument. In exercise physiology, *endurance fitness* is defined by assessing physiological response on an exercise ergometer (i.e. a machine, such as a treadmill or stationary cycle, devised to precisely control exercise intensity). By noting the change in response (e.g. in heart rate) to increments in exercise load/intensity, a measure of endurance fitness can be derived. Some people naturally (due to genetics) have lower cardiovascular responses to physical and psychological stress and at rest. Comparing fit and less fit people on different indicators of psychological well-being is, therefore, limited. Some naturally "fit" people may do little or no exercise and still be assessed as fitter than more active people on standard fitness tests. However, many studies have examined the effects of chronic exercise on psychological well-being, compared with inactive control groups. In one useful review, Biddle *et al.* (2000) conclude that chronic exercise is associated with increases in positive mood and affect (e.g. vigor and activation) and reductions in negative mood (e.g. tension, fatigue, and depression). Mutrie (2000; see also Lawlor & Hopker, 2001) concludes that chronic exercise reduces depression, while Fox (1997, 2000) reviews considerable evidence that shows improved physical self-perceptions and physical self-concept. Boutcher (2000) reports that exercise training improves cognitive functioning (i.e. speed and capacity to process information), and Taylor (2000) has confirmed previous evidence (Petruzzello *et al.*, 1991) that supports a positive effect of chronic exercise on trait anxiety (i.e. a disposition to be anxious). Other research has even begun to show beneficial effects of low to moderate intensity exercise (e.g. brisk walking), lasting only 10 minutes (e.g. Thayer, 1987; Ekkekakis *et al.*, 2000).

One of the complexities of this work is that there is undoubtedly personal meaning attached to exercise. For example, the thought of having to join a group of other exercisers may bring back memories of physical education classes and elicit fear of being breathless. Displaying our bodies in exercise settings may also bring out what is called social physique anxiety. On the other hand, exercise performed in supportive groups or with friends, and which provides a sense of mastery over time (e.g. becoming fitter or improving a movement skill), can facilitate anxiety reduction. The challenge for exercise scientists has been to identify the psychobiological versus psychosocial outcomes of different exercise intensities, durations, and frequencies. Initially, it was believed that the dose of exercise had to be sufficiently high to improve cardiovascular fitness before psychological benefits would accrue. It is now known that this is not necessarily the case. Reductions in trait anxiety can result from regular exercise at low to moderate intensity without observation of an improvement in cardiovascular fitness as determined from a fitness test. However, this finding may be due to the fact that fitter and more active people have tended to be involved in these studies and that there is less opportunity for them to improve anyway. Inactive and less fit people who are generally anxious are likely to improve fitness with chronic exercise of sufficient duration—at least 4 weeks—while concurrent improvements in anxiety will also be evident.

If chronic exercise (particularly of the aerobic type) is to be recommended for reducing one's disposition to be anxious and help manage stress, then some insight needs to be provided as to how this could possibly work. If the same effects could be observed from a more passive form of exercise (e.g. yoga, tai chi, or Alexander technique) with fewer environmental constraints, then it is likely that, disregarding the other physical benefits that accrue from this form of exercise, many would choose the easiest option. However, research has shown that low-intensity exercise does not have the same beneficial effects on health as moderate-intensity exercise, even when carried out for the same duration and frequency. To date, there is a much greater body of knowledge about moderate and vigorous aerobic exercise than less intensive (e.g. yoga, tai chi, and Alexander technique) or resistance exercise (e.g. circuit and weight training), but recent valuable work has begun to examine more closely forms of low-intensity activity that are sustainable, accessible, and popular (e.g. tai chi, particularly among older people).

One possible explanation for the anxiety reducing effects of chronic exercise is distraction. Regular mental focus on something that prevents rumination about ongoing worries and stress can certainly be useful. On the other hand, an exercise that demands only limited information processing may very well not have the same benefits; for example, walking alone at a low intensity can still allow for rumination. More quickly paced exercise forces the mind to think about the physical symptoms of the activity itself. Similarly, exercise with others (at a pace that still enables conversation) or in an environment that distracts or demands attention is also likely to be beneficial. Either way, exercise needs to be performed regularly to develop optimal attention control.

Another explanation is that exercise involves improvements in self-confidence and self-esteem. People may label themselves as "not the sporty kind" or "not very good at exercise." A hierarchical model of physical self-perceptions (Fox, 1997) would suggest that the more negative labels one has, the lower will be the person's self-perception across different domains (e.g. academic, musical, social, and physical). According to this theory, if there is only one domain in which a person feels good about him- or herself (e.g. music performance), then that person's self-esteem will be relatively fragile. Also, self-esteem and neuroticism (i.e. a disposition to be anxious) are negatively related—that is, people with low self-esteem tend to be more anxious. Exercise provides an excellent medium in which to experience mastery under the right conditions. First, performance can be easily assessed and monitored. At exercise facilities, trained staff can help with this, but it is equally easy to monitor improvement alone, anywhere. Assuming there are no health reasons or contraindications to exercise, after a warm up and stretch, a brisk walk or jog can be timed between two fixed points. Regular exercise will lead to improvements in this time or reductions in any perceived negative physical symptoms such a breathlessness or fatigue. More complex monitoring may involve taking a pulse by hand or with a heart rate monitor after the exercise, keeping the time and pace constant across assessments. Following 6–8 weeks of regular exercise, there is likely to be a reduction in heart rate of at least 5–10 beats per minute (bpm), depending on initial levels of fitness. Second, the improvement curve is likely to be particularly great for those who are least active and least fit. The feedback from self-monitoring provides a rapid sense of achievement after only a few sessions and weeks. As a word of caution, the experience of mastery is dependent on "goal orientation." If goals are set that involve comparison with others, then outcomes are often less positive. There are always people who may be better at a given task, so aiming to be better than others can be self-defeating. In contrast, if goals are centered on personal achievement (with self-referenced targets), then this can lead to a sense of mastery with greater improvements in affect and motivation to persist. As a further word of caution, particularly for people who have been sedentary, it is better not to seek rapid gains but to build up the exercise dose slowly.

A final explanation for how exercise reduces anxiety involves various physiological adaptations (for reviews, see Morgan, 1997; Biddle & Mutrie, 2001). Regular exercise participation may change some physiological systems that impact on the subjective appraisal of stress and, hence, on musical performance. Some researchers have focused on how the central nervous system adapts to regular exercise. There is evidence that chronic exercise reduces muscle tension (determined from self-report and electromyography). Stress hormones such as catecholamine (adrenaline and noradrenaline) and corticosteroids (e.g. cortisol) also appear to be reduced over time following chronic exercise. In terms of cardiovascular adaptations, resting heart rate and blood pressure are also reduced. It would also be easy to speculate that improved lung function could aid certain types of musicians (i.e. woodwind or brass players) through enhanced pulmonary or lung function, which often results from aerobic exercise training. Interestingly though, there is little or no literature on the specific physiological benefits of chronic exercise on particular performance specialties.

There have been at least two studies that have considered stress reactivity to a musical performance as a stressor (Abel & Larkin, 1990; Valentine *et al.*, 1995). The music stressor did elicit an increase in heart rate and systolic blood pressure, as might be expected. However, the research did not consider the role of cardiovascular fitness or chronic exercise as a moderator of these effects. Anxious people, smokers, less active people, and those with a family history of hypertension tend to be more responsive to mental and physical challenges. In other words, these people show greater increases (from rest) in cardiovascular indices (e.g. heart rate and blood pressure) in anticipation of and during psychosocial stressors. Some research suggests that following chronic exercise, there are small reductions in cardiovascular reactivity (Taylor, 2000). The importance for musicians is that, as a result of chronic exercise, if smaller changes in physiological symptoms of arousal are perceived, this may lead to lower perceptions of activation and enhanced feelings of calm.

One of the proposed ways in which regular exercise impacts on psychological outcomes may be simply from repeated benefits from single sessions of exercise. In other words, should someone stop exercising, the benefits would be quickly lost. There are mixed views about this; however, a considerable research literature exists on the effects of a single session of exercise on emotions, mood, and affect. The conclusions drawn from this literature are considered and the potential implications for musicians are explored in the next section.

9.3   Acute exercise

Extensive literature surveys (Petruzzello *et al.*, 1991; Taylor, 2000) have concluded that acute exercise can reduce self-reported state anxiety and physiological indices of stress (e.g. blood pressure). Research suggests that the physiological effects of vigorous exercise may last up to 24 hours—but not beyond 2 days—while the psychological impact seems to be more transitory. Stronger anxiety-reducing effects have been observed when the exercise is of moderate intensity, as compared with low and vigorous intensities. From a practical perspective, it is important that exercise should not be thrown blindly into a musician's pre-performance routine without rehearsal and refinement. The time between exercise and performance should depend on fitness and personal preference, gained from experience and trial-and-error before music rehearsals rather than performances. Given the range of emotions and moods attached to a musical performance, and indeed to specific musical works, it is impossible to give a blanket exercise prescription for eliciting optimal psychological states. The use of acute exercise requires individual exploration and experimentation.

There is evidence for an impact on basic affect (founded on reasonably well understood psychophysiological responses to exercise), but exactly how acute exercise impacts on specific emotions and mood is less well understood. A variety of mechanisms have been proposed. Distraction and mastery, as identified above, may play a part in gaining benefits from a single session of exercise before performance. Additional explanations include the release of endorphins (endogenous opioids), increase in core body temperature, and rhythmic contraction and relaxation of muscles to reduce tension, but no clear conclusions have been agreed (Morgan, 1997). Recent evidence also points to changes in brain activation associated with positive affect (Petruzzello *et al.*, 2001). It is likely that a number of psychological or physiological mechanisms are simultaneously involved or have greater or lesser impact, depending on variations in exercise intensity and duration.

Taylor (2000) has argued that a single session of exercise can reduce reactivity to a psychosocial stressor. In other words, the stress response (e.g. in terms of blood pressure change) is dampened or attenuated following exercise. It is likely that the effects will be greater for those with parental hypertension and could well be greater when the stressor has been appraised as particularly threatening, rather than just a challenge. One main criticism of this work is that it has typically employed laboratory-based stressors (or mental challenges) rather than naturalistic stressors, thereby raising issues about applicability to musical performance stress.

In order to address the questions raised in Section 9.1 earlier, the authors conducted two studies within the context of a large-scale research initiative, "Zoning In: Motivating the Musical Mind," aimed at optimizing the performance of music conservatory students (see also Chapters 10, 11, and 12 of this volume). In particular, the effects of regular and single sessions of exercise were explored to determine possible benefits for musicians on psychological and physiological indices of stress (Wasley & Taylor, 2002).

9.4   Studies with musicians

9.4.1   Chronic exercise and music performance

Initially, a musical performance was staged to simulate a natural stressor. The conservatory students were asked to prepare two compositions, each lasting 3–5 minutes. Assessors were in the audience and the performances were videotaped. On a separate day, students also underwent a sub-maximal fitness test and a laboratory-based stressor (i.e. a color–word Stroop test). Before and during both stressors, a variety of psychological and physiological indicators of stress were taken—heart rate, blood pressure, and state anxiety. Students were then assigned to one of two groups: the first (12 students) did 16 weeks of exercise training involving a weekly 1-hour group session at a local gym and an expectation to do at least 3–5 days of 30 minutes of moderate intensity exercise. The other group (9 students) had similar contact time in Alexander technique lessons. Finally, the performance, laboratory stressor, and fitness test were repeated, under identical conditions, 16 weeks later. The exercise group completed on average 13 contact sessions, and increased the amount of physical activity they did to an average of 180 minutes per week.

The results showed that, as expected, responses to the fitness test improved only for the exercise group, confirming sufficient involvement in the program among most of the students. The ability to utilize oxygen improved significantly, with no change in the Alexander group. Heart rate at rest and during the actual performance was also reduced by about 7 bpm among the exercise group (though not significantly so), with no change for the Alexander group (see Table 9.2). Interestingly, some individual heart rates were as high as 140 bpm during the actual performance, indicating a high level of both physical and emotional engagement in the performance. The exercise (but not the Alexander) group significantly reduced diastolic blood pressure after training, both at rest and before the performance.

Exercise training, therefore, appears to be valuable in reducing the physiological symptoms of occupational stress; however, the fact that there was no reduction in heart rate before the musical performance suggests that the anticipation of a stressor is not influenced by exercise training. It may be that being more fit does little to help cope with a passive stressor such as anticipating a musical performance, but when an active response to a stressor is needed (e.g. as in an actual performance), then the data suggest that being more fit results in a downregulation of the sympathetic nervous system (i.e. attenuation of arousal response).

In terms of general anxiety levels, both the exercise and Alexander groups showed a similar trend of reduced trait anxiety from before to after training; although, without a passive control group, it is not possible to attribute changes to the interventions. Also, the exercise group found the performance situation to be as anxiety eliciting as the Alexander group, but their transient state anxiety levels after performance were marginally lower,

Table 9.2 Mean heart rate (standard deviation in brackets) under three conditions (i.e. rest, before performance, and during performance), before and after involvement in a 16-week exercise or Alexander technique training program

Regime	Resting heart rate (bpm)		Heart rate before performance (bpm)		Heart rate during performance (bpm)	
	Before	After	Before	After	Before	After
Exercise	72.04	67.83	81.23	84.33	120.17	113.25
	(7.51)	(11.36)	(12.41)	(14.91)	(20.74)	(20.79)
AT	75.72	74.11	82.44	85.67	117.33	123.44
	(10.44)	(7.36)	(6.69)	(11.68)	(20.53)	(20.98)

suggesting that chronic exercise may have expedited recovery after this stressful event (Wasley & Taylor, 2002). Further work is needed to consider how regular exercise may influence both psychological and physiological post-performance recovery.

9.4.2   Acute exercise and music performance

In a second study with different students, the simulated musical performance described above was repeated, and a financial incentive (in the form of a prize to one winner) was used to increase the perceived pressure/competitiveness associated with the performance. Thirteen musicians performed on two occasions, and each was asked to select one of their two audiotaped performances to be sent to independent assessors to determine the winner. The students were also given a familiarization session, in which they were introduced to the experimental procedure; this was deemed necessary in order to reduce any concerns the students may have had about the monitoring of physiological indices or about the study in general. Before one performance, students undertook 20 minutes of moderately intense acute exercise, followed by 20 minutes of rest; they were then given a warm-up period on their instruments. Before the other performance, students sat quietly without playing for an equivalent period of time, before also engaging in their normal pre-performance activities. To control for order effects, half the students were assigned to the exercise condition first.

Students then listened to and selected one of their two performances to be put through to the competition. Even though the students had not rehearsed or practiced using exercise within a pre-performance routine, 9 of the 13 students selected their performance after acute exercise as the better of the two. Following the acute exercise, state anxiety was significantly lower than for the nonexercise event. Diastolic (but not systolic) blood pressure after exercise was also slightly lower before the performance, as compared with the resting condition. Mean changes in heart rate from baseline to during the performance was 18 and 23 bpm, following exercise and no exercise, respectively (a statistically significant difference).

9.4.3   Subjective responses from students

In addition to the data presented above, the students in both of these studies were interviewed about their subjective responses to the chronic and acute exercise interventions. As a sample, two are provided below verbatim. They provide valuable insight into some benefits that had not been expected, but stimulate further thoughts about the potential implications of physical exercise for enhancing musical performance.

A female oboist: I have always been fairly active but hadn't thought about exercising before a performance. Before a performance, I sometimes resorted to drinking alcohol or taking tranquilizers. The exercise program taught me how to build aerobic exercise into a pre-performance routine, and I no longer resort to alcohol or tablets. Now, I walk briskly for 25–30 minutes, ending about 90 minutes before performing. I then go through the rest of my routine, which involves rehearsal, imagery, and relaxation.

A male pianist: Previously, I couldn't eat before a performance and would go into it feeling hungry and empty. Now, I always do at least 20 minutes of exercise ending at least 2 hours before a performance, then shower and feel relaxed enough to eat a meal. After that, I go into my normal routine leading up to the performance. I wouldn't want to perform without exercising.

9.5   Guidelines for the musician

When the students in the above studies were first interviewed, their self-reported physical activity levels were below UK national recommendations for most students. A few were quite active, but most were keen to participate in the research in order to learn more about the benefits of exercise. No student had systematically incorporated exercise into his or her pre-performance routine (as described above). This section offers recommendations for physical activity and exercise for the musician, both from a general fitness perspective and for pre-performance. It is important to bear in mind that the following guidelines are general and that there is no one-size-fits-all approach. The following guidelines are provided for those who are not at present actively involved in exercise and who have, as is typical among musicians, a busy schedule.

General guidelines for regular exercise

◆ Incorporating more physical activity into your daily living contributes to your over-all health, but exercise, like other activities, has a risk attached to it. The level of risk depends on you (the exerciser), as well as the chosen activity and intensity. There are ways to appraise and reduce this risk, and this normally involves exercising within your ability until you are sure how hard you can push yourself. Also, you should ask yourself a number of questions which, if the answer is "yes," you may want to take necessary care. For example, do you suffer from asthma or another form of breath-ing difficultly? If yes, you should keep your medication with you just in case. Do you have an injury that may be negatively affected by the exercise? If yes, consider other forms of exercise that do not aggravate your condition. If you are in any doubt, visit your physician to discuss your intended program of exercise. This being said, do not let this put you off from planning and starting to become more physically active, as the benefits very often far outweigh the risks.

◆ The type of exercise in which you decide to engage can be a highly individual choice and may require trial and error. Broadly speaking though, all forms of aerobic activ-ity (e.g. walking briskly, jogging, swimming, and cycling) offer similar health bene-fits. Thus, regardless of changes in the year and the advantages and challenges to maintaining physical activity that this brings, it is important to know that the same health outcomes can be achieved through several routes. But obviously, the more you enjoy your choice, the more likely you are to maintain your activity.

◆ You may want to consider exercising with a friend to give the event a social aspect. This has been suggested as one option for enhancing motivation and making exer-cise more fun. Alternatively, joining a gym can be highly motivating, provide a safe exercise environment, and give structure to your exercise regime; however, fitness centers can be somewhat expensive, inconvenient, and daunting to the new exerciser. Again, it is a matter of your preference as to which approach you take. You can gen-erally achieve the same health and fitness results whether in a gym or not.

◆ Above all, it is important to keep your chosen exercise intensity in mind. The general program recommended in Table 9.3 starts with one session per week lasting between 20–30 minutes and focuses on moderate intensity activities, as this appears to afford

Table 9.3 General guidelines for engaging in regular (or chronic) exercise for aerobic fitness benefits (assuming a sedentary starting point)

Weeks	Number of sessions per week	Duration (minutes)	Intensity
1–4	1	20–30	Moderate
4–8	2	20–40	All moderate
8–16	2	20–60	All moderate
16 onwards	3	20–60	Two moderate (with one session more vigorous)

Note: For general health benefits, the aim should be to accumulate *at least* 30 minutes of moderate or vigorous activity on five or more days per week. This can be achieved through multiple short bouts of physical activity lasting only 10 minutes.

the best health outcomes. In moderate intensity exercise, you need only feel a little sweaty and mildly breathless, while still able to maintain a conversation. After 3–4 weeks, it is recommended that you increase to two sessions per week at the same intensity.

♦ This program requires two considerations, however. Firstly, you may find it useful to accumulate the suggested amount of exercise over two or more shorter sessions that add up to your goal. Secondly, the exercise program should progress from a generally easy start with incremental additions of time, frequency, and intensity to avoid injury and unnecessary, unpleasant post-exercise experience. It is relevant to remember that the adage "no pain, no gain" does *not* apply here. Yes, you must push yourself somewhat—but not beyond your limits. It has been observed that many people start exercise programs at unsuitable intensities and frequencies, which can then lead to injury, negative experiences, and ultimately dropping out of exercise. A steady approach will deliver a healthier and more enjoyable experience.

♦ There are numerous books on exercise, from simple texts on walking to highly technical guidelines set by the American College of Sports Medicine (2001). In addition to general guidelines, as noted above, you may want to explore how best to increase physical activity around musical practicing (such as during breaks) and performance.

Pre-performance guidelines

♦ As a first step, try monitoring how your physical activity patterns change before a performance. It is strongly recommended that the introduction of any moderate intensity exercise before a performance be initially rehearsed and any response closely monitored before attempting to use it within an actual pre-performance routine. This will enable you to work out what is best for you.

♦ As a general guide, your exercise should take place more than an hour before the performance, as this appears to allow for adequate recovery; however, the intensity at which you work will also impact on the amount of time required to recover.

◆ Try exercises that are suitable for the environment you are in. For example, go for a brisk, moderate intensity walk for 20 minutes or longer; also, use stairs that may be available in order to get to the desired intensity.

◆ An exercise session might be incorporated into getting to the performance location, but being late and rushing to a performance is highly discouraged, as this is likely to have a deleterious effect on the necessary calm and focus required for performing. Rather, acute exercise should be planned deliberately with time incorporated for recovery at the venue. Also, remember to rehydrate during or after exercise with sufficient fluid.

9.6   Conclusions

In terms of practical experience, research confirms that there are individual differences in how musicians respond to chronic and acute exercise. A process of trial and error to find the right intensity and duration is essential, with an adequate period after exercise for recovery. Clearly, exercise can play a particularly important role if the performer has a predisposition or learned response pattern to be overly anxious. Some musicians may fear that exercising will leave them too tired to practice and perform, but the often-cited notion that exercise leaves one fatigued is largely a mistake. Moderate-intensity exercise is advocated here, which is not likely to have this effect. In fact, there is growing evidence that moderate intensity exercise has revitalizing or energizing capabilities, in addition to reducing anxiety (Ekkekakis *et al.*, 2000). This chapter has focused on aerobic exercise, which has known health and stress management properties. Other exercise involving stretching and resistance training may also be integrated into an exercise program.

Acknowledgments

We wish to acknowledge the support of The Leverhulme Trust and the Royal College of Music, London, for the work reported in this chapter. Also, we would like to thank the David Lloyd Club (South Kensington, London) for generously providing exercise facilities, as well as the participating students for their enthusiastic support and involvement.

Further information and reading

Relevant material on the benefits of exercise, suggestions for exercise routines, and information on how to find a personal fitness instructor is available through the following websites: American College of Sports Medicine (*www.acsm.org*), The Exercise Register (*www.exerciseregister.com*), Fit Launch (*www.fitlaunch.com*), and Just Walk (*www.justwalk.com*; track your exercise and diet online). Further particulars of the research results presented in this chapter are provided at the project website for "Zoning In: Motivating the Musical Mind": *www.zoningin.rcm.ac.uk*. For additional reading, see:

American College of Sports Medicine. (2001). *ACSM's Resource Manual for Guidelines for Exercise Testing and Prescription*. London: Lippincott, Williams, and Wilkins.

Biddle, S. J., Fox, K., & Boutcher, S. H. (Eds.). (2000). *Physical Activity and Psychological Well-Being*. London: Routledge.

Franks, B. D., & Howley, E. T. (1998). *Fitness Leader's Handbook*. Champaign, IL: Human Kinetics.

Karageorghis, C. I., & Terry, P. C. (1997). The psychophysical effects of music in sport and exercise: A review. *Journal of Sport Behavior, 20*, 54–68.

McPherson, B. D. (Symposium Chair). (2001). *Medicine and Science in Sports and Exercise, 33* (June Supplement), S345–641.

Pate, R. R., Pratt, M., Blair, S. N., Haskell, W. L., Macera, C. A., Bouchard, C., Bucher, D., Ettinger, W., Heath, G. W., King, A. C., Kinska, A., Leon, A. S., Marcus, B. H., Morris, J., Paffenbarger, R. S., Patrick, K., Pollock, M. L., Rippe, J. M., & Sallis, J. W. (1995). Physical activity and public health: A recommendation from the Centers for Disease Control and Prevention and the American College of Sports Medicine. *Journal of the American Medical Association, 273*, 402–407.

Weinberg, R. S., & Gould, D. (1999). *Foundations of Sport and Exercise Psychology* (2nd ed.). Champaign, IL: Human Kinetics.

References

American College of Sports Medicine (2001). *ACSM's Resource Manual for Guidelines for Exercise Testing and Prescription*. London: Lippincott, Williams, and Wilkins.

Abel, J. L., & Larkin, K. T. (1990). Anticipation of performance among musicians: Physiological arousal, confidence, and state anxiety. *Psychology of Music, 18*, 171–182.

Batty, D., & Thune, I. (2000). Does physical activity prevent cancer? Evidence suggests protection against colon cancer and probably breast cancer. *British Medical Journal, 321*, 1424–1425.

Biddle, S. J., & Mutrie, N. (2001). *Psychology of Physical Activity: Determinants, Well-Being, and Interventions*. London: Routledge.

Biddle, S. J., Fox, K., & Boutcher, S. H. (Eds.). (2000). *Physical Activity and Psychological Well-Being*. London: Routledge.

Blair, S. N., Haskell, W. L., Ho, P., Paffenbarger, R. S., Vranizan, K. M., Farquhar, J. W., & Wood, P. D. (1985). Assessment of habitual physical activity by a seven-day recall of physical in a community survey and controlled experiments. *American Journal of Epidemiology, 122*, 794–804.

Bonaiuti, D., Shea, B., Iovine, R., Negrini, S., Robinson, V., Kemper, H. C., Wells, G., Tugwell, P., & Cranney, A. (2003). Exercise for preventing and treating osteoporosis in postmenopausal women (Cochrane Review). *The Cochrane Library, Issue 4*. Oxford: Update Software Ltd.

Boutcher, S. H. (2000). Cognitive performance, fitness, and ageing. In S. J. Biddle, K. Fox, & S. H. Boutcher (Eds.), *Physical Activity and Psychological Well-Being* (pp. 118–129). London: Routledge.

Ekkekakis, P., Hall, E. E., Van Landuyt, L. M., & Petruzzello, S. J. (2000). Walking in (affective) circles: Can short walks enhance affect? *Journal of Behavioral Medicine, 23*, 245–275.

Fox, K. R. (1997). The physical self and processes in self-esteem development. In K. Fox (Ed.), *The Physical Self: From Motivation to Well-Being* (pp. 111–140). Champaign, IL: Human Kinetics.

Fox, K. R. (2000). The effects of exercise on self-perceptions and self-esteem. In S. J. Biddle, K. Fox, & S. H. Boutcher (Eds.), *Physical Activity and Psychological Well-Being* (pp. 88–117). London: Routledge.

Kubitz, K. A., Landers, D. M., Petruzzello, S. J., & Han, M. (1996). The effects of acute and chronic exercise on sleep: A meta-analytic review. *Sports Medicine, 21*, 277–291.

Lawlor, D. A., & Hopker, S. W. (2001). The effectiveness of exercise as an intervention in the management of depression: Systematic review and meta-regression analysis of randomised controlled trials. *British Medical Journal, 322,* 1–8.

Lazarus, R. S., & Folkman, S. (1984). *Stress, Appraisal, and Coping.* New York: Springer.

Morgan, W. P. (1997). *Physical Activity and Mental Health.* Washington, DC: Hemisphere.

Moses, J., Steptoe, A., Mathews, A., & Edwards, S. (1989). The effects of exercise training on mental well-being in the normal population: A controlled trial. *Journal of Psychosomatic Research, 33,* 47–61.

Murphy, M., Nevill, A., Neville, C., Biddle, S. J., & Hardman, A. (2002). Accumulating brisk walking for fitness, cardiovascular risk, and psychological health. *Medicine and Science in Sports and Exercise, 34,* 1468–1474.

Mutrie, N. (2000). The relationship between physical activity and clinically defined depression. In S. J. Biddle, K. Fox, & S. H. Boutcher (Eds.), *Physical Activity and Psychological Well-Being* (pp. 46–652). London: Routledge.

NVC Arts (producer) (1998). *Maxim Vengerov Masterclass* [television broadcast], December 29. London: Channel 4.

Pate, R. R., Pratt, M., Blair, S. N., Haskell, W. L., Macera, C. A., Bouchard, C., Bucher, D., Ettinger, W., Heath, G. W., King, A. C., Kinska, A., Leon, A. S., Marcus, B. H., Morris, J., Paffenbarger, R. S., Patrick, K., Pollock, M. L., Rippe, J. M., & Sallis, J. W. (1995). Physical activity and public health: A recommendation from the Centers for Disease Control and Prevention and the American College of Sports Medicine. *Journal of the American Medical Association, 273,* 402–407.

Petruzzello, S. J., Hall, E. E., & Ekkekakis, P. (2001). Regional brain activation as a biological marker of affective responsivity to acute exercise: Influence of fitness. *Psychophysiology, 38,* 99–106.

Petruzzello, S. J., Landers, D. M., Hatfield, B. D., Kubitz, K. A., & Salazar, W. (1991). A meta-analysis on the anxiety-reducing effects of acute and chronic exercise: Outcomes and mechanisms. *Sports Medicine, 11,* 143–182.

Sallis, J. F., & Owen, N. (1999). *Physical Activity and Behavioral Medicine.* London: Sage.

Sothmann, M. S., Buckworth, J., Claytor, R. P., Cox, R. H., White-Welkley, J. E., & Dishman, R. K. (1996). Exercise training and the cross-stressor adaptation hypothesis. *Exercise and Sport Sciences Reviews, 24,* 267–287.

Steptoe, A. (1989). Stress, coping and stage fright in professional musicians. *Psychology of Music, 17,* 3–11.

Steptoe, A., & Cox, S. (1988). Acute effects of aerobic exercise on mood. *Health Psychology, 7,* 329–340.

Steptoe, A., & Fidler, H. (1987). Stage fright in musicians: A study of cognitive and behavioural strategies in performance anxiety. *British Journal of Psychology, 78,* 241–249.

Taylor, A. H. (2000). Physical activity, stress and anxiety: A review. In S. J. Biddle & K. Fox & S. H. Boutcher (Eds.), *Physical Activity and Psychological Well-being* (pp. 10–45). London: Routledge.

Thayer, R. E. (1987). Energy, tiredness, and tension effects of a sugar snack versus moderate exercise. *Journal of Personality and Social Psychology, 52,* 119–125.

US DHSS (1996). *Physical Activity and Health: A Report of the Surgeon General.* Pittsburgh, PA: Department of Health and Human Services, Centers for Disease Control and Prevention, and National Center for Chronic Disease Prevention and Health Promotion.

Valentine, E. R., Fitzgerald, D. F. P., Gorton, T. L., Hudson, J. A., & Symonds, E. R. C. (1995). The effect of lessons in the Alexander Technique on music performance in high and low stress situations. *Psychology of Music, 23*, 129–141.

Videman, T., Sarna, S., Battie, M. C., Koskinen, S., Gill, K., Paananen, H., & Gibbons, L. (1995). The long-term effects of physical loading and exercise lifestyles on back-related symptoms, disability, and spinal pathology among men. *Spine, 20*, 699–709.

Vuori, I. M. (2001). Dose-response of physical activity and low back pain, osteoarthritis, and osteoporosis. *Medicine and Science in Sports and Exercise, 33* (June Supplement), S551–S586.

Wasley, D., & Taylor, A. (2002). The effect of physical activity and fitness on psycho-physiological responses to a musical performance and laboratory stressor. In C. Stevens, D. Burnham, G. McPherson, E. Schubert, & J. Renwick (Eds.), *Proceedings of the Seventh International Conference on Music Perception and Cognition* (pp. 93–96). Adelaide, Australia: Causal Productions.

CHAPTER 10

ALEXANDER TECHNIQUE

ELIZABETH VALENTINE

The Alexander technique (AT) is a method of kinesthetic re-education developed by F. M. Alexander, who was born in Tasmania in 1869, came to live and work in England, and died in London in 1955. His career as an actor became jeopardized by periodic attacks of loss of voice, particularly when under stress. On finding that rest did not cure his problem and that the medical profession was unable to help him, he turned to his own resources, examining his manner of bodily use by observing himself in a mirror. He noticed that whenever he was on the point of reciting he would pull his head back and down, tighten his neck muscles, and suck in air through his mouth. Eventually, he managed to train himself to inhibit this maladaptive strategy of anticipatory tensing.

Alexander (1932) considered that the key to efficient control of bodily movement was the relation of the head to the neck and back, the "primary control" as he called it, a position of mechanical advantage. His view was that in general people develop habitual patterns of muscles, perhaps owing to the failure of instinctive control of the body to keep pace with civilization in the evolution to upright posture. Typically, the head is pulled back and down, as in the startle reaction, when performing simple acts like sitting down. He believed this was particularly insidious because kinesthetic feedback is unreliable and misleading. Alexander's aim was to re-educate people kinesthetically in what he termed "good use," a coordinated and balanced distribution of muscle tension throughout the body, resulting in an attentive state attainable under stress. Habitual, automatic reactions are inhibited and replaced by consciously controlled, directed actions. An important element is maintaining a state of openness with regard to the eventual act to be performed: thus, at the critical moment, a decision may be made to inhibit the intended action, to perform an alternative action, or to continue with the intended one.

Alexander preferred the term "posture" not to be used: Dart's (1947) "poise" gives a much better idea of what is intended. The aim of the technique is to condition the association of a new postural model to verbal instructions such as "direct the head forward and upward" or "lengthen and widen the back," first given overtly by the teacher but subsequently covertly by the student. Movements in accordance with the technique are characterized by economy of effort, a subjective sense of lightness, and a balanced and appropriate distribution of tension (not an absence of tension, but no more than is necessary). Such optimal functioning constitutes good use and deviations from it are termed "misuse." Similarities to the oriental martial arts and the concept of "flow" (Green & Gallwey, 1986; Csikszentmihalyi, 1992; Goleman, 1998) have not gone unnoticed (Gehman, 2002).

In this chapter, the principles of the technique are described and its application to music performance discussed. Although often regarded as on the fringe of science, an increasing number of studies have provided scientific evidence for both its anatomical and physiological underpinnings, and its beneficial effects on behavior and experience. Anatomical and physiological studies of AT in the general population are reviewed, followed by a consideration of studies on its effects in musicians, firstly physiological, and then behavioral and experiential. Although the evidence is limited and not always consistent, a number of studies have shown beneficial effects of training in AT on breathing, heart rate and blood pressure, posture and bodily use, quality of musical performance, and mental attitude. Finally, a list of resources is supplied where further information can be obtained both on the research that has been conducted and on how to find out more about the technique and to locate a teacher. Lessons are typically individually based, and training in AT is commonly available in music conservatories and university music departments.

10.1   Application of AT to music performance

Although considered something that can be of use to everyone, AT has been applied clinically in areas of pain management (Fisher, 1988; Bajwa *et al.*, 2001), Parkinson's disease (Stallibrass, 1997), and for the mentally and physically disabled (Maitland *et al.*, 1996). It has been popular in equitation and generally in the performing arts, especially ballet (e.g. Richmond, 1994; Bluethenthal, 1996). Given the fine neuromuscular coordination, and physical and mental strains and stresses to which performing musicians are subject, it is not surprising that AT has been popular among them. The technique has been endorsed by such eminent and diverse musicians as Adrian Boult, Julian Bream, Colin Davis, James Galway, Paul McCartney, Yehudi Menuhin, Sting, and Barry Tuckwell. It is taught at most, if not all, leading international music conservatories and has been applied to *voice* (Lewis, 1980; Duarte, 1981; Lloyd, 1986; Englehart, 1989; Rohmert *et al.*, 1990; Hudson, 2002); *wind instruments* (Bosch, 1997; Holm, 1997; Bosch & Hinch, 1999); *strings* (Tursi, 1959; Richter, 1974; Hamilton, 1986; Conable, 1993; McCullogh, 1996; Stein, 1999); and *keyboard* (Ben-Or, 1987; Kaplan, 1994).

Although group lessons are occasionally given, lessons are typically and preferentially one-to-one and hands-on. The teacher will guide the student's movements by light touch and verbal instructions. Attention is usually focused initially on familiar, daily actions—in which the student is taught to connect thought to movement—and is later extended and applied to specific areas of skilled performance, such as playing a musical instrument. The student may lie on the floor (or for teaching purposes, on a long wide table) in semi-supine position (i.e. on the back with the knees bent up pointing to the ceiling), thus allowing for a natural lengthening of the spine. Another common feature of a lesson is the movement from sitting to standing and vice versa. Such common everyday activities enable the teacher to demonstrate the importance of keeping the head and neck free, and the back lengthening at all times. Other activities include walking, bending, reaching, lifting, and breathing, which is of course crucially important to music performance. In each case, the teacher will help students become more aware of themselves, where they are, and how they move. She or he might draw their attention to the way they put on their shoes or jacket, pick up a bag, or open the door at the end of a lesson. Particularly in the case of a musician, the teacher will help the student become aware of maladaptive, habitual reactions that are often associated with underlying patterns of tension and anxiety (e.g. singers skewing their head to one side on high notes or string players arching their back) and encourage ease and freedom of movement. Of great importance to the musician is the proper support of the arms, hands, and fingers from the lower back. The student may also be given homework, which can include keeping a diary of "use" and reading relevant texts.

There is evidence that musicians both need and use therapeutic techniques to aid them in their work. Several studies have indicated that levels of anxiety are higher among musicians than in the general population. Watson and Valentine (1987) administered a number of personality inventories and a questionnaire about the use of complementary medical techniques to 60 members of the London Sinfonietta. Both sexes scored significantly above the norms for general or *trait* anxiety (see Chapter 1)—for instance, the sample mean on Spielberger's Trait Anxiety Inventory (Spielberger *et al.*, 1983) was 41.95 for men, compared with the norm of 34.89 for the general population, and 44.25 for women, compared with the norm of 34.79. This is consistent with the work of Kemp (1981), who also found that professional performing musicians scored significantly above population norms for anxiety, that music students were more anxious than nonmusic students, and that "talented" musicians were more anxious than "nontalented." In Watson and Valentine's sample, 53% reported using anxiety-reduction techniques of some kind. AT was easily the most frequently used technique, with 43% currently taking or having taken lessons. This suggests that AT is used by at least 20% of the general population of musicians (this allows for possible sampling bias; only 50% of the sample returned usable data).

10.2   AT and science

The work of eminent scientists such as George Coghill, Rudolph Magnus, and Charles Sherrington was invoked in support of Alexander's ideas, though in some cases now considered an unjustified extrapolation. Many famous people were numbered among Alexander's admirers, including John Dewey (McCormack, 1958), Aldous Huxley, George Bernard Shaw, and Nikolaas Tinbergen, who devoted much of his Nobel prizewinner's lecture to a discussion of Alexander's work. The theory, however, has remained on the fringe of science and medicine. Among psychologists, Alexander's admirers have included Harold Schlosberg and Tony Buzan.

Alexander developed his method of posture and movement re-education about the same time (i.e. soon after the turn of the twentieth century) as Sherrington's theories on the nature of proprioception were becoming known. His methods of releasing tension patterns in the neck coincided with the discovery of massive numbers of muscle spindles in the cervical musculature (Batson, 1996, in reviewing recent work relevant to the peripheral neuroanatomic basis of AT, remarks on the prescience of Alexander's conclusions, in the light of current knowledge in neuroscience). Alexander does not mention this work, though he may have known about it. Like Freud, he seems not to have felt the need to validate his ideas scientifically, perhaps considering that he had created a practical, experiential means of body learning, accessible through a method of "hands-on" instruction. Hence, while belief in the technique remains strong and practitioners are fulsome in its praise and testify to its benefits in their personal statements, rigorous objective data have been hard to come by (this is all the more surprising in view of the large number of musicians who use the technique and claim to benefit from it). This may be partly because of the ineffable nature of its effects, inherently difficult to describe verbally or quantify, and partly because it is subject to effects of expectation and suggestibility, or both of these.

In 1937, 19 physicians wrote to the *British Medical Journal* to urge that "as soon as possible, steps be taken for an investigation of Alexander's work" (Bouce-Porter *et al.*, 1937, p. 1137). Dewey undertook to get support for a scientific investigation from the Rockefeller Foundation, but Alexander set up too many requirements and it fell through. In 1949, a grateful student gave $500 (US) for research which was used for a pilot electromyographic study at Tufts University (see Section 10.3 below). Then Dewey died, and not long afterwards Alexander himself. As late as 1978, Wilfred Barlow wrote: "I appreciate only too well that the statistical background which doctors and scientists will eventually need is not very much in evidence" (p. 11).

There is a substantial literature on AT (for bibliographies, see Priest, 1992; Evans, 2000), not only in English, but also in French, German, Spanish, and Italian. Articles are scattered among professional journals, scientific periodicals, theses, and dissertations. Nevertheless, with very few notable exceptions, it is still the case that the majority of studies are anecdotal, lacking in adequate experimental controls, on small samples, or simply case studies. While considerable progress has been made on pharmacological and cognitive-behavioral therapeutic interventions for the treatment of performance anxiety (see Chapters 12 and 14 of this volume), there has been very little systematic investigation of the efficacy of AT on behavioral and experiential manifestations.

10.3   Anatomical and physiological studies on the general population

Most of the attempts to provide objective evidence of the effect of AT have focused on anatomical and/or physiological measurements. Some of the earliest research on AT was carried out by Wilfred Barlow on army cadets (see Barlow, 1998, for a review). He suspended a tape measure from the back of their heads, enabling measurement of the distance to the bottom of their necks. The vast majority showed a shortening of this distance (head retraction) by an inch or more as they sat down or stood up, which they were unable to prevent and of which they were unaware (see Figure 10.1). This confirms Alexander's view that kinesthetic sensations are unreliable.

Frank Pierce Jones (Jones *et al.*, 1963; see Jones, 1976, for a review), working at Tufts University in the 1950s and 1960s, measured muscle activity and movement patterns for guided and unguided movements using electromyography (i.e. electrical recording of muscle activity), X-ray and multiple-image photography, and a strain-gauge force platform (which measures directional forces). The X-ray photographs showed that employing the Alexander principle resulted in increased length of the sternomastoid muscles on the side of the neck, increased width of the discs between the neck vertebrae, and a forward movement of the center of gravity of the head. The multiple-image photographs showed that the movements were quicker and more direct. This work has

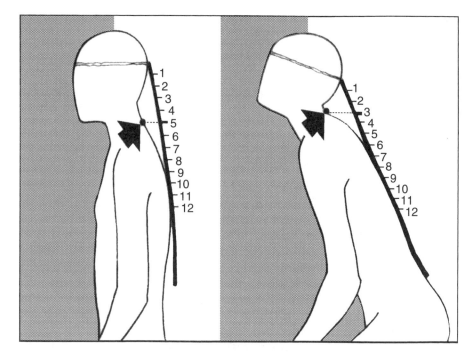

Figure 10.1 Pulling back the head when moving from a standing position (left) to sitting down (right). (From Barlow, 1998. © Orion Publishing group, used by permission.)

been criticized by Stevens (1987) on the grounds of artifacts due to touching the participant in the guided movements, slow sampling rates of the photography which induce various kinds of error, and outdated anatomical and physiological knowledge.

Stevens *et al.* (1989) repeated Jones's work, using more sophisticated electronic apparatus. Their results confirmed those of Jones in showing that guided movements, in which habitual postural adjustments of the head and neck are inhibited, require less force, show less muscle activity, and are quicker and smoother than habitual movements. In their study, guided sit-to-stand movements showed a decrease in head movements, ground reaction forces, and electromyographic activity in the trapezius, sternomastoid, and erector spinae muscles (located in the shoulders, neck, and back respectively).

Austin and his colleagues have investigated the effects of AT instruction on respiratory function in healthy adult volunteers. In an exploratory study, Austin and Pullin (1984) studied six normal volunteers using standard spirometric (i.e. lung capacity) and mouth pressure tests before and after a single lesson in the technique, but no differences were found. They then studied eight normal adult volunteers before and after a course of 20 weekly private lessons. The results showed significant increases in the following measures of respiratory function:

- forced vital capacity (i.e. the volume of air expelled by a forced maximal expiration from a position of full inspiration)

- peak expiratory flow (i.e. the maximum rate of airflow that can be achieved during a sudden forced expiration from a position of full inspiration)
- forced expiratory flow at 25% of forced vital capacity
- maximum voluntary ventilation
- maximal inspiratory pressure (i.e. the amount of air that can be inspired from normal expiration)
- maximal expiratory pressure (i.e. the amount of air that can be forcibly expired at the end of normal expiration); this increased for seven of the eight participants, but the change was not statistically significant.

Six of the eight participants reported a subjective sense of distinctly increased physical well-being and that performance of a favorite physical activity, such as skiing or playing the piano, had improved. Possible mechanisms suggested for the observed increases are decreased resting tensions of the respiratory muscles, decreased intra-abdominal pressures, and enhanced coordination of the respiratory muscles. The authors speculate that as lengthening and poise develop, compression of the torso by habitual muscular actions may lessen (i.e. the "normal" corseting effect on respiration may decrease). They conclude that AT appears to offer promise for improving respiratory function, by teaching improved use of the musculoskeletal system. One limitation of the study, however, is that there was no comparison control group.

In a study that did compare an experimental and a control group, Austin and Ausubel (1992) obtained further evidence that AT musculoskeletal education may enhance respiratory muscular function in normal adults. Following a course of 20 private AT lessons at weekly intervals, the experimental group (consisting of 10 participants) showed significant improvements on a number of spirometric measures:

- peak expiratory flow
- maximal voluntary ventilation
- maximal inspiratory pressure
- maximal expiratory pressure.

The control group (also of 10 participants), matched for age, gender, height, and weight, given no lessons, did not show any significant changes. Again, suggested mechanisms for the observed effects are increased length and decreased resting tension of muscles in the torso (which, in turn, may increase their strength), increased thoracic compliance (i.e. a measure of lung and chest recoil, the inverse of stiffness), and/or enhanced coordination.

10.4   Studies with musicians

10.4.1   Physiological studies

Doyle (1984) applied physiological measurements to musicians, undertaking photographic and electromyographic analysis of the head–neck relationship during violinists' initiation of the act of playing. He claimed that the demonstrated association between neck tonus and the attitudinal response in the player supports Alexander and discusses implications for the pedagogy of violin playing.

Nielsen (1988) assigned members of the Aarhus Symphony Orchestra to an exercise group (who ran 7 kilometers 3 times a week for 8 weeks), an Alexander group (who received 20 private lessons in the technique during the same period), and a beta-blocker group (who took 40 mg of propranolol 1.5 hours before the test concert). Measures of heart rate and blood pressure were taken just before the first rehearsal, the final rehearsal, and the concert on two separate occasions (i.e. before and after the intervention). Exercise led to a significant reduction in heart rate. Lessons in AT and beta-blockers led to significant reductions in systolic blood pressure and significantly reduced increases in systolic blood pressure from the final rehearsal to the concert.

It appears, therefore, that AT can be almost as effective as beta-blockers in preventing inappropriate responses to stress (the effect was somewhat stronger in the latter than in the former). Nielsen suggests that this may be by resolving the demands of the voluntary and reflex components of behavior in a more conscious way. The musicians reported that participation in the study had resulted in benefits for the orchestra as a whole, predominantly social but also musical. Of 13 members of the exercise group, 12 members of the Alexander group, and 7 members of the beta-blocker group, 10, 8, and 3 respectively reported that the intervention had led to lowered unwanted stress; 11, 10, and 2 respectively that they would like to continue with the training; and 11, 8, and 2 respectively that they would recommend their treatment to others. Exercise was reported to increase general well-being, and Alexander training to result in improved breathing and surplus energy with which to solve daily problems. Beta-blockers, however, were reported to produce indifference to the job, deterioration in concentration, feelings of being isolated, and hammering in the fingers and toes. As one participant said: "If you become totally de-stressed and cold after taking a beta-blocker, the result is that what you play becomes cold and uninteresting" (see Chapter 14 for further discussion).

10.4.2   Behavioral studies

Early work on the behavioral effects of AT was undertaken by Barlow (1956), who compared 44 students at the Central School of Speech (CSS; where posture was considered important), who were taught by conventional methods (verbal instructions, manual adjustment, and exercises), with 20 students from the Royal College of Music, who were sent to him for lessons in AT. The students were photographed by an independent investigator but scored by Barlow for postural faults, including retracted head (see Figure 10.2), dropped shoulders, rotated pelvis, lordosis, and internally rotated knees. He sanguinely remarks, "A given observer soon achieves a uniform pattern of scoring. My average scoring for the first and second year group only varied by 1%, which indicates that the method is accurate" (p. 671). The students were categorized as follows:

- excellent (0–3 faults)
- slight defects (4–5 faults)
- moderately severe defects (6–9 faults)

- severe defects (10–14 faults)
- very severe defects (over 16 faults).

Barlow claimed that the RCM group showed considerable improvement and the CSS group deterioration, but no statistical analysis was conducted. Applying Kendall's tau to the results shows that there is indeed statistically significant evidence of improvement in the RCM group but that the deterioration in the CSS group is not statistically significant. However, the difference between the two groups is highly significant. This is consistent with Barlow's conclusion that "postural re-education will be ineffective unless a new 'body schema' is taught, by associating the postural model with an improved postural awareness," but more evidence would be needed to demonstrate that this is indeed the crucial element in Alexander training, not to mention the need for the assessments to be made blind by an independent observer.

In addition, Barlow (1955; see also 1978) reported a study of 50 opera students from a London voice and drama college, who had on average 37 lessons in AT. However, the

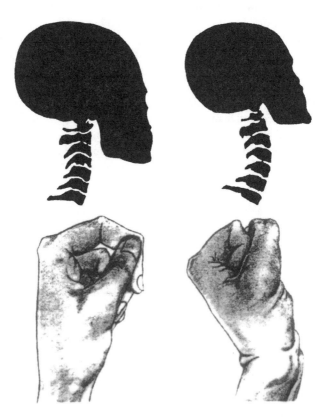

Figure 10.2 Skull and neck vertebrae, and "parallel" picture of hand and wrist. Cervical lordosis corrected by movement similar to wrist movement. (From Barlow, 1998. © Orion Publishing group, used by permission.)

study was unsystematic (he admits that "a statistician might like to see it all planned out a little more formally", p. 298), and the results are incompletely reported. Twenty of the students were subjected to Sheldon somatotype photography (while standing nude on a turntable!). Pictures for a selected five of these before and after re-education appear in the published report. Anthropocentric measurements were taken, and it is reported that "all the subjects with one or two exceptions show small but definite increases in standing and sitting height and shoulder width" (p. 300). A report was provided by two professors at the college, which included the following generalizations:

- In each case, there was marked physical improvement, which was usually reflected vocally and dramatically.

- In all cases, students since re-education were easier to teach.

- Each student reacted in a different characteristic way. The time it took to get results varied greatly between one student and another. The utilization of the approach depended largely on the student.

- Of eight students who entered a national singing competition, in which there were over 100 competitors, six reached the semifinal, which is quite out of proportion to what would be expected.

They concluded that "In our opinion, this approach is the best means we have yet encountered for solving the artist's problem of communication and should form the basis of training" (p. 300). However, there are a number of obvious criticisms of this study. Participants were not randomly assigned to the treatment, the sample included problem cases as well as "normals," there was no real control group, assessments were not free from observer bias, and the data are incompletely reported.

Jones (1972) made recordings of a singer when in the habitual mode and when the balance of the head was altered by the experimenter in accordance with the Alexander principle (however, note Stevens's criticism mentioned above). The singer reported that she sang more easily and with greater resonance and better breath control under the experimental conditions. The difference in the quality of singing was confirmed by other musicians who listened to the tape. A spectrogram confirmed increased richness of overtones and the virtual disappearance of breathing sounds during the experimental session.

Dennis (1987) randomly assigned 13 wind players to 20 lessons in AT or to a control group. Music performance was video-recorded and various measures of respiratory function, using standard spirometry and maximal static mouth pressures, were taken before and after training. For music performance, measures were taken of posture and movement during nonplaying, posture and movement during playing, breath control, and overall performance quality. The only significant difference between groups favored the control group, who showed a significantly greater improvement in maximal voluntary ventilation following training. No significant differences were obtained between the groups on the five other measures of respiratory function (forced vital capacity; forced expiratory volume at one second; peak expiratory flow; expiratory flow rates at 25%, 50%, and 75% of forced vital capacity; maximal inspiratory and expiratory pressures) or on any of the measures of musical performance (overall performance, posture and movement during playing and nonplaying, and breath control). It is important to note that, as wind players, these musicians may already have been performing at ceiling on respiratory function. As is often the case, subjective reports by the musicians suggested a range of beneficial effects of the lessons.

Using a design that avoided some of the methodological weaknesses of earlier studies, Valentine *et al.* (1995) aimed to investigate the experiential and behavioral effects of lessons in AT on music performance. Specifically, participants were randomly allocated to treatment and control conditions, and judges were blind to participants' condition assignment (i.e. they did not know which students had received lessons). Music students taking classes in performance were randomly assigned to an experimental group, which was offered a course of 15 lessons in AT, and to a control group. They included singers, violinists, cellists, pianists, organists, flautists, clarinetists, an oboist, and a trombonist. Physiological, behavioral, and self-report measures were taken on four occasions: in both a high-stress situation (an audition or a recital, subject to evaluation with serious consequences) and a low-stress situation (class performances, still subject to appraisal by the class teacher and peers), before and after treatment.

Measures of height and peak expiratory flow were included to test frequent claims that training in AT increases the realization of potential height and improves breath control. Heart rate mean and variance were chosen as measures of arousal under stress, as well as self-report questionnaires on mental state (i.e. a mood checklist and the Musical Performance Anxiety Self-Statement Scale, which measures a positive attitude to performance and task-focused attention; Craske *et al.*, 1988). Performances were video-recorded and subsequently rated by expert judges blind to participants' condition assignment, for degree of misuse by two Alexander teachers (other than those who gave the lessons) who specialize in teaching musicians, and for music performance by two music faculty members who specialize in teaching performance. Judgments of misuse (i.e. deviations from optimal performance in accordance with the principles of the Alexander technique) were made on a 7-point rating scale, drawn up and agreed by the two judges, where 1–2 indicated low levels, a generally good (above average) standard of use and coordination; 3–5 indicated more significant misuse likely to impair performance; and 5–7 indicated serious misuse. Judgments were made purely on the basis of visual information, with the sound turned down.

Positive effects of AT were obtained for physiological, performance, and self-report measures. The experimental group showed improvement relative to the control on the following measures:

- overall musical and technical quality
- heart rate variance
- self-rated anxiety
- positive attitude to performance.

Thus, quality of musical performance and positive attitude to performance increased, and heart rate variance and self-rated anxiety declined, as a result of training in AT. However, with the exception of heart rate variance, these effects were restricted to performance in the low stress class situations (it is worth noting, however, that the degree of stress is relative: mean heart rate was 102.19 beats per minute in the high-stress situations compared with 90.83 in the low-stress situations). There were no significant changes in height or peak flow as a result of the intervention.

There was good agreement between the two judges on overall musical quality and on technical quality (this is of interest in view of the skepticism concerning the validity of such "subjective" judgments). On the other hand, inter-rater agreement for judgments of misuse by the Alexander experts was very low. Qualitative comments made by one of the judges indicated that four participants in the experimental group, but none in the control group, were considered to have improved, whereas one participant in the experimental group and two in the control group were considered not to have shown improvement. There were no significant effects of training in AT on misuse as judged on the basis of video-recordings of behavior. This may indicate that it is difficult to assess misuse on the basis of purely visual information (which in addition may be limited in perspective).

The musicians' average ratings of general benefit derived from the course of lessons was 3.86 and for musical benefit was 4.77 (both on a scale from 1, not at all, to 7, very beneficial). Responses ranged from very little general effect to "marvelous, fantastic, terrific." All participants mentioned increased awareness of tension and improvement in the ability to relax. Some participants mentioned help with physical effects such as breathing or posture—for example, "helps poise," "induces a feeling of lifting up, being elongated" (two participants said they felt taller after lessons), "increases awareness of the relation of particular movements to overall body use," "eliminates bad habits," "avoids a bull-in-a-china-shop approach," "muscles don't become tense and bones are where they should be." Others emphasized mental attitudes towards playing (e.g. "teaches you how to go about setting yourself up to play," "decreases nervousness and uptightness in relation to performance," "releases tension, helps you relax"). Eight out of twelve participants said they would have more lessons if they could. Seven said they would definitely recommend lessons to someone else, three that they probably would, and two that they might possibly, depending on whether the person had tension problems and the abilities of the teacher. No one said they would definitely not recommend the technique.

In sum, these results suggest that AT may have beneficial effects on the quality of performance, the mental state of the performer, and may help to modulate increased variability of heart rate under stress. However, attention should be drawn to two cautionary qualifications. First, the sample size was small and the participants were predominantly female. Second, with the exception of heart rate variance, the effects of the experimental treatment were restricted to the low stress class situations and did not extend to the high stress recital situation. It is possible that 15 lessons were insufficient to develop the level of skill required to apply the technique in a state of high arousal, or that an enhanced ability to deal with performance anxiety is not the main benefit to be derived from the technique. Far more dramatic effects have been obtained with cognitive-behavioral methods (see Kendrick *et al.*, 1982; Sweeney & Horan, 1982; Clark & Agras, 1991; Chapter 12 of this volume). It is possible that demand characteristics may have contributed to the results, since it was considered necessary to inform the participants of the purpose of the study in order to enlist their cooperation, given the small size of the available sample. While demand characteristics may have affected the self-report measures, this is less plausible as an explanation for the more objective, physiological measures and independent behavioral ratings.

In a recent study (Valentine & Williamon, 2003), conservatory students were randomly assigned to various training groups: three groups received different kinds of neurofeedback and one group received AT lessons (students were also assigned to other interventions as part of the project "Zoning In: Motivating the Musical Mind"; see also Chapters 9, 11, and 12). The musicians in the neurofeedback training groups received 10 15-minute sessions over a period of 6–8 weeks. Those in the AT group received 12 30-minute sessions of one-to-one training on a weekly basis. Music performances before and after training were video-recorded. These were then randomly ordered and assessed by expert judges, external to the conservatory and blind to students' group membership, on perceived instrumental competence, musical understanding, and communication (each of which had three subscales) in addition to overall quality. Only one of the groups receiving neurofeedback (that receiving "alpha/theta" neurofeedback) showed significant changes on these rating scales as a result of training (for further discussion of the neurofeedback results, see Gruzelier *et al.*, 2002, and Chapter 11 of this volume). Following training, all four groups showed significant reductions in self-rated *state* anxiety (see Spielberger *et al.*, 1983, and Chapter 1) before performance. Video-recordings for the alpha/theta neurofeedback and the AT groups were rated for quality of bodily use by an experienced musician and AT practitioner, with extensive experience of teaching AT to musicians. She devised her own rating scales as follows (ratings were made from 1, very poor, to 7, excellent, purely on the basis of visual information with the sound turned down):

- head–neck–back relationship
- upper limb/back
- hips/balance
- direction of knees
- face and eyes
- breathing
- fingers
- thought direction
- inhibition
- overall impression/poise.

The AT group showed a significant improvement relative to the neurofeedback group on seven of the ten scales of "use": head–neck–back relationship, upper limb/back, face and eyes, fingers, thought direction, inhibition, and overall impression/poise (change scores, i.e. the difference between scores before and after training, were all significantly correlated with the exception of those among head–neck–back relationship, face and eyes, and breathing, suggesting that these are relatively independent of the rest and of each other). This is the first demonstration of the validity of judgments of AT use based on video-recorded performance and suggests not only that training in AT can enhance use but also that this can be demonstrated objectively. There were also some interesting differences among instruments on several of the scales: hips/balance, fingers, and thought direction. The greatest improvements were shown by singers.

Student feedback indicated a high degree of satisfaction and perceived benefit from the training: "I'd love it if the lessons were longer—half an hour goes very quickly"; "I really enjoyed and found useful the practical sessions—when I played piano or oboe and [the teacher] worked specifically with my needs"; "I found everything really interesting and incredibly helpful"; "I found the work we did with my instrument during lessons particularly valuable"; "Slowly making the Alexander technique a part of my life is a really fulfilling experience. I think it will always be part of my life from now on."

10.5   Conclusions

Although results have not always been consistent, there is now sufficient scientific research confirming that training in AT can:

- improve respiratory function
- minimize increases in heart rate and blood pressure under stress
- improve bodily use
- enhance the quality of musical performance.

Practitioners report improved mental attitudes, and increased awareness of ability to minimize tension. Results are best when general training in the technique can be integrated with work specifically directed at music performance in situ. For details of useful contacts and how to obtain further information, see "Further information and reading" below.

Acknowledgments

I should like to thank Judith Kleinman and Elisabeth Waterhouse for their help, and an anonymous reviewer for useful comments on a draft of this chapter. The research reported at the end of this chapter was supported by the Research Strategy Fund of Royal Holloway, University of London, and by the Royal College of Music, London.

Further information and reading

Additional information (including how to locate a teacher) can be obtained through the following professional associations: The Society of Teachers of the Alexander Technique (see *www.stat.org.uk* or write to STAT, First floor, Linton House, 39–51 Highgate Road, London NW5 1RS, UK), The American Society for the Alexander Technique (see *www.alexandertech.org* or write to AmSAT, 30 North Maple, P.O. Box 60008, Florence, MA 01062, USA), and Alexander Technique International (see *www.ati-net.com*). Further details of the project "Zoning In:

Motivating the Musical Mind" are available at *www.zoningin.rcm.ac.uk*. For additional reading on research conducted on the Alexander technique and what to expect in a lesson, see:

Books and journal articles

Alcantara, P. D. (1997). *Indirect Procedures: A Musician's Guide to the Alexander Technique*. Oxford: Clarendon Press.

Brennan, R. (1999). *The Alexander Technique Manual: A Step-by-Step Guide to Improve Breathing, Posture and Well-Being*. London: Little, Brown and Company.

Conable, B. (2000). *What Every Musician Needs to Know About the Body: The Practical Application of Body Mapping & the Alexander Technique to Making Music*. Portland, OR: Andover.

Gelb, M. (1981). *Body Learning*. London: Aurum.

Mackie, V., & Armstrong, J. (2002). *Just Play Naturally*. Aarhus, Denmark: Novis/Duende.

Rosenthal, E. (1987). The Alexander technique. What it is and how it works: Work with three musicians. *Medical Problems of Performing Artists, 2*, 53–57.

Articles in music periodicals

Anon (1989). The Alexander technique: From pupil to teacher. *Music Teacher, 68*(4), 19–20.

Babits, L., & Mayers, H. (1988). The path to productive practicing: An introduction to the Alexander technique. *American Music Teacher, 38*, 24–26 and 60.

Benham, B., Melborn, M., & Sanders, J. (1996). Three musicians talk about the Alexander Technique. *Journal of the International Double Reed Society, 24*, 121–127.

Bondurant, N. (1992). Movement, music, and the Alexander technique. *The Double Reed, 15*(1), 59–61.

Farkas, A. (1995). Coach's notebook . . . Exploring the Alexander technique and opera. *Opera Journal, 28*(3), 16–32.

Naylor, J. (1992). Getting better: Applying Alexander technique to instrumental study. *Music Teacher, 71*(7), 30–31.

Sanders, J. (2002). Freedom to breathe. *Strad, 113*, 631–635.

Stein, J. (1996). To schlep or not to schlep. *Music Teacher, 75*(5), 8–13.

References

Alexander, F. M. (1932). *The Use of Self*. New York: Dutton.

Austin, J. H. M., & Ausubel, P. (1992). Enhanced respiratory muscular function in normal adults after lessons in proprioceptive musculoskeletal education without exercises. *Chest, 102*, 486–490.

Austin, J. H. M., & Pullin, G. S. (1984). Improved respiratory function after lessons in the Alexander technique of musculoskeletal education. *American Review of Respiratory Disease, 129*, A275.

Bajwa, Z. H., Gupta, W., Warfield, C. A., & Steinman, T. I. (2001). Pain management in polycystic kidney disease. *Kidney International, 60*, 1631–1644.

Barlow, W. (1955). Anxiety and muscle tension. In D. F. O'Neill (Ed.), *Modern Trends in Psychosomatic Medicine* (pp. 285–309). London: Butterworth.

Barlow, W. (1956). Postural deformity. *Proceedings of the Royal Society of Medicine, 49*, 670–674.

Barlow, W. (1978). Research at the Royal College of Music. In W. Barlow (Ed.), *More Talk of Alexander* (pp. 190–195). London: Victor Gollancz.

Barlow, W. (1998). *The Alexander Principle: How to Use Your Body Without Stress.* London: Victor Gollancz.

Batson, G. (1996). Conscious use of the human body in movement: The peripheral neuroanatomic basis of the Alexander technique. *Medical Problems of Performing Artists, 11*, 3–11.

Ben-Or, N. (1987). The Alexander technique and performance. In C. Grindea (Ed.), *Tensions in the Performance of Music* (revised ed., pp. 84–95). London: Kahn and Averill.

Bluethenthal, A. (1996). Before you leap: The Alexander technique, an alternative approach to dance. *Dance Theatre Journal, 13*, 44–46.

Bosch, A. (1997). *The Use of the Alexander Technique in the Improvement of Flute Tone.* Unpublished masters dissertation, University of Pretoria, Pretoria, South Africa.

Bosch, A., & Hinch, J. (1999). The application of the Alexander technique for flute teaching: Two case studies. *British Journal of Music Education, 16*, 245–251.

Clark, D. B., & Agras, W. S. (1991). The assessment and treatment of performance anxiety in musicians. *American Journal of Psychiatry, 148*, 598–605.

Conable, W. (1993). The Alexander technique. *Journal of the Violin Society of America, 13*, 125–135.

Craske, M. G., Craig, K. D., & Kendrick, M. J. (1988). The musical performance anxiety self-statement scale. In M. Hersen & A. S. Bellack (Eds.), *Dictionary of Behavioral Assessment Techniques.* Oxford: Pergamon.

Csikszentmihalyi, M. (1992). *Flow: The Psychology of Happiness.* London: Rider.

Dart, R. (1947). The attainment of poise. *South African Journal, 21*, 764–791.

Dennis, R. J. (1987). *Music Performance and Respiratory Function in Wind Instrumentalists: Effects of the Alexander Technique on Musculoskeletal Education.* Unpublished doctoral dissertation, Columbia University, New York.

Doyle, G. (1984). *The Task of the Violinist: Skill, Stress and the Alexander Technique.* Unpublished doctoral dissertation, Lancaster University, Lancaster, UK.

Duarte, F. (1981). The principles of the Alexander technique applied to singing: The significance of the "preparatory set." *Journal of Research in Singing, 5*, 3–21.

Englehart, R. J. (1989). *An Electromyographic Study of Preparatory Set in Singing as Influenced by the Alexander Technique.* Unpublished doctoral dissertation, Ohio State University, Columbus, OH.

Evans, N. (2000). Alexander technique: An introduction and bibliography of recommended resources for the musician. *Brio: Journal of the United Kingdom Branch of the International Association of Music Libraries, Archives and Documentation Centres, 37*, 9–12.

Fisher, K. (1988). Early experiences of a multidisciplinary pain management programme. *Holistic Medicine, 3*, 47–56.

Gehman, S. (2002). *The Alexander Technique and Tai Chi Chuan?* Retrieved June 24, 2003, from *www.drizzle.com/~stacyg/ATforTaiChi.html.*

Goleman, D. (1998). *Working with Emotional Intelligence.* London: Bloomsbury.

Green, B., & Gallwey, W. T. (1986). *The Inner Game of Music.* New York: Doubleday.

Gruzelier, J. H., Egner, T., Valentine, E., & Williamon, A. (2002). Comparing learned EEG self-regulation and the Alexander Technique as a means of enhancing musical performance. In C. Stevens, D. Burnham, G. McPherson, E. Schubert, & J. Renwick (Eds.), *Proceedings of the*

Seventh International Conference on Music Perception and Cognition (pp. 89–92). Adelaide, Australia: Causal Productions.

Hamilton, B. (1986). *The Alexander Technique: A Practical Application to Upper String Playing.* Unpublished doctoral dissertation, Yale University, New Haven, CT.

Holm, C. P. (1997). *Corrective to Breathing Hindrances in Flute Performance, With Emphasis on the Alexander Technique.* Unpublished doctoral dissertation, Southern Baptist Theological Seminary, Louisville, KY.

Hudson, B. (2002). The effects of the Alexander technique on the respiratory system of the singer/actor. I: F. M. Alexander and concepts of his technique that affect respiration in singer/actors. *Journal of Singing, 59,* 9–17.

Jones, F. P. (1972). Voice production as a function of head balance in singers. *Journal of Psychology, 82,* 209–215.

Jones, F. P. (1976). *Body Awareness in Action: A Study of the Alexander Technique.* New York: Schocken.

Jones, F. P., Hanson, J. A., Miller, J. K., & Bossom, J. (1963). Quantitative analysis of abnormal movement: The sit and stand pattern. *American Journal of Physiological Medicine, 42,* 208–218.

Kaplan, I. (1994). *The Experience of Pianists Who Have Studied the Alexander Technique: Six Case Studies.* Unpublished doctoral dissertation, New York University.

Kemp, A. (1981). The personality structure of the musician: I. Identifying a profile of traits for the performer. *Psychology of Music, 9,* 3–14.

Kendrick, M. J., Craig, K. D., Lawson, D. M., & Davidson, P. O. (1982). Cognitive and behavioral therapy for musical-performance anxiety. *Journal of Consulting and Clinical Psychology, 50,* 353–362.

Lewis, P. P. (1980). *The Alexander Technique: Its Relevance for Singers and Teachers of Singing.* Unpublished doctoral dissertation, Carnegie Mellon University, Pittsburgh, PA.

Lloyd, G. (1986). *The Application of the Alexander Technique to the Teaching and Performing of Singing: A Case Study Approach.* Unpublished masters dissertation, University of Stellenbosch, Stellenbosch, South Africa.

Maitland, S., Horner, R., & Burton, M. (1996). An exploration of the application of the Alexander technique for people with learning disabilities. *British Journal of Learning Disabilites, 24,* 70–76.

McCormack, E. D. (1958). *Frederick Matthias Alexander and John Dewey: A Neglected Influence.* Unpublished doctoral dissertation, University of Toronto.

McCullogh, C. P. (1996). *The Alexander Technique and the Pedagogy of Paul Rolland.* Unpublished doctoral dissertation, Arizona State University, Tempe, AZ.

Nielsen, M. (1988). A study of stress amongst professional musicians. In C. Stevens (Ed.), *The F. M. Alexander Technique: Medical and Psychological Aspects* (pp. 14–16). Aalborg, Denmark: International School for the Alexander Technique.

Priest, J. (1992). *From Stage-Fright to Seat-Height: An Annotated Bibliography on the Alexander Technique and Music 1907–1992.* North Grosvenordale, CT: The author.

Richmond, P. (1994). The Alexander technique and dance training. *Impulse: The International Journal of Dance Science, Medicine, and Education, 2,* 24–38.

Richter, E. (1974). *The Application of the Alexander Technique to Cello Playing.* Unpublished doctoral dissertation, Florida State University, Tallahassee, FL.

Rohmert, F., Rehders, H., & Rohmert, G. (1990). Alexandertechnik: Auswirkungen der Korperaufrichtung auf das Klangspektrum der menschlinchen Stimme. In *Beitrage zum 1* (pp. 81–90). Kolloquium Praktische Musikphysiologie Koln: Schmidt.

Spielberger, C. D., Gorsuch, R. L., Lushene, R., Vagg, P. R., & Jacobs, G. A. (1983). *Manual for the State-Trait Anxiety Inventory (Form Y1)*. Palo Alto, CA: Consulting Psychologists Press.

Stallibrass, C. (1997). An evaluation of the Alexander Technique for the management of disability in Parkinson's disease: A preliminary study. *Clinical Rehabilitation, 11*, 8–12.

Stein, C. J. (1999). The Alexander technique: Its basic principles applied to the teaching and performing of stringed instruments. *American String Teacher, 49*, 72–77.

Stevens, C. H. (1987). *The Alexander Technique*. London: MacDonald.

Stevens, C. H., Bojsen-Møller, F., & Soames, R. (1989). Influence of initial posture on the sit to stand movement. *European Journal of Applied Physiology, 58*, 687–692.

Sweeney, G. A., & Horan, J. J. (1982). Separate and combined effects of cue-controlled relaxation and cognitive restructuring in the treatment of musical performance anxiety. *Journal of Counseling Psychology, 29*, 486–497.

Tursi, F. (1959). The problem of excessive psycho-physical tension in string performance. *American String Teacher, 9*, 6–8.

Valentine, E. R., & Williamon, A. (2003). Alexander technique and music performance: Evidence for improved "use". In R. Kopiez, A. C. Lehmann, I. Wolther, & C. Wolf (Eds.), *Proceedings of the Fifth Triennial ESCOM Conference* (pp. 145–147). Hanover, Germany: Hanover University of Music and Drama.

Valentine, E. R., Fitzgerald, D. F. P., Gorton, T. L., Hudson, J. A., & Symonds, E. R. C. (1995). The effect of lessons in the Alexander Technique on music performance in high and low stress situations. *Psychology of Music, 23*, 129–141.

Watson, P., & Valentine, E. (1987). The practice of complementary medicine and anxiety levels in a population of musicians. *Journal of the International Society for the Study of Tension in Performance, 4*, 26–30.

CHAPTER 11

PHYSIOLOGICAL SELF-REGULATION: BIOFEEDBACK AND NEUROFEEDBACK

JOHN H. GRUZELIER AND TOBIAS EGNER

A high degree of control over both mental and emotional processes is of particular importance to performing musicians. Musicians must attain high concentration levels when performing—without getting overly tense or excited. At the same time they must achieve a degree of mental relaxation, flexibility, and assurance in order to express their own creativity and individuality and to communicate this to an audience. EEG biofeedback, or "neurofeedback," is a technique that teaches the individual how to control the rhythmic electrical activity of the brain. Brain rhythms differ in frequency (or speed) and in amplitude (or voltage). The amount of activity at certain frequencies reflects information processing, such as focused concentration or day-dreaming, and aspects of arousal, such as being tense, awake, relaxed, or sleepy. Neurofeedback makes individuals aware of these processes by *feeding back* a representation of their own electrical brain activity and allowing them to change it. Since particular frequencies are closely associated with, for example, states of high concentration or deep relaxation, musicians can use this feedback to guide themselves into brain states that are beneficial for performing at their peak. This chapter provides a survey of the theoretical and clinical underpinnings of neurofeedback and reviews recent studies that have systematically examined this training and its application to music. First, however, it places neurofeedback in the broader context of general biofeedback training.

The real impetus for this review has been the surprising efficacy of neurofeedback in recent studies with music conservatory students. After neurofeedback training, students have shown substantive increases in ratings by experts on the overall quality of musical performance and on artistic aspects of performance such as "interpretative imagination," "musicality," "stylistic accuracy," and "emotional commitment and conviction." These were controlled studies and the results were replicated across two years of research (see Gruzelier *et al.*, 2002; Egner & Gruzelier, 2003). At the same time, neurofeedback training has produced improvements in cognitive and neurophysiological measures of attention and in semantic working memory in either the same musicians or in concurrent studies with medical students (Egner & Gruzelier, 2001, 2004a; Vernon *et al.*, 2003). These results contribute to growing evidence of performance enhancement due to neurofeedback in a diverse range of applications, and to what is anticipated to be a renaissance in the field of biofeedback training, both for optimizing performance in healthy individuals and for clinical applications.

11.1   Biofeedback

"Physiological self-regulation" describes voluntary control over functions of the central nervous system (CNS) and the peripheral nervous system (PNS), the latter comprising the somatic nervous system (SNS) and the autonomic nervous system (ANS; see Chapter 1 for an outline of the divisions of the human nervous system). Such control is acquired by means of "instrumental learning," which refers to the adjustment of behavior in response to the behavior's perceived consequences. These perceptions can then either act as positive or negative reinforcement (making the repetition of that behavior more likely) or as punishment (making the occurrence of the behavior less likely in the future). For any such trial-and-error learning to occur, the presence of feedback of a given behavior's consequences is essential. For instance, in order to learn to play the piano at an elementary level, it is crucial to receive tactile feedback from the fingers' interplay with the keyboard and auditory feedback in the shape of the sounds that are produced by this interaction.

Instrumental learning of psychomotor skills such as playing the piano, which are mediated by interaction between the CNS (the brain and spinal cord) and the SNS (motorneurons that innervate the musculoskeletal system), has never been subject to great controversy. On the other hand, the learning of voluntary control over ANS functions, such as heart rate and blood pressure, has historically been assumed to be impossible. However, the careful study of instrumental learning of ANS responses in animals has revealed that, provided accurate feedback linked to reinforcement, animals can achieve learned control over such autonomic measures as blood pressure and galvanic skin response (which reflects sweat gland activity; for a review, see Kimmel, 1974) and that control over these peripheral responses can be achieved in the absence of voluntary muscular changes (Miller & DiCara, 1967). These findings have provided an important foundation for the development of clinical applications in humans that make use of the individual's capacity for learned physiological self-regulation through a process called *biofeedback* training.

The biofeedback rationale holds that, if one can record a physiological response and *feed back* information about ongoing changes in this measure to the person from whom it is recorded, this feedback loop can enable instrumental learning of control over that physiological response. The progressive stages that comprise the successful therapeutical biofeedback training process have been identified by Stoyva and Budzynski (1993) as follows:

- acquiring awareness of the maladaptive response (e.g. high muscular tension)
- learning to associate certain changes in mental and bodily states with changes in the maladaptive response through the biofeedback process, leading to learned self-regulation
- the transference of the learned skill into everyday life.

Over the last three decades, this simple realization has spawned a great variety of effective clinical applications. For instance, biofeedback of blood pressure levels and electrodermal activity (i.e. skin conductance) has been employed in the treatment of hypertension (e.g. Benson *et al.*, 1971; Patel, 1973). Likewise, thermal biofeedback (e.g. finger temperature) has been used in the treatment of Raynaud's disease (e.g. Freedman *et al.*, 1983) and tension headache (see Blanchard & Andrasik, 1987). Probably the most widely used biofeedback modality is electromyography (EMG), which measures electric muscle activity. EMG biofeedback has been employed in the treatment of such diverse ailments as tension headaches (e.g. Reinking & Hutchins, 1981) and asthma (e.g. Kotses *et al.*, 1991), as well as for neuromuscular re-education after stroke (e.g. Basmajian *et al.*, 1975). Given that the most commonly reported medical problems in musicians are related to muscle and tendon injuries (Lockwood, 1989), EMG biofeedback constitutes a particularly promising treatment modality for performers.

Typically, however, EMG and other biofeedback regimes are employed as complementary therapeutic tools for general relaxation training in the treatment of many anxiety and stress-related conditions. It is likely that, in addition to primary gains associated with control over the specific physiological measure that represents the symptomatology of a given clinical problem, all of the mentioned biofeedback treatments lead to appreciable nonspecific relaxation effects. In fact, all biofeedback training protocols that address ANS functions appear to be geared at shifting the organism's ANS from an activated, sympathetic state (i.e. the "fight or flight" system) to a more relaxed, parasympathetic tone. Additional nonspecific factors that may contribute to biofeedback efficacy are an enhancement of general awareness of one's bodily state, as well as feelings of self-efficacy and control stemming from perceived success at the biofeedback task. From this portrayal of specific and nonspecific gains that can be derived from biofeedback training, it would appear quite obvious that the application of these techniques to issues related specifically to musicians and music performance could be a fruitful endeavor.

11.2   Biofeedback and music performance

A small number of research studies have explored benefits of biofeedback training within music (mostly specific to muscular control) and supplied promising results. For example, Morasky *et al.* (1981) studied the use of EMG biofeedback for reducing excess left-arm extensor muscle tension in string players. They reported that the performers learned to reduce muscular tension during playing and that these reductions were successfully transferred to their playing in the absence of feedback. Morasky *et al.* (1983) performed a similar study involving clarinet players, where forearm extensor EMG feedback was again found to facilitate significantly reduced tension that generalized beyond the feedback condition itself. In order to allay fears that a more relaxed muscle tone would negatively affect musical performance, they also showed that performance speed in playing trills and scales, which would have been most affected by this particular muscle relaxation, remained at comparable levels to pre-training performances.

Biofeedback regimes have also been employed to help musicians with specific career-threatening clinical symptoms. For instance, Levee *et al.* (1976) reported a case study of a woodwind player suffering from tics due to high tension in throat and facial muscles. Specific EMG biofeedback, targeting the muscle groups in question, led to successful symptom reduction and improved (self-reported) musical performance ability. Similarly, LeVine (1983) documented dramatic improvements in a professional violinist suffering from functional palsy (also known as "craft palsy," of which writer's cramp and focal dystonia are examples) after she participated in a mixed course of behavioral therapy and thermal biofeedback.

Further intriguing examples of EMG biofeedback as a pedagogical tool in music include its application for removing unwanted left-hand tension in violin and viola players by feeding back muscle activity recorded from the adductor pollicis muscle. Self-rated improvements in muscle tension were evident even at 5-month follow-up interviews (LeVine & Irvine, 1984). Montes *et al.* (1993) found that EMG feedback training of activity of the abductor pollicis brevis muscle in pianists facilitated peak amplitude and relaxation rate values in this muscle group during thumb attacks in trills, a pattern of muscular activity that is seen in advanced pianists but not in beginners. From this brief survey of biofeedback applications in general and some peer-reviewed publications of its specific use in relation to music performance, it can be summarized that biofeedback training in principle could be employed to address profession-related clinical symptoms, general clinical and nonclinical levels of tension and anxiety, and as an instrument-specific pedagogical aid. It has to be stressed, however, that the use of objective performance measures for determining the benefits of such interventions has been almost entirely absent from this literature.

11.3   Neurofeedback

A different feedback modality to those discussed above is one that taps directly into the self-regulation of brain activity: biofeedback of the electroencephalogram (EEG) or neurofeedback. The EEG is commonly recorded via noninvasive electrodes attached to the scalp with paste or gel. These sensors allow for the measurement of minute electric potentials (i.e. brain rhythms or "brainwaves") emanating from the cortical neuronal populations just beneath the scalp electrode. This brainwave activity can be analyzed, by means of filtering or mathematical transformation, in terms of the amount of activity present in different "frequency bands" (i.e. at different speeds of brainwaves).

The body of knowledge concerned with mechanisms underlying cerebral rhythmic activity is elaborate, but nevertheless far from complete. In a general sense, rhythmic activity recorded at the scalp is the sum of electrical field potentials generated by cortical neurons in the vicinity of the electrode site, with one scalp electrode possibly integrating activity from neurons across 10 cm^2 of cortical surface (Nunez, 1995a). As random fluctuations in electrical potentials cancel each other out, any electrical activity detectable at the scalp necessitates approximately synchronous activity of a large number of neurons (for further discussion of the principles underlying fundamental characteristics and measurement of the human EEG, see Rosenweig & Leiman, 1989; Nunez, 1995b; Gazzaniga, 2000).

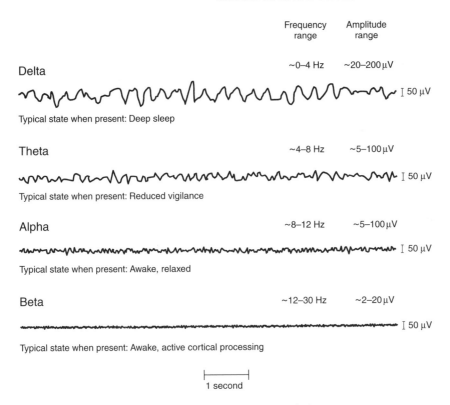

Figure 11.1 Spectral components and characteristics of human brain rhythms.

The feasibility of modifying aspects of the EEG by means of instrumental learning has been demonstrated in animals by supplying a food reward for the production of a particular frequency component of the EEG. For example, it has been shown that cats (Wyrwicka & Sterman, 1968) as well as rhesus monkeys (Sterman *et al.*, 1978) readily learn to enhance brainwaves at specific frequencies in their EEG. In humans, intentional modulation of brain activity is usually achieved by displaying an approximately real-time representation of some EEG parameter to the trainee participant (thus providing biofeedback), paired with reinforcement to facilitate successful instrumental learning of the desired response.

The idea of employing EEG frequency-band activity as a feedback criterion in biofeedback training partly stems from the close association observed between the speed of EEG frequencies and the arousal state of the organism. For example, very slow brainwaves in the so-called "delta" range (~0–4 Hz) are primarily found in the human EEG during deep sleep. Slightly faster "theta" waves (~4–8 Hz) on the other hand are often associated with drowsiness and early sleep stages, while the adjacent "alpha" frequency (~8–12 Hz) is characteristic of a relaxed, waking state. Faster frequencies in the

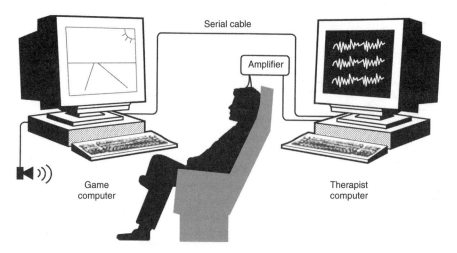

Figure 11.2 The neurofeedback loop. Scalp electrodes are attached, with reference and ground electrodes attached to the earlobes. The EEG signal is filtered into different frequency bands and displayed to the experimenter or therapist. For the training of high frequencies (e.g. beta and SMR), the frequency components may be translated into a graphic computer-game display, visible to the participant. For lower frequencies (e.g. alpha and theta), the participant listens in a reclining position with eyes closed to sounds through headphones (e.g. waves on the shore, a babbling brook, a Thai gong). (From Neurocybernetic, 1998. © EEG Spectrum International, Inc., used by permission.)

"beta" (~12–30 Hz) and "gamma" range (above 30 Hz) are associated with more aroused, active cortical processing during mental operations in the alert brain (see Figure 11.1).

It is important to stress that this association between EEG rhythms and arousal/activational state of the organism is but one of many functional correlates of EEG activity and, as such, constitutes only a convenient simplification. For instance, in the context of carrying out different tasks, any one particular brain rhythm may reflect many diverse functional states of neural communication, and may be generated through different processes by various anatomical structures. Furthermore, many aspects of EEG generation and functional significance are very much under active research and, as of yet, not entirely understood.

In the typical neurofeedback set-up, EEG activity is recorded from a single scalp electrode, and referenced and grounded to electrodes attached to the earlobes. The recorded signal is then filtered in order to extract activity in the frequency bands of interest, and ongoing changes in activity in these bands are relayed in real time to the trainee participant, usually in the form of audio-visual feedback similar to a computer game (see Figure 11.2). The trainee gets rewarded (e.g. by winning points) for producing the desired changes in brainwave patterns, and over the course of a number of training sessions (which typically last between 15–30 minutes each) learns to self-regulate the EEG activity.

11.4   Neurofeedback and attention

A line of pioneering neurofeedback research was set in motion by Sterman's experiments on cats in the 1960s (for a review, see Sterman, 1996). Sterman and associates noted that during learned suppression of a previously conditioned response (pressing a bar for food), a particular brain rhythm emerged over the cats' sensorimotor cortex (Roth *et al.*, 1967; Wyrwicka & Sterman, 1968; Sterman & Wyrwicka, 1967; Sterman *et al.*, 1969). This rhythm was characterized by a frequency range of 12–20 Hz, with a spectral peak in the area of 12–14 Hz, and has since been referred to as the "sensorimotor rhythm" (SMR; Roth *et al.*, 1967). The researchers decided to study this distinct rhythm directly, attempting to teach the cats to produce SMR through instrumental learning, by making a food reward contingent on the occurrence of SMR "bursts" (Wyrwicka & Sterman, 1968; Sterman *et al.*, 1969). Cats learned this feat of EEG self-regulation with apparent ease, and the behavior associated with SMR production was one of behavioral stillness, with SMR bursts regularly preceded by a drop in muscle tone.

In a serendipitous twist, Sterman's laboratory was also commissioned to establish dose-response functions of a highly epileptogenic rocket fuel. When using the cats that had previously taken part in SMR conditioning, these cats were found to display elevated epileptic seizure thresholds compared to untrained cats. This research was successfully extrapolated to humans, where it was repeatedly documented that epileptic motor seizure incidence could be lowered significantly by SMR feedback training (Sterman & Friar, 1972; Sterman *et al.*, 1974; Sterman & MacDonald, 1978; Lantz & Sterman, 1988; for a review, see Sterman, 2000).

In acknowledgement of the apparent quieting effect of SMR training on the excitability of the sensorimotor system, Lubar and coworkers applied a protocol of SMR enhancement to the treatment of attention deficit hyperactivity disorder (ADHD; Lubar & Shouse, 1976). These researchers reported that enhancement of SMR with concurrent suppression of slow-wave theta activity (4–8 Hz) resulted in attentional improvements primarily facilitated by reduced motor hyperactivity (Lubar & Shouse, 1976; Shouse & Lubar, 1979). Subsequently, the training of SMR has often been complemented or substituted by another training protocol that combines suppression of theta activity with increments in higher beta components, such as the beta-1 band (15–18 Hz). These types of "beta" protocols have been conceptualized as targeting improvements in attentiveness (e.g. Lubar & Lubar, 1984).

The application of beta/SMR protocols to attentional disorders has since evolved into probably the most widely employed application within the field of neurofeedback. However, only rather recently have appropriately controlled studies begun to supply a proper scientific basis for the training's efficacy. For instance, Rossiter and LaVaque (1995) and Fuchs *et al.* (2003) have reported that beta/SMR neurofeedback has led to significant improvements in laboratory attention tests, as well as observational ratings of behavior, in children with ADHD; these improvements were at comparable levels to those seen with stimulant medication. Furthermore, Monastra *et al.* (2002) have shown that an extensive course of beta band training in addition to standard pharmacological treatment can lead to lasting benefits even after medication has been suspended. These studies have provided evidence for neurofeedback's potential for enhancing attentional function in clinical groups, and offer the promise of possible applications to improving attentional abilities in healthy people (see Section 11.6).

11.5   Neurofeedback and relaxation

In what is believed to be the first ever application of neurofeedback training, Kamiya (1962) found that participants who were made aware of alpha-frequency bursts (8–12 Hz) in their EEG recorded from the occipital scalp regions (i.e. at the back of the head) could eventually identify alpha in the absence of feedback. They also appeared to be able to increase voluntarily the incidence of alpha rhythms, and they reported the subjective experience of the "alpha state" as being relaxing and peaceful. This initiated the pursuit of neurofeedback research that aimed to use EEG frequency characteristics as criteria for allowing the brain to be guided into different functional and activational states. Following this line of inquiry, a number of studies reported alpha density enhancement accompanied by a reduction in anxiety (and/or physiological arousal) by means of alpha feedback training (Kamiya, 1969; Brown, 1970; Budzynski & Stoyva, 1972; Hardt & Kamiya, 1978). This endeavor, however, did not always result in reliable replication of the subjective and physiological states originally associated with the "alpha state." Participants did not always succeed in actually enhancing alpha activity above pre-feedback levels (Lynch et al., 1974), and in some studies, the behavioral and phenomenological effects could be attributed to social variables such as positive expectancies (Pressner & Savitzky, 1977) and perceived success at the biofeedback task (Plotkin & Rice, 1981).

More recently, an alpha/theta neurofeedback protocol that has been conceptualized as an "EEG-based relaxation therapy" (Peniston & Kulkosky, 1999, p. 158) has emerged as a complementary therapeutic tool in the treatment of alcoholism (Peniston & Kulkosky, 1989, 1990; Saxby & Peniston, 1995), as well as post-traumatic stress disorder (PTSD; Peniston & Kulkosky, 1991). The protocol is geared at facilitating a rise in levels of theta (4–8 Hz) over alpha (8–12 Hz) activity in a state of eyes-closed relaxation. Normally, upon closure of the eyes and onset of relaxation, the EEG displays high-amplitude rhythmic alpha activity. When the organism deactivates further, alpha activity slowly subsides and slower theta (and delta) activity gradually becomes predominant (see Broughton & Hasan, 1995; De Gennaro et al., 2001). The point in time when theta activity supersedes alpha activity (the so-called "theta/alpha crossover") is in this context commonly associated with loss of consciousness and the onset of early sleep stages (i.e. sleep stage I). By teaching trainees to raise theta over alpha activity while not falling asleep, the alpha/theta protocol aims to teach people to enter a state of deep relaxation and deactivation consciously, apparently resembling a meditative state that would normally be unconscious.

Initial development of this kind of protocol (e.g. Budzynski & Stoyva, 1972) was based on the proposed association between alpha activity and subjective phenomenology of relaxation, as well as the implication of elevated theta amplitudes in certain types of meditative (Anand et al., 1961) and "reverie" states (Green et al., 1970). The application of alpha neurofeedback to alcoholism was originally justified only in terms of the high levels of anxiety reported among alcoholics (Passini *et al.*, 1977). Subsequent research (Gabrielli *et al.*, 1982) has furthermore confirmed the negative correlations between alcoholism and alpha activity first reported by Funderburk (1949), as well as increased alpha band levels in alcoholics after alcohol consumption (Pollock *et al.*, 1983).

Peniston and Kulkosky have developed a treatment protocol that customarily combines alpha/theta neurofeedback with various other relaxation-inducing techniques, such as thermal (finger temperature) biofeedback, respiratory and autogenic instructions, and systematic desensitization procedures (Peniston & Kulkosky, 1999). The application of this combined treatment package, as an additional intervention to conventional therapy, has resulted in spectacular improvements in relapse rates in alcoholics (Peniston & Kulkosky, 1989; Saxby & Peniston, 1995). Dramatic symptom reductions in veterans with combat-related PTSD have also been reported from the same program of intervention (Peniston & Kulkosky, 1991). However, given the heterogeneous nature of their treatment package, it has been impossible to assess unambiguously the specific importance of the contribution of alpha/theta neurofeedback to the therapeutic process, and it has been suggested that it may be no different from alternative relaxation techniques (Taub & Rosenfeld, 1994; Graap & Freides, 1998). Even the basic feasibility of gaining voluntary control over this specific EEG signature has long remained unsubstantiated. However, in a recent study, Egner *et al.* (2002) have demonstrated that accurate alpha/theta feedback did successfully facilitate learned control over these frequency components and led to significantly elevated theta-to-alpha ratios in comparison with relaxation under noncontingent feedback conditions.

Regardless of the ambivalent status of its scientific evaluation, the alpha/theta neurofeedback protocol has gained considerable popularity with biofeedback practitioners in application to a number of tension- and anxiety-related clinical conditions and, as such, could provide a potential tool for addressing similar issues commonly found in musicians.

11.6 Neurofeedback and performance enhancement in musicians

It is clear that peak performance in music requires tremendous control over the brain processes underlying shifts of attentional and activational states. Working on the basis that such control is of central importance to the musician, one could argue that a program of experimental application of the clinical neurofeedback paradigms described previously could be applied to music with professionally significant consequences. In recent research based at a music conservatory, the authors have conducted two studies to examine the strength of this line of reasoning. In particular, the studies were carried out as part of the project "Zoning In: Motivating the Musical Mind" (see also Chapters 9, 10, and 12), with the intention of establishing the impact of these neurofeedback training paradigms on laboratory-based behavioral and neurophysiological measures of attention and on the quality of music performance.

11.6.1   Enhancing attention

In the first study, a group of music students were trained on both an attention-targeting beta1/SMR neurofeedback protocol (i.e. 10 15-minute sessions of both beta-1 and SMR training) and a relaxation-targeting alpha/theta neurofeedback protocol (also 10 15-minute sessions). The assessment of attention performance was carried out employing a computerized test displaying two classes of stimuli: (1) "targets," which require the participant to respond as quickly and accurately as possible (by pushing a response switch) and (2) "nontargets," which require the participant to refrain from responding. Thus, two types of errors can be incurred on such a task: (1) errors of *omission* (i.e. failing to respond to a target stimulus) and (2) errors of *commission* (i.e. erroneously responding to a nontarget stimulus). Respectively, these errors are held to reflect inattentiveness and impulsiveness. A further attention measure, derived from signal detection theory (Green & Swets, 1966), is termed "perceptual sensitivity" or "d prime" (d') and takes into account both of these error types by expressing a ratio of hit rate to false alarm rate.

From the emergent data, it was established that 10 training sessions of both beta-1 and SMR neurofeedback led to a significant reduction in errors (Egner & Gruzelier, 2001). More specifically, students showed a significant reduction in commission errors as compared with measures taken before training. When exploring the link between the process of learned EEG self-regulation and this reduction in impulsive mistakes, it was found that the relative success at enhancing the SMR was highly positively correlated with reduced commission errors, meaning that participants who did well on the SMR feedback task tended to decrease the amount of impulsive mistakes after training. These findings support the notion that learned SMR enhancement is associated with improved response inhibition and constitute the first evidence for cognitive performance enhancement through neurofeedback in healthy volunteers (Egner & Gruzelier, 2001).

It was furthermore established that SMR neurofeedback training can also improve the incidence of omission errors (inattentive mistakes) in healthy subjects (Egner & Gruzelier, 2004a), and recent findings even suggest that memory function can be enhanced by similar means (Vernon *et al.*, 2003). In addition, the attention-enhancing potential of beta-1 neurofeedback has been corroborated by electrocortical performance measures related to selective attention processes. Specifically, beta-1 neurofeedback training is associated with increments in the P300 event-related brain potential (Egner & Gruzelier, 2001; Egner & Gruzelier, 2004a), which has been conceptualized as representing activity in neuronal sources responsible for updating relevant stimulus environment information in working memory (Donchin & Coles, 1988; see Chapter 7 of this volume for a short discussion of working memory). While these data offer support for the general feasibility of employing neurofeedback for improving cognitive performance in healthy individuals, they might be of no meaningful consequence at all for the enhancement of such a complex blend of requirements as live musical performance.

11.6.2   Achieving peak performance

The variable of relevance to the issue of achieving peak performance is, of course, the measurement of music performance quality itself. While some form of quantitative evaluation of music performance quality has long formed a routine part of the assessment policies within music schools and conservatories, the issue of reliable measurement of such seemingly subjective concepts as a performer's musical interpretation is, not surprisingly, an issue of some debate. The use of performance measures as dependent variables in music psychology research has gained popularity in recent years (e.g. Juslin & Laukka, 2000; Williamon & Valentine, 2000, 2002), and the actual process of performance evaluation is under active investigation (Thompson & Williamon, 2003). Attempts at quantifying quality judgments of musical performance in order to achieve reliable assessments have typically involved having expert evaluators complete structured evaluation forms that elicit judgments along a range of performance aspects (e.g. "technical ability" versus "artistic expression"; see Chapter 4 for a discussion of performance assessment schemes).

The purpose of the music performance measurements in the neurofeedback research was to assess performance variables of high ecological validity and pedagogical relevance; therefore, it seemed appropriate to employ an evaluation scheme by which students are assessed customarily. For this reason, the marking scheme of the Associated Boards of the Royal Schools of Music (Harvey, 1994) was adapted to take into account segmented aspects of performance quality (including "instrumental competence," "musicality," and "communicative ability"), as well as overall performance quality (see Table 11.1 for a listing of the four main assessment categories and the adapted sub-scales).

While examination assessments within a conservatory are normally carried out on live performances by teachers both internal and external to the institution, in the context of a scientific investigation, this type of evaluation procedure would seem to introduce potential sources of bias. Foremost, the assessors would be aware of the order of pre- and post-training performances, which might induce expectations of improved performances. In order to exert maximum control over such biases, the performances

Table 11.1 Music performance evaluation scales and Pearson product-moment correlation coefficients between change scores in music performance evaluation and alpha/theta learning (from Egner & Gruzelier, 2003). Major evaluation categories are in italics, with their associated sub-scales following below

	Alpha/theta learning
Overall quality	$r = 0.47$, $p = 0.038$
Instrumental competence (i.e. technical ability)	$r = 0.50$, $p = 0.029$
Level of technical security	$r = 0.39$, $p = 0.086$
Rhythmic accuracy	$r = 0.65$, $p = 0.003$
Tonal quality and spectrum	$r = 0.39$, $p = 0.140$
Musicality	$r = 0.54$, $p = 0.017$
Stylistic accuracy	$r = 0.58$, $p = 0.007$
Interpretative imagination	$r = 0.48$, $p = 0.037$
Expressive range	$r = 0.53$, $p = 0.016$
Communicative ability	$r = 0.55$, $p = 0.013$
Deportment	$r = 0.45$, $p = 0.052$
Communication of emotional commitment and conviction	$r = 0.51$, $p = 0.021$
Ability to cope with situational stress	$r = 0.44$, $p = 0.052$

here were videotaped, randomized, and then evaluated only by experienced assessors external to the institution and blind as to the order of performances and to experimental group membership of the students. In order to assess whether any changes in music performance ratings were related to pre-performance anxiety, the Spielberger's State Anxiety Inventory (Spielberger *et al.*, 1983) was administered to each participant just before performance.

As mentioned earlier, a group of music students took part in a mixed course of beta-1/SMR and alpha/theta training in the first study (Gruzelier *et al.*, 2002; Egner & Gruzelier, 2003). Prior and subsequent to the training program, the students were assessed on the quality of their performances. The impact of participation in this mixed course of beta-1/SMR and alpha/theta neurofeedback was assessed in comparison with a no-training control group, as well as with a randomly selected subgroup of neurofeedback participants who engaged in additional interventions. These additional training components consisted of a physical exercise regime (see Chapter 9) and a course of "mental skills training" composed of interventions derived from sports psychology (see Chapter 12). These comparison groups were conceived in order to allow for the assessment of neurofeedback's impact on performance as a stand-alone intervention versus a subcomponent of a more elaborate training program, while controlling for the presumed natural progression in performance quality resulting from the standard conservatory training (through the no-training control group).

The blind rating scores of music performance quality before and after training obtained from two expert judges were averaged for each rating scale for each student. It was found that improvements in performance were evident in the neurofeedback-only group, but neither in the neurofeedback group engaging in additional interventions nor in the no-training control group (see Figure 11.3). The neurofeedback group improved most markedly on ratings of overall quality of performance and of their "communication of emotional commitment and conviction."

Interestingly, an alpha/theta training learning index, reflecting increasing ease and depth of relaxation across the training process, correlated highly positively with music

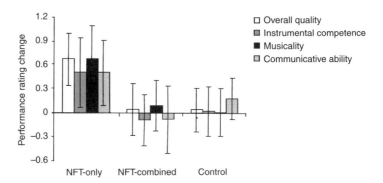

Figure 11.3 Mean music performance rating change scores (i.e. scores from the post-training performance minus those of the pre-training performance, on a 10-point rating scale) on the main evaluation categories for neurofeedback-only (NFT-only), neurofeedback and additional interventions (NFT-combined), and a no-training control group. The whiskers indicate mean ± standard error.

performance improvements. As can be seen in Table 11.1, alpha/theta learning was significantly associated (i.e. $p < 0.05$) with trends of improvement in 9 out of 13 rating criteria, including the main four. Neither the SMR nor the beta-1 protocols were related to improvements in music performance. Furthermore, differential improvement rates between the experimental groups in this study were not related to pre-performance state anxiety, as generally decreased anxiety levels between the first and second performances did not differ between groups.

These findings supply evidence for a potential benefit of neurofeedback on a highly ecologically valid music performance measure. The fact that music performance quality changes were not related to SMR and beta-1 learning suggests that improvements were not mediated by attention-related variables, whereas the fact that alpha/theta learning correlated highly with changes in virtually all music evaluation categories would seem to point to a single, pervasive factor mediating these correlations. Given the nature of the alpha/theta protocol and these relationships, a prime candidate for effect mediation would appear to be pre-performance anxiety, but the data did not support this assumption.

In order to clarify the seemingly strong association between alpha/theta neurofeedback and performance enhancement, a quasi-replication study was devised (Gruzelier et al., 2002; Egner & Gruzelier, 2003), where participants were randomly allocated to one of the following: an alpha/theta, SMR, or beta-1 neurofeedback training group, a physical exercise program, or a mental skills training program. As before, music performances were assessed before and after training. In addition, a further comparison group was integrated into the study consisting of students involved in a course of Alexander technique training, as this technique is considered an established tool for improving performance in music conservatories worldwide. This program engaged participants in a comparable amount of one-to-one interaction as the neurofeedback intervention (see Chapter 10 for further discussion of the Alexander technique).

Analysis of music performance ratings from three expert judges blind to the experimental conditions revealed that the alpha/theta group displayed significant improvements, while neither the beta-1 nor the SMR group exhibited any post-training performance changes. Similarly, students from the Alexander technique, physical exercise, and mental skills training groups showed no post-training changes. In the alpha/theta group, evaluation scores for "musicality," "stylistic accuracy," "interpretative imagination," and "overall quality" were all significantly improved (see Figure 11.4). These increments represent average alpha/theta group improvements between 13.5% and 17%, with a mean improvement rate of 12% across all evaluation scales. Individual participants displayed improvements of over 50% on some evaluation criteria. As in the first study, all groups reported significantly less pre-performance anxiety before the post-training performance, with no differences between groups.

In the previous study, alpha/theta learning correlated with musical improvements across all evaluation categories. Here, the protocol's performance enhancing effects proved to be replicable particularly with respect to parameters on the "musicality" evaluation category (see Table 11.1). These data could be interpreted as indicating that alpha/theta training led especially to improvements on attributes of artistic expression (as opposed to technical skills), which in turn improved overall performance. These

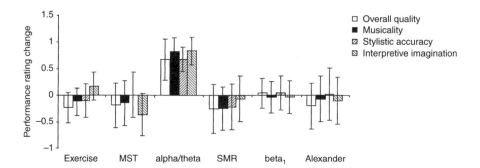

Figure 11.4 Mean music performance rating change scores (i.e. scores from the pre-training performance minus those of the post-training performance, on a scale of 1–10) for the exercise, mental skills training (MST), alpha/theta, SMR, beta₁, and Alexander technique groups. The whiskers indicate mean ± standard error on a 10-point rating scale of musical evaluation criteria (from Egner & Gruzelier, 2003).

results suggest that alpha/theta training appears reliably to enhance artistic aspects of musical performance skills, independently of training on additional neurofeedback protocols and that these effects are superior to the other interventions in this respect. These data confirm a significantly beneficial effect of alpha/theta training on a highly ecologically valid and pedagogically relevant performance measure. Indeed, the improvements were equivalent to two academic grades within the conservatory's assessment system. These effects cannot be accounted for by invoking practice, motivational, or generic neurofeedback factors. An explanation based on generic relaxation can also be discounted on the grounds that, once again, the alpha/theta training was not associated with a greater decrease in pre-performance anxiety than that seen in other groups. Additionally, a mental skills training group, which engaged in extensive relaxation training, showed no detectable performance improvements.

The size of the performance improvements implies great potential for the implementation of this application in music performance contexts. But how does alpha/theta training achieve these remarkable effects? In theoretical terms, the data do not appear to fit with a conceptualization of training efficacy primarily based on relaxation. The need to look beyond a mere relaxation model is further emphasized by a study showing that significantly different theta-to-alpha ratios between real and false alpha/theta feedback conditions were not reflected in differences in reports of subjective relaxation (Egner *et al.*, 2002).

When inspecting EEG changes within the sessions across the training process, an increase in the production of theta amplitudes has been noted (Egner & Gruzelier, 2004b). EEG theta activity has been implicated in a number of mental and affective states ostensibly unrelated to relaxational processes. Furthermore, the clinical efficacy of alpha/theta training in patients suffering trauma and chronic drug addiction, extending in recent evidence to young offenders with crack and cocaine misuse, implies a more powerful impact than can be achieved with relaxation and anxiety reduction alone. Theta is generated throughout the cortex in hypnogogic states and following training in meditation and hypnosis (Vaitl *et al.*, 2003); its production can often outlast the experience itself (Williams & Gruzelier, 2001). These states are typically associated with pleasure, and in the case of meditation, theta production has been positively associated with ratings of bliss (Aftanas & Golocheikine, 2001). Accordingly, theta appears associated with enhanced feelings of well-being as well as with relaxation; in the words of one participating music student: "it lets the mind breathe" (Gruzelier *et al.*, 2002).

Relevant too is the growing evidence of the role of theta in a range of memory control processes, enabling a fluent retrieval of memories into conscious awareness and working memory (Klimesch, 1996; Burgess & Gruzelier, 1997; Sarnthein *et al.*, 1998; Klimesch *et al.*, 2001). It is self-evident that memory control processes are exercised to the hilt in musical performance, when both virtuoso technical accomplishment and artistry are demanded.

Intriguingly, a bold theory of the relation between theta, dreams, and survival by Winson (2002) chimes with the findings presented here. Winson has long observed that across species theta from the hippocampus (a structure situated deep in the brain's limbic system) is generated both in situations that challenge survival and in dream sleep. Consistent with the evidence of the importance of theta for memory control processes, he posits that theta assists in making available to memory information that is necessary for survival. This follows his observations of survival behavior in animals, which (though species-specific) is united by the occurrence of theta. Theta also occurs in all species during dream sleep, which serves the purpose of facilitating access to memory control processes of information regarding events that threaten survival in order to deal more effectively with any recurrence of threat. The process of alpha/theta training, in fact, involves the transient entering and re-entering of dream-like states. Let us consider that the typical music student's career trajectory has taken 10 years or so of singular dedication to the practice and performance of music at the highest level. Now his or her musical ability and career ambition is under the challenge of a stressful performance to be judged by teachers and other experts. Accordingly, the exercise of theta-related processes through alpha/theta training may well facilitate success, for the successful student orchestrates a dazzling technical and artistic display that is dependent on memory control processes. This involves a complex coordination of sensory-motor, postural, and respiratory functions, together with the expression and modulation of emotion and the expression of creative and artistic ability (as is inherent in the concept of musicality).

A further line of interpretation of these results stems from considerations of the post-training effects of alpha/theta neurofeedback on the EEG amplitudes in different frequency bands across the whole scalp. From measuring whole-head multi-channel EEG activity during rest, there is evidence for alpha/theta training being related to a reduction in high beta-frequency activity (15–30 Hz) over frontal brain regions (Egner *et al.*, 2003). The training's effect of reducing frontal beta band activity could quite readily be interpreted as reflecting decreased agitation and negative affect, based on associations between frontal beta activity and depression (Pollock & Schneider, 1990) and post-traumatic stress (Begic *et al.*, 2001), and with stress responses to brief painful stimulation in nonclinical groups (Chen *et al.*, 1989; Chen, 2001). Based on these data, a theoretical account of alpha/theta neurofeedback efficacy has to integrate its apparent role in reducing vigilant arousal and its positive effects on artistic expression in musical performance.

Irrespective of the precise mechanisms underlying the training effects, the findings presented here have important implications with respect to both the psychological and physical well-being of musicians. The significant enhancement of performance skills may in the long run alleviate excessive worry about performing, the most commonly cited impediment to musicians' successful careers (Fishbein *et al.*, 1988; Steptoe, 1989). Furthermore, the enhancement of artistic aspects of performance warrant application to the performing arts in general.

Although a theoretical link between functional correlates of theta activity (as well as alpha/theta training effects on frontal beta activity) and improved artistic expression in music performance can easily be envisaged, no effect mediation has yet been established. However, the remarkable neurofeedback training effects demonstrated in these studies should serve as a motivation for empirically addressing the exact mechanisms underlying the training in the future. Firstly, further clarification of the precise nature of the alpha/theta effects is required for advancing the theoretical framework. With regards to subjective phenomenology, a wide scope of self-report measures assessing the experiences associated with the training process could prove elucidating for pinpointing psychological mediators of the training's efficacy. Furthermore, the impact of alpha/theta training on arousal states within training sessions, as well as at post-training, could be assessed by peripheral physiological measures, such as the skin conductance response. The monitoring of whole-scalp EEG changes within each training session would also be of great interest, above all in order to elucidate the origin of the theta activity generated during the training and the way in which the training may affect frontal beta band activity.

Of more immediate practical concern to the musician and educator are the questions of who is most likely to benefit from the training, how to optimize the nature and duration of the training, and how long the effects may be expected to last. These issues are at the present moment unresolved but under active investigation. Elaborate psychometric testing could possibly allow one to determine personality trait predictors of likely responsiveness to alpha/theta neurofeedback and successful performance enhancement. It is also conceivable that particular instrument groups are more likely to benefit from this intervention than others.

The relevance of applying this technique to music performers hinges decidedly on its potential to evoke long-term effects. The research to date does not permit any inferences regarding this important aspect, as all post-training music performance measures were taken within a time-span of maximally four weeks after the last training session. In the future, studies that involve regular follow-up assessments over a longer interval will have to be conducted in order to determine whether the costs of neurofeedback training (both in terms of time and money) as a performance enhancement tool are justified by long-term returns.

11.7   Conclusions

The field of learned physiological self-regulation through means of biofeedback holds promising potential for enhancing musical performance (see Table 11.2 for a summary

Table 11.2 A summary of the clinical and music performance benefits of biofeedback and neurofeedback

	Clinical benefits	Music performance benefits
Biofeedback		
Blood pressure	Treatment of hypertension (Benson *et al.*, 1971; Patel, 1973)	
Electrodermal	Treatment of hypertension (Benson *et al.*, 1971; Patel, 1973)	
Thermal	Treatment of Raynaud's disease (Freedman *et al.*, 1983) Treatment of tension headaches (Blanchard & Andrasik, 1987)	Treatment of functional palsy in a professional violinist (LeVine, 1983)
EMG	General relaxation training Treatment of tension headaches (Reinking & Hutchins, 1981) Treatment of asthma (Kotses *et al.*, 1991) Neuromuscular re-education after stroke (Basmajian *et al.*, 1975)	Reduction of left arm tension in string players (Morasky *et al.*, 1981; LeVine & Irvine, 1984) Reduction of forearm tension in clarinet players (Morasky *et al.*, 1983) Reduction of tension in facial muscles of a woodwind player (Levee *et al.*, 1976) Facilitation of peak amplitude and relaxation rate values in pianists' trills (Montes *et al.*, 1993)
Neurofeedback		
SMR	Treatment of epilepsy (Sterman & MacDonald, 1978; Lantz & Sterman, 1988) Treatment of attention deficit hyperactivity disorder (Rossiter & LaVaque, 1995; Fuchs *et al.*, 2003)	Improved attention performance in music students (Egner & Gruzelier, 2001, 2004a)
Beta	Treatment of attention-deficit hyperactivity disorder (Rossiter & LaVaque, 1995; Monastra *et al.*, 2002; Fuchs *et al.*, 2003)	Enhanced attention-related P300 event-related brain potential in music students (Egner & Gruzelier, 2001, 2004a)
Alpha	Reduction of anxiety in anxiety-prone students (Hardt & Kamiya, 1978) and in alcoholics (Passini *et al.*, 1977)	
Alpha/theta	Treatment of alcoholism (Peniston & Kulkosky, 1989, 1990) and posttraumatic stress disorder (Peniston & Kulkosky, 1991)	Improved music performance in music students (Egner & Gruzelier, 2003)

of emergent findings). Biofeedback of peripheral nervous system measures, notably EMG activity, has successfully been employed as an educational aid and as a therapeutic tool in reducing muscular tension in string and wind players. More recently, an exciting new possibility of improving music performance has arisen through the use of EEG biofeedback of alpha and theta frequencies. Research has shown that alpha/theta neurofeedback can facilitate replicable improvements in music performance skills in conservatory students. These effects were not related to learning of a relaxation technique per se, nor to reduced pre-performance anxiety levels. In order to understand fully the way in which the alpha/theta protocol produces its effects, the training process will have to be monitored closely by assessing both cerebral and peripheral electro-physiological responses and by elucidating in detail the resultant phenomenology.

Acknowledgments

This research was supported by grants from The Leverhulme Trust, the Research Strategy Fund of Royal Holloway, University of London, and the Royal College of Music, London.

Further information and reading

Additional information on physiological self-regulation, biofeedback, and neurofeedback can be obtained from the websites of the following societies: the Association for Applied Psychophysiology and Biofeedback (*www.aapb.org*), the Society for Neuronal Regulation (*www.snr-jnt.org*), and the European chapter of the Society for Neuronal Regulation (*www.e-isnr.org*). Further particulars of the research results presented in this chapter are provided at the project website for "Zoning In: Motivating the Musical Mind": *www.zoningin.rcm.ac.uk*. For related reading, see:

Evans, J. R., & Abarbanel, A. (Eds.) (1999). *Introduction to Quantitative EEG and Neurofeedback.* London: Academic Press.

Freeman, W. J. (1999). *How Brains Make Up Their Minds.* London: Weidenfeld & Nicolson.

Gazzaniga, M. S. (Ed.) (2000). *Cognitive Neuroscience: A Reader.* Oxford: Blackwell.

Hatch, J. P., Fisher, J. G., & Rugh, J. D. (Eds.) (1987). *Biofeedback: Studies in Clinical Efficacy.* New York: Plenum.

Nunez, P. L. (Ed.) (1995b). *Neocortical Dynamics and Human EEG Rhythms.* Oxford: Oxford University Press.

Shapiro, D., Barber, T. X., DiCara, L. V., Kamiya, J., Miller, N. B., & Stoyva, J. M. (Eds.) (1972). *Biofeedback and Self-Control.* Chicago: Aldine.

References

Aftanas, L. I., & Golocheikine, S. A. (2001). Human anterior and frontal midline theta and lower alpha reflect emotionally positive state and internalized attention: High-resolution EEG investigation of meditation. *Neuroscience Letters, 310,* 57–60.

Anand, B. K., China, G. S., & Singh, B. (1961). Some aspects of electroencephalographic studies in yogis. *Electroencephalography and Clinical Neurophysiology, 13,* 452–456.

Basmajian, J. V., Kukulka, C. J., Narajan, M. G., & Takebe, K. (1975). Biofeedback treatment of foot drop after stroke compared with standard rehabilitation technique: Effects on voluntary control and strength. *Archives of Physical Medicine and Rehabilitation, 56,* 231–236.

Begic, D., Hotujac, L., & Jokic-Begic, N. (2001). Electroencephalographic comparison of veterans with combat-related post-traumatic stress disorder and healthy subjects. *International Journal of Psychophysiology, 40,* 167–172.

Benson, H., Shapiro, D., Tursky, B., & Schwarz, G. E. (1971). Decreased systolic blood pressure through operant conditioning techniques in patients with essential hypertension. *Science, 173,* 740–741.

Blanchard, E. B., & Andrasik, F. (1987). Biofeedback treatment of vascular headache. In J. P. Hatch, J. G. Fisher, & J. D. Rugh (Eds.), *Biofeedback: Studies in Clinical Efficacy* (pp. 1–79). New York: Plenum.

Broughton, R., & Hasan, J. (1995). Quantitative topographic electroencephalographic mapping during drowsiness and sleep onset. *Journal of Clinical Neurophysiology, 12*, 372–386.

Brown, B. B. (1970). Recognition of aspects of consciousness through association with EEG alpha activity represented by a light signal. *Psychophysiology, 6*, 442–452.

Budzynski, T. H., & Stoyva, J. M. (1972). Biofeedback techniques in behavior therapy. In D. Shapiro, T. X. Barber, L. V. DiCara, J. Kamiya, N. B. Miller, & J. M. Stoyva (Eds.), *Biofeedback and Self-Control* (pp. 437–459). Chicago: Aldine.

Burgess, A. P., & Gruzelier, J. H. (1997). Short duration synchronization of human theta rhythm during recognition memory. *NeuroReport, 8*, 1039–1042.

Chen, A. C. N. (2001). New perspectives in EEG/MEG brain mapping and PET/fMRI neuroimaging of human pain. *International Journal of Psychophysiology, 42*, 147–159.

Chen, A. C. N., Dworkin, S. F., Haug, J., & Gehrig, J. (1989). Topographic brain measures of human pain and pain responsivity. *Pain, 37*, 129–141.

De Gennaro, L., Ferrara, M., & Bertini, M. (2001). The boundary between wakefulness and sleep: Quantitative electroencephalographic changes during the sleep onset period. *Neuroscience Letters, 107*, 1–11.

Donchin, E., & Coles, M. G. H. (1988). Is the P300 component a manifestation of context updating? *Behavioral and Brain Sciences, 11*, 357–374.

Egner, T., & Gruzelier, J. H. (2001). Learned self-regulation of EEG frequency components affects attention and event-related brain potentials in humans. *NeuroReport, 12*, 4155–4159.

Egner, T., & Gruzelier, J. H. (2003). The effects of neurofeedback training on the spectral topography of the healthy electroencephalogram. Manuscript submitted for publication.

Egner, T., & Gruzelier, J. H. (2004a). EEG Biofeedback of low beta band components: Frequency-specific effects on variables of attention and event-related brain potentials. *Clinical Neurophysiology, 115*, 131–139.

Egner, T., & Gruzelier, J. H. (2004b). The temporal dynamics of electroencephalographic responses to alpha/theta neurofeedback training in healthy subjects. *Journal of Neurotherapy, 8*, 43–57.

Egner, T., Strawson, E., & Gruzelier, J. H. (2002). EEG signature and phenomenology of alpha/theta neurofeedback training versus mock feedback. *Applied Psychophysiology and Biofeedback, 27*, 261–270.

Egner, T., Zech, T. F., & Gruzelier, J. H. (2003). *The effects of neurofeedback training on the spectral topography of the healthy electroencephalogram.* Manuscript submitted for publication.

Fishbein, M., Middelstadt, S. E., Ottati, V., Strauss, S., & Ellis, A. (1988). Medical problems among ICSOM musicians: Overview of a national survey. *Medical Problems of Performing Artists, 3*, 1–8.

Freedman, R. R., Ianni, P., & Wenig, P. (1983). Behavioural treatment of Raynaud's disease. *Journal of Consulting and Clinical Psychology, 51*, 539–549.

Fuchs, T., Birbaumer, N., Lutzenberger, W., Gruzelier, J. H., & Kaiser, J. (2003). Neurofeedback treatment for attention-deficit/hyperactivity disorder in children: A comparison with methylphenidate. *Applied Psychophysiology and Biofeedback, 28*, 1–12.

Funderburk, W. H. (1949). Electroencephalographic studies in chronic alcoholics. *Electroencephalography and Clinical Neurophysiology, 1*, 369–370.

Gabrielli, W. F., Mednick, S. A., Vlovka, J., Pollack, V. E., Schulsinger, F., & Itil, T. M. (1982). Electroencephalograms in children of alcoholic fathers. *Psychophysiology, 19*, 404–407.

Gazzaniga, M. S. (Ed.). (2000). *Cognitive Neuroscience: A Reader.* Oxford: Blackwell.

Graap, K., & Freides, D. (1998). Regarding the database for the Peniston alpha-theta EEG biofeedback protocol. *Applied Psychophysiology and Biofeedback, 23*, 265–272.

Green, D. M., & Swets, J. A. (1966). *Signal Detection Theory and Psychophysics.* New York: Wiley.

Green, E. E., Green, A. M., & Walters, E. D. (1970). Voluntary control of internal states: Psychological and physiological. *Journal of Transpersonal Psychology, 2*, 1–26.

Gruzelier, J. H., Egner, T., Valentine, E., & Williamon, A. (2002). Comparing learned EEG self-regulation and the Alexander Technique as a means of enhancing musical performance. In C. Stevens, D. Burnham, G. McPherson, E. Schubert, & J. Renwick (Eds.), *Proceedings of the Seventh International Conference on Music Perception and Cognition* (pp. 89–92). Adelaide, Australia: Causal Productions.

Hardt, J. V., & Kamiya, J. (1978). Anxiety change through electroencephalographic alpha feedback seen only in high alpha subjects. *Science, 201*, 79–81.

Harvey, J. (1994). *These Music Exams.* London: Associated Board of the Royal Schools of Music.

Juslin, P. N., & Laukka, P. (2000). Improving emotional communication in music performance through cognitive feedback. *Musicæ Scientiæ, 4*, 151–183.

Kamiya, J. (1962). *Conditioned Discrimination of the EEG Alpha Rhythm in Humans.* Paper presented at the Western Psychological Association, San Francisco, CA.

Kamiya, J. (1969). Operant control of the EEG alpha rhythm and some of its reported effects on consciousness. In C. T. Tart (Ed.), *Altered States of Consciousness* (pp. 519–529). New York: Wiley.

Kimmel, H. D. (1974). Instrumental conditioning of autonomically mediated response in human beings. *American Psychologist, 29*, 325–335.

Klimesch, W. (1996). Memory processes, brain oscillations and EEG synchronisation. *International Journal of Psychophysiology, 24*, 61–100.

Klimesch, W., Doppelmayr, M., Yonelinas, A., Kroll, N. E., Lazzara, M., Rohm, D., & Gruber, W. (2001). Theta synchronisation during episodic retrieval: Neural correlates of conscious awareness. *Cognitive Brain Research, 12*, 33–38.

Kotses, H., Harver, A., Segreto, J., Glaus, K. D., Creer, T. L., & Young, G. A. (1991). Long-term effects of biofeedback induced facial relaxation on measures of asthma severity in children. *Biofeedback and Self-Regulation, 16*, 1–21.

Lantz, D., & Sterman, M. B. (1988). Neuropsychological assessment of subjects with uncontrolled epilepsy: Effects of EEG biofeedback training. *Epilepsia, 29*, 163–171.

Levee, J. R., Cohen, M. J., & Rickles, W. H. (1976). Electromyographic biofeedback for relief of tension in the facial and throat muscles of a woodwind musician. *Biofeedback and Self-Regulation, 1*, 113–130.

LeVine, W. R. (1983). Behavioural and biofeedback therapy for a functionally impaired musician: A case report. *Biofeedback and Self-Regulation, 8*, 101–107.

LeVine, W. R., & Irvine, J. K. (1984). In vivo EMG biofeedback in violin and viola pedagogy. *Biofeedback and Self-Regulation, 9*, 161–168.

Lockwood, A. H. (1989). Medical problems of musicians. *New England Journal of Medicine, 321*, 51–53.

Lubar, J. F., & Shouse, M. N. (1976). EEG and behavioural changes in a hyperkinetic child concurrent with training of the sensorimotor rhythm (SMR): A preliminary report. *Biofeedback and Self-Regulation, 3*, 293–306.

Lubar, J. O., & Lubar, J. F. (1984). Electroencephalographic biofeedback of SMR and beta for treatment of attention deficit disorders in a clinical setting. *Biofeedback and Self-Regulation, 9*, 1–23.

Lynch, J. J., Paskewitz, D. A., & Orne, M. T. (1974). Some factors in the feedback control of human alpha rhythm. *Psychosomatic Medicine, 36*, 399–410.

Miller, N. E., & DiCara, L. (1967). Instrumental learning of heart rate changes in curarized rats: Shaping and specificity to discriminative stimulus. *Journal of Comparative and Physiological Psychology, 63*, 12–19.

Monastra, V. J., Monastra, D. M., & George, S. (2002). The effects of stimulant therapy, EEG biofeedback, and parenting style on the primary symptoms of attention-deficit/hyperactivity disorder. *Applied Psychophysiology and Biofeedback, 27*, 231–249.

Montes, R., Bedmar, M., & Martin, M. S. (1993). EMG biofeedback of the abductor pollicis brevis in piano performance. *Biofeedback and Self-Regulation, 18*, 67–77.

Morasky, R. L., Reynolds, C., & Clarke, G. (1981). Using biofeedback to reduce left arm extensor EMG of string players during musical performance. *Biofeedback and Self-Regulation, 6*, 565–572.

Morasky, R. L., Reynolds, C., & Sowell, L. E. (1983). Generalization of lowered EMG levels during musical performance following biofeedback training. *Biofeedback and Self-Regulation, 8*, 207–216.

Neurocybernetics (1998). *Biofeedback Program User's Manual* (Version 2.3). Canoga Park, CA: EEG Spectrum International, Inc.

Nunez, P. L. (1995a). Mind, brain, and electroencephalography. In P. L. Nunez (Ed.), *Neocortical Dynamics and Human EEG Rhythms* (pp. 133–194). Oxford: Oxford University Press.

Nunez, P. L. (Ed.). (1995b). *Neocortical Dynamics and Human EEG Rhythms*. Oxford: Oxford University Press.

Passini, F. T., Watson, C. B., Dehnel, L., Herder, J., & Watkins, B. (1977). Alpha wave biofeedback therapy in alcoholics. *Journal of Clinical Psychology, 33*, 292–299.

Patel, C. H. (1973). Yoga and biofeedback in the management of hypertension. *Lancet, 2*, 1053–1055.

Peniston, E. G., & Kulkosky, P. J. (1989). Alpha-theta brainwave training and beta endorphin levels in alcoholics. *Alcoholism: Clinical and Experimental Results, 13*, 271–279.

Peniston, E. G., & Kulkosky, P. J. (1990). Alcoholic personality and alpha-theta brainwave training. *Medical Psychotherapy, 3*, 37–55.

Peniston, E. G., & Kulkosky, P. J. (1991). Alpha-theta brainwave neurofeedback for Vietnam veterans with combat-related post-traumatic stress disorder. *Medical Psychotherapy, 4*, 47–60.

Peniston, E. G., & Kulkosky, P. J. (1999). Neurofeedback in the treatment of addictive disorders. In J. R. Evans & A. Abarbanel (Eds.), *Introduction to Quantitative EEG and Neurofeedback* (pp. 157–179). London: Academic Press.

Plotkin, W. B., & Rice, K. M. (1981). Biofeedback as a placebo: Anxiety reduction facilitated by training in either suppression or enhancement of alpha brainwaves. *Journal of Consulting and Clinical Psychology, 49*, 590–596.

Pollock, V. E., & Schneider, L. (1990). Quantitative, waking EEG research on depression. *Biological Psychiatry, 27,* 757–780.

Pollock, V. E., Volavka, J., Goodwin, D. W., Mednick, S. A., Gabrielli, W. F., Knop, J., & Schulsinger, F. (1983). The EEG after alcohol in men at risk for alcoholism. *Archives of General Psychiatry, 40,* 857–864.

Pressner, J. A., & Savitsky, J. C. (1977). Effect of contingent and noncontingent feedback and subject expectancies on electroencephalogram biofeedback training. *Journal of Consulting and Clinical Psychology, 45,* 713–714.

Reinking, R. H., & Hutchins, D. (1981). Follow-up to: "Tension headaches: What form of therapy is most effective?". *Biofeedback and Self-Regulation, 6,* 57–62.

Rossiter, T. R., & LaVaque, T. J. (1995). A comparison of EEG biofeedback and psychostimulants in treating attention deficit hyperactivity disorders. *Journal of Neurotherapy, 1,* 48–59.

Roth, S. R., Sterman, M. B., & Clemente, C. C. (1967). Comparison of EEG correlates of reinforcement, internal inhibition, and sleep. *Electroencephalography and Clinical Neurophysiology, 23,* 509–520.

Sarnthein, J., Petsche, H., Rappelsberger, P., Shaw, G. L., & von Stein, A. (1998). Synchronization between prefrontal and posterior association cortex during human working memory. *Proceedings of the National Academy of Sciences of the United States of America, 95,* 7092–7096.

Saxby, E., & Peniston, E. G. (1995). Alpha-theta brainwave neurofeedback training: An effective treatment for male and female alcoholics with depressive symptoms. *Journal of Clinical Psychology, 51,* 685–693.

Shouse, M. N., & Lubar, J. F. (1979). Operant conditioning of EEG rhythms and ritalin in the treatment of hyperkinesis. *Biofeedback and Self-Regulation, 4,* 299–312.

Spielberger, C. D., Gorsuch, R. L., Lushene, R., Vagg, P. R., & Jacobs, G. A. (1983). *Manual for the State-Trait Anxiety Inventory (Form Y1).* Palo Alto, CA: Consulting Psychologists Press.

Steptoe, A. (1989). Stress, coping and stage fright in professional musicians. *Psychology of Music, 17,* 3–11.

Sterman, M. B. (1996). Physiological origins and functional correlates of EEG rhythmic activities: Implications for self-regulation. *Biofeedback and Self-Regulation, 21,* 3–33.

Sterman, M. B. (2000). Basic concepts and clinical findings in the treatment of seizure disorders with EEG operant conditioning. *Clinical Electroencephalography, 31,* 45–55.

Sterman, M. B., & Friar, L. (1972). Suppression of seizures in an epileptic following sensorimotor EEG feedback training. *Electroencephalography and Clinical Neurophysiology, 33,* 89–95.

Sterman, M. B., & MacDonald, L. R. (1978). Effects of central cortical EEG feedback training on incidence of poorly controlled seizures. *Epilepsia, 19,* 207–222.

Sterman, M. B., & Wyrwicka, W. (1967). EEG correlates of sleep: Evidence for separate forebrain substrates. *Brain Research, 6,* 143–163.

Sterman, M. B., Wyrwicka, W., & Roth, S. R. (1969). Electrophysiological correlates and neural substrates of alimentary behavior in the cat. *Annals of the New York Academy of Sciences, 157,* 723–739.

Sterman, M. B., MacDonald, L. R., & Stone, R. K. (1974). Biofeedback training of the sensorimotor electroencephalogram rhythm in man: Effects on epilepsy. *Epilepsia, 15,* 395–416.

Sterman, M. B., Goodman, S. J., & Kovalesky, R. A. (1978). Effects of sensorimotor EEG feedback training on seizure susceptibility in the rhesus monkey. *Experimental Neurology, 62,* 735–747.

Stoyva, J. M., & Budzynski, T. H. (1993). Biofeedback methods in the treatment of anxiety and stress disorders. In P. M. Lehrer & R. L. Woolfolk (Eds.), *Principles and Practice of Stress Management.* London: Guilford Press.

Taub, E., & Rosenfeld, J. P. (1994). Is alpha/theta training the effective component of the alpha/theta therapy package for the treatment of alcoholism? *Biofeedback, 22,* 12–14.

Thompson, S., & Williamon, A. (2003). Evaluating evaluation: Musical performance assessment as a research tool. *Music Perception, 21,* 21–41.

Vaitl, D., Birbaumer, N., Gruzelier, J., Jamieson, G., Kotchoubey, B., Kübler, A., Lehmann, D., Miltner, W. H. R., Ott, U., Pütz, P., Sammer, G., Strauch, I., Strehl, U., Wackermann, J., Weiss, T. (2003). *Psychobiology of altered states of consciousness.* Manuscript submitted for publication.

Vernon, D., Egner, T., Cooper, N., Compton, T., Neilands, C., Sheri, A., & Gruzelier, J. H. (2003). The effect of training distinct neurofeedback protocols on aspects of cognitive performance. *International Journal of Psychophysiology, 47,* 75–85.

Williamon, A., & Valentine, E. (2000). Quantity and quality of musical practice as predictors of performance quality. *British Journal of Psychology, 91,* 353–376.

Williamon, A., & Valentine, E. (2002). The role of retrieval structures in memorizing music. *Cognitive Psychology, 44,* 1–32.

Williams, J. D., & Gruzelier, J. H. (2001). Differentiation of hypnosis and relaxation by analysis of narrow band theta and alpha frequencies. *International Journal of Clinical and Experimental Hypnosis, 49,* 185–286.

Winson, J. (2002). The meaning of dreams. *The Hidden Mind: Scientific American,* special edition, 54–61.

Wyrwicka, W., & Sterman, M. B. (1968). Instrumental conditioning of sensorimotor cortex EEG spindles in the waking cat. *Physiology and Behavior, 3,* 703–707.

CHAPTER 12

MENTAL SKILLS TRAINING

CHRISTOPHER CONNOLLY AND AARON WILLIAMON

For decades, elite athletes have enhanced their performance by exploiting advancements in applied psychology and science. An important constituent of the training received by these performers has focused on the interplay between mental and physical skills. Indeed, any witness to elite sporting achievement can appreciate that physical exactitude and excellence go hand in hand with mental agility, determination, focus, and an unimpeded vision of the performance outcome. Thus, the potency and worth of pursuing holistic body–mind training approaches for developing both physical and mental skills have been taken as self-evident by sports trainers and coaches.

Clearly, the same argument can be made for musical performance. A concert soloist performing Dvořák's Cello Concerto, for example, will need to be in command of a number of psychological features, not least among these are the ability to fuse his or her musical ideas with those of the conductor and other ensemble members, to communicate effectively that combined vision to the audience, and to manage any excess anxiety that may accompany the event. In music, as with sports, it is very often the case that the skills needed to master such demands are accrued through years of hard work, training, experience, and self-reflection. This chapter aims to offer performers a range of musically validated techniques for honing their mental skills in order to perform at the peak of their personal abilities. The chapter emerges from work with conservatory students as part of the multidisciplinary project "Zoning In: Motivating the Musical Mind," which examined the efficacy of several interventions for enhancing musical performance (see also Chapters 9, 10, and 11). Considering the wide applicability of mental skills training (also referred to as "cognitive-behavioral" training) to other performance domains, it was hypothesized that particular techniques within the cognitive-behavioral repertory would be of use to highly skilled musicians. The objective of the mental skills program, therefore, was to design and pilot a curriculum of training derived from applied sports psychology. Within the program, a total of 58 students took part in both group and individual training sessions.

This chapter lays the foundation for mental skills training in music, first, through introductions to relaxation and mental rehearsal techniques. It then builds upon this by examining how mental skills can be used to prepare for and meet the demands of specific performance situations and to set and achieve long-term performance goals. Exercises found to be most effective by the participating conservatory students are provided as a guide for how mental skills can be practiced, and readers are strongly encouraged to make note of how the techniques can be employed toward their own musical and personal development. It is important to stress that mental skills should be learned and developed in the same way as any musical skill—that is, they should be practiced regularly. People who get the most from this training find ways of integrating techniques into their everyday lives, alongside and in ways complementary to physical engagement in the domain.

12.1   Relaxation

"Arousal" is the degree of activation in the body, and as is described in Chapter 1, level of arousal can have an impact on performance preparation and quality. A relaxed state is characterized by an absence of unnecessary activity and tension; it is a period of stillness, in which the need for activity or any sense of deficiency is subjugated or at least interrupted for a period. In terms musical performance, relaxation techniques can be used (1) to manage levels of *over*arousal that can interfere with pre-, during-, and post-performance functioning and (2) to control general life and occupational stress that can detract from physical and psychological well-being.

Firstly, a number of studies in music have produced notable results when using cognitive-behavioral interventions to reduce the "stage fright" typically associated with physical, mental, and emotional arousal (Kendrick *et al.*, 1982; Sweeney & Horan, 1982; Nagel *et al.*, 1989; Clark & Agras, 1991). Although the degree of arousal appropriate for performance will vary between individuals and with the particular performance occasion, relaxation training can help instill an awareness of bodily and mental states. This awareness can then be used, for example, to reduce muscle tension that interferes with the coordination of physical skills or to quiet distracting, rational "chattering" in the mind. In this sense, it augments focus on the task at hand. Of course, degrees of relaxation and tension exist on a continuum of arousal, but when used as part of a pre-performance routine, relaxation techniques can and should be paired with mental alertness. Achieving a relaxed, lethargic state will be of no benefit to the performer, particularly as part of an overall performance cycle; therefore, relaxation techniques that are to be implemented before a performance should be practiced and tested well in advance of any crucial performance.

Secondly, relaxation techniques also offer broad, lifestyle benefits, which may then impact on practice and performance activities. For instance, they can regenerate the body, mind, and emotions through the induction of a positive state of being; they can be used to enhance learning and recall; and they can improve sleep and energy conservation (see Woolfolk *et al.*, 1976). In fact, research suggests that skills are best learned in a relaxed state, and by interspersing periods of learning with relaxation sessions, more can be absorbed without deterioration of learning (Benson, 1975).

Relaxation techniques tend to be either physical (e.g. the reduction of tension in muscles) or mental (e.g. the visualization of a natural, quiet scene). Both can be used to reach either a deep, sustained level of relaxation or a momentary, less profound state; the depth to which one relaxes will depend on the time and focus devoted to the exercise. Practice of deeper methods of relaxation is best carried out after, rather than before, a musical activity (e.g. after an intensive practice session) and more generally as part of an overall daily routine (e.g. before an evening meal and going to sleep, when they can be particularly beneficial for combating fatigue and excess worry). Momentary relaxation can be used in relation to musical performance in a number of ways: before warming up on the instrument (to determine a sense of physical, mental, and emotional state), in gaps during practice and performance (to reduce unnecessary tension and refocus thoughts on the task), as part of warming down (to reduce the build up of tension and re-establish a balanced physical state), and before practicing any form of mental rehearsal (see Section 12.2).

Exercise 12.1:   Introduction to relaxation

The following steps can be used as a guide to relaxation. As with all exercises presented in this chapter, you may want to have someone read these points aloud to you at first or tape record them, so that you are then free to experience the effects without having to remember each step. With time and practice, the steps will come naturally.

- Sit down. Put your feet flat on the floor, with your hands placed easily on your lap. Close your eyes.
- First, pay attention to the sounds outside of the room; then, within the room; then, notice your own thoughts.
- Pay attention to the contact you make with the chair and floor, and notice your breathing.
- Take a deep breath in for four counts; hold it for four, and let it out slowly to the count of either four or eight.
- As you continue to breathe, easily pay attention to the muscles around your face: your forehead, the muscles around your eyes, cheeks, mouth, jaw, and neck. As you exhale, imagine all tension draining away through your shoulders and on through your arms, wrists, hands, and fingers.
- Notice how your chest relaxes, as well as your back, and your stomach, waist, and pelvis.
- Pay attention to your thighs, and notice any tension you may find in them. On your next outbreath, imagine all of the tension draining away through your knees, calves, ankles, feet, and into the floor, leaving you calm, relaxed, and alert.
- Remain in this state for a few minutes before taking three deep breaths, stretching, and opening your eyes.

How we breathe has a considerable impact on our state of physical, mental, and emotional arousal. Deep-centered breathing from the abdomen can be relaxing and energizing. Stopping to take a few slow, steady breaths can help to center focus on the here-and-now and to check mental state. The following exercise can be used to release tension just before the start of a performance or in short gaps between successive performance events.

Exercise 12.2:   Breathing through the body

For this exercise, you will be breathing in a similar way as in the exercise above, relaxing three areas of your body with each exhale. It is worth noting that one physiological symptom of performance anxiety is hyperventilation, which is an abnormally increased pulmonary ventilation. Therefore, in high-anxious situations, it is advisable to clear the lungs of air *before* taking in deep breaths.

Exercise 12.2 (*Continued*)

- Start breathing from the center of your body (just behind your navel). Draw in air slowly through your nose for a count of four. As you inhale this long, slow breath, allow the air to fill your belly out, like a balloon filling with air.
- Hold your breath for a count of four.
- Now, slowly exhale for a count of eight, and as you do, release any tension from your forehead, jaw, and neck through your shoulders and arms and on through to your fingers.
- Inhale for four and hold for four in the same way.
- Slowly exhale for a count of eight, releasing any tension from your chest and stomach and relaxing all of your vertebrae down your spine.
- Inhale for four and hold for four in the same way.
- And now, slowly exhale for a count of eight, releasing any tension from your hips and thighs through your lower leg and ankle, all the way to your toes.

Reflections on relaxation

- When you were relaxing, what physical sensations did you notice? What did you notice about your thoughts?
- What did you feel during the relaxation, and what do you feel now?
- Where and when might you practice this technique? Why?

12.2   Mental rehearsal

12.2.1   Introduction to mental rehearsal

Mental rehearsal is the cognitive or imaginary rehearsal of a physical skill without overt muscular movement. The basic idea is that the senses—predominantly aural, visual, and kinesthetic for the musician—should be used to create or recreate an experience that is similar to a given physical event. Everyone has the capacity to rehearse mentally, and in making the most of this, musicians would be well served when developing their mental rehearsal (as recommended in Chapter 5) to activate their analysis and ear training skills, their abilities to notice and attend to movements and touch, their knowledge of style and history of music, and their powers of reflection and memorization.

Some inconsistency has emerged within the music research literature regarding the extent to which mental rehearsal can positively impact performance skills (e.g. Rubin-Rabson, 1937, 1941; LaBerge, 1981; Ross, 1985; Coffman, 1990; Jones, 1990; Kopiez, 1990a, 1990b, 1991). This is not surprising, however, given the wide disparity in the methods employed in the research, including core differences in the groups of musicians recruited to take part (i.e. their level of skill and instrument specialization), the procedure implemented (i.e. the amount of time given for mental rehearsal, the selection and length of the pieces to be rehearsed, and the purpose of the rehearsal itself), and the outcome measures of the performance skill. What is clear from the extant literature is that musicians themselves vary considerably in their use of mental rehearsal (see Grøndahl, 1987). It seems also that the points of most practical significance are that (1) informed physical practice at the highest levels of musicianship can hardly take place without some sort of cognitive or mental activity and (2) only through committed, personal effort can the musician expand, differentiate, and fully exploit his or her repertory of mental strategies.

With regard to the former point, evidence suggests that mental and physical practice are inextricably linked on a psychophysiological level. Hale (cited in Freymuth, 1993) found that internal imagery produced the same muscle activity that would have been used in the actual movements (see further evidence provided by Stippich *et al.*, 2002). In addition, Bird and Wilson (1988) studied electroencephalographic (EEG) and electromyographic (EMG) data obtained from student conductors and their teacher during imagery. The results showed that, despite large individual differences, the teacher and the more skilled students produced more repeatable EEG patterns than the less skilled students. In addition, the teacher displayed EMG patterns during mental rehearsal that were similar to those of the actual performance. Given that conductors are by necessity forced to engage in much mental rehearsal, these findings suggest that, with practice, mental rehearsal can indeed be an effective supplement to physical rehearsal. As such, it can then be integrated into the musician's practice routine so as to avoid the musculoskeletal problems that may arise from overpracticing (see Chapter 3 for further discussion).

Findings presented by Rubin-Rabson (1937, 1941), Ross (1985), and Coffman (1990) all provide support for the notion that combining physical and mental practice can be favorable for musical learning. Gabrielsson (1999) concludes, however, that "it seems the less advanced the person is on the instrument and the more difficult the music is, the more important is the motor practice" (p. 507). But what exactly can musicians gain from integrating mental rehearsal into their regular practicing routines? Interview data with the conservatory students mentioned above suggest that mental rehearsal can be used as follows:

- To improve learning and memory

  A horn player: "I had to play pieces from memory for my final [recital]. I found that really difficult because I've never done anything from memory before. I spent an awful lot of time playing the music through my head, without it in front of me, playing it through, seeing what it felt like."

- To make practice more efficient

  A clarinetist: "My fundamental practicing has been a lot more focused. I achieve things in a shorter amount of time . . . because I make sure I am doing it properly."

- To overcome technical difficulties and develop skills

  A pianist: "Mental rehearsal helps with body/mind awareness, which helps correct technical difficulties in pieces; rather than go over and over, I try and fix it the first time."

- To heighten sensory awareness

  A cellist: "I am more aware of my sound, more aware of what I am doing, more aware of what I can do. . . . I experiment . . . and have clarity of thought for executing something difficult."

- To gain more interest in the music itself

  An oboist: "Mental practice made me aware of other things I wanted to check out about the piece. . . . When you start thinking about playing the music rather than just doing it, it helps."

- To refocus attention during performance

  A singer: "I use quick images and color when I notice my attention drift during a performance."

- To enhance general confidence and resilience on stage

  A violinist: "I think it's the self-confidence. The confidence in my own performance. . . . You have rehearsals before a concert, and often that's just to remind yourself how it all goes and how it works with other instruments. . . . That's what I'm basically doing, but I'm just cutting out the actual, physical side of it—doing it mentally—which seems to work just as well."

- To achieve greater control over negative emotions

  A horn player: "By imagining myself performing, I think it takes away the fear of the unknown—unknown places, unknown circumstances."

- To establish a greater connection and presence with an audience

  A flute player: "I'm closer to the music, I suppose, than I have ever been before and hopefully, therefore, the audience is too. They're closer to what they've come to experience. . . . I link images with the music, and this helps me to project my feelings and the meaning of the music."

- To achieve peak experience.

  A violinist: "I had the first real performance after last year's course of mental skills on Thursday of last week. There were 800 people in the audience, and I was being sponsored to play. So, it was quite important. It was lovely because I went on, and the pieces were internalized from when I learned them last summer, so it was a question of bringing them out. For the first time, I forgot I was playing—not forgot, although I was communicating with the audience, I detached myself from them and concentrated on the music and let the music bridge, rather than myself playing a violin and looking at the audience. It was the music. I looked around while I was playing, and I felt very easy. . . . The high afterwards was great."

Plainly, the above benefits may not apply universally to all musicians. In fact, specific benefits are likely to vary depending, for instance, on the individual's current technical skill, personal preferences for learning and self-reflection, the conditions under which a particular piece is to be performed, and most importantly, how and the extent to which mental rehearsal techniques are practiced. Ultimately, it is not a question of adopting either a mental or physical approach, but rather how to make the most of both approaches. The two simply are not mutually exclusive at the highest levels of performance.

Research on motor skill acquisition has identified conditions and situations in which mental rehearsal is optimally effective. For example, the person should have prior experience in executing the task (or one similar to it). Also, mental rehearsal can be particularly effective during the early stages of learning, when novel insights and ideas about the task can be formulated, and during the later stages to reinforce cultivated performance strategies. Furthermore, the performer should endeavor to imagine responses in muscles that would actually perform the movement (Weinberg, 1982). In addition, years of hands-on experience in the field of sports psychology have led to several guiding principles for mental rehearsal (see Loehr, 1987; Martens, 1987; Syer & Connolly, 1991, 1998; Butler, 1996), which include the following:

◆ Practice regularly, especially in the morning (May *et al.*, 1993; Yoon *et al.*, 2000; Hasher *et al.*, 2002).

◆ It is better to carry out short, regular mental rehearsal sessions (e.g. of 5–10 minutes) than long, infrequent sessions (Weinberg, 1982).

◆ Start with relaxation, so that clear signals can be communicated between mind and body. You need to be relaxed and alert at the same time.

◆ Mentally rehearse specific skills or qualities you are working on in your technical training, above and close to your current level of performance.

◆ Be positive; move toward what you want to focus on, not on aspects that do not contribute directly to improving your performance. Stay in control of what you rehearse.

◆ Use all of your senses, so that you believe that you are actually in the situation executing the skill. Keep working to improve the clarity and vividness of mental images; include emotions and feelings.

◆ Notice how you visualize. Do you observe yourself performing as if on a screen (externally), or do you see, hear, and feel from within your body (internally)? Both strategies can be useful (see Section 12.3.2 below). In general, when you are correcting skills, it is helpful to observe externally (from the outside) until the skill is corrected, and then to experience it from an internal perspective, noticing the physical sensations and feelings associated with the skill.

In short, to use mental rehearsal successfully for performance enhancement, relaxation should come first, focus should be intently on the task at hand, the experience should be realistic, and it should be practiced regularly.

Exercise 12.3:   Developing imagery skills

Mental rehearsal for performance enhancement is not just visual. Rather, it involves using all of the senses. This introductory exercise is intended to develop such imagery.

◆ Before visualizing, take a moment to relax. Let yourself imagine, one after another, the following sensory experiences:

◆ Now *see*: A sunset over the ocean, white clouds racing over the sky, your musical instrument, the face of a friend, a building that you like, a rose as it opens and blooms. . . .

◆ Now *hear*: The sound of a rainstorm on a tin roof, church bells ringing in the distance, the applause of the audience at the end of a concert, the sound of wind in the trees, your favorite piece of music, the voice of a famous singer. . . .

Exercise 12.3 (*Continued*)

◆ Now *feel*: The sun on your back on a hot day, jumping into a cold bath or pool, the grasp of a firm handshake, walking barefoot on grass, your fingers moving when you play your instrument. . . .

◆ Now *smell*: Your favorite perfume, a newly mowed lawn, burnt toast, a new musical instrument. . . .

◆ And now *taste*: A lemon as you bite into it, a cool refreshing drink, your favorite food. . . .

◆ Let the scene fade, slowly stretch, and open your eyes.

Exercise 12.4:   Developing control of your mental rehearsal

It is important that you have control over your experience during mental rehearsal. The following exercise can be helpful in developing this.

◆ Sit down in a place where you will not be disturbed. Uncross your legs and arms. Close your eyes, and relax from your head downward.

◆ In your imagination, walk into a practice room. Notice what the room looks like.

◆ See your instrument (or any object generally related to your performance, such as a music stand or a page of a score). Notice details in what you see.

◆ Walk around it. Notice what you can see and hear as you do this.

◆ Look at the instrument from above, and then from below.

◆ Now, imagine your instrument growing and make it larger. Then, see it getting smaller, first back to its normal size and then smaller still.

◆ Now, change its color. What color is it?

◆ Take a breath, and go back to the beginning. Walk into the room again.

◆ See your instrument again. What details do you notice now?

◆ Reach toward your instrument and touch it. Notice what it feels like, its texture. Either pick it up or put yourself into a position ready to play it.

◆ Notice how you make contact with the instrument. Take time to "feel right," and stay with this feeling for a moment.

◆ Begin to play and listen. What can you hear?

◆ Stop playing. Breathe.

◆ Begin to play again and listen.

◆ Stop playing. Breathe. Do this a few more times, but when your attention begins to waver or you begin to lose control of your imagery, finish the practice.

◆ Stop playing, put the instrument down, and leave the room.

◆ Let the scene fade, and slowly bring your attention back to your present environment.

Exercise 12.5:   Skill development mental rehearsal

Skill development mental rehearsal complements the physical practice of a skill. Adding this process to your weekly training can increase confidence and speed the learning process. You may also develop a greater awareness of what you are doing. Choose a specific skill or piece of music you want to practice. You may want to choose a piece that you need to memorize, are having technical difficulties with, or want to practice communicating to an audience.

- Before visualizing, take a moment to relax as you have practiced previously. Notice how the more you train yourself to relax, the easier it becomes.
- See yourself in a place where you can practice or perform the skill you want to improve. Create as real and as genuine a scene as possible, incorporating information from all your senses.
- Now, see yourself approaching your instrument, and when you have reached it, prepare to play. Find the place that feels right, as you did before. Notice what you do to prepare yourself.
- Begin to play. Notice what you can see and hear as you observe yourself. How do you use your arms and head? How is your body positioned? How do you use your legs and feet? Notice as much detail as possible.
- Take a deep breath, and now watch the same scene from somewhere else—a different viewpoint, closer or further away. Again, pay attention to all the details. Listen to the music, and take note of what you can see.
- Rewind the image to the beginning, and this time step into the image of yourself in the scene. You are now inside your body looking through your own eyes. As you play, notice what you can see and hear, and notice physical sensations and feelings. Notice what parts of your body seem most alive. Notice where you are relaxed and where you are tense. Be aware of all the sensations and feelings you identify with this practice. Notice what your whole body feels like when you are playing.
- Rewind and repeat this one more time, this time focusing on different parts of your body or different aspects of your technique.
- Stop the practice. Take a breath, move away from your instrument, and leave the room.
- Let the scene fade, and slowly bring your attention back to your present environment.

Reflections on mental rehearsal

- What did you discover about using all your senses?
- Which sense was the easiest to evoke? Which was the most difficult? What happened when you explored your physical sensations and feelings?
- What did you notice about your ability to control your visualization?
- What did you see and hear yourself doing when you observed yourself playing?
- What did you notice when you looked from a different viewpoint?
- What skills do you want to improve using mental rehearsal?

12.2.2 Evocative symbols and images

Images, sounds, symbols, and words can evoke certain feelings and physiological changes in us. Indeed, music teachers have long used metaphors to suggest new musical ideas and to encourage students to express music in particular ways. In one study of 135 music students, 81% at one point had been taught to express music through this method, and 42% ranked it as most effective, compared with "felt emotion" (preferred by 39%) and "aural modeling" (preferred by 25%; Lindström *et al.*, 2003). The aim of mental skills training in relation to evocative symbols and images is to develop within performers the ability to exploit symbols and images for themselves and, subsequently, to make the mental rehearsal in which they engage all the richer and more detailed. To do so, it is helpful to be aware of images, stories, and sounds that may naturally emerge when practicing and performing. As such, one's intuition, imagination, and emotion are stimulated.

Exercise 12.6:   Developing qualities in performance

For this exercise, you will be playing through a piece of music in your mind.

- Start by using a relaxation exercise to prepare yourself for mental rehearsal.
- Imagine that you are about to perform a piece of music. Look around you, and notice what you can see and hear.
- When you are ready, begin playing. Pay attention to your physical sensations as you play. Play everything perfectly. Notice the sound you are creating and how you feel when you hear the music played in this way.
- When you are fully immersed in the music and the experience, take a deep breath. As you exhale, notice what image the music evokes in you. Notice what the image, metaphor, symbol, or object is. Stay with the image, and let it continue to get clearer in your mind.
- Now, continue to play the passage while maintaining the image in your mind.
- As you finish the piece, notice what you are feeling.
- Gradually let the scene fade, and when you are ready, open your eyes.

Over the coming week, imagine this image or symbol, and in your imagination, play the piece with this quality. As soon as you are able, evoke this same quality by imagining the image or symbol before playing the piece physically.

Reflections on developing qualities in performance

- What image or symbol was evoked when you expressed the music?
- How will you use this symbol or image in practice and performance?

Exercise 12.7:   Acting "as if"

Acting "as if" is like acting a part, performing as if you were someone or something else that represents a quality you want to emphasize in your performance. The someone or something will be very specific to you.

- Before starting the mental practice, identify someone who expresses a performance quality that you would like to emulate.
- Use a relaxation exercise that you find works best for you.
- Observe this person in a specific situation where he or she expresses this quality. Step into the situation yourself and imagine being this person in this situation. Notice physical sensations, and notice what it feels like to be the person.
- Keep this image in your mind, and imagine playing a piece of music you want to perform. Notice what you see, hear, and feel subjectively when you play like this person with the qualities that they possess.
- And as you finish the piece, let the scene fade. When you are ready, bring your attention back to your present environment.

Over the coming week, take the best qualities you discover about yourself or the "model performer" in this exercise, and play the piece with these qualities in your imagination. Before you physically practice the piece, picture this image and allow it to evoke the quality you want to express in the music. In practice, you may want to try playing the piece as if you are this person. Many people find this exercise can be very effective. Some, however, prefer to use only themselves as a model. This can be done equally well, and you may want to model yourself on one of your own "peak performances" when you played at your very best.

Reflections on acting "as if"

- What did you notice when you acted the part of the other person?
- What quality of performance was evoked?
- What did you notice about your performance when you played the music with this quality?

12.3 Using and developing mental skills for specific performance situations

12.3.1 The pre-performance routine

Partington (1995) found that highly skilled musicians give a central role to physical and mental strategies that enable them to feel confident and ready to perform. During the one or two days before a performance, he found that the performers deeply immersed themselves in musical, physical, and mental preparation aimed at allowing them to perform at their best. They developed preparation routines through personal experience. On the day of the performance, they displayed a wide range of individual differences in preparation. Technical and physical readying included staying connected with the music through easy practicing, not changing interpretation, and ensuring adequate sleep and nutrition. To prepare themselves mentally, some strove to feel excited and ready to perform, yet not too anxious. To achieve this, some simply "took it easy;" others used relaxation techniques or positive imagery; and some engaged in constructive internal dialogue and reasoning. The final stages of preparation (i.e. the few hours before performance) were also highly individualized. To avoid anxiety associated with waiting, some arrived only 15 minutes before playing. Others arrived 1–2 hours beforehand and worked through a systematic physical and mental warm-up that sometimes consisted of reviewing the score through audiation, engaging in an internal dialogue to achieve an appropriate orientation to play, or completing a predetermined warm-up on their instrument. In the minutes just before going on stage, some of the musicians attempted to create a mood in themselves appropriate for their intended expression of the music, while others struggled to isolate themselves or remain relaxed through easy playing.

Despite the clear individual differences emerging from Partington's account, it was clear that each player made a systematic, patient effort to nurture and maintain a state optimal for concert performance. Two key factors seemed to apply in facilitating this process: (1) a long-term commitment to high-quality physical, technical, and artistic preparation and (2) the development of an individualized, flexible pre-performance routine that includes physical activity, nutrition, and rest, as well as warming up using mental, emotional, technical, and musical strategies.

Exercise 12.8:   Optimizing performance preparation and review

The following will help you optimize your performance preparation over time and will encourage you to incorporate mental and emotional strategies, as well as physical.

◆ Think back to your last important performance, and write down answers to the questions that follow:

◆ How did you prepare physically, emotionally, and mentally?

◆ What worked well?

◆ What, if anything, do you want to change?

◆ What else could you have done?

Once you have answered these questions, think back to how you *reviewed* the success of that performance and write down answers to the following questions:

◆ How did you review your performance physically, emotionally, and mentally?

◆ What worked well?

◆ What, if anything, do you want to change?

◆ What else could you have done?

Exercise 12.9:   Developing consistency in preparation

Consistency in preparation leads to consistency in performance. Segment your preparation on concert day into four sections: (1) the morning of the performance day, (2) the afternoon of the performance day, (3) arrival at the performance venue, (4) 10 minutes before performing. Within each section, consider what you are doing to prepare technically, musically, mentally, and emotionally. It is vital that you be specific.

In addition, when warming up, you may find it is useful to pay attention and tune into five different factors that can affect your performance:

◆ The place where you are to perform (identify supportive factors and distractions in the environment; make yourself at home).

◆ Yourself (what are your physical sensations, thoughts, and feelings?).

◆ The people you are with, especially others with whom you are going to perform.

◆ Your technical and artistic intentions.

◆ The way in which you will meet and convey these intentions.

It is best to start with a simple routine and use trial and error to try out variations on this in situations where you are able to experiment. Begin to integrate the results of your experimentation into your preparation for actual performances when you feel ready. Importantly, ensure that there is sufficient flexibility within your routine so that you can adjust it to changing external circumstances (adapted from Emmons & Thomas, 1998).

12.3.2 Concentration

It is common to find musicians asking themselves why they have difficulty focusing in high-pressure performance situations. Being able to concentrate and "shift" one's focus of attention is a salient component of musical expertise (Williamon *et al.*, 2002), which is typically acquired over years of practice and training (see Chapter 2 for an extensive discussion). Still, to make the most of this training in intense performing environments, it can be helpful for performers to understand some mechanics of concentration.

Concentration can differ and vary in duration and intensity. High concentration is an unwavering awareness of a specific subject to the momentary exclusion of other subjects. For musical performance, such concentration should ideally take the form of a relaxed state of being alert. Moreover, the performer should be mentally agile enough to change focus rapidly and smoothly in conjunction with the flow of relevant factors and external events. In work with athletes, Nideffer (1976) developed a model that is helpful in becoming aware of how to direct attention before, during, and after a performance. The model recognizes that concentration can be broken down into two key dimensions: direction (internal or external) and width (broad or narrow). These dimensions, in turn, form four quadrants of concentration (see Figure 12.1).

In terms of concentration training, performers need to maintain awareness of themselves and what is happening around them, allowing only the most relevant factors to come into momentary focus at the expense of all else. Practicing concentration and shifting the focus of attention can help performers become aware of where attention is actually drawn and why it is there, and then to break outdated patterns of undesirable thought or unproductive behaviors. Performers can then become more closely familiar with parts of their performance that are within their control, and can interrupt or distance themselves from distractions or worries that stem from sources beyond their control.

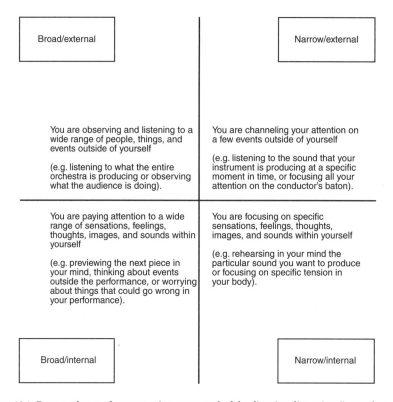

Figure 12.1 Four quadrants of concentration, composed of the direction dimension (internal or external) and the width dimension (broad or narrow; adapted from Nideffer, 1976).

In terms of when performers should concentrate, an obvious answer is throughout the entire performance event, but many performances offer periods of more and less activity. These can demand continual change in the direction, span, and intensity of concentration. Discovering where best to focus attention during periods of inactivity requires practice. Generally speaking, changing focus between external and internal and between broad and narrow gives the performer a way to review and refocus. When the focus of attention is on distractions that are unhelpful or irrelevant for performance, it is important to redirect attention to task-relevant cues. The ability to do this can be enhanced by identifying occasions or moments when distraction habitually occurs. Once counterproductive patterns in attentional focus have been identified, mental skills training can then be directed toward managing or (when possible) replacing negative habits with more appropriate ones. It is important to mention that when seeking to change behaviors, a negative habit needs to be replaced with a more productive habit: simply stopping a habit without substituting another for it can result in the negative habit eventually reasserting its presence.

Exercise 12.10:   Identifying drifts in attention

◆ Review your last few performances and notice when and where your attention drifted. Attentional drifts very often result when you are focusing on factors that are unhelpful to your performance. Concentrate on what you need to do, not what to avoid.

◆ Are you distracted by factors in the environment?

◆ Are you distracted by past or future experiences?

◆ Are you distracted by task-irrelevant thoughts?

◆ What patterns do you notice?

Exercise 12.11:   Concentration and focused breathing

◆ Breathe from the center of your body.

◆ Hold your breath for a count of 4.

◆ Then, for a count of 4, exhale through your mouth, and allow the air to flow out of your belly.

◆ Repeat for 10 more times. Count the number of breaths you take. See how many times you can count up to 10 without distraction.

Review of focused breathing

◆ How many times were you able to count to 10 without being distracted?

◆ Where did your attention drift?

◆ What helped you maintain your focus on the here and now?

Exercise 12.12:   Shuttling

This is an exercise designed to help you avoid getting stuck in the "middle zone," a term that describes situations in which you are physically doing one thing (e.g. performing a movement of a piece) while mentally doing another (e.g. thinking about how you will be performing a technically difficult passage in the next movement). This preliminary "drill," which should be practiced with a partner, will help you develop your ability to control attention and learn to shift your attention intentionally.

◆ Close your eyes, and tune in to some sensation, feeling, thought, sound, or image from inside and say "now I am aware of. . . ." For example: "now I am aware of my breathing," or "now I am aware of a pain in my leg," or "now I am feeling silly," etc.

◆ Then, open your eyes, and say "now I am aware of . . .", adding something from outside, such as "now I am aware of the sunlight" or "now I am aware of your eyes."

◆ Repeat the process, shuttling your attention inside and out; first an inside statement, and then an outside statement for a few minutes.

Exercise 12.12 (*Continued*)

♦ Let your partner do the same.

♦ Now, try the same exercise again with your eyes open all the time.

Reflections on shuttling

♦ Did you find it easier to shift your attention in or out?

♦ How aware were you of your internal experience; your external experience?

Exercise 12.13:   Zooming in and out

When you are anxious, your attention narrows, and your ability to shift attention lessens—that is, your ability to shift attention from either broad to narrow or internal to external is hampered. This can have a negative effect on your performance, particularly if your ability to pick out and pay attention to salient performance cues is reduced. The purpose of this exercise is to practice shifting your attention across all four quadrants shown in Figure 12.1.

Nervous zoom

♦ Imagine a time when you were very nervous or anxious. Recall the whole experience; notice what you can see, hear, and feel. Step into the experience, only as much as you feel comfortable. Stay with this feeling.

♦ Pay attention to what is happening inside of you. First, focus on a specific feeling, sensation, thought, image, or sound. Now broaden your internal lens. Keep broadening and narrowing your internal lens, and notice what you become aware of each time.

♦ Now, shift your attention outside. Zoom your external lens in and out.

♦ Shuttle your internal and external lenses from broad to narrow and vice versa a few more times.

♦ Stop, stand up, and shake out the feeling of nervousness.

Confident zoom

♦ Imagine a time when you were confident and assured. Step into the whole experience, noticing what you see, hear, and feel. Stay with this feeling.

♦ Pay attention to what is happening inside of you. First, focus on a specific feeling, sensation, thought, image, or sound. Now broaden your internal lens. Keep broadening and narrowing your internal lens, and notice what you become aware of each time.

♦ Now, shift your attention outside. Zoom your external lens in and out.

♦ Shuttle your internal and external lenses from broad to narrow and vice versa a few more times. In each, try to achieve a greater flexibility in shifting your attention.

Reflections on zooming in and out

♦ During the nervous zoom, where did your attention switch to most easily? What impact does switching from broad internal to broad external have on your state?

♦ During the confident zoom, what did you notice about your ability to switch your attention?

Exercise 12.14:   The present moment technique

This exercise can help you to focus on the here and now—the present moment. It is a simple exercise that takes 30 seconds and can help you refocus *during* a performance.

◆ For 10 seconds, focus all of your attention externally, and notice the visual or auditory detail of what you are looking at or listening to.

◆ For 10 seconds, focus all of your attention on your breathing and total body awareness.

◆ For the last 10 seconds, imagine playing your next phrase perfectly. Breathe deeply, and then play it.

There are several additional strategies that can be adopted that may have a positive effect on enhancing concentration. These include (1) building and practicing a stronger pattern (e.g. adopting the five-point warm-up procedure described in Exercise 12.9), (2) strengthening the attraction of the object or action on which attention must be placed, (3) deliberately paying attention to the distraction (i.e. treating it as if it has a life of its own; discovering its "needs" and making a contract to deal with it later), (4) "making friends" with the distraction (i.e. practicing in an environment where distractions are simulated and/or finding a way to view the distraction positively), and (5) removing the focus from emotional distraction to physical or mental patterns (e.g. if the distraction is emotionally charged anxiety and tension, a physical technique such as Exercise 12.2 could be used to relax). It is important to stress that the selection of the "right" strategy(s) for each musician will inevitably depend on that individual's experimentation and preferences. Ultimately, intense and consistent concentration is most likely to be possible when the performer is well prepared artistically, when he or she has developed clear intentions for the performance.

12.3.3   Ideal performance states and simulation

What a musician focuses on during a performance seems to be one of the keys to perceived inspiration (Partington, 1995). Experienced performers concentrate on a range of features when making music, including making a personal statement, conveying beauty, and establishing a rapport with the audience (see Chaffin *et al.*, 2002). They are often aware that the consequences of concentrating on playing each note with technical perfection are generally disappointing and can lead to high anxiety about making an error, disappointment following the error, and a generally cool response from the audience to an accurate (yet unmoving) rendition of a piece. Furthermore, they seem to focus on doing, not on *how* to do what they are doing. The following are characteristics associated with individuals in peak performance states (for further discussion, see Csikszentmihalyi & Csikszentmihalyi, 1988; Csikszentmihalyi, 1990; Syer & Connolly, 1991, 1998):

● energized, yet relaxed (a subtle balance of quiet intensity)

● confident (an expectation of success; lapses in performance do not undermine self-belief)

- focused (absorbed in the moment; focused solely on the task at hand)
- effortless and automatic (mind and body working in unison; little or no conscious thought involved; instincts and intuition "just let the performance happen")
- fun (incomparable enjoyment)
- in control (full control of the situation, no matter what).

The purpose of this section is to assist musicians in attaining peak performance states. The exercises covered previously provide the foundation for this. Relaxation training helps generate a relaxed state, which is vital to peak performance; mental rehearsal helps to fine tune performance and develop skills; a consistent routine before both practice and performance allows for adequate mental, physical, and emotional preparation and warm-up. The exercises below can help the performer use mental rehearsal to re-experience peak performance states both mentally and in actual performance.

Exercise 12.15:   Top performance mental rehearsal

- First, relax yourself to ensure that your mind, body, and emotions are quiet.
- Imagine yourself walking into a big room, and in front of you, you see a chair and a large screen. Sit down, and watch a film of your best ever performance. Notice what you are doing to prepare yourself, and when you begin playing, notice what the music sounds like. Notice how you are expressing yourself, the positioning of your body, and your facial expression. As you come to the end of your performance, notice what you look and sound like.
- Having just finished watching yourself, what is your response? What are you feeling?
- Rewind the film back to the beginning, and this time, choose another camera angle—perhaps from above or behind—and then play the film through again. What can you see and hear? What is different when you look from this angle? Complete the performance.
- Now, see yourself about to perform again, and this time, imagine yourself getting up from your chair and stepping into the film. You are now about to play from the inside, looking through your own eyes.
- Prepare yourself and play. Give your best performance. Notice where and what you are paying attention to, notice what the music sounds like, and notice how you are expressing yourself. In particular, pay attention to the physical sensations when you play. What are the key aspects of your performance? Complete the performance and notice what you are feeling now.
- Give the performance from inside for a second time. Focus on the key aspects of your performance and hold onto the feelings that are specific to when you play your best. Complete the performance and return to your seat, where you can see yourself on the screen again.
- Watch yourself one more time, performing at your very best, and notice your response. As the performance finishes, notice what you are feeling and bring this feeling back with you to your present environment.

Reflections on top performance mental rehearsal

◆ What did you notice when you observed and heard your performance from the outside?

◆ What focus and feeling did you associate with your best performance?

◆ What are you going to do before future performances to evoke this state in yourself?

Exercise 12.16:   Simulating performance

Before you do this visualization, it helps if you have seen the venue in which you are going to be performing.

◆ Notice the details of the room and what the room sounds like.

◆ Relax your mind and body in the usual way and now recall the memory of a moment in your musical career when you felt you were in the "right place at the right time"— just one moment, the first that occurs to you. This is a moment when your performance was seemingly flawless, when you seemed to know in advance what was going to happen.

◆ Notice what you are doing, where you are, and who you are with. Above all, notice your physical sensations and what it feels like to be performing in this way. Play through this moment once or twice more, focusing on both your physical and mental sensations.

◆ Hold these feelings and imagine you have arrived at the venue for an upcoming performance. Find a place in the venue where you can momentarily store your equipment and feel at home. Walk into the room where you will be playing and notice what you see and hear as you walk around. Perhaps go to back of the room and notice what you can see from the audience's point of view. Now walk onto the stage and look around and listen carefully to the room. Make yourself at home on stage.

◆ Imagine that you have now completed your warm-up routine, and when you are ready, step out to perform. As you do so, bring the experience and feeling of being in the right place at the right time with you. Notice how you feel as you step out onto the stage and ready yourself. Notice the audience that you are communicating with and the place you are in now. Focus on yourself, and notice what you are feeling. Now play.

◆ Notice what you can see and hear as you play, and pay attention to your physical sensations and feelings. Play your performance perfectly. For a moment, float out of your body and notice what you can see and hear from the audience's perspective. Notice how you are responding as a member of the audience. Now, float back into yourself and complete your performance. As you finish, notice what and how you feel, and then bring yourself back to your present environment.

Reflections on simulated performance

◆ What did you feel when you were in the right place at the right time?

◆ When and where will you use this visualization again?

12.4   Using mental skills for long-term learning and preparation for performance

As detailed throughout the rest of this book, there are several qualities that performers should incorporate into their long-term performance preparation. These include maintaining high-quality individual and group practice (e.g. the adoption of a systematic practice approach, selecting an appropriate environment for practice with minimal internal and external distractions, and using a warm-up routine that prepares the body and mind to play), technical preparation and learning (e.g. the removal of extraneous and unwanted physical movements and tension), and artistic preparation and expression (e.g. seeking to make a personal statement in interpreting and expressing music and working to communicate that statement to the audience).

Mental skills training can also be used to help performers realize their long-term goals. Essential ingredients to any long-term preparation plan include the ability to (1) assess performance quality, (2) set goals and plan, (3) take action toward meeting those goals, and (4) monitor progress. In terms of the first, it is important to acknowledge one's current performance ability in order to conceive of how performance can be improved (see Chapter 4 for a discussion on how to increase the power of one's "microscope" for assessing performance quality). Second, setting challenging and specific goals can lead to better performances than setting goals merely to "do my best" or not setting goals at all. Goals provide direction, maintain motivation, increase effort, direct attention, and improve learning (Reitman, 1965; Simon, 1973; Wessels, 1982; see also Chapters 2 and 5 of this volume). Third, this action plan must be implemented. Finally, it is important to review set goals regularly in order to update and adjust the plan accordingly. The following exercise can assist long-term preparation; it will take about an hour, and since it is potentially an important step in planning career choices, it should be done with undivided attention.

Exercise 12.17:   Choosing and prioritizing goals; deciding on actions and scheduling

Choosing goals

◆ To do this, you will need five sheets of paper.

◆ On the first sheet, write "LIFETIME GOALS." Now, write as many such goals as you can for 5 minutes. Write down anything that comes to your mind.

◆ Take the second sheet and write "1 TO 3 YEAR GOALS," and do the same.

◆ Take the third sheet and write "3 TO 12 MONTH GOALS," and do the same.

◆ Take the forth sheet and write "1 MONTH GOALS," and do the same.

Prioritizing goals

◆ Review each piece of paper in turn and decide on the goals that are most important to you (e.g. those that you are most excited about).

- ◆ Choose the three goals that are most important to you and that have a sense of urgency about them. Write "A" beside them.

- ◆ Write "B" next to three of the remaining important goals. These goals either do not have the same urgency or are not as important as the "A" goals.

- ◆ Now, write "C" next to the remaining goals. There is neither the same importance nor urgency for these, but at some point in the future, you may want to review their relative importance.

Deciding on actions and scheduling

- ◆ On the fifth sheet, draw up a table with the following headings in the left-hand column: (1) Specific actions for 1 MONTH "A" goals, (2) Specific actions for 1 MONTH "B" goals, (3) Specific actions for 3 TO 12 MONTH "A" goals, (4) Specific actions for 1 TO 3 YEAR "A" goals, and (5) Specific actions for LIFETIME "A" goals. In the right-hand column, beside each of these five headings, write "when."

- ◆ Look at your 1 MONTH goals. For each "A" goal, choose three actions you will take in the coming week. For each "B" goal, choose one action you will take in the coming week. Schedule each item with a date to be completed.

- ◆ Look at your 3 TO 12 MONTH goals. For each "A" goal, choose one action you will take in the coming week. Schedule each item with a date to be completed.

- ◆ Look at your 1 TO 3 YEAR goals. For each "A" goal, choose one action you will take in the next month. Schedule each item with a date to be completed.

- ◆ You now have a number of specific actions to do over the next month. How are you going to remember to pay attention to these actions?

- ◆ After 2 weeks, review your progress and decide to what extent you have achieved your 1 MONTH goals, and then schedule further actions.

- ◆ Also, look at your LIFETIME goals. For each "A" goal, choose one action you will take in the next year. Schedule each item with a date to be completed and review these actions monthly.

This exercise should be reviewed and revised on a fortnightly or monthly basis. Once a year, you may want to conduct the whole exercise again, putting aside your previous goals setting exercise. After you have completed the exercise again, you may then contrast your goals of the previous year with the newly developed ones to see how you have progressed in your career path and your priorities.

12.6 Conclusions

Mental skills are integral to performance success. The ability to guide oneself consistently into a calm, focused, flexible, goal-oriented state of mind is so central to performance that renowned pedagogues have long championed its use. Karl Leimer, for example, teacher of the famous pianist Walter Gieseking, advocated mental training for all of his students, most notably in relation to memorization but also for refining technique and developing the "inner ear" (see Gieseking & Leimer, 1932/1972). As for the general benefits of mental training, Leimer remarks:

To practice the piano five, six, or seven hours daily is generally done without concentration and is at the same time injurious to the health. The mental study demanded by the method here outlined is naturally very strenuous, and pupils afflicted with mental inertness greatly dislike it. But it is the only way in which really good and astonishing results can be obtained (p. 48).

Leimer continually stressed the importance of practicing mental skills but remarked that "when pupils assert that they make use of mental study, it is usually only talk" (p. 49). The purpose of this chapter has been to provide musicians with some representative mental skills exercises that they can apply within the framework of their own performance schedules and their own identified goals. Performers are encouraged to experiment with the exercises presented, adapt them where necessary, and reflect on how their mental and physical skills can interact to enhance their performance. To promote the development of metacognitive skills (as discussed in Chapter 5; also see Nielsen, 1999; Barry & Hallam, 2002), reflective guiding questions have been provided along with the exercises presented here.

Despite the fact that mental skills training is largely specific to the individual, one factor that generalizes across all potential users is that mental skills must be practiced regularly and should be viewed as a long-term commitment. By adopting and sticking with a personalized mental skills regime (embedded within a larger program of high-quality physical practice), the benefits can manifest themselves in ways that are both personally and professionally meaningful.

Acknowledgments

We would like to thank David Buswell and Mark Mercer for their assistance on earlier drafts of this chapter and The Leverhulme Trust and the Royal College of Music, London, for their support of our efforts to develop a mental skills training curriculum for music students.

Further information and reading

Further details of mental skills training and sports psychology can be obtained from the websites of the following organizations: the Exercise and Sports Psychology Division of the American Psychological Association (*www.psyc.unt.edu/apadiv47*), the Association for the Advancement of Applied Sports Psychology (*www.aaasponline.org*), and the European Federation of Sport Psychology (*www.psychology.lu.se/Fepsac*). Additional information on the material presented in this chapter is provided at the project website for "Zoning In: Motivating the Musical Mind": *www.zoningin.rcm.ac.uk*. For further reading on mental skills, see:

Emmons, S., & Thomas, A. (1998). *Power Performance for Singers: Transcending the Barriers.* Oxford: Oxford University Press.

Godøy, R. I., & Jørgensen, H. (Eds.). (2001). *Musical Imagery.* Lisse, The Netherlands: Swets and Zeitlinger.

Martens, R. (1987). *Coaches Guide to Sports Psychology.* Champaign, IL: Human Kinetics.

Nideffer, R. M. (1976). *The Inner Athlete.* New York: Thomas Crowell.

Partington, J. T. (1995). *Making Music.* Montreal: Carleton University Press.

Syer, J., & Connolly, C. (1991). *Think to Win.* London: Simon and Schuster.

Syer, J., & Connolly, C. (1998). *Sporting Body, Sporting Mind* (2nd ed.). London: Simon and Schuster.

References

Barry, N. H., & Hallam, S. (2002). Practice. In R. Parncutt & G. E. McPherson (Eds.), *The Science and Psychology of Music Performance: Creative Strategies for Teaching and Learning* (pp. 151–165). Oxford: Oxford University Press.

Benson, H. (1975). *The Relaxation Response.* New York: Morrow.

Bird, E. I., & Wilson, V. E. (1988). The effects of physical practice upon psychophysiological response during mental rehearsal of novice conductors. *Journal of Mental Imagery, 12,* 51–64.

Butler, R. J. (1996). *Sports Psychology In Action.* Oxford: Butterworth-Heinemann.

Chaffin, R., Imreh, G., & Crawford, M. (2002). *Practicing Perfection: Memory and Piano Performance.* Mahwah, NJ: Erlbaum.

Clark, D. B., & Agras, W. S. (1991). The assessment and treatment of performance anxiety in musicians. *American Journal of Psychiatry, 148,* 598–605.

Coffman, D. D. (1990). Effects of mental practice, physical practice, and knowledge of results on piano performance. *Journal of Research in Music Education, 38,* 187–196.

Csikszentmihalyi, M. (1990). *Flow: The Psychology of Optimal Experience.* New York: Harper and Row.

Csikszentmihalyi, M., & Csikszentmihalyi, I. S. (Eds.). (1988). *Optimal Experience: Psychological Studies of Flow in Consciousness.* Cambridge: Cambridge University Press.

Emmons, S., & Thomas, A. (1998). *Power Performance for Singers: Transcending the Barriers.* Oxford: Oxford University Press.

Freymuth, M. (1993). Mental practice for musicians: Theory and applications. *Medical Problems of Performing Artists, 8,* 141–143.

Gabrielsson, A. (1999). The performance of music. In D. Deutsch (Ed.), *The Psychology of Music* (2nd ed., pp. 501–602). London: Academic Press.

Gieseking, W., & Leimer, K. (1932/1972). *Piano Technique.* New York: Dover. (Original work published in 1932.)

Grøndahl, D. (1987). *Thinking Processes and Structures Used by Professional Pianists in Keyboard Learning.* Unpublished masters dissertation, Norwegian Academy of Music, Oslo.

Hasher, L., Chung, C., May, C. P., & Foong, N. (2002). Age, time of testing, and proactive interference. *Canadian Journal of Experimental Psychology, 56,* 200–207.

Jones, A. R. (1990). *The Role of Analytical Prestudy in the Memorization and Retention of Piano Music with Subjects of Varied Aural/Kinesthetic Ability.* Unpublished doctoral dissertation, University of Illinois, Urbana-Champaign, IL.

Kendrick, M. J., Craig, K. D., Lawson, D. M., & Davidson, P. O. (1982). Cognitive and behavioral therapy for musical-performance anxiety. *Journal of Consulting and Clinical Psychology, 50,* 353–362.

Kopiez, R. (1990a). *Der Einfluss kognitiver Strukturen auf das Erlernen eines Musikstücks am Instrument.* Frankfurt am Main, Germany: Peter Lang.

Kopiez, R. (1990b). Der Einfluss grafischer vs. verbal-analytischer kognitiver Strukturierung mentalen Erlernen eines Musikstücks. *Jahrbuch der Deutschen Gesellschaft für Musikpsychologie, 7*, 147–155.

Kopiez, R. (1991). Structural aids to the cognitive practice of music: Graphic or verbal analysis? *Psychologica Belgica, 31*, 163–171.

LaBerge, D. (1981). Response to Robert G. Sidnell. In *Documentary Report of the Ann Arbor Symposium. Applications of Psychology to the Teaching and Learning of Music* (pp. 39–41). Reston, VA: Music Educators National Conference.

Lindström, E., Juslin, P. N., Bresin, R., & Williamon, A. (2003). "Expressivity comes from within your soul": A questionnaire study of music students' perspectives on expressivity. *Research Studies in Music Education, 20*, 23–47.

Loehr, J. E. (1987). *Mental Toughness Training For Sports*. Harrisonburg, VA: R. R. Donnelley and Sons.

Martens, R. (1987). *Coaches Guide to Sports Psychology*. Champaign, IL: Human Kinetics.

May, C. P., Hasher, L., & Stoltzfus, E. R. (1993). Optimal time of day and the magnitude of age differences in memory. *Psychological Science, 4*, 326–330.

Nagel, J., Himle, D., & Papsdorf, J. (1989). Cognitive-behavioural treatment of musical performance anxiety. *Psychology of Music, 17*, 12–21.

Nideffer, R. M. (1976). *The Inner Athlete*. New York: Thomas Crowell.

Nielsen, S. G. (1999). Learning strategies in instrumental music practice. *British Journal of Music Education, 16*, 275–291.

Partington, J. T. (1995). *Making Music*. Montreal: Carleton University Press.

Reitman, W. R. (1965). *Cognition and Thought: An Information Processing Approach*. New York: Wiley.

Ross, S. L. (1985). The effectiveness of mental practice in improving the performance of college trombonists. *Journal of Research in Music Education, 33*, 221–230.

Rubin-Rabson, G. (1937). *The Influence of Analytical Pre-Study in Memorizing Piano Music*. New York: Archives of Psychology.

Rubin-Rabson, G. (1941). Studies in the psychology of memorizing piano music: VI. A comparison of two forms of mental rehearsal and keyboard overlearning. *Journal of Educational Psychology, 32*, 593–602.

Simon, H. A. (1973). The structure of ill-structured problems. *Artificial Intelligence, 4*, 181–202.

Stippich, C., Ochmann, H., & Sartor, K. (2002). Somatotopic mapping of the human primary sensorimotor cortex during motor imagery and motor execution by functional magnetic resonance imaging. *Neuroscience Letters, 331*, 50–54.

Syer, J., & Connolly, C. (1991). *Think to Win*. London: Simon and Schuster.

Syer, J., & Connolly, C. (1998). *Sporting Body, Sporting Mind* (2nd ed.). London: Simon and Schuster.

Sweeney, G. A., & Horan, J. J. (1982). Separate and combined effects of cue-controlled relaxation and cognitive restructuring in the treatment of musical performance anxiety. *Journal of Counseling Psychology, 29*, 486–497.

Weinberg, R. S. (1982). The relationship between mental preparation strategies and motor performance: A review and critique. *Quest, 33*, 195–213.

Wessels, M. G. (1982). *Cognitive Psychology.* New York: Harper and Row.

Williamon, A., Valentine, E., & Valentine, J. (2002). Shifting the focus of attention between levels of musical structure. *European Journal of Cognitive Psychology, 14*, 493–520.

Woolfolk, R. L., Carr-Kaffashan, K., & Lehrer, P. M. (1976). Meditation training as a treatment for insomnia. *Behavior Therapy, 7*, 359–365.

Yoon, C., May, C. P., & Hasher, L. (2000). Aging, circadian arousal patterns, and cognition. In D. C. Park & N. Schwarz (Eds.), *Cognitive Aging: A Primer* (pp. 151–171). Hove, UK: Psychology Press.

CHAPTER 13

FEEDBACK LEARNING OF MUSICAL EXPRESSIVITY

PATRIK N. JUSLIN, ANDERS FRIBERG,
ERWIN SCHOONDERWALDT, AND JESSIKA KARLSSON

One of the recurrent themes in treatises on music is that music is expressive (Davies, 1994). Although this notion seems generally accepted among scholars, the concept of expression itself has remained elusive. This is reflected to some extent in both research and education. In research on music performance, many different approaches to expression have been adopted (for reviews, see Gabrielsson, 1999, 2003), but few attempts have been made to integrate different approaches into a coherent framework (Juslin *et al.*, 2002). Within music education, studies have indicated that the explicit teaching of expressive skills has largely been neglected (Tait, 1992; Persson, 1993; Rostwall & West, 2001) and that the teaching that is available seems to be based on folk theory and tradition, rather than on empirically validated knowledge (Persson, 1996). Why is this so?

First, the nature of musical expressivity does not lend itself easily to formalized description. For instance, much knowledge about expressivity is tacit and, therefore, difficult to express in words (Hoffren, 1964). Second, researchers have not been able to provide music teachers with theories that can guide the development of novel strategies for teaching expressive skills (Juslin & Persson, 2002). Expression in music performance is usually studied in isolation from any concerns with teaching of expressivity (Palmer, 1997), and studies of teaching strategies rarely investigate the nature of expressivity itself (Marchand, 1975). Yet, these aspects should not be separated because the development of new and perhaps more effective methods of teaching expressivity may benefit from a more complete understanding of the nature of expressivity.

Fortunately, research carried out during the last decade or so makes it possible to develop more theoretically informed teaching strategies aimed at expressive skills. The purpose of this chapter is to consider how theory and research on expressivity may inform day-to-day practice in the music profession. First, a critical discussion of traditional views on expressivity is provided, and some of the myths that surround the concept of expressivity are dispelled. Then, a revised view of expressivity based on modern research is proposed. Finally, a new and empirically based approach to learning expressivity, termed *cognitive feedback* (CFB), is described and evaluated. The bulk of this chapter is devoted to expression of emotion, but in the process, other important issues regarding expressivity are considered. The focus is on psychological research rather than philosophical inquiry (for a review of the latter, see Davies, 1994).

13.1   The nature of expressivity

One necessary requirement for the development of a good teaching strategy is to have a theory of the skill that is desired. A natural point of departure is to look at how music performers and researchers have traditionally conceptualized expressivity and then to propose a revised view based on current research on expressivity. It should be noted from the outset that the discussion is restricted to Western music, especially classical and popular music from the eighteenth century to the present day.

13.1.1   Common myths about expressivity

Views on expression and emotion have changed over time (Ratner, 1980; Cook & Dibben, 2001) as have, without doubt, the expressive features of performance themselves. Certain views have, however, been remarkably consistent across time and musical styles. Below, five myths about expressivity are considered, which may have had a negative impact on the teaching of expressivity in music education. Some of these myths stem from historical treatises and folk theories, and certainly not all students and teachers today subscribe to them. However, the discussion below highlights key issues that are helpful in understanding the context of the novel teaching strategy presented later.

Expressivity is a completely subjective entity that cannot be studied objectively

Much has been written about expressivity by philosophers, musicologists, and musicians—often with the implication that there is something *mysterious* about expressivity. Different authors have defined expressivity in strikingly different ways. This has led to the belief that expressivity is a completely "subjective" quality that cannot—or at least should not—be described in scientific terms (Hoffren, 1964; cf. Howard, 1989). Musicians are often unable, or unwilling, to define expressivity or to probe its underlying mechanisms: "great interpretation certainly is a mystery" (Dubal, 1985, p. 62); "the interpretation should speak for itself" (Menuhin, 1996, p. 329); "expressiveness should not be demystified, this could make the expression itself disappear" (teacher cited in Laukka, in press); "the most inspired performances are always those that are inexplicable from a logical point of view" (Ruth Laredo, cited in Dubal, 1985, p. 245).

Does this mean that it is impossible to study expressivity objectively? Not necessarily; acoustic correlates of expressivity can readily be obtained and manipulated in music performances, and listeners' judgments of expressivity can be systematically and reliably related to such acoustic correlates (see Section 13.1.2 below). Note that one common teaching strategy aimed at developing expressive skills, modeling, actually presumes that there are objective correlates of expressivity: the teacher's performance provides an acoustic model of what is desired from the student and the student is required to learn simply by imitating the teacher (Dickey, 1992). The problem is that the student is required to pick up relevant features of the model, and that it may be difficult for a student to know precisely what to listen for and how to represent it in terms of specific skills (Lehmann, 1997; see Woody, 1999, for data supporting this view).

You must feel the emotion in order to convey it to your listeners

"A musician cannot move others unless he too is moved," C. P. E. Bach (1778/1985) argued in his book on the true art of playing keyboard instruments (p. 152). This idea is common even among today's students (Lindström *et al.*, 2003) and teachers (Laukka, in press). Focusing on felt emotions may help a performer to naturally translate emotions into appropriate sounds, but felt emotion does not guarantee that the emotion will be communicated to listeners—neither is it necessary to feel an emotion in order to communicate it successfully. A listener has no direct access to the performer's emotion. What reaches the listener is the sound properties of the music. Emotion is communicated only to the extent that the sound properties contain information about emotion.[1] As noted by Sloboda (1996), students rarely monitor the expressive outcome of their own performances. Instead, they monitor their own intention and "take the intention for the deed" (p. 121). Indeed, recent questionnaire data indicate that 50% of students at conservatories listen to recordings of their own performances "seldom" or "never" (Lindström *et al.*, 2003). This is unfortunate, since listening to the performance may reveal just how far from the intended expression the actual sounds are. Some professional musicians do listen to their own performance: "It can be very instructive. When I hear it back, I think 'did I really play it *that* fast?' or 'Why didn't I give that section more poetry or feeling?' This never fails to amaze me" (Murray Perahia, cited in Dubal, 1985, p. 260).

Undoubtedly, focusing on felt emotions may help a performer to activate existing schemata for emotional expression, and a performer can use emotional memories as a means to self-induce moods (Stanislavski, 1937/1988; Persson, 1993). This is not an all-encompassing strategy, however, because a performer must be able to accomplish a convincing expression, regardless of what he or she feels (which could be nervousness, exhilaration, or intense concentration, depending on the specific circumstances). This is all the more true considering that a performer may need to move swiftly between different expressions within the same piece of music. Emotional engagement is not necessarily bad, but it cannot substitute for teaching that addresses the actual playing in specific and informative ways (see also Tait, 1992).

Explicit understanding is not beneficial to learning expressivity

Treatises on art often focus on intuition: "The artist activates . . . aesthetic experience through an intuitive combination of sensory stimuli" (Eibl-Eibesfeldt, 1989, p. 685). This is true also of musicians: "ultimately, the paramount role is that of intuition. For me the determining factor in creativity, in bringing a work to life, is that of musical instinct" (Casals, 1970, p. 97). It seems to be generally agreed that musicians are usually not aware of the details of how their expressive intentions are realized in performance (Sloboda, 1996), although there are individual differences among performers in this regard. To the extent that expressive features are used *tacitly*, this presents a problem for the teaching of expressivity, which relies to a large extent on verbal instruction (Tait, 1992). Moreover, because expert performers do not consciously think about how to apply expressive features in performance, one might wrongly conclude that students do not benefit from thinking about how to apply such features, even in early learning stages.

The notion that learning of expressive skills is "best left untouched" by conscious thoughts reflects a misunderstanding that pervades commonsense teaching based on tradition and folklore. It is important to note that willfully applied, goal-directed strategies normally undergo automation as a result of practice. For instance, although a performer may initially have to apply expressive features in a conscious manner, soon the associations between features and emotions become internalized by that performer and no longer in need of conscious control. Recent studies have shown that explicit instruction is beneficial to learning expressivity. Woody (1999), for example, noted that "the most effective approach for expressive performance involves conscious identification and implementation of specific expressive features" (p. 339; see Chapter 5 of this volume for a discussion of the benefits of metastrategies for individual learning and practice).

Emotions expressed in music are very different from everyday emotions

The most popular idea among musicians and others about what music expresses is emotion (e.g. Budd, 1985; Davies, 1994; Juslin & Sloboda, 2001; Lindström *et al.*, 2003; Laukka, in press). However, several authors have argued that the emotions expressed in music are very different from the emotions expressed in everyday life (e.g. Lippman, 1953; Swanwick, 1985). It is often suggested that music expresses emotions so subtle and complex that they cannot be described in words—that is, they are *ineffable* (Raffman, 1993). There are certain aspects of music experience that are difficult to describe in words, but this does not necessarily apply to emotions (note that most Western languages have several hundreds of emotion words that can be used to describe emotional nuances). Perhaps, listeners confuse the subtlety and variety of the music itself with the emotions actually expressed? The notion that emotions expressed in music are ineffable is not helpful in music education. How could teachers say anything about the ineffable?

An arguably more fruitful approach is to regard emotions expressed in music as similar to those expressed outside of music (Davies, 1994; Juslin, 2001). The acoustic factors used to express emotions in performance (e.g. tempo, sound level, articulation, timbre) gain much of their power from the nonverbal communication of emotions. For instance, there is evidence that performers' expression of emotions in music largely reflects the nonverbal aspects of speech (see Section 13.2). Hence, if one defends the notion that musical emotions are different from everyday emotions, music students are effectively robbed of their most powerful sources of expressive form.

One of the most common strategies for teaching expressive skills (and apparently the most popular among music students; see Lindström *et al.*, 2003) is the use of metaphors, which presumes that emotions expressed in music are similar to everyday emotions. Metaphors are useful because emotions experienced in a nonmusical context can help shape musically relevant emotions. Musical emotions touch deeply not because they are so different from everyday emotions, but because they are so similar. However, the problem with metaphors is that they depend on the performer's personal experience with words and images. For that reason, metaphors may be ambiguous as directions to a performer (e.g. Persson, 1996; but see Barten, 1998, for a positive view). Still, the fact that music students find extramusical sources, such as life situations, useful in developing expression (see Woody, 2000; Lindström *et al.*, 2003) suggests that emotions expressed in music have much in common with emotions in everyday life.

Expressive skills cannot be learned

The four myths about musical expressivity described thus far will tend to reinforce the fifth—namely, that expressive skills cannot be learned. If expressivity is completely subjective and passive and has nothing to do with an explicit understanding or emotions as they are known, it will obviously be difficult to teach expressivity to students. Expertise in music performance is often viewed as the synthesis of *technical* and *expressive* skills (Sloboda, 1996; Gabrielsson, 1999). However, technical aspects of playing are often regarded as learnable skills, whereas expressive aspects are regarded as instinctive (Boyd & George-Warren, 1992, pp. 104–105). Some teachers conceive of expression as "something that cannot be taught," a view that is shared by some students: "there is no technique to perform expressively. You have to use your soul" (student cited in Woody, 2000, p. 21).

As discussed by Sloboda (1996), one consequence of this view is that musical expressivity is wrongly believed to reflect only musical talent that is beyond learning and development. True enough, expressive skills sometimes reflect the emotional sensitivity of the musician in regard to musical sounds (as suggested by the personality concept of *auditory style*; see Brodsky *et al.*, 1994). But this does not mean that it is impossible to develop expressive skills through training. This is really an empirical question: studies that have addressed this issue have demonstrated that expressive skills can be improved by instruction and training (Marchand, 1975; Johnson, 1998; Woody, 1999; Juslin & Laukka, 2000; Sloboda *et al.*, 2003; see also Section 13.2.4 below).

Perhaps, the critical issue is *how* expressivity is being taught to students. Essential to the learning process is the provision of informative feedback. Technically, *feedback* has been defined as "the process by which an environment returns to individuals a portion of the information in their response output necessary to compare their present strategy with a representation of an ideal strategy" (Balzer *et al.*, 1989, p. 412). Consideration of this definition suggests that the traditional teaching strategies mentioned earlier (i.e. modeling and metaphors) rarely provide informative feedback, for they do not provide the performer with a comparison of his or her current performance strategy with an optimal strategy. Could empirical research help to address this problem?

13.1.2   Perspectives from empirical research

Experimental studies of music performance have been conducted for at least 100 years (Gabrielsson, 1999). Researchers have investigated performance expression mainly by measuring various acoustic parameters in the performance and relating these measures to a musical notation. In this particular context, expression usually refers to the "systematic variations" or "deviations" in timing, dynamics, timbre, and pitch that form the so-called *microstructure* of a performance, and differentiate it from another performance of the same music (Palmer, 1997). Sometimes, attempts have been made to relate such acoustic properties to the perceived expression of the performance, as evident from listener judgments.

Much like the individual performer who first learns to play a musical instrument, studies of expressivity in music performance have progressed from a consideration of basic principles of expression (e.g. how does the performer convey the phrase structure?) toward more subtle and individualistic aspects (e.g. what makes a performance truly special?). However, it is fair to say that researchers are still struggling with the problem of how to account for the microstructure of a typical performance of music. Contributing to the difficulty are the vast number of factors that, in principle, may

Table 13.1 Examples of factors that may influence expressivity in music performance (based on Juslin, 2003)

	Examples of factors
Piece-related	The musical composition itself Notational variants of the piece Consultations with composer or composer's written comments Musical style/genre
Instrument-related	Acoustic parameters available Instrument-specific aspects of timbre, pitch, etc. Technical difficulties of the instrument
Performer-related	Performer's structural interpretation Performer's expressive intention with regard to the mood of the piece Performer's emotion-expressive style Performer's technical skill Performer's motor precision Performer's mood while playing Performer's body language Performer's interaction with co-performers Performer's perception of/interaction with audience
Listener-related	Listener's musical preferences Listener's musical expertise Listener's personality Listener's current mood Listener's state of attention
Context-related	Acoustics Sound technology (e.g. recording technique, stereo equipment) Listening context (e.g. recording, concert) Other individuals present Visual performance conditions Larger cultural and historic setting Whether the performance is formally evaluated

influence expressivity in music performance (see Table 13.1). Music performance is a complex process affected by numerous factors related to the music: the instrument, the performer, the listener, and the social context. As a result of the practical limitations associated with experimental studies, researchers have been forced to bracket most of the factors shown in Table 13.1 and to focus instead on the core principles of music performance (discussed later in this section) that transcend a specific time and place (in certain styles of music in the Western world, at least).

Still, some consistent themes have emerged from this field of research, one of which is that performance expression is best conceived of as a multidimensional phenomenon, which may be decomposed into different subcomponents. That is, there are different kinds of expressivity that arguably make different contributions to the aesthetic impact of a given performance. Expressive features may serve different and sometimes opposing functions. The exact nature of these components of expressivity is still being discussed by researchers. However, drawing on previous research, Juslin (2003) argues that expressivity derives from five main sources (collectively referred to as the GERMS model):

1. *Generative rules (G)* that mark the structure in a musical manner (Clarke, 1988). By means of variations in such parameters as timing, dynamics, and articulation, a performer is able to communicate group boundaries (Gabrielsson, 1987), metrical accents (Sloboda, 1983), and harmonic structure (Palmer, 1996). Generative features may increase the emotional impact of the music, but do so mainly by enhancing the expression that is inherent in the structure of the piece. Hence, part of the expression reflects the *structure* of the piece performed—as filtered through the performer's interpretation.

2. *Emotional expression (E)* that serves to convey emotions to listeners (Juslin, 1997a). By manipulating overall features of the performance, such as tempo, timbre, and loudness, a performer is able to play the same structure with different emotional characters. Often the performer will try to support the emotional character suggested by piece-specific features (e.g. melody, harmony), although by contradicting the expression of the piece to some degree, the performer may convey "conflicting," "mixed," or "complex" emotions.

3. *Random fluctuations (R)* that reflect human limitations in motor precision (Gilden, 2001). It has been revealed in several studies that even when expert performers attempt to play perfectly even time intervals (e.g. in a tapping task), there are still small and involuntary fluctuations in timing in their performance. Practice instills consistency in speed, precision, and fluency—among other things—but it seems that the small random variations contribute to the "living" character of music; the slight unpredictability that makes every performance absolutely unique (Juslin *et al.*, 2002).

4. *Motion principles (M)* that hold that tempo changes should follow natural patterns of human movement (e.g. gesture). A pleasing performance is one in which the expressive microstructure satisfies basic constraints of animate motion (Shove & Repp, 1995). For instance, Friberg and Sundberg (1999) showed that final ritards of music performances that are preferred by listeners tend to follow a tempo curve similar to that of runners' decelerations.[2]

5. *Stylistic unexpectedness (S)*, which reflects a performer's deliberate attempt to deviate from stylistic expectations concerning performance conventions in order to add tension and unpredictability to the performance (e.g. Meyer, 1956, p. 206). This aspect is probably the least researched so far, but it may be critical to developing a truly original interpretation.

All of these components reflect psychophysical relationships among acoustic characteristics of the performance (specific patterns of information) and psychological characteristics of the human listener (e.g. categorical perception). In reality, all five components occur together in complex interactions, but for certain purposes (e.g. research, teaching), it may be useful to consider them separately. The reasons for this are that the components have different origins, display different characteristics, and are processed partly by different regions of the brain (Juslin, 2003). Juslin *et al.* (2002) made an attempt to simulate the first four of the GERMS components in synthesized performances of music, and a listening test indicated that all four components contributed to the perceived expressivity of a performance, although in different degrees. Statistically, the emotion component (E) had the largest impact on listeners' judgments.

What are the implications of the GERMS model for music education? One is that, at certain stages, the different aspects of expressivity may need to be taught separately because they have different characteristics. According to the GERMS model, a performance should (1) convey the generative structure of the music, (2) express emotions, (3) exhibit motor precision, (4) be suggestive of human motion and gesture, and (5) deviate from stylistic expectations in aesthetically pleasing ways. The conveying of structure (G) is probably the aspect that has received most attention in research and education, perhaps because it is the most tangible aspect: "structure can be seen, heard, demonstrated" (Epstein, 1995, p. 126). Certainly, there is no substitute for a thorough understanding of the musical structure in shaping a musical interpretation. This aspect of expressivity may be guided by structural analysis, by consulting the composer or his or her writings, and also by exploring visual graphs of performance parameters alongside the notation (e.g. Riley-Butler, 2001). The motion component (M) may be trained by using techniques outlined by Davidson and Correia (2002), such as asking the student to conduct the expression in the playing of the teacher and developing nonverbal narratives of physical gesture for individual phrases. The stylistic unexpectedness component (S) requires extensive knowledge about musical styles and performance conventions, as well as an ability to conceive of the performance structure in terms of a narrative of musical expectations that can be experimented with in creative ways. The aspect of expressivity in most need of a formalized teaching strategy is emotional expression (E).

Expression of emotions: Summary of findings

Research on emotional expression, as manifested specifically in *performance features* (e.g. timing, timbre) as opposed to features of the composition (e.g. melody, harmony), have matured in the last decade (Juslin, 2001). Most of these studies have used a procedure in which musicians were asked to play various pieces of music in order to express specific emotions (e.g. tenderness). The performances were recorded and used in listening tests to see whether listeners could (accurately) recognize the intended expression.[3] In addition, many studies have analyzed the acoustic features of the performances to investigate *how* each emotion was expressed. Below, the key findings from this research are summarized (for more extensive treatment, see Juslin & Laukka, 2003).

1. Professional performers are able to communicate basic emotions (happiness, sadness, anger, fear, tenderness) to listeners with accuracy about as high as in facial and vocal expression of emotions (Juslin & Laukka, 2001, 2003). Amateur performers communicate emotions less effectively and tend to apply the expressive features inconsistently (Juslin & Laukka, 2000; Rohwer, 2001).

2. The communicative process appears to operate on a fairly broad level of emotion categories, whereas finer distinctions within these categories are difficult to convey (Juslin & Lindström, 2003; Juslin, 1997c), at least without additional context (lyrics, program notes, visual cues).

Table 13.2 Summary of acoustic features used to express 12 "basic" and "complex" emotions by professional performers (adapted from Juslin & Lindström, 2003)

	Acoustic feature						
	Tempo	Sound level	Articulation	Timbre*	Attack*	Vibrato extent*	Vibrato rate*
Anger	↑	↑	=	↑	↑	↑	=
Contentment	↓	=	↑	=	↓	↓	↓
Curiosity	=	=	↓	=	↓	↑	=
Disgust	=	↑	↓	=	↑	=	↑
Fear	=	↓	↓	↓	↑	=	↑
Happiness	↑	↑	↓	=	↑	↓	=
Jealousy	↑	↑	=	↑	=	↑	↓
Love	↓	=	↑	=	↓	=	↓
Pride	=	↑	=	↑	↑	=	↑
Sadness	↓	↓	↑	↓	↓	↓	↓
Shame	↓	↓	↓	↓	=	=	↑
Tenderness	↓	↓	↑	↓	↓	↓	=

Note: ↑ indicates a high value, ↓ indicates a low value, = indicates a medium value. A high value indicates (respectively for each cue) fast (versus slow) tempo, high (versus low) sound level, legato (versus staccato) articulation, much (versus little) high-frequency energy in the spectrum, fast (versus slow) attack velocity, large (versus small) vibrato extent, and fast (versus slow) vibrato rate ($N = 216$, except * $N = 144$).

3. The timbre of specific musical instruments may affect the effectiveness of the communicative process to some extent (e.g. Behrens & Green, 1993).

4. Many studies have attempted to describe the "code" (the acoustic means) that performers use to convey each emotion. This has shown that performers manipulate variables such as tempo, sound level, articulation, timbre, timing, attack, decay, intonation, portamento, and vibrato to express different emotions (Juslin, 2001). Both mean levels and patterns of variability in these variables may influence the perceived expression (Juslin, 1997b; Juslin & Madison, 1999). Table 13.2, for example, summarizes, in a simplified fashion, patterns of acoustic features used by professional performers to express 12 "basic" and "complex" emotions (on guitar, piano, and saxophone). In reality, the emotional expression will often change rapidly within a piece, or even within a single note. Many different musical styles have been studied (classical music, folk music, rock, opera, jazz), but it is not yet known whether the obtained relationships hold for other cultures as well.

5. Whether researchers' descriptions of acoustic features used to express various emotions are valid can be confirmed by creating synthesized performances of music on the basis of these findings. Synthesized performances with appropriate acoustic settings can express emotions as reliably as human performers (Juslin, 1997b; see also Bresin & Friberg, 2000).

6. An extensive review of 145 studies (101 speech and 44 music studies) strongly indicates that patterns of acoustic features used to convey each emotion largely derives from the nonverbal features of emotional speech (Juslin & Laukka, 2003), as suggested by Spencer (1857).

7. The expression created by overall features such as tempo can be enhanced by accents on specific notes in the melodic structure (e.g. those with much melodic tension; Lindström, 2003).

8. The communication of emotion in music is generally successful despite individual differences in the use of acoustic features among both performers and listeners (e.g. Juslin, 2000), and despite the fact that different musical instruments provide different features at the musician's disposal.

13.2   A novel approach: Feedback-learning of musical expressivity

In a project called "Feedback-learning of Musical Expressivity" (Feel-ME), the authors aim to develop new methods for teaching expressive skills based on recent advances in musical science, psychology, technology, and acoustics. *Cognitive feedback* (CFB), an empirically based approach to learning expressivity, has been developed and implemented in user-friendly computer software. A number of computer programs aimed at enhancing performance skills have been created, as computers have become both less expensive and more easy to use (Webster, 2002). None of these programs, however, seems to focus on emotional expression.

13.2.1   Criteria for a useful teaching strategy

One requirement for teaching emotional expression is that it improves the communication of emotion as effectively as possible. However, the ultimate goal should be to provide performers with the tools they need to develop their own personal expression (originality is often emphasized as an important criterion for an artistic work). To achieve a creative interpretation of a piece of music, the performer may wish the emotional expression to be clear or ambiguous, stable or variable, specific or general. But only detailed knowledge about the relationships among expressive features and their perceptual effects will help the performer to achieve the desired effects on listeners reliably. This knowledge may serve as the core from which interpretations are developed, with knowledge about the particular musical instrument, piece, style, and composer. Given these aims, what are the specific criteria for a useful teaching strategy?

◆ First, it is essential that the teaching strategy is well-suited to the nature of the communicative process as described in research. Such communication involves a number of acoustic features that are used largely tacitly by performers and listeners. A useful teaching strategy should take these characteristics into account, and help to render transparent the communicative process.

◆ Second, the teaching strategy should include the three elements required for *deliberate practice* (Ericsson *et al.*, 1993): (1) a well-defined task, (2) informative feedback, and (3) opportunities for repetition and correction of errors.

◆ Third, the teaching strategy should allow the performer to compare his or her playing with an "optimal" (or reference) model, in accordance with the definition of feedback discussed earlier.

◆ Fourth, the teaching strategy should relate sound properties of the performance to experiential concepts (e.g. emotion) relevant in interpretation. Previous strategies focus either on acoustic aspects (e.g. modeling) or experiential aspects (e.g. metaphors), but a useful strategy should preferably resolve this dualism by describing the relationships between the two.

◆ Finally, the efficacy of the teaching strategy should have been empirically demonstrated.

Below, a teaching strategy is presented that meets these criteria. First, however, a general model is outlined that is suited to describing the communicative process.

13.2.2   The lens model

Communication of emotion requires that there is both a performer's intention to express an emotion and recognition of this same emotion by a listener.[4] The performer may, for instance, wish to highlight an emotional quality of a piece of music (e.g. to bring out love and joy in Beethoven's Appassionata; Dubal, 1985, p. 107). Emotional communication requires a controlled application of dynamic contrasts in various expressive features: fast–slow, loud–soft, staccato–legato, bright–dark, and so on. These features have some peculiar characteristics that are essential to understand in order to devise an efficient teaching strategy.

   One way of capturing the characteristics of the communicative process is to conceptualize it in terms of a variant of Brunswik's (1956) *lens model*. The lens model was originally intended as a model of visual perception but was later used mainly in studies of human judgment (Cooksey, 1996). The lens model (see Figure 13.1) can be used to illustrate how musicians express emotions by means of a set of *cues* (e.g. tempo, sound level, timbre) that are uncertain, but partly redundant (the cues covary to some extent).

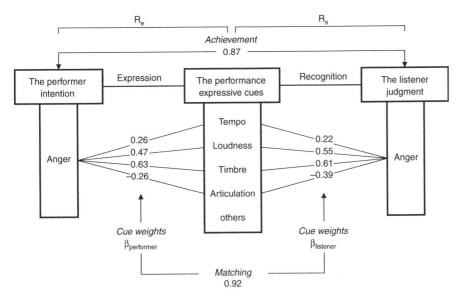

Figure 13.1 A Brunswikian lens model of communication of emotion in music performance. The cue weights should be interpreted as follows: positive (as opposed to negative) signs indicate, respectively for each cue, fast (versus slow) mean tempo, high (versus low) sound level, sharp (versus soft) timbre, and legato (versus staccato) articulation (for details regarding methodology, see Juslin, 2000).

The expressed emotions are recognized by listeners, who use the same cues to recognize the expression. The cues are uncertain because they are not perfectly reliable indicators of the intended expression. Thus, for instance, fast tempo is not perfectly correlated with expression of happiness, because fast tempo is also used in expression of anger. None of the cues are completely reliable when used in isolation, but by integrating the values of various cues, performers and listeners can achieve reliable expression and recognition, respectively. This is not simply a matter of pattern matching (as suggested by Table 13.2), since cues contribute in a mainly additive fashion to listener judgments (Juslin, 1997b). This can explain how the communication can be successful on different musical instruments, which provide different cues. Redundancy between cues partly reflects how sounds are produced on instruments (e.g. a harder string attack produces a tone that is both louder and sharper in timbre). There are several indices in the lens model that are key in understanding the communicative process (for a description of how each index is measured, see Juslin, 2000):

- *Achievement* (r_a) refers to the relationship between the performer's expressive intention and the listener's judgment. It is a measure of how well the performer succeeds in communicating a particular emotion to listeners.
- *Cue weight* (β_1, β_2, β_3 . . .) refers to the strength of the relationship between an individual cue, on the one hand, and expressive intentions and listeners' judgments, on the other (indexed by correlation statistics). Cue weights indicate how individual cues are used by performers and listeners, respectively (e.g. that the performer uses fast tempo in expression of anger).
- *Matching* (G) refers to the degree of similarity between the performer's and the listeners' utilization of acoustic cues, respectively. For effective communication to occur, the performer's use of cues (i.e. their cue weights) must be reasonably matched to listeners' use of cues.
- *Consistency* (R_e and R_s) refers to the degree of consistency with which the performer and listener, respectively, are able to utilize the various cues. Other things equal, the communication will be more effective if the cues are used in a consistent manner.

The important point is that the upper limit of communication accuracy is set by the degree of matching, performer consistency, and listener consistency. If the emotional communication is *not* successful, this may be because (1) performer and listeners use the cues differently (poor matching), (2) the performer uses the cues inconsistently, and (3) the listeners use the cues inconsistently. By analyzing these indices separately, one can interpret the success of communication in a particular situation. This information is needed in order to be able to improve the communicative process (Juslin, 2000; see also Hursch *et al.*, 1964).

The lens model has several important implications. First, perfect accuracy of communication cannot be expected. If the acoustic cues are uncertain, it means that the communicative process is uncertain too. Second, to understand the success of the communication in a specific situation, both expression and recognition of emotions must be described in terms of the same concepts. The model implies that the extent to which the emotional expression of a piece of music is recognized depends equally on the sender and the receiver. Third, because the cues are partly redundant, more than one cue utilization strategy could lead to the same level of accuracy (e.g. Juslin, 2000). Since there is no pressure toward uniformity in utilization of cues, performers can communicate successfully with listeners, without having to compromise their unique playing styles. The key is to profit from the cue redundancy through *vicarious functioning* of cues (Brunswik, 1956)—one cue may substitute for another to some extent. Of course, there are clear limits to this tolerance, and the use of vicarious functioning requires a certain kind of knowledge (detailed in Section 13.2.3). Further, this flexibility comes with a price: redundancy limits the information capacity of the communication because the same, rather than unique, information is conveyed by many cues. This explains why performers find it hard to communicate anything other than broad categories of emotion (Juslin & Lindström, 2003).

13.2.3   Cognitive feedback

The lens model offers a useful tool for improving the communication of emotions in music. Recall that emotional communication in music performance involves a large number of acoustic cues that are used by both performers and listeners. Both expression and recognition of emotion are made by integrating these cues. Such integration requires knowledge about the *relationships* between performers, cues, and listeners. The notion of CFB is to allow the performer to compare a model of his or her playing to an "optimal" model of playing. This is obviously a feature of feedback as such; however, it is important to understand how this is accomplished in the present method. Several of the performer's manipulations of acoustic cues are audible to listeners in general and to music teachers in particular. Nevertheless, it is extremely difficult for a human perceiver to infer the statistical relationships that exist among expressive intentions, acoustic cues, and listener impressions (see Figure 13.1), let alone the relationships among the cues themselves. It is well-known from extensive research on human judgment that judges are usually unable to verbalize the basis of their own judgments, especially in situations that involve many uncertain cues (Cooksey, 1996). CFB benefits from a statistical method (i.e. regression analysis) that makes it possible to describe the complex relationships with a precision that human perceivers would find difficult to achieve (e.g. Juslin, 2000). The authors recently implemented CFB in computer software. In the following summary of the basic procedure of CFB (Box 13.1), the plain text explains what the user (i.e. the musician) is doing in each phase, and the text in *italics* explains what the software is doing in each phase. This is to highlight that, although the principles by which CFB is generated are complicated, the actual use of the software is relatively straightforward.

It should be noted that using this software may comprise two different aspects of learning expressivity: (1) a "normative" aspect that involves trying to maximize communication accuracy through effective use of cues (the three phases described in Box 13.1 may be repeated as many times as judged necessary, e.g. until a certain level of matching is accomplished), and (2) an "aesthetic explorative" aspect that means that the performer may simply experiment with different ideas for interpretation, and check how listeners would be likely to perceive the resulting expression. The latter aspect

Box 13.1 CFB: Basic procedure

◆ In the first phase, the performer records a set of different performances of the same melody with the goal of expressing particular emotions (e.g. happiness, sadness, anger, tenderness) that are selected at the outset. The performer should record several versions of each emotional expression to obtain a representative sample of performances. The recording of each version can be repeated until the performer is satisfied with the result. When the performer has recorded the performances, he or she requests feedback from the software.[5]

◆ *Performances are recorded and acoustic cues are automatically analyzed by the software. The recording is first segmented into tone boundaries from an analysis of both sound level and pitch. Potential tone onsets and offsets are detected by identifying areas of similar pitch and substantial dips in the sound level. An example of the segmentation is presented in Figure 13.2. For each detected tone, the following cues are computed: pitch (in semitones), sound level (dB, upper quartile of sound level within onset–offset), instantaneous tempo (notes per second), articulation (percentage of pause duration), attack velocity (dB/s), spectral content (dB, difference between high and low spectral content, i.e. a correlate of perceived timbre), vibrato rate (Hz), and extent of vibrato (semitones). Then, statistical analysis is used to model the correlations between the performer's expressive intentions and the acoustic cues. This produces indices of consistency and cue weights for the performer (explained in Section 13.2.2). The performer's model is also mathematically related to a stored model of*

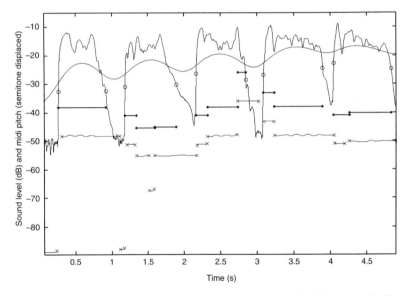

Figure 13.2 Automatic extraction of musical notes. This is an example of the onset and offset detection applied to a short phrase played on the violin. The upper two lines show the sound level and the "smoothed" sound level. Circles indicate tone onset and offset as indicated by sound level detection. The lines with crosses at the bottom are the tones suggested by the pitch analysis. The resulting tones from the combination of pitch and sound level analysis are the thick lines in the middle. (For clarity, the pitch graphs are displaced by −110 and −120 semitones, respectively.)

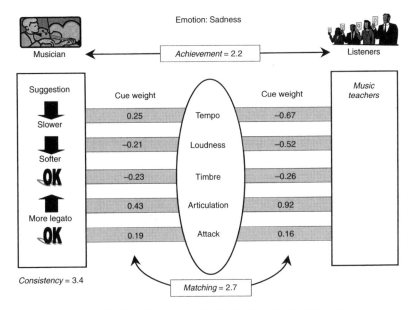

Figure 13.3 The graphical interface for cognitive feedback used in the CFB software.

listeners' judgments of emotion in music performances. This listener model was obtained from listening tests in which listeners were asked to judge the emotional expressions of a wide range of performances with varying emotional expression. Statistical analysis was used to model the correlations between listeners' judgments and acoustic cues, thus producing a general model that may be used to simulate new listener judgments. From this, the program obtains indices of achievement, matching, consistency, and cue weights. This information is finally transformed to a graphical interface, according to set criteria (for further details, see Juslin et al., 2003).

◆ In the second phase, the performer receives CFB from the software: this consists of a visual and numerical description of the performer's use of cues, the listeners' use of cues, the degree of matching between performer's and listeners' cue weights, the consistency of the performer's use of cues, and the achievement. All this is shown in a graphic interface that resembles the lens model (see Figure 13.3). This makes it possible to compare directly how performers and listeners use the same cues in the performances. Instances of poor matching are highlighted by arrows that signal that a change in utilization of a cue in a specific direction is recommended. The recommendation is also expressed verbally (e.g. "softer"). If the performer is using cues in an inconsistent manner, this will also be apparent. Quantitative indices of the lens model—achievement, matching, consistency—are converted to "scores" (1–5). From this point, the performer should try to revise his or her use of cues in accordance with provided feedback (e.g. to use more legato articulation in expression of sadness).

◆ In the final phase, the user repeats the first task once again (i.e. recording of performances with the same emotional expressions). The aim is to see whether the performer has improved his or her accuracy by changing the use of cues in the ways recommended by the feedback. Thus, it can easily be examined which cues are used effectively and

> **Box 13.1** (*Continued*)
>
> which cues need continued attention. The performer may also request statistics on the progress over repeated feedback cycles.
>
> ◆ *The computer software again records and analyzes the acoustics of the performances, and uses simulated listener judgments to obtain updated lens model indices, which may be compared with previous findings. Information from successive feedback cycles are stored in the computer software and can be retrieved at will from a database to plot learning curves for achievement, matching, and consistency, as well as changes in cue weights.*

is further enhanced by the possibility to select models of different types of listeners (e.g. music teachers, expert performers, or laymen) for the simulation of listeners' judgments.

13.2.4   Research on cognitive feedback

A pilot study evaluated the efficacy of the CFB procedure (although using manual acoustic measurements), and indicated that the method is highly effective (Juslin & Laukka, 2000). Eight pop/rock guitarists (aged 16–29) at an intermediate level of skill went through one cycle of CFB (the three phases described in Box 13.1) playing three different pieces of music. The results indicated that CFB yielded about a 50% increase in accuracy after a single feedback session, as shown by listening tests. Moreover, a questionnaire suggested that the performers reacted positively to the CFB and believed that it had improved their skills. In contrast, a no-training contrast group did not improve its accuracy.

After these promising findings, the authors began developing computer software that could provide automatic feedback to musicians. Research is currently underway to evaluate the usability of the software. *Usability* is the quality that arises from a well-functioning interplay between (1) a task, (2) a user who is solving the task, and (3) a system that supports the user in solving the task. Four features of usability are regarded as important in the evaluation (Briggs, 1987): *efficacy* (does the software improve the communication?), *user satisfaction* (how is the software experienced by the user?), *user understanding* (has the user adequate knowledge regarding the software?), and *training cost* (how quickly can the user learn to use the software?). In one study (Juslin *et al.*, 2003), 36 semi-professional jazz/rock guitarists (aged 21–49) were randomly assigned to one of three conditions:

1. *CFB provided by the computer software*: After a brief interactive exploration of the software supervised by the experimenter, the participant was instructed to go through one cycle of CFB as described above in Section 13.2.3. The melody used was "When the Saints" and the emotions to be expressed were happiness, sadness, anger, and fear. Measures of achievement were obtained before (pre) and after (post) feedback. The participant also completed a questionnaire regarding usability.

2. *Teacher feedback*: The participant carried out the same task as in condition 1, except that the feedback was provided by a teacher. The teacher was allowed to use any kind of verbal instruction (e.g. metaphors, technical directions) to help the participant improve the emotional expression.

3. *No feedback (contrast group)*: The participant received no feedback, but simply performed the musical material (same as in conditions 1 and 2) twice (pre- and posttest) with a break in between.

Figure 13.4 presents the main findings from this study in terms of measures of achievement (pre and post) for each of the three conditions. The largest improvement

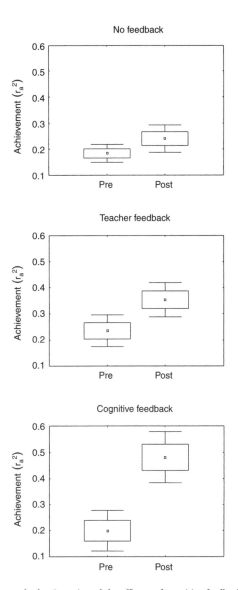

Figure 13.4 Results from a study that investigated the efficacy of cognitive feedback from the CFB software in comparison with teacher feedback and a no-feedback contrast condition (from Juslin *et al.*, 2003). Markers indicate the mean level of achievement (squared), boxes indicate the standard error of the estimate, and whiskers indicate 95% confidence intervals around the mean.

in achievement occurred for the CFB group, followed by the teacher group, and the no-feedback group. In sum, CFB seems to be highly effective in improving performers' communication of emotions.

13.2.5   Generality of the CFB approach

The present approach offers a certain level of generality, since the basic procedure of CFB (recording, analysis, simulation of listener judgments, feedback) can, in principle, be used with any style of music. What is required to adapt the CFB software to a specific style is (1) that all acoustic parameters that are relevant to the style are featured in the acoustic analysis and (2) that the listener model used to simulate listener judgments is based on listening tests in which musical examples, emotion terms, and listeners are appropriate for the musical style of interest. Could the CFB software work with music performance based in a different cultural context? Again, there is nothing in the basic procedure of CFB as such that precludes its use with regard to music from other cultures. In the current version of the software, the acoustic cue extraction and the listener models were based on characteristics of Western music (e.g. classical music, pop music, jazz), but both of these parts of the software could, in principle, be adapted to other cultural settings.

However, there are also some limitations of the CFB approach to learning expressivity. For example, in its current form, the software can only analyze cues from monophonic performances of music (melody). Thus, the software is mainly suitable for single line, solo instruments, such as the violin, flute, guitar, saxophone, and voice. Still, researchers are currently attempting to develop cue extraction for polyphonic performances as well. Another limitation of the CFB software is that it is restricted to fairly brief extracts of music; the software analyzes cues in terms of average measures across each recorded performance, and these measures are not meaningful for longer pieces where the expression may change substantially. One solution to this problem could be to practice the various sections of a longer piece in short segments that are appropriate for the CFB software.

There are also some conceptual problems. The issue of developing expressive performance raises the crucial question of what constitutes an "optimal" performance. Arguably, this issue spans many different artistic aspects, including originality, recognition, arousal, beauty, emotion, balance, and personal expression. In this chapter, the focus has been on only one of these aspects—namely, emotional expression. In the very specific context of the CFB software, it is easy to define what constitutes an optimal performance: an optimal performance is one that communicates the intended emotion reliably to listeners by incorporating cues in accordance with how listeners use the same cues in their judgments of expression. As this is only one aspect of expressivity, performers obviously have to develop other aspects as well, using other means (see Section 13.1.2).

It is not clear whether music performers at all skill levels would benefit from using the CFB software. Obviously, the student must be able to manipulate various acoustic cues independently in order to benefit from the detailed feedback. Hence, the software may be too demanding for novices. On the other hand, expert musicians may already have perfected many of the features addressed by the software. Thus, the software may be most useful for performers at an intermediate skill level.

13.2.6 Implications for music education

The use of computer feedback brings certain advantages: it (1) can provide critical feedback but in a nonthreatening environment, (2) is easily available, (3) provides possibilities for flexible and individually-based learning, and (4) explicitly describes cues that are typically embedded in tacit knowledge. There could be drawbacks as well. First, the usefulness of computer feedback depends on the availability of computers, and not all institutions or individuals may have access to these. Fortunately, some recent estimates show that the availability of computers in music educational contexts is steadily increasing (Webster, 2002). Second, one may fear that use of CFB could lead to standardized performances of music. It must be emphasized that the decision about how to interpret the music is left to the performer. The CFB software only serves to help performers achieve intended interpretations more reliably, whatever those may be, by giving performers a better understanding of cue–emotion relationships. Third, computers lack a human touch that may be highly valued by the student. However, the teacher could play a supporting role also when using computer-assisted teaching strategies, especially in shaping aesthetic judgment and achieving balance among different aspects of expressivity. One final problem with computer-based instruction (CBI) is that students seem to have a negative attitude toward using computers in music teaching (Lindström *et al.*, 2003). Such skepticism may be unwarranted; studies that have compared CBI with traditional approaches suggest that CBI can be just as effective as teacher-based instruction (Taylor, 1981; Webster, 2002).

13.3   Conclusions

A number of conclusions can be drawn from the evidence outlined in this chapter. First, expressivity is an empirically tractable problem: acoustic correlates of expressivity have been identified and simulated (Section 13.1.2) and important aspects of the communicative process can now be modeled in a systematic way (Sections 13.2.2–13.2.4). This research has various limitations but shows that it is time to discard the view that expressivity is a mystery, impossible to describe in scientific terms. Second, music teaching should incorporate up-to-date theories and findings about expressivity to replace the common myths about musical expressivity described in Section 13.1.1. Third, although traditional teaching strategies (e.g. the use of metaphors) may be useful, teaching of expressivity should at some stage, at least, address the actual sound properties of the performance (Woody, 1999) and should help the student to relate sound properties to experiential properties. Finally, CFB as provided in user-friendly software offers an efficient method of teaching emotional expressivity to students that could complement traditional teaching strategies.

Findings from a questionnaire study indicate that the majority of music students would like to practice more on expressivity than is currently the case, and that most of them are willing to try out new teaching strategies (Lindström *et al.*, 2003). This chapter has attempted to show that new strategies for teaching expressivity are indeed within reach. Adopting these strategies in music education will require openness among students and teachers. Some of the traditional views on expressivity may need to be revised in the light of empirical findings; however, all aspects of musical expressivity may never be fully explained. Be that as it may, it must not prevent practitioners from making an effort to improve teaching and learning of musical expressivity on the basis of empirical research.

Acknowledgments

The writing of this chapter was supported by the Bank of Sweden Tercentenary Foundation. We are grateful to Aaron Williamon, Peter Johnson, Chris Gayford, Caroline Minassian, and two anonymous reviewers for helpful comments on an earlier version of this chapter.

Notes

1. An important exception to this is when the *visual* impression of a performer may influence the listeners' experience of the music (see Chapter 4). Listeners may be much more likely to engage emotionally with a performance if they believe the performer is also engaged, as suggested by facial expressions and body language. However, such features may be either feigned or genuine expressions, just like the sounds produced by the performer.

2. A subset of movement patterns in performance expressivity are those involuntary patterns that reflect instrument-specific constraints in combination with anatomical constraints of the human body. These patterns should be distinguished from a performer's intentional attempt to render a performance with a certain motion character (Juslin *et al.*, 2002).

3. In this chapter, the focus is on *expression* and *recognition* of emotion, rather than on the more labile process of *induction* of emotion, which is influenced by a number of factors outside the performer's control (see Chapters 4, 16, 18, and 19 in Juslin & Sloboda, 2001).

4. Certainly, performers may not always strive to achieve communication. Sometimes, the artist may prefer to create complex and ambiguous scenarios for the listener or simply try to discover the composer's intention. However, questionnaire research indicates that musicians commonly attempt to express specific emotions in their performances (Lindström *et al.*, 2003).

5. It should be apparent that this procedure requires that the performer momentarily sets aside his or her concerns with the composer's intentions regarding the piece for the sake of the practice. As it happens, performers usually find it interesting and thought-provoking to attempt many different interpretations of the same piece of music.

Further information and reading

Musicians, teachers, researchers, and others interested in receiving more information about the CFB software are encouraged to contact the authors. For further information, see the "Feedback-learning of Musical Expressivity" website: *www.psyk.uu.se/hemsidor/musicpsy.*

References

Bach, C. P. E. (1778/1985). *Essay on the True Art of Playing Keyboard Instruments* (W. J. Mitchell, Trans.). London: Eulenburg Books. (Original work published in 1778).

Balzer, W. K., Doherty, M. E., & O'Connor, R. (1989). Effects of cognitive feedback on performance. *Psychological Bulletin, 106,* 410–433.

Barten, S. S. (1998). Speaking of music: The use of motor-affective metaphors in music instruction. *Journal of Aesthetic Education, 32*, 89–97.

Behrens, G. A., & Green, S. B. (1993). The ability to identify emotional content of solo improvisations performed vocally and on three different instruments. *Psychology of Music, 21*, 20–33.

Boyd, J., & George-Warren, H. (1992). *Musicians in Tune: Seventy-Five Contemporary Musicians Discuss the Creative Process.* New York: Fireside.

Bresin, R., & Friberg, A. (2000). Emotional coloring of computer-controlled music performance. *Computer Music Journal, 24*, 44–62.

Briggs, P. (1987). Usability assessment for the office: Methodological choices and their implications. In M. Frese, E. Ulich, & W. Dizda (Eds.), *Human Computer Interaction in the Workplace* (pp. 381–401). Amsterdam: Elsevier.

Brodsky, W., Sloboda, J. A., & Waterman, M. G. (1994). An exploratory investigation into auditory style as a correlate and predictor of music performance anxiety. *Medical Problems of Performing Artists, 9*, 101–112.

Brunswik, E. (1956). *Perception and the Representative Design of Experiments.* Berkeley, CA: University of California Press.

Budd, M. (1985). *Music and the Emotions: The Philosophical Theories.* London: Routledge.

Casals, P. (1970). *Joys and Sorrows.* London: MacDonald.

Clarke, E. F. (1988). Generative principles in music performance. In J. A. Sloboda (Ed.), *Generative Processes in Music: The Psychology of Performance, Improvisation, and Composition* (pp. 1–26). Oxford: Clarendon Press.

Cook, N., & Dibben, N. (2001). Musicological approaches to emotion. In P. N. Juslin & J. A. Sloboda (Eds.), *Music and Emotion: Theory and Research* (pp. 45–70). Oxford: Oxford University Press.

Cooksey, R. W. (1996). *Judgment Analysis.* London: Academic Press.

Davidson, J. W., & Correia, J. S. (2002). Body movement. In R. Parncutt & G. E. McPherson (Eds.), *The Science and Psychology of Music Performance: Creative Strategies for Teaching and Learning* (pp. 237–250). Oxford: Oxford University Press.

Davies, S. (1994). *Musical Meaning and Expression.* Ithaca, NY: Cornell University Press.

Dickey, M. R. (1992). A review of research on modeling in music teaching and learning. *Bulletin of the Council for Research in Music Education, 113*, 27–40.

Dubal, D. (1985). *The World of the Concert Pianist: Conversations with 35 Internationally Celebrated Pianists.* London: Victor Gollancz.

Eibl-Eibesfeldt, I. (1989). *Human Ethology.* New York: Aldine.

Epstein, D. (1995). A curious moment in Schumann's Fourth Symphony: Structure as the fusion of affect and intuition. In J. Rink (Ed.), *The Practice of Performance: Studies in Musical Interpretation* (pp. 126–149). Cambridge: Cambridge University Press.

Ericsson, K. A., Krampe, R. T., & Tesch-Römer, C. (1993). The role of deliberate practice in the acquisition of expert performance. *Psychological Review, 100*, 363–406.

Friberg, A., & Sundberg, J. (1999). Does music performance allude to locomotion? A model of final ritardandi derived from measurements of stopping runners. *Journal of the Acoustical Society of America, 105*, 1469–1484.

Gabrielsson, A. (1987). Once again: The theme from Mozart's piano sonata in A major. A comparison of five performances. In A. Gabrielsson (Ed.), *Action and Perception in Rhythm and Music* (pp. 81–103). Stockholm: The Royal Swedish Academy of Music.

Gabrielsson, A. (1999). The performance of music. In D. Deutsch (Ed.), *The Psychology of Music* (2nd ed., pp. 501–602). London: Academic Press.

Gabrielsson, A. (2003). Music performance research at the millennium. *Psychology of Music, 31,* 221–272.

Gilden, D. L. (2001). Cognitive emissions of 1/f noise. *Psychological Review, 108,* 33–56.

Hoffren, J. (1964). A test of musical expression. *Council for Research in Music Education, 2,* 32–35.

Howard, V. A. (1989). Expression as hands-on construction. In H. Gardner & D. Perkins (Eds.), *Art, Mind, & Education* (pp. 133–141). Chicago: University of Illinois Press.

Hursch, C. J., Hammond, K. R., & Hursch, J. L. (1964). Some methodological considerations in multiple-cue probability studies. *Psychological Review, 71,* 42–60.

Johnson, C. M. (1998). Effect of instruction in appropriate rubato usage on the onset timings and perceived musicianship of musical performances. *Journal of Research in Music Education, 46,* 436–445.

Juslin, P. N. (1997a). Emotional communication in music performance: A functionalist perspective and some data. *Music Perception, 14,* 383–418.

Juslin, P. N. (1997b). Perceived emotional expression in synthesized performances of a short melody: Capturing the listener's judgment policy. *Musicæ Scientiæ, 1,* 225–256.

Juslin, P. N. (1997c). Can results from studies of perceived expression in musical performances be generalized across response formats? *Psychomusicology, 16,* 77–101.

Juslin, P. N. (2000). Cue utilization in communication of emotion in music performance: Relating performance to perception. *Journal of Experimental Psychology: Human Perception and Performance, 26,* 1797–1813.

Juslin, P. N. (2001). Communicating emotion in music performance: A review and a theoretical framework. In P. N. Juslin & J. A. Sloboda (Eds.), *Music and Emotion: Theory and Research* (pp. 309–337). Oxford: Oxford University Press.

Juslin, P. N. (2003). Five facets of musical expression: A psychologist's perspective on music performance. *Psychology of Music, 31,* 273–302.

Juslin, P. N., & Laukka, P. (2000). Improving emotional communication in music performance through cognitive feedback. *Musicæ Scientiæ, 4,* 151–183.

Juslin, P. N., & Laukka, P. (2001). Impact of intended emotion intensity on cue utilization and decoding accuracy in vocal expression of emotion. *Emotion, 1,* 381–412.

Juslin, P. N., & Laukka, P. (2003). Communication of emotions in vocal expression and music performance: Different channels, same code? *Psychological Bulletin, 129,* 770–814.

Juslin, P. N., & Lindström, E. (2003). *Musical expression of emotions: Modeling composed and performed features.* Manuscript submitted for publication.

Juslin, P. N., & Madison, G. (1999). The role of timing patterns in recognition of emotional expression from musical performance. *Music Perception, 17,* 197–221.

Juslin, P. N., & Persson, R. S. (2002). Emotional communication. In R. Parncutt & G. McPherson (Eds.), *The Science and Psychology of Music Performance: Creative Strategies for Teaching and Learning* (pp. 219–236). Oxford: Oxford University Press.

Juslin, P. N., & Sloboda, J. A. (Eds.). (2001). *Music and Emotion: Theory and Research.* Oxford: Oxford University Press.

Juslin, P. N., Friberg, A., & Bresin, R. (2002). Toward a computational model of expression in music performance: The GERM model. *Musicæ Scientiæ, Special Issue 2001–2002*, 63–122.

Juslin, P. N., Friberg, A., Karlsson, J., Lindström, E., & Schoonderwaldt, E. (2003). *Once more with a feeling: Feedback-learning of expressivity in music performance.* Manuscript submitted for publication.

Laukka, P. (2004). Instrumental music teachers' views on expressivity: A report from music conservations. *Music Education Research, 6*, 45–56.

Lehmann, A. C. (1997). Acquired mental representations in music performance: Anecdotal and preliminary empirical evidence. In H. Jørgensen & A. C. Lehmann (Eds.), *Does Practice Make Perfect? Current Theory and Research on Instrumental Music Practice* (pp. 141–163). Oslo: Norwegian State Academy of Music.

Lindström, E. (2003). The contribution of immanent and performed accents to emotional expression in short tone sequences. *Journal of New Music Research, 32*, 269–280.

Lindström, E., Juslin, P. N., Bresin, R., & Williamon, A. (2003). "Expressivity comes from within your soul": A questionnaire study of music students' perspectives on expressivity. *Research Studies in Music Education, 20*, 23–47.

Lippman, E. A. (1953). Symbolism in music. *Musical Quarterly, 39*, 554–575.

Marchand, D. J. (1975). A study of two approaches to developing expressive performance. *Journal of Research in Music Education, 23*, 14–22.

Menuhin, Y. (1996). *Unfinished Journey.* London: Methuen.

Meyer, L. B. (1956). *Emotion and Meaning in Music.* Chicago: University of Chicago Press.

Palmer, C. (1996). Anatomy of a performance: Sources of musical expression. *Music Perception, 13*, 433–453.

Palmer, C. (1997). Music performance. *Annual Review of Psychology, 48*, 115–138.

Persson, R. S. (1993). *The Subjectivity of Musical Performance: An Exploratory Music-Psychological Real World Enquiry into the Determinants and Education of Musical Reality.* Unpublished doctoral dissertation, University of Huddersfield, Huddersfield, UK.

Persson, R. S. (1996). Concert musicians as teachers: On good intentions falling short. In A. J. Cropley & D. Dehn (Eds.), *Fostering the Growth of High Ability: European Perspectives* (pp. 303–320). Norwood, NJ: Ablex.

Raffman, D. (1993). *Language, Music, and Mind.* Cambridge, MA: MIT Press.

Ratner, L. G. (1980). *Classic Music: Expression, Form, and Style.* New York: Schirmer.

Riley-Butler, K. (2001). *Teaching Expressivity through Feedback and Replication.* Paper presented at the Meeting of the Society for Music Perception and Cognition, Kingston, Canada.

Rohwer, D. (2001). Instrumental music students' cognitive and performance understanding of musical expression. *Journal of Band Research, 37*, 17–28.

Rostwall, A.-L., & West, T. (2001). *Interaktion och Kunskapsutveckling* [Interaction and Learning. A Study of Music Instrument Teaching]. Unpublished doctoral dissertation, KMH Förlaget, Stockholm.

Shove, P., & Repp, B. H. (1995). Musical motion and performance: Theoretical and empirical perspectives. In J. Rink (Ed.), *The Practice of Performance: Studies in Musical Interpretation* (pp. 55–83). Cambridge: Cambridge University Press.

Sloboda, J. A. (1983). The communication of musical metre in piano performance. *Quarterly Journal of Experimental Psychology, 35A*, 377–396.

Sloboda, J. A. (1996). The acquisition of musical performance expertise: Deconstructing the "talent" account of individual differences in musical expressivity. In K. A. Ericsson (Ed.), *The Road to Excellence: The Acquisition of Expert Performance in the Arts and Sciences, Sports, and Games* (pp. 107–126). Mahwah, NJ: Erlbaum.

Sloboda, J. A., Minassian, C., & Gayford, C. (2003). Assisting advanced musicians to enhance their expressivity—An intervention study. In R. Kopiez, A. C. Lehmann, I. Wolther, & C. Wolf (Eds.), *Proceedings of the Fifth Triennial ESCOM Conference* (p. 92). Hanover, Germany: Hanover University of Music and Drama.

Spencer, H. (1857). The origin and function of music. *Fraser's Magazine, 56*, 396–408.

Stanislavski, C. (1937/1988). *An Actor Prepares.* London: Methuen. (Original work published in 1937).

Swanwick, K. (1985). *A Basis for Music Education.* Windsor, UK: NFER-Nelson.

Tait, M. (1992). Teaching strategies and styles. In R. Cowell (Ed.), *Handbook of Research on Music Teaching and Learning* (pp. 525–534). New York: Schirmer.

Taylor, J. A. (1981). *Introduction to Computers and Computer-Based Instruction in Music.* Tallahassee, FL: Center for Music Research, Florida State University.

Webster, P. R. (2002). Computer-based technology and music teaching and learning. In R. Colwell & C. Richardson (Eds.), *The New Handbook of Research on Music Teaching and Learning* (pp. 416–439). Oxford: Oxford University Press.

Woody, R. H. (1999). The relationship between explicit planning and expressive performance of dynamic variations in an aural modeling task. *Journal of Research in Music Education, 47*, 331–342.

Woody, R. H. (2000). Learning expressivity in music: An exploratory study. *Research Studies in Music Education, 14*, 14–23.

CHAPTER 14

DRUGS AND MUSICAL PERFORMANCE

ROBERT WEST

Musical performance can be among the most difficult and demanding of human activities and generally occurs in situations when the personal cost of failure or even suboptimal performance is very high. It is not surprising, therefore, that individuals who earn a living by performing often turn to artificial aids to help them cope either emotionally or physically (Wesner *et al.*, 1990). Use of "psychotropic" drugs (i.e. drugs that affect the mind and behavior) has been linked to music certainly for centuries and probably since both were discovered by our ancestors. The question is: can they genuinely help the performer? If the answer to this is yes, we must also ask who might benefit and is there a price to pay? This chapter provides a wide-ranging review of psychotropic drug effects and their implications for musical performance. There is actually very little direct evidence linking the two, but research on drug effects more generally can provide useful clues and practical guidance for the performing musician.

14.1 Musical performance as a psychomotor task

Before scrutinizing drug effects, it is worth briefly considering musical performance as a "psychomotor task;" this should help to set these effects in context. Psychomotor performance refers to the execution of tasks requiring physical actions to achieve a predetermined goal (Lemon, 1999; see also Chapter 8 of this volume). At its simplest, it can involve pressing a button as quickly as possible in response to a tone or a light, and it includes tasks as varied as typing and driving a car. Musical performance is a particular kind of psychomotor task which is self-initiated (i.e. the musician starts when he or she is ready) and largely self-contained (i.e. other than group improvisation, it involves executing an internal plan rather than responding to a changing environment). Figure 14.1 shows a simplified overview of this kind of task. Schlaug (2001) provides a very interesting review of the development of musical skill and how this relates to changes in brain function.

Psychomotor performance involves a wide range of component activities or processes, each of which may in principle be affected in different ways by different drugs. Musical information needs to be stored, recalled, or derived from a score or extemporized. Sensory information needs to be monitored and used to initiate and control action sequences within certain parameters. Most obviously, there is a need for fine control of one's muscles so that notes are played or sung as intended with the

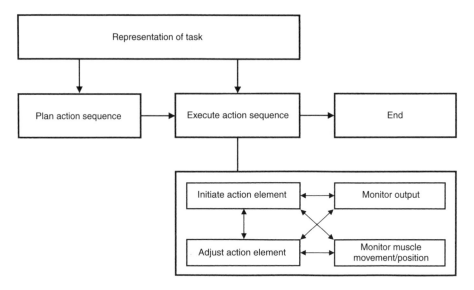

Figure 14.1 Elements of psychomotor performance for self-initiated, self-contained tasks.

required quality and intonation. This requires very precise and often very rapid movements. All of this takes place in a context where the performer knows he or she is being subject to evaluation, possibly by hundreds, thousands, or even millions of people. Performers also put great pressure on themselves to achieve what they consider to be perfection.

14.1.1   The effects of anxiety on psychomotor performance

It is well recognized that a little anxiety can improve performance but that a high level can be anything from mildly unpleasant to disastrous (Fredrikson & Gunnarsson, 1992). Individuals differ in their propensity to experience anxiety; this manifests itself first in childhood and does not change much over the years (Chorpita & Barlow, 1998). However, individuals can be more or less successful in finding ways of coping with it or masking or suppressing it. Simple task elements involving rapid responses can benefit from even quite high levels of anxiety but more complex task elements requiring problem solving or fine muscle control can be badly affected (see Table 14.1). Anxiety can also affect the way information is processed. Anecdotally, there are reports that it tends to expand one's sense of time—pauses can seem very long.

All of this can give some guide to the way in which drugs might affect performance, but in practice, much depends on the dose, the dosing methods, and contextual and individual factors. Indeed, the only way to know for sure whether a drug will have a particular effect is to test it in the context in which it will be used in people who are likely to use it. Unfortunately, there is very little research of this kind in the literature. However, current evidence is provided below and conclusions are drawn where possible.

Table 14.1 Aspects of musical performance, and their relationship with anxiety and level of arousal

Activity	Effect of high anxiety	Optimum arousal level
Recall of musical information	Interferes	Low
Perception of time	Expands	Moderate
Coordination of movement	Interferes	Moderate
Fine control of muscles	Interferes (e.g. tremor)	Moderate
Monitoring of muscle activity	Not known	Not known
Monitoring of sound output	Not known	Not known
Monitoring of external sounds	Not known	Not known
Speed of movement	Increased	High

14.2   Types of drug

Drugs that affect the mind or performance can be classified in many ways. One system for classifying drugs is according to their effects on mental state. Drugs can be thought of as "stimulant" if they increase alertness, wakefulness, or agitation. They are "sedative" if they have the opposite effects. Drugs that relieve anxiety are said to have "anxiolytic" properties, just as drugs that help relieve depressed moods are known as "antidepressants." Some drugs, independent of stimulant or sedative properties, induce a feeling of well-being; these have "euphoriant" actions. Some drugs can induce distorted perceptions; these are "hallucinogens."

Drugs are also classified according to their effects on physiological systems. For example, drugs that mimic the body's naturally occurring neurotransmitters (i.e. chemicals released that transmit a signal between nerve cells and, thereby, enable our nervous system to encode and process information and function) are labeled by the neurotransmitter they mimic: "cholinergic" drugs mimic a neurotransmitter called acetylcholine; "dopaminergic" drugs mimic dopamine; "adrenergic" drugs mimic adrenaline, and so on.

This section starts with the most commonly used licit, nonprescription drugs (alcohol, caffeine, and nicotine), then considers prescription drugs (antidepressants, beta-blockers, and tranquilizers), and finally drugs that are used illicitly and are subject to abuse (amphetamines, cocaine, ecstasy, hallucinogens, and opiates). Of course, there are many other drugs that could be considered, but the ones reviewed here are probably the most significant for performers.

14.2.1   Lifestyle drugs

Alcohol

Alcohol is very much a part of many musicians' lives. This may be partly because of lifestyle or possibly the personality characteristics of people who become musicians. However, there are numerous anecdotal reports of musicians who consciously use alcohol to help them cope with the stress of performing. There is little doubt that, acutely, alcohol can "dull the senses;" it can also ease feelings of anxiety. Unfortunately, the intoxicating and sedating effects of alcohol impair performance on most tasks

(Ellinwood *et al.*, 1981; Horne & Gibbons, 1991; Grant *et al.*, 2000; Farquhar *et al.*, 2002). Alcohol also increases impulsiveness (Nagoshi *et al.*, 1991). Intoxicated individuals are often not aware of the level of impairment because alcohol appears to disrupt this perception as well (Lubin, 1977; Ridderinkhof *et al.*, 2002). Moreover, consuming alcohol in large quantities over a period of time leads to a chronic increase in anxiety and neuropsychological problems (Eckardt *et al.*, 1980; Capitani *et al.*, 1983; Schaeffer *et al.*, 1989; Beatty *et al.*, 2000; Di Sclafani *et al.*, 2002).

In this way, musicians who start using alcohol to calm their nerves before performing can become trapped in a downward spiral, in which they come more and more to rely on alcohol and without it become ever more anxious. This is compounded, of course, by the fact that alcohol adversely affects technique. Coordination, memory, and muscle control are impaired in a dose–response manner (Burns & Moskowitz, 1980; Chait & Perry, 1994). For performers who experience severe anxiety about performing, there may be a difficult line to tread between the need to control the nerves enough to perform and the effect of alcohol on that performance.

Of equal concern is that excessive drinking, particularly bingeing (i.e. drinking large quantities on a single occasion), is damaging to physical health. Consistently drinking above 21 units per week by a man or 14 units by a woman increases risk of liver damage, heart disease, and other organ damage (a unit is 330 ml of ordinary strength beer, a medium sized glass of wine, or a single measure of spirit). In addition, excessive drinking is linked with an increased risk of accidental injury or death and involvement in violence both as a victim and a perpetrator. These latter effects are probably linked to the effect of alcohol in removing inhibitions (de Wit *et al.*, 2000). This loss of inhibition is a double-edged sword because many drinkers, particularly if they are socially anxious, feel that they are funnier and more attractive when they drink (and to be fair, some are).

In fact, moderate drinking probably has beneficial psychological and physical effects. It seems to reduce risk of heart disease, possibly by reducing the amount of low-density lipoprotein (a fat that damages the arteries) in the blood. Psychologically, it is linked with greater social integration and feelings of adjustment. Some have argued that alcohol can increase creativity. This has not been studied much, but an interesting study of well-known writers and musicians suggests that for most of them alcohol had the opposite effect (Ludwig, 1990).

Alcohol dependence is quite common, affecting 5–10% of the adult population in the USA and UK, and more in countries such as Russia. It is characterized by compulsive use, strong cravings, and drinking to relieve withdrawal symptoms. These symptoms include anxiety and often physical symptoms such as tremor and even on occasions seizure. It has a strong genetic component (Nestler, 2000). If one or more parent is or has been alcohol dependent, the offspring are significantly more likely to develop problems of the same kind. It is very difficult for a musician to perform to an acceptable standard if he or she is severely alcohol dependent, and eventually, something has to give.

Treatment for alcohol dependence involves an initial period of "detoxification" in which abstinence from alcohol is made more comfortable with the use of drugs such as benzodiazepines (Edwards *et al.*, 2003). The detox can be undertaken with the patient as either an outpatient or an inpatient, depending on the person's life circumstances and the severity of dependence. After this, the patient is usually given an extended period of counseling, often supplemented by the drug Campral (acamprosate) which can help reduce the cravings. While many alcoholics respond well to this treatment protocol, relapse is very common, and for a large proportion of alcoholics (but not all), their condition is best conceived of as a chronic condition that can be improved for quite long periods but is ever-present. The goal of the sufferer, as well as of various treatment agencies, is to keep it at bay as often and for as long as possible. It has been suggested that it is possible for people who are alcohol dependent to resume a life of "controlled drinking" rather than total abstinence; while there are clearly instances where this has occurred, it is rare.

Where all this leaves the musician is debatable. The majority can gain the benefits of alcohol while retaining control over their drinking; however, onset of dependence is insidious. The alcohol "abuser" is typically in no position to detect the downward spiral, perhaps because alcohol is affecting his or her judgment. Given the strong genetic contribution to alcohol dependence, perhaps an individual could use his or her own family history as a guide to assessing how far he or she can go with alcohol consumption before running into difficulties. Another approach is to monitor one's drinking—to ensure that one goes at least a few days in any given month without drinking and to ensure that one does not exceed the maximum recommended level over a period of time. Musicians who feel the need for something to relax them should consider other, less harmful approaches, including exercise (see Chapter 9), counseling, and prescription medications (see Section 14.2.2 below).

Caffeine

Caffeine is a mild central nervous system stimulant (Battig, 1991; Donovan & DeVane, 2001; Mandel, 2002). It is a member of the group of chemically related alkaloids known as methylxanthines. In moderate doses (i.e. less than 400 mg per day), which can be obtained from no more than a few cups of coffee, it can improve vigilance and endurance and reduce fatigue (Tarnopolsky, 1994; Spriet, 1995; Graham, 2001; Smith, 2002). A typical cup of "real" coffee contains about 100 mg of caffeine, and soft drinks such as colas contain up to 50 mg. At these doses, it has not been found to have adverse health effects (Nawrot *et al.*, 2003). In fact, there is some evidence that it can have a modest effect in opening the airways and easing breathing difficulties. However, in higher doses, it can increase feelings of anxiety and has been reported to impair fine muscle control. It can also have adverse effects on the cardiovascular system and calcium balance. In women, there is some evidence that in high doses it may affect fertility and fetal development. Thus, while it may be invaluable in keeping the musician awake and alert, it is not necessarily harmless.

Heavy caffeine use over a long period can lead to withdrawal symptoms during abstinence (Griffiths & Chausmer, 2000; Dews *et al.*, 2002). A common symptom is headache, although drowsiness and other symptoms are also reported. It has been reported that a proportion of regular caffeine users develop cravings and show signs of compulsive use, but there is little evidence of this from controlled studies. Given that caffeine is relatively benign, the pressure on users to abstain is not great and so it is not clear what proportion of users would find it impossible to abstain if they had to.

For the musician, it makes sense to consider caffeine in moderate doses as a potentially useful tool when alertness needs to be maintained or to mitigate the effect of alcohol (Liguori & Robinson, 2001; Drake *et al.*, 2003), but it would probably be unwise to maintain a high dose for long periods or, obviously, to use the drug if it appears to be impairing ability to execute fine movements.

Nicotine

Nicotine is very rapidly absorbed from cigarette smoke (West & Shiffman, 2003). It is also obtained from other tobacco products such as cigars and pipes. A smoker will typically absorb 10–20 mg of nicotine each day—about 1 mg from each cigarette. Nicotine is also absorbed, albeit more slowly, from smokeless tobacco products such as nasal or oral snuff and chewing tobacco. There is also a wide range of pure nicotine delivery systems available such as nicotine chewing-gum, inhaler, skin patch, lozenge, and nasal spray. These are marketed as aids to stopping smoking but, in principle, can also be used instead of smoking; pure nicotine does not cause cancer, so they are much less harmful than cigarettes.

Nicotine affects the central and peripheral nervous system by partially mimicking the effects of a naturally occurring neurotransmitter called acetylcholine (RCP, 2000). It has complex effects on the body, and there are many misunderstandings about what these are. Its most noticeable effects are essentially "stimulant;" causing an increase in heart rate and blood pressure, sweating, a slight "buzz," and feelings of agitation. Nicotine also causes feelings of nausea in individuals who are not used to it or who take more than they are used to.

The hands of smokers typically shake more than those of nonsmokers. When smokers stop, the tremor reduces within a few hours as nicotine leaves the body. Of course, nervousness at performing in public also typically causes tremor. It may be that the effect of nicotine would aggravate this problem, but that has not been tested.

There is some research to show that nicotine can increase the speed of simple movement tasks such as tapping on a keyboard (West, 1993). It is plausible that this would help with passages that require fast movement. It is also possible that nicotine withdrawal would cause problems with this, but no scientific studies have been conducted on this.

Musicians who smoke might be concerned that they would experience an increase in anxiety when they stop. Contrary to what many people believe, smoking does not typically calm the nerves (West, 1993). The idea that it calms the nerves probably arises out of the fact that, when abstaining, smokers experience unpleasant withdrawal symptoms, such as irritability and restlessness, and smoking makes these go away. Strangely, although anxiety itself is listed as a nicotine withdrawal symptom in the American Psychiatric Association diagnostic manual, many studies actually find a decrease in anxiety within a week of stopping smoking and an increase if the smoker relapses (West & Hajek, 1997). One thing is clear; musicians who stop smoking can expect to experience less chronic stress than if they continue, quite apart obviously from the health benefits which accrue.

One potentially important nicotine withdrawal symptom is impaired ability to concentrate (RCP, 2000). Obviously this could be a problem for musicians, but it can be ameliorated by using one of the pure nicotine delivery systems that are available.

Smokers who fail to stop smoking experience diseases of old age about 12 years earlier than nonsmokers and die an average of 8 years earlier. Lung cancer and heart disease are well known as two of the causes of death. Less well-known is "chronic obstructive pulmonary disease," in which there is a progressive deterioration in ability to breathe. Any smoker who is beginning to experience breathlessness or a chronic cough should stop immediately, as they may well be on a steep decline in lung function. The good news is that stopping halts the accelerated decline straight away. For people who play wind instruments, the importance of maintaining lung function is obvious.

Musicians who perform in clubs and pubs can be exposed to quite high levels of smoke from other people's cigarettes. Although the effects of such exposure are considerably less than from active smoking, there is an increase in risk from lung cancer and heart attack. Passive smoking can also trigger asthma attacks and other respiratory problems. This has led to legislation to protect nonsmokers from exposure to tobacco smoke in some countries, and in the future, it is likely that smoking restrictions will extend further, affecting clubs and music venues.

In summary, it is unlikely that tobacco use significantly improves musical performance, but in addicted users, there may be impairment during periods of abstinence. Pure nicotine products may mitigate these effects. Musicians, like any other smokers, would be well advised for the sake of their mental and physical health to try their best to stop and keep trying until they succeed. They should use proven treatment approaches, including nicotine replacement therapies (gum, patch, etc.), bupropion (Zyban), and behavioral support. In the UK, one should simply be able to go to a general practitioner to get an immediate referral to the specialist stop smoking treatment service, which is paid for by the national health service.

14.2.2   Prescription drugs

Antidepressants

Like anyone else, musicians can suffer from depression. In fact, depression as a clinical syndrome is much more common than most people realize. About 1 in 7 people will suffer at least one bout in their lives, and many are plagued by repeated occurrences. One of the common symptoms is an inability to motivate oneself to do anything, in many cases even to get out of bed. This is accompanied by feelings that one is worthless as a person, sometimes irritability, and often suicidal thoughts; one is overwhelmed by a sense of hopelessness. Obviously, this is not good news for the performing musician, who has to get up on stage and ply his or her craft.

There are several different classes of antidepressant on the market. One of these is the *tricyclics*; the name derives from their chemical structure which includes three hydrocarbon rings. Commonly used examples are imipramine (Tofranil) and nortriptyline (Pamelor, Aventyl). They can help about 20–30% of users to recover within a couple of months who would not have done otherwise (surprising as it may seem, about a quarter to a third of depressive episodes resolve within about 3 months by themselves). They can also be effective against anxiety. However, they are not without side-effects. The most common are dry mouth, a slight tremor, fast heartbeat, constipation, sleepiness, and weight gain. Depending on the instrument one plays, these could in principle affect performance, and this needs to be taken into account by the prescribing doctor.

The second and probably most popular class of antidepressants are called *selective serotonin re-uptake inhibitors* (SSRIs). Probably the best known of these is fluoxetine (Prozac), but there are many others, such as paroxetine (Seroxat) and fluvoxamine (Luvox). These do not seem to be more effective in treating depression than the older tricyclic antidepressants, but users generally find the side-effects more tolerable. In the first couple of weeks of taking these, some users feel sick and some more anxious. They can also interfere with sexual functioning. However, these symptoms, if they occur, generally resolve after a few weeks. Paroxetine and other drugs in this class have recently come under scrutiny because of concerns that they might cause anxiety disturbances or even suicide attempts in some users.

The third main class of antidepressants in common use is the *monoamine oxidase inhibitors* (MAO inhibitors). These block the breakdown of the neurotransmitters dopamine, noradrenaline, and serotonin, making them more readily available in the central nervous system. These drugs can be quite effective, and there is little evidence that they impair psychomotor performance (Tiller, 1990).

In general, antidepressants clearly have a potential role for musicians who are suffering from clinical depression or anxiety, and the effect on performance is likely to be modest (Hindmarch, 1992; Linnoila *et al.*, 1993). However, there is no particular reason for a musician to use an antidepressant as a performance-enhancing medication or to control anxiety specifically related to performance.

Beta-blockers

Beta-blockers are drugs that block the action of a naturally occurring neurotransmitter, noradrenaline, in the autonomic nervous system (see Chapter 1). These drugs are available only on prescription and are not suitable for people who have low blood pressure, bronchial asthma, or some other conditions. They were developed to control high blood pressure. Apart from reducing blood pressure, they reduce other physical symptoms of overarousal and anxiety, including tremor (Brantigan *et al.*, 1978, 1979, 1982). For this reason, many musicians regularly take beta-blockers to control "stage fright" (Neftel *et al.*, 1982). In fact, one survey found that about 20% of orchestral musicians in the USA took beta-blockers for performance anxiety. One can take the pill an hour or so before an important performance, and the effect lasts several hours. There is reasonably strong evidence that they are indeed quite effective at this and can improve performance as a result (Lidén & Gottfriess, 1974; James *et al.*, 1977, 1978, 1983; Pearson & Simpson, 1978; James, 1984; James & Savage, 1984; Gates *et al.*, 1985). However, these drugs do not deal with the emotional experience of anxiety and should not be considered a panacea by any means.

There are quite a few different brands of beta-blocker which differ slightly in their action. Drugs such as metoprolol (Lopresor) and atenolol (Tenormin) are "beta-1 selective". This means they block the beta-1 form of the noradrenaline receptor, which is found primarily in the heart, but not the "beta-2" receptors, which are found in the lungs. As a result, they are less likely to cause bronchoconstriction and breathing difficulties. Propranolol (Inderal) is a beta-1 and beta-2 antagonist. A dose of 40 mg (less than that typically used to control blood pressure) is recommended to control "situational anxiety".

Like any drug, beta-blockers have side effects, although these are generally mild. In someone who has normal blood pressure, they can cause dizziness from low blood pressure, particularly when suddenly getting up ("postural hypotension"). They can also cause tiredness or reduce physical endurance (Kaiser *et al.*, 1981; Bengtsson, 1984; Cupido *et al.*, 1994) and may have a modest effect on speed of reactions (Broadhurst, 1980). Beta-blockers are not known to be addictive.

In summary, views vary about the appropriateness of using beta-blockers to ease symptoms of anxiety and help performance. Taken infrequently (e.g. before important auditions) and under the supervision of a doctor, they may benefit many musicians. However, it is also important to consider other methods of controlling anxiety at its source. This can include exercise, self-help guides, and cognitive-behavioral therapy (Clark & Agras, 1991; see Chapters 9 and 12 of this volume).

Tranquilizers

The most commonly used tranquilizers today are benzodiazepines such as diazepam (Valium) and chlordiazepoxide (Librium). These are used to control anxiety (anxiolytics) or aid sleep (hypnotics). They work by enhancing the inhibitory actions of a naturally occurring neurotransmitter called GABA. In this respect, they are quite similar to alcohol.

There are many different drugs in this class, some of which are short-acting and some longer-acting. They differ in the extent to which they cause sedation (de Wit *et al.*, 1993). In general, their effects on ability to perform complex tasks and tasks requiring vigilance are as one would expect from sedative drugs: they impair it (Erwin *et al.*, 1986; Kunsman *et al.*, 1992; Simpson & Rush, 2002). Impairment is made worse when alcohol is taken as well (Lister & File, 1983). It is possible that, in individuals with very high levels of anxiety, they could lead to a net improvement by combating the deterioration caused by that anxiety, although this has not been adequately tested.

Benzodiazepines are also used illicitly as recreational drugs for their subjective effects (Evans *et al.*, 1990). Concerns have also been expressed that users can become dependent on them, and it is true that there is often a rebound increase in anxiety and sleeplessness when people come off them. However, it is not clear how much this is just a re-emergence of a problem that the drugs have been suppressing. In that event, it seems that there is a decision to be made as to whether the benefits of continuing with long term use of the drugs outweigh the costs.

Because of their sedative properties, benzodiazepines are probably not very suitable for performance anxiety. However, they can have a role to play in treating clinical anxiety disorders or dealing with anxiety associated with an acute traumatic event such as a bereavement.

Newer tranquilizers have been developed that seem to be suffer less from problems of performance impairment and sedation (Mattila *et al.*, 1982). Most notable among these is buspirone (Goldberg, 1984). If a drug is needed to treat clinical anxiety, it is certainly worth considering one of these modern anxiolytics. Antidepressants (see above) are also commonly used nowadays in the treatment of anxiety disorders. These have a range of side effects but little effect on psychomotor performance.

14.2.3   Illicit drugs

Performers appear more likely than the general population to take illicit drugs, particularly those musicians who are involved in jazz, rock, blues, and other modern idioms. In many cases, the usage is recreational, but in others, the motivation may be related to musical performance *per se*. The drugs discussed in this section (listed alphabetically) are classified as illicit because they are frequently used illicitly (i.e. their possession or use without authority constitutes a criminal offence). However, this is for presentational purposes only; in many cases there are also licit uses, and some drugs considered in previous sections can also be used illicitly.

Amphetamines

Amphetamines are stimulants that, like caffeine, increase feelings of agitation and arousal (Koelega, 1993). They work by stimulating release of the neurotransmitters dopamine and noradrenaline in the central nervous system and also blocking their re-uptake back into the nerve terminals, making them more available. They are chemically similar to the drug ephedrine, which was once used as a decongestant and diet pill. The three main types in use are amphetamine sulfate (Benzedrine), dexamfetamine (Dexedrine), and methamphetamine (Methedrine). They can improve endurance and performance on tasks that are physically demanding, and there is some evidence that they can mitigate the effect of alcohol on psychomotor performance (Perez-Reyes *et al.*, 1992). Unlike caffeine they can also produce a strong feeling of well-being and increase self-confidence. These are attractive attributes for musicians, who have a demanding schedule or feel that they need to maintain a high energy level in their performance. Amphetamines can help with breathing disorders because they dilate the bronchioles. They have also been used as weight loss pills. Unfortunately, sessions of amphetamine use are often followed by a "crash" or period of feeling depressed and tired. This can act as a stimulus to take more of the drug.

Amphetamines can be ingested in a variety of ways but probably most commonly as pills. "Ice" is recrystallized methamphetamine hydrochloride and is a potent stimulant. It generally takes the form of clear crystallized chunks that can be smoked. Amphetamines can also be sniffed and even injected.

Unfortunately, amphetamines can also create feelings of paranoia and stimulate aggressive behavior (Schiorring, 1981; de Wit *et al.*, 2000). Some users become addicted to them, although the pattern of addiction is generally not the same as for nicotine and alcohol, where there is regular use throughout the day. Amphetamine use more commonly involves bingeing on large quantities on specific occasions, often at weekends. Heavy amphetamine use can lead to psychosis and to serious physical effects including cardiac arrest.

Although it may be tempting to use amphetamines to keep up one's energy levels, maintain an attractive weight, and to feel good, for many users the harm outweighs the benefits, and musicians should treat these drugs with caution.

Cannabis

Cannabis is the most widely used illicit drug in the world, and of course, it is a staple among entertainers and musicians of all kinds. About 30% of adults in the UK have tried cannabis, and about 7% are current users. The average of lifetime use in Europe is around 20%, with about 7% being current users; figures for other English-speaking countries are very similar. The active ingredient in cannabis is tetrahydrocannabinol or THC. This produces a range of effects that include a sense of well-being, a feeling of relaxation, and enhanced sociability (Heishman *et al.*, 1997). It also results in increased appetite, difficulty in concentrating, a distorted sense of time, and altered perceptions, and can in high doses lead to hallucinations (Perez-Reyes *et al.*, 1988; Chait & Perry, 1994; Liguori *et al.*, 2002). Physical effects include increased heart rate and decreased muscle tone. The psychomotor impairment caused by cannabis is modest (Pickworth *et al.*, 1997) but exacerbated when consumed with alcohol (Perez-Reyes *et al.*, 1988; Liguori *et al.*, 2002).

There is a heated debate about the harmfulness of this drug. Physically, the main harm would be expected to arise from smoking it, particularly with tobacco. The extent of the risk has yet to be quantified, but it is likely that there is at least some because inhaling smoke particles on a regular basis in itself damages the respiratory system. On the psychological side, the potential for addiction appears to be similar to that for alcohol, with approximately 1 in 10 users developing a clinical dependence syndrome involving compulsive use. There is some evidence that high levels of chronic use can lead to intellectual impairment, although the effects are generally quite subtle (Schwartz *et al.*, 1989). Perhaps of greater concern is the likelihood that use precipitates psychiatric disturbance in susceptible individuals. Users are more likely to develop psychotic symptoms and to attempt suicide than nonusers, even once other predisposing factors have been taken into account.

Advising musicians (particularly hip-hop, pop, jazz, rock musicians, and suchlike) to avoid taking cannabis is probably akin to advising a dog not to bark. However, it is important to be aware that its effects may detract from performance, and it is not without risks.

Cocaine

Cocaine is very similar to amphetamines, with possibly a greater potential to induce feelings of well-being. It works in a somewhat similar manner by blocking re-uptake of the neurotransmitters dopamine and noradrenaline into the nerve terminals, thereby increasing their potency. It is also easy to take in rapidly acting forms either through sniffing into the nose (cocaine hydrochloride powder) or through inhaling the "freebase" form produced by heating cocaine hydrochloride and baking soda ("crack"). Subjectively, the main difference from amphetamines is probably that there is less agitation.

Unfortunately, perhaps more than amphetamines, cocaine can be addictive and can come to take over the life of the user. There is some evidence of neurological problems with chronic use (Di Sclafani *et al.*, 2002). Chronic use can also damage the parts of the brain that are involved in feeling pleasure, so that normal sources of pleasure lose their attractiveness. As with amphetamines, a bout of cocaine use is often followed by a "crash" or period of depression.

Also as with amphetamines, the physical effects of cocaine use include constricted peripheral blood vessels, dilated pupils, and increased temperature, heart rate, and blood pressure. Even in first-time users, cocaine can cause cardiac arrest. It can also interact with alcohol to cause liver damage (Hoyumpa, 1984). The duration of cocaine's psychological effects depends on the route of administration. The faster the absorption, the more intense the "high" but the shorter the duration of action. The high from sniffing may last 15–30 minutes compared with perhaps 5–10 minutes from smoking. As with amphetamines, high doses of cocaine and/or prolonged use can trigger paranoia. Chronic cocaine snorting can result in ulceration of the mucous membrane of the nose and can damage the nasal septum enough to destroy it.

It is possible to recover from problem use of cocaine. As yet there is little scientific evidence that specific treatments improve the chances of recovery, but cognitive-behavioral therapy and contingency management (where rewards and punishments are used to maintain abstinence, checked by urine analysis) have shown some limited effect. A number of medications are also being tried as treatments for cocaine dependence, but at present, there is no clear evidence that they are of lasting benefit.

Ecstasy

Ecstasy (MDMA) is a stimulant quite similar chemically to amphetamines. The main effect on the brain is to increase the release of the neurotransmitters serotonin (5-hydroxytryptamine) and dopamine. The drug remains in the system and is active for several hours. Physiological effects are similar to other stimulants; it can increase alertness and physical energy. In addition, it raises body temperature, and this has been blamed for a number of deaths among users. Users report that taking ecstasy makes them feel more sociable, with heightened sensory awareness. There is slight "depersonalization", an altered sense of time and greater feeling of warmth toward others.

Deaths from ecstasy have achieved prominence in the media, although they are rare considering the number of users. Concerns have been raised about the long-term damage that taking ecstasy might inflict. There is some evidence that ecstasy can cause damage to the nerves that normally produce serotonin, and it has been speculated that this may cause chronic depression in heavy users. Chronic use has also been found to be associated with memory deficits and impairment on tasks involving complex information processing (Simon & Mattick, 2002).

For the musician, the benefits of the increased energy and greater sense of sociability and well-being produced by ecstasy have to be weighed against the significant risk of longer term mental health problems and memory impairment.

Hallucinogens

Hallucinogens (or "psychedelic drugs") are a class of drugs characterized by the sensory distortions that they induce. Best known among these is lysergic acid diethylamide (LSD). These drugs were popular among rock and pop musicians in the 1960s because at that time there was considerable interest in altered states of consciousness and expanding one's experiences. Recently they have become popular again with young people. The dangers in using them lie in the distorted perception of reality they create during acute intoxication, which can lead to self-harm. In the longer term, there is a risk of a chronic syndrome of unpredictable recurrence of the drug effects ("flash-backs") and possibly longer-term mood disturbance (Strassman, 1984).

Acute intoxication with these drugs makes controlled performance extremely difficult. Some have argued that it might assist with more free-form extemporization, though scientific evidence for this is lacking.

Opiates

Opiates are a class of drug made from the opium poppy. They include opium itself, morphine, and diacetylmorphine (diamorphine or heroin). Methadone is a synthetic opiate which is longer acting. These drugs have powerful pain-relieving properties because they mimic the actions of naturally occurring "endogenous" opiates in the brain. They can also produce a powerful feeling of euphoria or well-being, particularly heroin and opium (Hill & Zacny, 2000). Of course, they are also highly addictive.

Heroin is the most commonly used illicit form of the drug in countries such as the UK and USA. It can be sniffed, smoked, or injected. In all cases it carries a risk of death from overdose due to respiratory suppression—the user stops breathing. A large proportion of overdoses occur not because the drug is unusually pure or because it has been taken in larger quantities than normal, but because it is taken with alcohol or benzodiazepines which compound the effect. Overdose is the most common cause of death in heroin users, but death from HIV, hepatitis and other infections, suicide, and homicide are also quite common. A heroin addict is about 30 times more likely to die in a given year than the average adult of the same age.

After a few weeks of regular use the body adapts, and users experience withdrawal symptoms when they abstain. Sometimes overdoses occur when a user has abstained for a while (e.g. when in prison) and then resumed taking the drug without compensating for the loss of tolerance. In a chronic opiate user, abstinence will bring on withdrawal symptoms within a few hours. They peak at about 2–4 days and are usually gone within a week or two. These include gastrointestinal upset, "goose bumps," shivering, yawning, sweating, and muscle cramps. Some have likened them to a bout of flu. They are not life-threatening. Many people think that it is the need to avoid these withdrawal symptoms that keeps people addicted to heroin. Certainly, heroin users report fear of withdrawal symptoms as a major factor keeping them seeking out the drug; however, there is far more to heroin dependence than this. Chronic heroin users continue to get a rush or high from the drug and will typically relapse back to the drug even after they have gotten over the withdrawal symptoms.

There are many famous examples of musicians—particularly in rock, blues, jazz, and pop—who have become addicted to heroin. As with drugs such as cocaine and alcohol, how far this reflects their temperament or their lifestyle is difficult to determine; neither is it clear whether opiates have any beneficial effect in terms of creativity or musical expression. They are probably not as damaging as alcohol to the execution of a performance. Chronic illicit opiate and methadone use has been linked with some intellectual and psychomotor impairment (Mason, 1977; Darke *et al.*, 2000;

Specka *et al.*, 2000; Mintzer & Stitzer, 2002), but patients on long-term opiate treatment for pain control do not appear to be impaired (Fishbain *et al.*, 2003).

However, the control that these drugs come to exert over the individual's life can be so profound that indirectly they make it impossible to continue a musical career. While the situation varies considerably, many heroin addicts are often "busy people." Their life is dominated by acquiring the means to obtain the drug, obtaining it, using it, and then starting the cycle over again. This leaves little time or energy to pursue work and relationships.

Treatment for heroin addiction typically involves trying either to stabilize the patient on prescribed methadone to enable him or her to lead as normal a life as possible or to assist the patient to come off opiates altogether. In the latter case, the regimen consists of medication, such as methadone or buprenorphine, to control withdrawal symptoms, accompanied by counseling to help the patient adapt to life without drugs. The medication is then gradually withdrawn. In practice, this is rarely effective, and it is more common these days (at least in the UK) to try to manage the heroin addict's condition by maintaining him or her on a long-term methadone or buprenorphine program designed to minimize the need to use street heroin. Some treatment centers will provide patients with heroin on prescription, although this is still controversial and whether it confers any benefit over methadone is not clear.

In fact, most heroin addicts also take other drugs such as cocaine, cannabis, benzodiazepines, and amphetamines, and almost all smoke cigarettes. This raises the question of how far to go in treating dependence on these other drugs. In general, drug treatment programs tend to focus on heroin and stimulant use and not worry too much about cannabis, alcohol, or smoking.

For musicians, the direct effect of opiates on performance is probably less of a problem than the more general effect on lifestyle and motivation, coupled obviously with a substantial increase in risk of early death.

14.3   Conclusions

Drugs are an important part of all our lives. Society's views on drugs are inconsistent across time and across drugs and have more to do with the way it regards the groups who use the drugs than the effects of the drugs themselves. As performers, musicians have particular traits and needs that seem to make them more likely to use a variety of drugs, either recreationally or to help them cope. The need to maintain a high energy level, performance anxiety, and boredom when traveling all probably contribute to self-medication by musicians. Acutely, drugs such as alcohol, cocaine, and amphetamines no doubt do, on occasion, meet a need on the part of the musician. Unfortunately for many, the cost in terms of dependence and the adverse effects of intoxication is high and sometimes disastrous.

Before closing this chapter with some general observations, it is important to note that how far an individual experiences problems with a drug is related to his or her psychological makeup and life circumstances. Use of a drug such as heroin or alcohol may result in a miserable short life, or the user may be able to retain control and reap the benefits while experiencing few of the adverse effects. Heroin addicts often turn out to have other psychiatric problems, which would be there even without the addiction, and so do alcoholics. It would be tempting, therefore, to imagine that one could inspect one's own personality and lifestyle and make an informed decision about drug taking. In practice, however, this turns out not to be a very successful strategy. Most of us simply do not have the self-insight to achieve it. The "sensible" advice to performing musicians, therefore, is:

- Drink alcohol in moderation, but avoid intoxication while performing.
- By all means, drink coffee or use caffeine if you need to maintain alertness, but watch out for its effects on your ability to execute fine movements.
- Do not smoke tobacco; it will probably bring on diseases of old age and premature death.
- If you suffer badly from performance anxiety, consider getting a prescription for beta-blockers from your doctor, but also consider exercise and psychological treatments (see Chapters 9 and 12 of this volume).
- Unless you suffer from a clinical anxiety disorder or depression, avoid tranquilizers and antidepressants; even if you do suffer clinical anxiety or depression, consider psychological treatments rather than pills.
- If you use cannabis, it is safer not to smoke it; be aware that it is not a safe drug and that it can be addictive.
- It is best to avoid stimulants such as amphetamines, cocaine, and ecstasy; the acute euphoriant effects may carry a price that you would prefer not to pay in terms of long-term damage to the brain.
- Probably steer clear of hallucinogens; the "expansion of your mind" may carry a price of short- and long-term effects you would want to do without.
- Avoid heroin; it is among the most addictive of all drugs, and there is a good chance it will ruin your life.

Of course, this advice is easier to give than to follow.

Acknowledgments

I would like to thank Andy McEwen, Andrew Preston, Mike Gossop, and Aaron Williamon for helpful comments on this chapter.

Further information and reading

For additional information on drugs and addiction, see the websites of the Society for the Study of Addiction (established since 1884) at *www.addiction-ssa.org* or Addiction Search at *www.addictionsearch.com*. Recommended books for further reading on this topic include:

Gossop, M. (2000). *Living with Drugs*. London: Ashgate Publishing.

Heather, N., & Robertson, I. (1997). *Problem Drinking*. Oxford: Oxford University Press.

Shapiro, H. (2003). *Waiting for the Man: The Story of Drugs and Popular Music.* London: Helter Skelter Publishing.

West, R., & Shiffman, S. (2003). *Smoking Cessation.* Oxford: Healthcare Press.

References

Battig, K. (1991). Coffee, cardiovascular, and behavioral effects current research trends. *Reviews on Environmental Health, 9,* 53–84.

Beatty, W. W., Tivis, R., Stott, H. D., Nixon, S. J., & Parsons, O. A. (2000). Neuropsychological deficits in sober alcoholics: Influences of chronicity and recent alcohol consumption. *Alcoholism: Clinical and Experimental Research, 24,* 149–154.

Bengtsson, C. (1984). Impairment of physical performance after treatment with beta blockers and alpha blockers. *British Medical Journal, 288,* 671–672.

Brantigan, C. O., Brantigan, T. A., & Joseph, N. (1979). The effect of beta blockade on stage fright. *Rocky Mountain Medical Journal, 76,* 227–233.

Brantigan, C. O., Brantigan, T. A., & Joseph, N. (1982). Effect of beta blockade and beta stimulation on stage fright. *American Journal of Medicine, 72,* 88–94.

Brantigan, T. A., Brantigan, C. O., & Joseph, N. (1978). Beta-blockade and musical performance. *Lancet, 2,* 896.

Broadhurst, A. D. (1980). Comparison of effect on psychomotor performance of single doses of propranolol and acebutolol. *Current Medical Research and Opinion, 7,* 33–37.

Burns, M., & Moskowitz, H. (1980). Effects of diphenhydramine and alcohol on skills performance. *European Journal of Clinical Pharmacology, 17,* 259–266.

Capitani, E., Della Pria, M., Doro, G., & Spinnler, H. (1983). Is memory impairment greater than cognitive impairment in moderate chronic alcoholics? *Italian Journal of Neurological Sciences, 4,* 443–449.

Chait, L. D., & Perry, J. L. (1994). Acute and residual effects of alcohol and marijuana, alone and in combination, on mood and performance. *Psychopharmacology, 115,* 340–349.

Chorpita, B. F., & Barlow, D. H. (1998). The development of anxiety: The role of control in the early environment. *Psychological Bulletin, 124,* 3–21.

Clark, D. B., & Agras, W. S. (1991). The assessment and treatment of performance anxiety in musicians. *American Journal of Psychiatry, 148,* 598–605.

Cupido, C. M., Hicks, A. L., McKelvie, R. S., Sale, D. G., & McComas, A. J. (1994). Effect of selective and nonselective beta-blockade on skeletal muscle excitability and fatiguability. *Journal of Applied Physiology, 76,* 2461–2466.

Darke, S., Sims, J., McDonald, S., & Wickes, W. (2000). Cognitive impairment among methadone maintenance patients. *Addiction, 95,* 687–695.

de Wit, H., Dudish, S., & Ambre, J. (1993). Subjective and behavioral effects of diazepam depend on its rate of onset. *Psychopharmacology, 112,* 324–330.

de Wit, H., Crean, J., & Richards, J. B. (2000). Effects of d-amphetamine and ethanol on a measure of behavioral inhibition in humans. *Behavioral Neuroscience, 114,* 830–837.

Dews, P. B., O'Brien, C. P., & Bergman, J. (2002). Caffeine: Behavioral effects of withdrawal and related issues. *Food and Chemistry Toxicology, 40,* 1257–1261.

Di Sclafani, V., Tolou-Shams, M., Price, L. J., & Fein, G. (2002). Neuropsychological performance of individuals dependent on crack-cocaine, or crack-cocaine and alcohol, at 6 weeks and 6 months of abstinence. *Drug and Alcohol Dependence, 66*, 161–171.

Donovan, J. L., & DeVane, C. L. (2001). A primer on caffeine pharmacology and its drug interactions in clinical psychopharmacology. *Psychopharmacology Bulletin, 35*, 30–48.

Drake, C. L., Roehrs, T., Turner, L., Scofield, H. M., & Roth, T. (2003). Caffeine reversal of ethanol effects on the multiple sleep latency test, memory, and psychomotor performance. *Neuropsychopharmacology, 28*, 371–378.

Eckardt, M. J., Ryback, R. S., & Pautler, C. P. (1980). Neuropsychological deficits in alcoholic men in their mid thirties. *American Journal of Psychiatry, 137*, 932–936.

Edwards, G., Marshall, E. J., & Cook, C. C. H. (2003). *The Treatment of Drinking Problems: A Guide for the Helping Professions* (4th ed.). Cambridge: Cambridge University Press.

Ellinwood, E. H., Linnoila, M., Easler, M. E., & Molter, D. (1981). Onset of peak impairment after diazepam and after alcohol. *Clinical Pharmacology and Therapeutics, 30*, 534–538.

Erwin, C. W., Linnoila, M., Hartwell, J., Erwin, A., & Guthrie, S. (1986). Effects of buspirone and diazepam, alone and in combination with alcohol, on skilled performance and evoked potentials. *Journal of Clinical Psychopharmacology, 6*, 199–209.

Evans, S. M., Funderburk, F. R., & Griffiths, R. R. (1990). Zolpidem and triazolam in humans: Behavioral and subjective effects and abuse liability. *Journal Pharmacology and Experimental Therepeutics, 255*, 1246–1255.

Farquhar, K., Lambert, K., Drummond, G. B., Tiplady, B., & Wright, P. (2002). Effect of ethanol on psychomotor performance and on risk taking behavior. *Journal of Psychopharmacology, 16*, 379–384.

Fishbain, D. A., Cutler, R. B., Rosomoff, H. L., & Rosomoff, R. S. (2003). Are opioid-dependent/ tolerant patients impaired in driving-related skills? A structured evidence-based review. *Journal of Pain and Symptom Management, 25*, 559–577.

Fredrikson, M., & Gunnarsson, R. (1992). Psychobiology of stage fright: The effect of public performance on neuroendocrine, cardiovascular, and subjective reactions. *Biological Psychology, 33*, 51–61.

Gates, G. A., Saegert, J., Wilson, N., Johnson, L., Shepherd, A., & Hearne, E. M. (1985). Effect of beta blockade on singing performance. *Annals of Otology, Rhinology, and Laryngology, 94*, 570–574.

Goldberg, H. L. (1984). Buspirone hydrochloride: A unique new anxiolytic agent. Pharmacokinetics, clinical pharmacology, abuse potential, and clinical efficacy. *Pharmacotherapy, 4*, 315–324.

Graham, T. E. (2001). Caffeine, coffee, and ephedrine: Impact on exercise performance and metabolism. *Canadian Journal of Applied Physiology, 26* (Supplement), S103–119.

Grant, S. A., Millar, K., & Kenny G. N. (2000). Blood alcohol concentration and psychomotor effects. *British Journal of Anaesthesia, 85*, 401–406.

Griffiths, R. R., & Chausmer, A. L. (2000). Caffeine as a model drug of dependence: Recent developments in understanding caffeine withdrawal, the caffeine dependence syndrome, and caffeine negative reinforcement. *Japanese Journal of Psychopharmacology, 20*, 223–231.

Heishman, S. J., Arasteh, K., & Stitzer, M. L. (1997). Comparative effects of alcohol and marijuana on mood, memory, and performance. *Pharmacology, Biochemistry, and Behavior, 58*, 93–101.

Hill, J. L., & Zacny, J. P. (2000). Comparing the subjective, psychomotor, and physiological effects of intravenous hydromorphone and morphine in healthy volunteers. *Psychopharmacology, 152*, 31–39.

Hindmarch, I. (1992). A review of the psychomotor effects of paroxetine. *International Clinical Psychopharmacology, 6* (Supplement 4), 65–67.

Horne, J. A., & Gibbons, H. (1991). Effects on vigilance performance and sleepiness of alcohol given in the early afternoon ("post lunch") vs. early evening. *Ergonomics, 34*, 67–77.

Hoyumpa, A. M. (1984). Alcohol interactions with benzodiazepines and cocaine. *Advances in Alcohol & Substance Abuse, 3*, 21–34.

James, I. M. (1984). Practical aspects of the use of beta-blockers in anxiety states: Situational anxiety. *Postgraduate Medical Journal, 60* (Supplement 2), 19–25.

James, I., & Savage, I. (1984). Beneficial effect of nadolol on anxiety-induced disturbances of musical performance in musicians: A comparison with diazepam and placebo. *American Heart Journal, 108*, 1150–1155.

James, I. M., Griffith, D. N., Pearson, R. M., & Newbury, P. (1977). Effect of oxprenolol on stage-fright in musicians. *Lancet, 2*, 952–954.

James, I. M., Pearson, R. M., Griffith, D. N. W., Newbury, P., & Taylor, S. H. (1978). The effect of beta-adrenoceptor blockade on the somatic manifestations of anxiety. A study of stage fright. *Journal of Psychosomatic Research, 22*, 327–337.

James, I. M., Burgoyne, W., & Savage, I. T. (1983). Effect of pindolol on stress related disturbances of musical performance: Preliminary communication. *Journal of the Royal Society of Medicine, 76*, 194–196.

Kaiser, P., Rossner, S., & Karlsson, J. (1981). Effects of beta-adrenergic blockade on endurance and short-time performance in respect to individual muscle fiber composition. *International Journal of Sports Medicine, 2*, 37–42.

Koelega, H. S. (1993). Stimulant drugs and vigilance performance: A review. *Psychopharmacology, 111*, 1–16.

Kunsman, G. W., Manno, J. E., Przekop, M. A., Manno, B. R., & Kunsman, C. M. (1992). The effects of temazepam and ethanol on human psychomotor performance. *European Journal of Clinical Pharmacology, 43*, 603–611.

Lemon, R. N. (1999). Neural control of dexterity: What has been achieved? *Experimental Brain Research, 128*, 6–12.

Lidén, S., & Gottfries, C.-G. (1974). Beta-blocking agents in the treatment of catecholamine-induced symptoms in musicians. *Lancet, 11*, 529.

Liguori, A., & Robinson, J. H. (2001). Caffeine antagonism of alcohol-induced driving impairment. *Drug and Alcohol Dependence, 63*, 123–129.

Liguori, A., Gatto, C. P., & Jarrett, D. B. (2002). Separate and combined effects of marijuana and alcohol on mood, equilibrium, and simulated driving. *Psychopharmacology, 163*, 399–405.

Linnoila, M., Stapleton, J. M., George, D. T., Lane, E., & Eckardt, M. J. (1993). Effects of fluvoxamine, alone and in combination with ethanol, on psychomotor and cognitive performance and on autonomic nervous system reactivity in healthy volunteers. *Journal of Clinical Psychopharmacology, 13*, 175–180.

Lister, R. G., & File, S. E. (1983). Performance impairment and increased anxiety resulting from the combination of alcohol and lorazepam. *Journal of Clinical Psychopharmacology, 3*, 66–71.

Lubin, R. A. (1977). Influences of alcohol upon performance and performance awareness. *Perceptual and Motor Skills, 45,* 303–310.

Ludwig, A. M. (1990). Alcohol input and creative output. *British Journal of Addiction, 85,* 953–963.

Mandel, H. G. (2002). Update on caffeine consumption, disposition, and action. *Food and Chemical Toxicology, 40,* 1231–1234.

Mason, M. F. (1977). Drug impairment reviews: Opiates, minor tranquilizers. *NIDA Research Monograph, Series 11,* 44–60.

Mattila, M. J., Aranko, K., & Seppala, T. (1982). Acute effects of buspirone and alcohol on psychomotor skills. *Journal of Clinical Psychiatry, 43,* 56–61.

Mintzer, M. Z., & Stitzer, M. L. (2002). Cognitive impairment in methadone maintenance patients. *Drug and Alcohol Dependence, 67,* 41–51.

Nagoshi, C. T., Wilson, J. R., & Rodriguez, L. A. (1991). Impulsivity, sensation seeking, and behavioral and emotional responses to alcohol. *Alcoholism: Clinical and Experimental Research, 15,* 661–667.

Nawrot, P., Jordan, S., Eastwood, J., Rotstein, J., Hugenholtz, A., & Feeley, M. (2003). Effects of caffeine on human health. *Food Additives and Contaminants, 20,* 1–30.

Neftel, K. A., Adler, R. H., Kappeli, L., Rossi, M., Dolder, M., Kaser, H. E., Bruggesser, H. H., & Vorkauf, H. (1982). Stage fright in musicians: A model illustrating the effect of beta blockers. *Psychosomatic Medicine, 44,* 461–469.

Nestler, E. J. (2000). Genes and addiction. *Nature Genetics, 26,* 277–281.

Pearson, R. M., & Simpson, A. F. (1978). Effect of oxprenolol in stage fright in musicians. *Transactions of the Medical Society of London, 95,* 46–53.

Perez-Reyes, M., Hicks, R. E., Bumberry, J., Jeffcoat, A. R., & Cook, C. E. (1988). Interaction between marijuana and ethanol: Effects on psychomotor performance. *Alcoholism: Clinical and Experimental Research, 12,* 268–276.

Perez-Reyes, M., White, W. R., McDonald, S. A., & Hicks, R. E. (1992). Interaction between ethanol and dextroamphetamine: Effects on psychomotor performance. *Alcoholism: Clinical and Experimental Research, 16,* 75–81.

Pickworth, W. B., Rohrer, M. S., & Fant, R. V. (1997). Effects of abused drugs on psychomotor performance. *Experimental and Clinical Psychopharmacology, 5,* 235–241.

Ridderinkhof, K. R., de Vlugt, Y., Bramlage, A., Spaan, M., Elton, M., Snel, J., & Band, G. P. (2002). Alcohol consumption impairs detection of performance errors in mediofrontal cortex. *Science, 298,* 2209–2211.

RCP (2000). *Nicotine Addiction in Britain.* London: Royal College of Physicians.

Schaeffer, K. W., Parsons, O. A., & Errico, A. L. (1989). Performance deficits on tests of problem solving in alcoholics: Cognitive or motivational impairment? *Journal of Substance Abuse, 1,* 381–392.

Schiorring, E. (1981). Psychopathology induced by "speed drugs". *Pharmacology, Biochemistry, and Behavior, 14* (Supplement 1), 109–122.

Schlaug, G. (2001). The brain of musicians: A model for functional and structural adaptation. *Annals of the New York Academy of Sciences, 930,* 281–299.

Schwartz, R. H., Gruenewald, P. J., Klitzner, M., & Fedio, P. (1989). Short-term memory impairment in cannabis-dependent adolescents. *American Journal of Diseases of Children, 143,* 1214–1219.

Simon, N. G., & Mattick, R. P. (2002). The impact of regular ecstasy use on memory function. *Addiction, 97,* 1523–1529.

Simpson, C. A., & Rush, C. R. (2002). Acute performance-impairing and subject-rated effects of triazolam and temazepam, alone and in combination with ethanol, in humans. *Journal of Psychopharmacology, 16,* 23–34.

Smith, A. (2002). Effects of caffeine on human behavior. *Food and Chemical Toxicology, 40,* 1243–1255.

Specka, M., Finkbeiner, T., Lodemann, E., Leifert, K., Kluwig, J., & Gastpar, M. (2000). Cognitive-motor performance of methadone-maintained patients. *European Addiction Research, 6,* 8–19.

Spriet, L. L. (1995). Caffeine and performance. *International Journal of Sport Nutrition, 5* (Supplement), S84–S99.

Strassman, R. J. (1984). Adverse reactions to psychedelic drugs: A review of the literature. *Journal of Nervous and Mental Disease, 172,* 577–595.

Tarnopolsky, M. A. (1994). Caffeine and endurance performance. *Sports Medicine, 18,* 109–125.

Tiller, J. W. (1990). Antidepressants, alcohol, and psychomotor performance. *Acta Psychiatrica Scandinavica, Supplement 360,* 13–17.

Wesner, R., Noyes, R., & Davis, T. L. (1990). The occurrence of performance anxiety among musicians. *Journal of Affective Disorders, 18,* 177–185.

West, R. (1993). Beneficial effects of nicotine: Fact or fiction? *Addiction, 88,* 589–590.

West, R., & Hajek, P. (1997). What happens to anxiety levels on giving up smoking? *American Journal of Psychiatry, 154,* 1589–1592.

West, R., & Shiffman, S. (2003). *Smoking Cessation.* Oxford: Healthcare Press.

EPILOGUE
A note on future directions for enhancing musical performance

Research aimed at enhancing musical performance demands ingenuity and persever-ance, as overcoming the methodological obstacles inherent to this area is no trivial undertaking. The studies reported throughout this book provide models for how such obstacles can be surmounted in future work. There are, nonetheless, a number of fun-damental issues that need to be addressed in subsequent efforts to enhance perform-ance. In my own reading of the existing research, four areas seem particularly important for further development:

• the refinement of systems used to measure performance enhancement

• the exploration of individual differences and responses to performance enhance-ment strategies and techniques

• the investigation of the long-term impact of interventions

• the study of how distinct approaches to enhancing performance can be combined.

First, those engaged in this research must not only be clear about which aspects of performance are responsive to enhancement through a given intervention, but also about how that enhancement can be measured reliably and consistently. As shown throughout this book, there is a multitude of ways to measure enhancement, but to date there is insufficient knowledge, in many cases, of the extent to which these meth-ods are comparable and how they interrelate. Grassroots work aimed at establishing "industry standard" scales, systems, and levels of accepted impact could offer signifi-cant research and pedagogical benefits and could also save valuable time and resources for future generations of researchers. (This, of course, would not rule out the possibility of devising entirely novel systems of measurement, which seems necessary for investiga-tions of unique performance characteristics, but it would enable benchmarks to be established against which new measurement systems could be compared and con-trasted.) A natural next step would be to accumulate large stores of performance-related data—psychological, physical, and musical—across a range of reasonably controlled and monitored conditions. These databases could then be shared and added to interna-tionally, in order to build up a more informative picture of the demands of perfor-mance and the ways in which musicians across the world respond to those demands.

Second, it is a common pattern within psychological research to work toward an understanding of principles and mechanisms that govern the functioning of all humans. From these endeavors, one can learn a great deal about the full extent of human behavior and achievement. In performance enhancement research, however, there seems to be tremendous potential for identifying how individual musicians differ with respect to their skills and how they respond idiosyncratically to different performance contexts and interventions. Understanding how individual variability arises within the confines of generalizable psychological mechanisms would certainly benefit any research initiative aimed at enhancing performance. In fact, one goal toward which research in this area should be geared is the identification of intervention-specific predictor variables, enabling the immediate assessment of whether a performer could indeed benefit from an intervention. Aside from attributes of the person (e.g. personality traits and musical abilities), these predictor variables should also be oriented around the musician's performance genre and his or her instrumental specialization.

Third, efforts should be made to determine the extent to which performance enhancement benefits will last over the long-term and how musicians should engage with an intervention over the course of their careers. This information could have an immediate impact on decisions to apply an intervention in educational and professional environments. For instance, a particularly effective technique may be of little practical value to an educational institution if the yield on investment (in terms of time, personnel, and expense) is comparatively short-lived and unfavorable. Thus, it is important where possible to pursue research agendas that are longitudinal in nature so that long-term benefits (or side-effects) can be documented.

Finally, much research (particularly in relation to the techniques discussed in Part III of this book) has been aimed at determining the effects of only one type of intervention on performance. This is understandable, as it is impossible to know the precise source of a given benefit if the musician is exposed to an elaborate cocktail of strategies. Still, for those approaches for which singular benefits have been identified, much could be gained by pairing them with complementary physical and psychological interventions. A performer cannot achieve excellence only by isolating and refining a limited range of skills; likewise, it seems reasonable to argue that the full potential for performance enhancement research lies in exploring how musicians' physical and psychological abilities can be enhanced in unison.

Other such methodological issues have been raised throughout this book (see, for example, Chapters 1, 11, and 13), and still others will invariably arise as the discipline expands and develops. It is vital, in my view, that systematic attempts be made to address such issues rigorously in future research. In this way, a greater theoretical and practical understanding of musical performance—as well as the educational and professional contexts in which it occurs—can be achieved, and research to enhance performance can begin to offer even richer benefits for practitioners.

Aaron Williamon

INDEX